Two Americans

TWO AMERICANS

——•◆•——

TRUMAN, EISENHOWER, AND A DANGEROUS WORLD

William Lee Miller

Alfred A. Knopf · New York · 2012

THIS IS A BORZOI BOOK
PUBLISHED BY ALFRED A. KNOPF

Library of Congress Cataloging-in-Publication Data
Miller, William Lee.
Two Americans : Truman, Eisenhower, and a dangerous world / William Lee Miller.—1st ed.
p.   cm.
"Borzoi book."
Includes bibliographical references and index.
ISBN 978-0-307-59564-5
1. Presidents—United States—Biography.   2. Political culture—United States—History—
20th century.   3. Political leadership—United States—Case studies.   4. Truman, Harry
S., 1884–1972.   5. Eisenhower, Dwight D. (Dwight David), 1890–1969.   6. United
States—Politics and government—1945–1953.   7. United States—Politics and
government—1953–1961.   I. Title.
E747.M63 2012
973.09'9—dc23
[B] 2011033891

Jacket image: General Dwight D. Eisenhower talking with President Harry S Truman,
June 1, 1945. Photo by Marie Hansen / Time-Life Pictures/Getty Images
Jacket design by Darren Haggar

Manufactured in the United States of America
First Edition

To the memory of

Tom Appleby

and of

Tom Sorensen,

political companions

CONTENTS

Two Americans

CHAPTER ONE

Boy's Life

I

GEORGE KENNAN, the diplomat and thinker whose understanding of world politics was of importance in shaping America's conduct during the Cold War, tells in his *Memoirs: 1950–1963* about a return, after many years spent representing the United States abroad, to the American Middle West, from which he had originally come. Superficially, his encounter was not edifying. Walking around Chicago—to which he had gone to give a lecture—he experienced a series of depressing sights and encounters. Nevertheless, he wrote:

> I knew myself to be back in the part of the world to which I truly belonged—a part of the world which, in memory, I loved as one can only love the place in which one grew up. I believed then deeply in the Middle West and still do—in its essential decency, its moral earnestness, its latent emotional freshness. I viewed it, and view it now, as the heart of the moral strength of the United States. This was precisely why I was so sensitive to its imperfections.

"Latent emotional freshness" is a quality not many, perhaps, would think to ascribe to the American Middle West. With further visits, Kennan came to an unlikely metaphor: "Increasingly, under the impression of this and other visits at mid-century, I came to see this native region as a great slatternly mother, sterile when left to herself yet immensely fruitful and creative when touched by anything outside herself." And then he saw this as a condition common to many countries: "But was this not, I often asked myself, the character and function of all these regions, everywhere across the world, that would respond to the French meaning of the word 'province'?"

Kennan and his ideas would have their strongest effect (although not always the one he wanted them to have) in the presidencies of two men from the U.S. provinces—Harry S Truman and Dwight David Eisenhower. This book is a brief narrative of the lives and careers of those two men. Part of the reason I chose to interweave their stories is to compare and contrast these men, in their relationships to the great issues with which they dealt and to each other (they came to have a considerable antagonism, as we shall see; their interaction is an interesting part of the story). Another reason for telling their story jointly is that, together, their careers reveal central aspects of American culture at crucial moments in history. Both were president at times that required important national decisions.

During the fifteen and three-fourths years of the presidencies of these two Middle Americans, bracketed by two Harvard men, the 175-year-old United States underwent a major change in the role that it would thenceforth play in the drama of world affairs. The nation rejoined Europe, entered its first peacetime alliance since the time of the Founders, undertook its first permanent global commitments, and coped for the first time in human history with a man-made destructive power that could destroy civilization. The history of the decades to follow—four decades of Cold War, with the bomb looming over them—was much affected by what happened in those Truman and Eisenhower years.

II

FIRST, as to Dwight Eisenhower: You could not ask for a purer sample of the American Middle West than the Eisenhower family in the small town of Abilene in the state of Kansas—very near the geographical center of the country and near the center of the national culture, as well.

David Dwight Eisenhower (his name in that order originally) was the third of seven boys—six of whom lived beyond infancy—born to David Eisenhower and Ida Elizabeth Stover, an unpretentious and impecunious couple of German Mennonite background in the town of Abilene. After the first two boys were born, their parents wished for a girl, but (like Abraham Lincoln and his wife) they kept having boys. Although farming had been the primary occupation of his forebears, and although the Reverend Jacob Eisenhower, Dwight's impressive multitasking grandfather, was able to give each of his sons 160 acres of Kansas farmland, Dwight's father, David, did not want to be a farmer. He got a college degree from a marginal institution called Lane University in Lecompton, Kansas, but had trouble making a living. He met and married Ida Stover at that university. He tried with a partner named Milton Good to make a living in a dry goods store, but that effort failed; in family lore and some biographies, the failure is blamed on Good's having absconded with the store's earnings, but a later biographer, who gave the story a more careful look, found that

that was a stretch;* David Eisenhower just was not a good salesman. After his failure with the store, he went at first by himself to Denison, Texas, where there was a laborer's job on the Missouri-Kansas-Texas, or "Katy," Railroad. His wife and family followed, and the next boy was born there. This was David Dwight, who, when his first and middle names were reversed, became Dwight. When he became a world figure, some in Texas tried to claim him, but he was in Texas only as an infant; he always made clear that Abilene, Kansas, was his hometown. After the David Eisenhower family had been in Denison for about three years, the River Brethren back in Abilene offered David Eisenhower a job at the Belle Spring Creamery, which the Brethren operated on the outskirts of Abilene, and the family returned there for all of Dwight's youth. David, the more somber parent, worked from six to six as a mechanic at the creamery throughout Dwight's boyhood. Ida was an able mother to the bourgeoning crew of boys, much praised by her most famous son, including one full chapter devoted to her in his book of reminiscences, *At Ease*.

Abilene was a town of some four thousand residents and had once briefly been the center of some lively history. Not long after the Civil War, the railroad reached the town, and promptly there was a stockyard at the northern end of Chisholm Trail, on which cattle were brought from Texas to the market. With the cattle came rough-riding cowboys. Abilene suddenly became notorious as the center of saloons, gambling houses, bawdy houses, and daily shootings. Among the town marshals who tried to bring law and order was a figure of legend, "Wild Bill" Hickock, who would be the town's most famous resident until another son of Abilene landed in England in June 1942.

But by the time the Eisenhowers and the Stovers reached Abilene, that colorful historic moment was over and Abilene had subsided into small-town ordinariness. The reasons those families came had nothing to do with cattle or the railroad or gunfights; they were part of a communal move undertaken by their religious group, the River Brethren.

The religious underpinnings of the normative American midwestern small town would be pluralistically Protestant, sectarian, individualistic, evangelical—in other words, not liturgical, communal, or Catholic, but also not secular. There would be multiple Protestant churches, leaning toward the free churches. In the special circumstance of Abilene, the River Brethren were one of them.

---

* Carlo D'Este tells the true story of the failed dry goods store, which does not include any absconding (see pp. 18–19). Dwight told the family's mistaken version briefly in his memoir *At Ease* (see p. 31).

The Eisenhauers of Bavaria, then of Switzerland, then, briefly, of Holland, then, later—in the early eighteenth century—of "Penn's woods" in the New World, and still later, after the Civil War, of Kansas, were, throughout all these moves, Mennonites. This religious affiliation was a chief cause of their frequent moves. The Stovers, the family of Dwight Eisenhower's mother, Ida Stover, had a similar history and were also long-time Mennonites. In the New World, both families came to be members of a subgroup of Mennonites, given their name, the River Brethren, because they carried on baptisms in the Susquehanna River.

The Mennonite heritage, which lasted so long and held together in such an impressive way, came right up to the edges of Dwight Eisenhower's youth and life—but then abruptly evaporated. In its European origins it had the cultural strength of a sect—a group with distinctive affirmations that has to some extent withdrawn from, and rejected elements of, the broader culture. A follower of Menno Simons (thus a "Mennist" or "Mennonite") was to *obey* the magistrate in all lawful and worldly things—but not himself to *be* the magistrate. Education was to be simple, Bible-based, and provided within the community. Farming was to be the primary occupation. There was to be no swearing, no taking of oaths, for an explicit biblical injunction forbade it. There was to be no marriage outside the group—a reason, presumably, that the Anabaptist line of the Eisenhowers and Stovers ran without a break through the centuries. Above all, there was to be no killing, no participation in war, no service to the worldly power of the state as a soldier. The pacifist principles of all branches of the Anabaptists was one of the reasons they were so often persecuted in Europe, which, in turn, is one of the reasons they moved so often, and why many finally made their way to that great haven for the persecuted in the New World, the Quaker colony whose very name many in eighteenth-century Europe would speak of with warm respect and admiration: Pennsylvania.

Then, after the Civil War, the River Brethren, like many Americans, saw rich lands and new opportunities in the West; encouraged by the Homestead Act and the spread of railroads, they moved there. This decision was not made by individual families, but by the whole sect's reaching a communal consensus to move to the rich farmland of Dickenson County, Kansas, where Abilene was located.

In the New World, the sectarian distinctiveness faded. In the haven of Pennsylvania, industriously working their farms and making their honest but shrewd business deals, the Mennonites were not as far outside the structures of power, or so far over on the fringes of society, as they had been in Europe. Pennsylvania as a colony and then America as a nation welcomed all religious groups, put none in a preferred place, and sanctioned no official persecution. And then in Kansas, though the River Brethren made the move as a communal venture, they were not enclosed within their own community as closely as they had been in the enclave of the Pennsylvania Dutch. The Mennonite heritage persisted in Dwight's home and in that of his parents: His mother had such a mastery of the Bible that she not only won prizes but also prided herself on not having to look up any biblical quotation, reciting it from memory instead. His father learned enough Greek that he could read the New Testament in that language. It was he who said grace before the family's meals. There were daily readings from the Bible. But in the generations of David and Ida Eisenhower and then of their boys, the pluralism of the New World, the openness and dynamism of the American West, and the acids of modernity did their work on the centuries-old heritage of the Mennonite sect. After the disillusioning experience of his business failure, David Eisenhower began to search the Scriptures as well as his heart, and he carried the fissiparous tendency of sectarian Protestantism to its logical end—as an independent individual thinker joined to no church. His wife turned to a narrower sect of more recent origin, becoming a Jehovah's Witness. None of their six sons, successful in various middle-class undertakings, had the remotest connections to the River Brethren in adulthood. When Dwight went to West Point, he had to attend compulsory chapel services, whose enforced attendance he used in later life as an excuse for not going to any church. There is almost no evidence of his Mennonite youth in the speeches or letters of the mature Eisenhower; the Mennonite heritage would appear only in anecdotes. In Kensington in the early stages of World War II, when the time came to tell family stories in Telegraph Cottage, after Kay Summersby had told tales of her Irish childhood, the central figure in the "family" there, General Eisenhower, would tell about his uncle Abraham, a River Brethren minister, the Reverend Abraham Lincoln Eisenhower, who could gather a crowd anytime he wanted to by going out into the streets, stretching his arm upward, pointing, and shouting, "This way to heaven!"

It is rather a clear symbol of the evaporation of the Mennonite heritage in his life that when Dwight Eisenhower was considering a college education and sought admission to Annapolis or West Point, he does not appear to have been inhibited in the slightest by the fact that going to those places meant becoming a warrior. Some biographers mention in passing the irony of the great military commander with a pacifist mother who wept

when he went off to West Point to become a soldier—the only time her
youngest son, Milton, had seen her weep. But that certainly did not deter
Dwight.

In the future, the Mennonite heritage would mean this to the supreme
commander and president: that unlike his new friend Winston Churchill,
he did not come into power conscious of a family heritage of outranking
others and holding power. Quite the opposite. The Eisenhowers had out-
ranked nobody.

Another main feature of the normative small town in the American hinterland is the dominant role of the public schools. Abilene did not have
enough Catholics for there to be Catholic schools, nor enough rich people
for there to be private schools; everybody went to public school. Ike went
to Lincoln Grade School and Garfield Junior High, the schools in Abilene
named for Republican presidents. Dwight was often bored, but he liked
the exactitude of spelling and of math, and the detail of history. When
he had achieved the White House, one of his teachers was interviewed by
Dave Garroway on the new medium of television:

> GARROWAY: Mrs. Wolf, how old was the President when he was your
> student?
> MRS. WOLF: He was nine years old, Mr. Garroway.
> G.: What sort of student was he?
> MRS. W.: Well, Mr. Garroway, you remember only two types of
> students—the exceptionally bright and the exceptionally ornery. The
> President was neither. Still, I remember him as a well-behaved boy. I
> would describe him as an average bright student.

Abilene was big enough to have its own high school and small enough
to have only *one* high school. The high school that Dwight Eisenhower
entered in the fall of 1904 did not yet have its own building; instead, it
occupied the first floor of the redbrick pseudo-Romanesque city hall. That
structure also housed the volunteer fire department, so when an alarm
rang, every high school boy was perforce a volunteer. While Ike was a
freshman, Abilene built a new two-story high school building. When
Eisenhower graduated in 1909, his class, as was common, had more girls
than boys: twenty-five girls, nine boys.

The education one received in such schools was overwhelmingly practical and down-to-earth, as would be all of Dwight Eisenhower's formal
education. After Abilene's public schools, that education took place
entirely within the context of the army—at West Point from 1911 to 1915,
at the U.S. Army Command and General Staff College at Fort Leaven-

worth from 1925 to 1926, and at the Army War College at Fort Leslie J. McNair in Washington in 1928. Kenneth S. Davis wrote of Eisenhower's days in West Point: "His sharp externalized mind would fit easily into a system of education which was, in the narrowest and most rigid sense, technical and scientific." But Ike did like to read history, and during his career he would surprise and impress associates with his memory of historical facts.

In their self-interpretation, these small mid-American towns were little democracies, societies without sharp class distinctions. "Everybody" knew "everybody." The schools would be seen as repositories and nurturers of democratic virtue. In the first Eisenhower biography, Kenneth S. Davis, himself a Kansan, wrote that "generally speaking, a man here is judged pretty much for what he himself is. Family means little; there are no 'old families.' Class means virtually nothing; the average Kansan is hardly aware that there is such a thing as a 'class.' " On the occasion of Dwight Eisenhower's triumphant return to Abilene, the heroic general "Swede" Hazlett, his boyhood friend from Abilene, the one who first got him interested in the service academies and who himself went to Annapolis and into the navy, wrote Ike a letter. He penned it by hand on "17 June, 1945" on University of North Carolina NROTC stationery (as "Professor of Naval Science and Tactics"). He celebrated Ike's return after V-E Day to the hometown they shared. "Welcome Home!" he began. "Welcome back to that good little town where there was never any difference between 'north of the tracks' and 'south of the tracks' and where we both received our first lessons in the kind of democracy that counts!" In 1947, Ike himself wrote that Abilene represented "a society which, more than any other I have encountered, eliminated prejudices based upon wealth, race, creed."

But was Abilene so perfect a democracy? A skeptic might observe that large parts of the nation and the world (speaking of races and creeds) were not represented in Abilene's rather pure white Protestant world. Dwight Eisenhower would have one close Catholic friend in Abilene, "Six" Mac-Donell, a man who would later be an accomplished left-handed pitcher, but it was a Protestant world—no Jews, few Catholics. The number of Negroes (the term used at the time) in Abilene was minuscule. The 1910 census listed 4,118 citizens in the town, only 110 of whom were Negroes— so small a number as to be out of sight, out of mind. Ike grew up in a white world. And as to the absence of "class": One is reminded that John Dollard, who wrote the classic sociological study *Caste and Class in a Southern Town,* knew, of course, that the little town he wrote about had a caste system—a sharp racial divide—but was told that the white world

was free of class distinctions. When he got there, he found that the outstanding fact about the place was, actually, its class distinctions. One may
notice in the letter from Swede Hazlett that when he said there was no
difference between the north and the south of Abilene, that difference was
the first and only item he mentioned. In *At Ease,* Ike wrote that when they
all attended Garfield School, the hostility between boys from the north
side and those from the south led to fights, like one in which he was the
south-side representative.

In this rather pure sample of American boyhood, there was a primary
emphasis on physical activity. In the household of six boys, there was
rivalry and competition, particularly between Edgar ("big Ike") and
Dwight ("little Ike"). The center of the young Eisenhowers' life was not
the church or the school, but the playing field and the outdoors. Little Ike
wrote to Big Ike many years after their boyhood adventures that it would
not be difficult to "make you and me look like Tom Sawyer and Huck
Finn." Dwight's early years were an idyll of American midwesternness.
There were lots of chores to be performed and evaded in the small Eisenhower home. There was also lots of horseplay and fighting and competition. And sports were of enormous importance—especially baseball and
football, which were at the center of young Dwight's life. Playing on
the teams was a major reason he wanted to go to West Point; he was chagrined when he was not chosen for the football varsity in his plebe, or
first, year.

"One of my reasons for going to West Point," he wrote, "was the hope
that I could continue an athletic career. It would be difficult to overem-
phasize the importance I attached to participation in sports. . . . In high
school and afterward I had some local reputation as a center fielder." There
was even a report, not much elaborated on by biographers and covered
with a certain mystery, that he played a bit of semipro baseball. As a plebe
at West Point, he was considered too small and light to make the football
varsity. But he did make it thereafter, and played in several games, until in
a game against Tufts he was tackled in a way that twisted his knee and
ended his football career. In the years to come, every man from Tufts he
met apologized for being the one who had tackled him on that day.

On one of the great occasions of Dwight Eisenhower's life, the victory
celebration at the Guildhall in London on June 12, 1945, at which he was
made an honorary citizen of London and presented with the Duke of
Wellington's sword, he explicitly said, "I come from the very heart of
America." Moreover, although he acknowledged that London was bigger
and older than Abilene, he nevertheless, with the innocent or pseudo-

innocent audacity of one born not far from Mark Twain's birthplace, and without any apparent sense of incongruity, placed these two locations (London, England, and Abilene, Kansas) in a kind of parallel spiritual equality. For the great freedoms of humankind, "a Londoner will fight. So will a citizen of Abilene."

It is a striking fact—considering Abilene and the Eisenhowers—that something in the family and perhaps the town equipped all of these sons of a poor family to make successful lives in a larger world: There were no black sheep. Arthur became a banker in Kansas City, Missouri; Edgar, a well-to-do lawyer in Tacoma, Washington; Roy, the only brother to stay in the state of Kansas, a pharmacist in Junction City; Earl, an electrical engineer for a power company in Pennsylvania and then a general manager of a publication and a legislator in Illinois; Milton, the youngest, and the most eminent brother before Dwight achieved fame, became a high federal bureaucrat and then president of three major universities in succession. At some point in the doldrums of peacetime, Dwight might have been regarded as the least successful brother.

One might add this further striking fact: Whatever the sturdy midwestern virtues of Abilene, the whole raft of Eisenhower boys got away from there.

No doubt Dwight's affectionate nostalgia for Abilene was genuine and its merits real. Nevertheless, when it came time to pick a place in which to retire, he chose not Abilene, but Gettysburg.

III

THE AMERICAN MIDDLE WEST featured in the life of Harry Truman not only with regard to the geographical location of the small town he came from but also because he spent some years outside that town as a farmer. In his early childhood, before they moved to Independence, his family had lived on farms, especially the farm of his formidable maternal grandfather, Solomon Young, near Grandview, Missouri, south of Independence, which furnished fond bucolic memories for Truman. Then, in 1906, when he was twenty-two, family necessity called him back from his bank job in the city to join his maternal grandmother, his father, and his mother on that Solomon Young farm of his childhood. The growing American mythic memory of Harry Truman may not include, to the degree that his life did, his role as a farmer. He spent eleven years as a farmer, from 1906 until he went into the army in 1917, from his twenty-second until his thirty-third year. He spent more time being a farmer than any other president of the United States, but he did so from necessity, not desire; that is not what he wanted to be or to do.

Truman was born in 1884, six years before Dwight Eisenhower, in another small town in the midst of the cows and wheat and pigs and corn and grain elevators of the nation's great midsection. Independence, Missouri, was fewer than 170 miles east of Abilene (today, by the Truman Road and the Eisenhower Highway, 163.3 miles). The proximity of the two towns was such that when, in the fall of 1904, Harry Truman, as a young bank clerk, was boarding "with some of the bank boys" at Mrs. Trow's boardinghouse at 1314 Troost Avenue in Kansas City, the nearest big town, one of the other bank boys boarding there was Arthur Eisenhower, Dwight's eldest brother, who had also gone to the nearest big city to become a bank clerk. Mrs. Trow charged the future president and the brother of another future president five dollars a week for breakfast, dinner, and a room (two to a room), and according to Harry Truman, she was "a cook you read about but seldom see."

As the Eisenhowers had moved from Pennsylvania in a great trek to Kansas, so the Trumans had moved in another great migration from Kentucky to Missouri. Missouri, admitted to the Union as a slave state in 1821 as part of the Missouri Compromise, was in its politics regularly Democratic. The Trumans and the Youngs (Truman's mother was a Young) had been Scots-Irish Democrats when they made their trek from Kentucky; their county was named Jackson, after the great Democratic party hero Andrew Jackson. The Civil War reinforced the heavily Democratic leaning of Missouri, of Jackson County, and of Independence. Among Harry Truman's early memories would be the great torchlight parade celebrating Grover Cleveland's second victory, in the presidential race in 1892; Harry's father, John Truman, a livestock trader and farmer who was a very active Democrat, would play a prominent role in that celebration.

Young Harry Truman was a different sort from Dwight Eisenhower, in part because of his eyes. From the time he was six, he was prevented from playing sports and roughhousing by the thick glasses he had to wear for his "flat eyeballs." He always had a book, and later claimed to have read everything in the town library, including the encyclopedias. He took piano lessons for a large part of his youth. Some of his best friends were girls, especially his cousins Ethel and Nellie Roland. One might expect the big Ikes and little Ikes of his town to have applied to him the appellation most dreaded of all for an American boy in an American town: "sissy." One day in the auditorium of the Truman Library, a small boy "whose ears had grown up but not his face" asked Truman, "Mr. President, was you popular when you was a boy?" "Why, no," Truman replied. "I was never popular. The popular boys were the ones who were good at games and had big, tight fists. I was never like that. Without my glasses I was blind as a bat, and to tell the truth, I was kind of a sissy. If there was any danger of getting into a fight, I always ran. I guess that's why I am here today."* David McCullough discovered other recollections from Truman's boyhood friends: "He wasn't considered a sissy exactly, only different, 'serious.' " McCullough quoted one of these friends:

> They wanted to call him a sissy, but they just didn't do it because they had a lot of respect for him. I remember one time we were playing . . . Jesse James or robbers and we were the Dalton brothers out in Kansas . . . and we were arguing about them . . . we got the history mixed up . . . but Harry came in and straightened it out, just who were the Dalton brothers and how many got killed. Things like that the boys had a lot of respect for. They didn't call him sissy.

Being the expert on how many of the Dalton boys got killed makes Harry sound like Tom Sawyer soberly adducing "the authorities."

In 1910, Harry Truman, working in Kansas City, spent twenty-five dollars of his own hard-earned money for a twenty-five-volume set of Mark Twain's works.

When they moved into the town of Independence, the Trumans were not part of the upper crust. Bess Wallace's mother, apparently throughout her son-in-law's entire life, including his serving as leader of the free world, never quite got over the feeling that he did not come from as high a social level as the Wallaces had expected a daughter of theirs to marry. Bess Wallace was the granddaughter of George Porterfield Gates, who had done well after the Civil War as a partner in the Waggoner-Gates Milling Company of Independence, making the "Queen of the Pantry" flour; the Wallaces were a cut or two higher than the Trumans in the social hierarchy of Independence.

Harry's father, John Truman, invested and lost heavily just at the time that his son would have gone to college; the money was not there, so young Harry went to work instead. He was, presumably, the last American president never to have attended college.

Independence, like Abilene, was overwhelmingly white and Protestant, not only in numbers but in culture. After he left Independence for the

---

* Alonzo Hambry began his Truman biography with this anecdote (see p. 3). It came originally from Merle Miller, *Plain Speaking: An Oral Biography of Harry S Truman* (see pp. 31–32).

army and for Kansas City, Harry Truman would have a Jewish buddy, business partner, and lifelong friend, Eddie Jacobson. His company in the army during the Great War, Battery D of the 129th Field Artillery, would be composed of Irish and German Catholics from Kansas City, and the priest who was their chaplain would be a lifelong friend. But all of that was later, after he had left home.

Truman attended the public schools of Independence, graduating from Independence High School in 1901 in a class of only forty-one students, thirty of them, including Bess Wallace, girls. Another of the eleven boys was Charlie Ross, the class intellectual and valedictorian, who later would be press secretary to President Truman.

Harry Truman's reading of and interest in, and *memory of,* history, especially American history and classical Greek and Roman history, were to be salient aspects of his vivid personality all his life, often surprising and impressing people with much superior formal educations, including biographers and Washington journalists. In the first summer he was president of the United States and suddenly conferring with the great leaders of England and Russia at Potsdam, he was taken to see the ruin of Berlin. He would write in his diary on July 16, 1945, about Hitler's devastation: "I thought of Carthage, Baalbek, Jerusalem, Rome, Atlantis, Peking, Nineveh, Scipio, Ramses II, Titus, Herman, Sherman, Genghis Khan, Alexander, Darius the Great."

When you consider the heritage of slavery and the Civil War, the picture of the two towns—Independence and Abilene—in other ways much alike, is radically altered. They are *not* alike with respect to the Civil War.

They were on opposite sides not just of the Civil War but also of the bloody border war that preceded it. The Civil War began in western Missouri and eastern Kansas not in 1861, but in 1854, when Stephen Douglas's bill for "squatter sovereignty" virtually invited a war over whether Kansas Territory would be slave or free. Bushwhackers from Missouri and Jayhawkers and Red Legs from Kansas raided, looted, and killed. Independence and Jackson County, Missouri, were at the center of one side of the ensuing war; the tiny unincorporated village of Abilene was a little beyond the western edge of the other side.

Harry Truman, who knew the history of all this, had family connections to the notorious William Quantrill, who, when you get far enough away from Independence, is described as the bloodthirsty leader of the bloody border ruffians and who, among other awful deeds, killed most of the citizens of Lawrence, Kansas, in a bloody raid. (For many in Independence, however, Quantrill was a hero. Merle Miller, visiting Independence for his interviews with Truman, met an old resident who told him, "If we'd had a few more like Quantrill we'd have won the War Between the States.")

The different attitudes on the other side of the border are suggested by the name of the school that Ike's father, David Eisenhower, attended and where he met his future wife, Ida Stover: Lane University. It was a small United Brethren school in Lecompton, Kansas, which had, with extreme presumption, been given its doubly dubious name—dubious because it was far from being a university and also because it was named for a man who was almost Quantrill's Kansas equivalent, the notorious Jim Lane.

James Henry Lane, the "Grim Chieftain of Kansas," led his raids, too, and one of them struck the farm of Solomon Young, Truman's maternal grandfather. Young himself was away at the time; Truman's grandmother, who was there, never forgot it, and, in fact, she entered a formal claim against the "Union" forces under Lane for their depredations. The brutality of this raid lived on in the Young and Truman family memories. In his autobiographical fragments, Harry Truman described what Lane did to his grandmother: "Jim Lane, a Kansas hero, had burned her house, killed four hundred of her hogs, cut the hams out and set the carcasses lie to rot. On top of that he forced her to make biscuits for the men until all her fingers were blistered."

Jim Lane, a hero in Kansas and a villain in Missouri, a colorful scamp, got himself elected as one of the first senators from Kansas, and he contributed two thousand dollars in cash to the new institution of higher education on the site of the proposed pro-slavery state government in Lecompton. Lane University eventually merged with another small college, which, in turn, merged with another, but that school closed after the crash of 1929.

Stories about the senior Mrs. Truman's indignant rejection of Lincoln abound in the Truman literature. For example, Clark Clifford tells this story about Martha Ellen Young Truman and her relationship to Abraham Lincoln: One evening when she had just arrived from Missouri for a stay at the White House, the president made a small joke that played on his mother's southern roots. "Tonight, Mother," he said, his eyes dancing, "we are going to give you a special treat, a chance to sleep in the most famous room in the White House, the Lincoln Room, and in the very bed in which Abraham Lincoln slept." There was quiet in the group for a moment, and Mrs. Truman—brought up on the myths of the old Confederacy by parents who had owned slaves—looked at her daughter-in-law and said, "Bess, if you'll get my bags packed, I'll be going back home this evening." Led by the president, everyone in the room started howling with laughter. The president's mother, realizing that it was a joke, finally joined in.

IV

HARRY S TRUMAN and Dwight David Eisenhower, the last American presidents to be born in the nineteenth century, would have much in common. They were both, as we have seen, grandsons of farmers. They were both sons of fathers who were respected but whose lives were interrupted by failure; both were children of forceful mothers in strong families. As we have seen, they were both small-town boys (in 1890, Abilene's population was 3,547; Independence's, 6,380). Each of them was born, as the result of reverses in his father's work life, in small towns (Truman in Lamar, Missouri, population 2,036; Eisenhower in Denison, Texas, population 10,768). They were both from the lower-middle class (John Truman, a mule trader; David Eisenhower, a mechanic at a dairy); both were educated in the small town's public schools; both were brought up in a low-church Protestant denomination (Truman a Baptist, Eisenhower an Anabaptist). Both would occasionally refer to the planet Earth, as no other recent president would be likely to do, as "God's footstool." Both were graduated, as we have noted, in a class with more girls than boys from the small town's one high school.

They were both externally minded sons of the middle border, active, purposeful. They both did well in school. They both liked history. They both were drawn to generals. They both admired Robert E. Lee, and both of them admired and knew about Hannibal. Neither of them was likely to become a lyric poet or a metaphysician.

Both worked hard when young (Truman at J. H. Clinton's Drug Store; Eisenhower at the Belle Springs Dairy). Neither had an assured college future. Harry Truman wanted to go to West Point but accidentally (because of his eyes) could not; Dwight Eisenhower had no particular desire to go there but accidentally did go.

They were both conscientious midwesterners with a strong sense of duty. They would both spend their entire careers in public service. They were both honest with respect to money. Neither one of them would own the house that he lived in until his entire career was over. Truman lived and died probably the poorest of twentieth-century presidents, certainly the poorest of the last fifty years. Eisenhower, in spite of book sales and rich friends, would not be among the richest.

Both married "above themselves" and had lifelong marriages. Harry

Truman displayed a spectacular devotion to Bess Wallace from the time he met her in the Presbyterian Sunday school when he was six until he died at eighty-eight. Through twenty-nine years of courtship and fifty-three years of marriage, he was faithful, apparently, despite life in the army in France, innumerable road trips as a traveling politician, regular attendance at American Legion conventions, and months of living alone in Washington, eating in Hot Shoppes, while Bess and Margaret went back to Independence. Dwight Eisenhower kept his marriage together through twenty-five years in the military camps of a peacetime army, seventeen different places of residence, a radical four-year wartime separation while he lived on another continent from his wife and became famous, as well as the focus of gossip because of his relationship with his driver, Kay Summersby, and then through twenty-four more years of fame, power, and retirement.

Both men had a straightforward, uncomplicated patriotism. The chief living moral model for both of them would be the same man: George Marshall. Truman chose him instead of the slippery Franklin Roosevelt; Eisenhower preferred him to the flamboyant Douglas MacArthur.

Although members of the Lost Generation, neither of them was lost. Although members of their generation engaged in the "revolt from the village" after the Great War and lived in Paris, neither of these villagers revolted. Neither went to Paris, or to anywhere else in Europe, except when sent there by the army.

V

WHEN JACQUELINE KENNEDY ONASSIS DIED, *Newsweek* contrasted the glamour of the White House during the Kennedys' brief occupancy with the atmosphere under the two previous presidents, who were lumped together—the Eisenhowers and the Trumans—as the Kennedys' "dowdy" predecessors.

Arthur Schlesinger, Jr., in *A Thousand Days*, describing Presidents John F. Kennedy and Franklin Roosevelt, said they were both "patrician, urbane, cultivated, inquisitive, gallant." The last of these words might by applied by some sympathetic interpreters to one or the other of the two men we are dealing with in these pages, or to both of them, but no one would apply Schlesinger's whole sequence to either. They were not patrician or urbane. Truman, on being asked what he did on his first day after becoming president, famously said, "I took the grips up to the attic." Eisenhower, responding to applause in a London theater soon after he had left

France after the victory in World War II, said, "It is good to be back in a country where I can *almost* speak the language."

They were both gregarious, friendly, card-playing joiners, with circles of friends all their lives. Dwight Eisenhower loved to play bridge, read endless Luke Short pulp Westerns, and could sing forty verses of "Abdul Abulbul Amir" (some authorities say fifty verses). Harry Truman loved to play poker, drank bourbon, wore excessive flowered sport shirts in Key West, and was an active Mason, Shriner, Elk, and Moose.

Harry Truman and Dwight Eisenhower, two ordinary, honorable Americans, did not have particularly "successful" careers. They were not instant, early successes—not the young men "going places" of American myth. They did not spring up life's ladder with rapid steps. No distinguished elder said to either of them, at their early display of dazzling abilities, what Emerson said to Walt Whitman: "Young man, I salute you at the outset of a great career." They were not expected to have particularly brilliant careers.

These two nondazzlers were not mediocrities, however. They were well regarded by their peers. They were able and honorable men who did their jobs, just as thousands of others were doing their jobs. They went about their work in the institutions in which life had, somewhat accidentally, placed them—in the various camps of the peacetime army, in the political institutions of Jackson County, Missouri; at Fort Houston, near San Antonio; at Fort Oglethorpe, in Georgia; at Camp Colt, near Gettysburg; at Camp Meade, in Pennsylvania; at a farm near Grandview, Missouri; in the National Guard; in Battery D of the 129th Field Artillery; at the haberdashery at Twelfth and Baltimore; at the Kansas City Automobile Club; at the county commission of Jackson County.

These able, intelligent, honorable men were recognized as such by their peers in their particular circles (the political sphere of Jackson County, Missouri; the peacetime army of the United States). Both had experiences in the larger world and gained some recognition and achievement beyond the ordinary. Truman was the respected and even beloved Captain Harry of Battery D of the 129th Field Artillery in the Great War; the energetic and *honest* road-building judge of the county court; a senator who investigated the defense industries. His merit was recognized not only by the inner core of United States senators but by (to name two surprises) Louis Brandeis and Bernard Berenson. Eisenhower was an early theorist of tank warfare and wrote a pioneering article on the subject in 1920; and he was the top graduate of the army's Command and General Staff School in 1926. If not himself a world-class bridge player, he could play with someone who was, his friend General Gruenther. His merit was recognized not only by each of the other top American generals of the century—Pershing, MacArthur, and, of course, Marshall—but also by the little-known but much-respected military intellectual Fox Conner.

But such achievements and recognitions come into sharp focus only *after* these men had achieved world fame. No one, including their close associates, would have named either of them, in 1939, as a man who would soon become a world leader at the very highest level.

Eisenhower was a major for sixteen years, and expected to retire as one. Harry Truman, the ex-captain, ex-haberdasher, ex–county judge, almost lost his Senate seat in 1940, at age fifty-six, in the Democratic primary in Missouri.

They did not have the youthful triumphs and great expectations that marked the early careers of, for example, Douglas MacArthur and Thomas E. Dewey—two men whose lives would intersect with both of theirs significantly.

Douglas MacArthur, whose father was a graduate of West Point and a famous general, graduated from West Point in 1903, *first* in his class. Dwight Eisenhower, whose father was a member of a pacifist sect and a mechanic in a dairy in a small town in Kansas, graduated from West Point in 1915, *sixty-first* in his class.

In the Great War, Douglas MacArthur rose to the rank of brigadier general, commanding the famous Forty-second ("Rainbow") Division. Dwight Eisenhower, desperate to get overseas, was kept at home, training others to go, and at the end of the war, he was living in a former college fraternity house at Gettysburg College, with the temporary rank of major, after which he returned to the rank of captain. Harry Truman started that war as a private in the Missouri National Guard, fought in France as a first lieutenant in an artillery unit, and rose at the end of the war to the rank of captain, then left the army and went into the business of selling shirts.

In 1925, when Douglas MacArthur became the youngest major general in the United States Army, Dwight Eisenhower, having crept up to the rank of major, was serving as a recruiting officer, having served the previous fall as backfield coach to the Third Corps Area football team at Camp Meade, in Maryland, and at Fort Logan, in Colorado. A year later, in June 1926, there was a grand reunion of all the Eisenhower brothers in Abilene, and each of the other five had brighter prospects and was making more money than Major Eisenhower. Arthur was a vice president of a leading Kansas City bank; Edgar was a prominent lawyer in Tacoma; Roy was a pharmacist in Junction City; Earl was an engineer in Pennsylvania; Milton was a high-ranking official in the Agriculture Department. "David and Ida," Stephen Ambrose wrote, "justly proud of them all, may have wondered when Dwight would get going."

Harry Truman, meanwhile, was paying off his debts from his failed efforts to sell men's shirts at Twelfth and Baltimore in Kansas City; had just been defeated for the post of county judge in Jackson County, Missouri; was selling memberships in the Kansas City Automobile Club; and was studying law in night school, an effort that he would soon have to abandon.

In 1930, Douglas MacArthur would be appointed chief of staff of the United States Army, with the rank of full general; if he had died in that year, when he was just fifty years old, he already would have been one of a handful of the most notable American military men of the century, but he went on to yet further glory. He was appointed chief of staff of the army not once, but twice—not by one president only, but by two (Hoover and Roosevelt). He went on to be field marshal of the Philippine Army; the commander of Allied Forces in the Southwest Pacific, general of the army, and commander of U.S. forces in the Pacific in World War II; head of the Allied delegation that received the Japanese surrender aboard the battleship *Missouri;* supreme commander of the Allied occupation forces in Japan, a unique sort of proconsul; and commander of the United Nations forces in the Korean War. He would personally direct the amphibious landing at Inchon, a model military operation that will be studied through the ages, yet another historic military accomplishment to add to those he had already accumulated in World Wars I and II. One of his subordinates in the 1930s, in Washington and the Philippines, and for longer than most people would realize (seven years), was a lieutenant colonel whose career was more or less static while MacArthur ascended from glory to glory: Dwight David Eisenhower.

One of the myriad veterans of that early step on MacArthur's path to glory, World War I, who wanted to go to West Point, could not even go there because of his eyes and was not accepted (although he tried to be accepted) for service in World War II, and whose military career after he was mustered out in 1919 was confined to bourbon and poker reunions with his buddies, was Harry S Truman. Nevertheless, in the early morning of April 11, 1951, Harry S Truman of the Missouri National Guard, the sometime captain in the field artillery, sent a telegram to the "Supreme Commander, Allied Powers; Commander in Chief, United Nations Command; Commander in Chief, Far East; and Commanding General, U.S. Army, Far East." It began, "I deeply regret that it becomes my duty as

President and Commander in Chief of the United States military forces to replace you . . ."

When Harry Truman was making his abortive stab at studying law in night school in Kansas City in 1925, Thomas E. Dewey, then just twenty-three years old and graduating from a real daytime law school at Columbia University, would spring upward in success and in fame, becoming known as a gang-busting district attorney in his early thirties; a candidate for governor of the nation's largest state at thirty-six; and as governor of New York at forty. He was reelected governor when he was only forty-four by the largest margin in the state's history. He became his party's nominee for the nation's highest office at forty-two, and he was his party's nominee again, assured of certain victory, four years later. There he was, in a full-page picture in *Life* magazine, only forty-six years old, projected to be the next president of the United States, the first president to be born in the twentieth century, Thomas E. Dewey. But time and chance happeneth to us all. President Dewey's public career was effectively over before he was fifty. If Harry Truman and Dwight Eisenhower had died at the age of fifty, we would never have heard of either of them.

But they did not die at fifty. Each of these men, after a lifetime of comparative obscurity, was grasped by the hand of history in the turbulent 1940s and suddenly hurled upward, past thousands of others, to awesome, unimaginable heights. There would be a preliminary elevation, big enough by ordinary standards, which would prove to be a staging area (to a second term in the United States Senate and the chairmanship of the committee to investigate the war effort; to the war-plans division of the War Department in Washington), and then in an incredibly compressed period (Eisenhower June 24, 1942–December 7, 1943; Truman July 21, 1944–April 12, 1945), each was catapulted up through layer upon layer of human function and preferment, past all peers, past all erstwhile superiors, to a unique position at the very top, to what Stephen Ambrose would call "the most coveted command in the history of warfare," and to the office with the most potent amalgam of physical and moral power ever assembled on God's footstool.

CHAPTER TWO

Two Warriors, First War

I

IN THE GREAT WAR, the civilian Harry Truman, the bank clerk and future haberdasher, proved himself a leader, was promoted, was commended, went overseas, was shot at, and held command of a body of men under fire. The warrior Dwight Eisenhower, the future supreme commander, proved himself a leader, was promoted (temporarily), was commended (belatedly), did not go overseas, was not shot at, and did not hold command of a body of men under fire.

Truman would be given responsibility beyond what he expected; would do his conscientious best; would succeed; and would end the war with the commendation of his superiors, the lifelong devotion of his men, and a new confidence in himself.

Eisenhower would hope to have an overseas command, would be dismayed at being sent instead to camps in the United States to train young men for battle; would each time do a good job anyway; would each time be commended; would each time request overseas assignment; would be dismayed at being sent instead to yet another camp to train yet more men for battle.

Eisenhower would be awarded the Distinguished Service Medal for the "unusual zeal, foresight, and marked administrative ability in the organization, training, and preparation for overseas" of the troops in his last assignment—but those troops never actually went overseas, and the medal was awarded ten years after the war was over.

When the Great War ended, it had been, for Harry Truman, a great fulfillment and source of self-discovery; for Dwight Eisenhower, it had been a great frustration.

But in a different way it was almost as important in the shaping of Dwight Eisenhower as of Harry Truman. What Eisenhower did in the first war—training officers, building and commanding a camp from scratch, learning about tanks, coping with diverse authorities—may have been more valuable for what he would do in World War II than would have been the narrow focus on the immobile trench warfare in World War I.

And the frustration of missing the war, of not being sent overseas to do what he had been trained to do, would fuel a new ambition in the hitherto rather relaxed midwestern army football coach.

Still, it was hard. John Keegan, the military historian, wrote about a soldier who saw action on the other side in this war, Adolf Hitler, saying that he would become a military snob—not a snob of rank, but a combat snob. There would be combat snobs from all the armies, and Dwight Eisenhower felt he would be subject to their slurs for the rest of his career. A biographer of Montgomery would write: "[N]ot until Air Marshal Broadhurst flew him over the battlefield of Mareth in April 1943 had Eisenhower ever seen a dead body." Even as late as September 1944, when the supreme commander, Dwight Eisenhower, took over the direct command of the Allied land armies in France, subordinating General Montgomery, a British major, Peter Earle, who was close to Montgomery, would scathingly describe the new commander as "Colonel Eisenhower of the Operations Divisions, the US War Department, who had never seen a shot fired in his life."

Harry Truman, in his different line of work, would not be subject to such slurs. His service in the war would be the foundation of the rest of his life, getting him away from the farm and providing customers for his store and voters for his political career.

When President Woodrow Wilson gave his war speech on April 2, 1917, symbolically the beginning of the bloody twentieth century for Americans, future president Harry Truman volunteered and helped get other men to volunteer.

The United States in 1917 was not a superpower, not a major power; in fact, it was not any kind of power, except potentially. David Fromkin has noted that when Wilson gave his war speech, the U.S. Army was smaller than the army commanded by General Washington, forces designed for Indian fighting in the eighteenth century. In her own view of herself, the United States had left old Europe behind, and that meant, among many other things, that she had transcended and disengaged from the balances of power, the alliance systems and calculations of national interest of the Old World. She had taken a tiny step back into that world in 1898, in a "splendid little war" with Spain; with Wilson's war speech in April 1917, she took a giant step into that realm in which wars would henceforth be neither little nor splendid.

Harry Truman out on the farm in Missouri thought Wilson was a great man. When at the Democratic National Convention in 1912 there had been a contest for the presidential nomination, although strong contender

Champ Clark came from Missouri and had the support of Harry's father, young Harry supported Governor Woodrow Wilson of New Jersey. He was thrilled when Wilson won both the nomination and, in a three-way race, the presidential office. He was further thrilled when Wilson was reelected in 1916. And then there was the lasting thrill of Wilson's war speech, which Truman never forgot.

Wilson's war speeches were among the most extraordinary oratorical performances in American history. In eloquence and in intellectual power, no speeches by President Harry Truman, or by President Dwight Eisenhower, or perhaps by any other president later in that turbulent century, could match them. But they were very "American" speeches, in a sense not altogether complimentary: noble, idealistic, "moral"—but also tainted with a national self-righteousness and naïveté. Forced by Germany's U-boat attacks on America's merchant shipping into a war he had long tried to stay out of, Wilson justified American entry into it in the highest moral terms. The United States fought not for territory, not for national advantage, not for "selfish" purposes, but for right, for peace, for democracy. The United States would fight its own war—separate from the European powers—against Germany (not, originally, against the other central powers).

However Wilson's war speech may sound to us now that this extraordinary chain of world events (1914–1919) is over, it was a thrilling speech to many, perhaps most, Americans at the time, including a farmer near Grandview, Missouri.

Harry Truman, already overage, with bad eyes, needed on the farm, and no longer a member of the Missouri National Guard (with which he had drilled and camped from 1905 to 1911), was not called up or drafted, and could responsibly have stayed home—but he joined anyway. He volunteered for the first war at thirty-three and tried to volunteer for the second at fifty-six.

When in April a new field artillery battery was formed out of elements of the Missouri National Guard, he was made first lieutenant. When on August 5, 1917, his units of the Missouri National Guard became the 129th Field Artillery, attached to the 35th Division, Truman became an officer in the U.S. Army. That would be Truman's military home throughout the war, and, in a sense, forever.

For Truman, service in war was a patriotic duty, interrupting his life's work; for Eisenhower, it *was* his life's work. So it was deeply disappointing to Eisenhower when he was given his first assignment, in September 1917.

He was sent to Fort Oglethorpe, in Georgia, to train officer candidates. Harry Truman, meanwhile, was sent to Camp Doniphan at Fort Sill, in Oklahoma, to be one of the officer candidates somebody else trained.

The United States not only came late to the 1914 war; it also came unprepared. Even after the United States declared war in April 1917, there was another long wait while this unwarlike nation trained some armed forces. Harry Truman trained for six months in Oklahoma, trained again for five weeks at an artillery school in France, and drilled in two other places in France before he and his regiment went to the front less than three months before the war's end. Dwight Eisenhower trained officers at Fort Oglethorpe and at Fort Leavenworth; began to train with the new weapon, the tank, at Camp Meade; commanded a camp, training a new tank corps at Camp Colt; and would have been ready to join in the great American offensive in the spring of 1919 had there been a great American offensive then.

The American lateness applied to supplies as well as to men. In the second world war of the twentieth century, American *production* would be a primary cause of victory, supplying not only the nation's own armies but also, most important, this time, beginning even before the United States was in the war, Great Britain and Russia: fur-lined boots, trucks, planes, guns, ninety-day wonder ships, supplies of all kinds, a key to victory. This was *not* the case in the first war. In this first war, Dwight Eisenhower's training for tank warfare lacked one important feature: tanks. When he finally did get three of them, they were of French manufacture.

The light artillery cannon that Harry Truman learned about in France, four of which then served as his artillery unit's reason for being, were not of American manufacture, either. They were the famous French 75mm cannon, with elements the French kept secret, the "devil gun" to Germans. (A young officer on General Pershing's staff in the first war, George C. Marshall, was determined that in another war the story of the guns would be very different, as indeed would prove to be the case.)

Harry Truman's marriage was postponed by the war; Dwight Eisenhower's was hastened by it. When in the spring of 1916 American entry into the European war seemed increasingly likely, Ike and Mamie pushed back the date and were married at her parents' home in Denver in July. When Ike was sent to Fort Oglethorpe the next year, Mamie stayed behind in San Antonio, where they had been living at Fort Sam Houston; she was pregnant. Their son Doud David, whom Mamie called "Icky," was born in September, while his father was at camp in Georgia.

Bess Wallace was willing to marry Harry Truman before he went off to war, too, but, as one of his biographers says, "incredibly," the faithful, besotted Harry told her not yet, because he might return a cripple. So he went off to war, engaged but not married, and showered Bess with letters.

At Camp Doniphan in Oklahoma, a few hundred miles to the north of Ike and Mamie down in Texas, Harry Truman, in addition to his other duties, was put in charge of the canteen, where he and Eddie Jacobson sold apples, candy, soda pop, pencils, and pens, cut hair, and repaired uniforms. This was the first manifestation of Truman and Jacobson—the Kansas City store the two men would form after the war.

Both Eisenhower and Truman proved to be not only good leaders but also good instructors, good trainers. At first, Eisenhower was training and Truman was being trained, but later Truman was trained to train others. Of the best of his instructors in Oklahoma, an artillery authority named Robert M. Danford, later to be head of field artillery for the whole army, Truman was to write:

> He taught me more about handling men and the fundamentals of artillery fire in six weeks than I'd learned in six months. . . . It seemed to be the policy of all high-ranking artillery officers . . . to make a deep dark mystery out of the firing of a battery. They taught us logarithms, square root, trigonometry, navigation and logistics but never did tell us that all they wanted to do was to make the projectile hit the target. Danford told us that.

In March 1918, Harry Truman was sent to Europe, and saw sights he would not have seen and had experiences he would not have had back in Missouri; he would spend the next year crisscrossing France, courtesy of the U.S. Army.

In March 1918, Dwight Eisenhower had just completed four months seeing sights he had seen before and having experiences he had had before, crisscrossing the plains of Kansas, courtesy of the U.S. Army. He was an instructor of provisional officers at the Army Service Schools at Fort Leavenworth, leading novice officers—among them a Minnesota boy from Princeton named F. Scott Fitzgerald—in calisthenics.

Truman, one of ten officers and one hundred men selected to leave in advance of the regiment to receive further special training, sailed on March 29 on the *George Washington,* the ship that nine months later would take President Wilson on his famous postwar trip to the conference at Versailles. Truman landed in Brest, on the northwestern tip of France, where Wilson also would land. Wilson's landing would be the first time an American president would visit Europe while in office.

For two pleasant weeks after arriving in Brest, Truman stayed in "a beautiful place," a room in the Hôtel des Voyagers that looked "more like some count's bedroom than a hotel room." He was then sent by train five hundred miles across northern France to Chaumont, in Lorraine, Pershing's headquarters. While attending an "elite artillery school," he was put up in "an old Chateau with a beautiful garden, a moat, a fine park, and a church with a chime clock and the most beautifully toned bell I ever heard." At this point he wryly observed: "The hardships of the war are sure easy to bear so far."

Truman "went to school like a damned kid" in the field artillery school in Montigny-sur-Aube; he did fairly well—but not too well. If he had been a notch or two better, he would have suffered in France the fate of Eisenhower back in the States: being kept behind to train another batch when the men went to the front.

After artillery school, Truman carried with him all his new knowledge about how to make the projectile hit the target. He took it back west across northern France to Angers, on the Loire, where he was reunited with the rest of the 129th Field Artillery, which had crossed the water later, and less pleasantly, than he. After a month, he and his regiment moved north and slightly west to Camp Coetquidan in Brittany, an old campsite of Napoléon. That was where he learned that he was to be captain of Battery D—a key moment in his life. After a last layer of drilling, Harry and the regiment were taken back east across France to the front by way of Paris, then along the Marne, past Château-Thierry, and southeast to the Vosges Mountains in Alsace, near the Swiss border. First came combat in the Vosges, then reserve duty at Saint-Mihiel, then combat in the Meuse-Argonne, and then sector service near Verdun. And there was much marching in between.

After the armistice, they were kept in France, drilling and being annoyed by the officers and catching influenza (although there was more of this "Spanish flu" at home: the fearful report of casualties reversed direction), while the peace negotiations went on in Paris. On passes, Truman went to Nice, Paris again, Marseille, and Monte Carlo. In April 1919, he and his regiment returned to the United States and were mustered out, and he and Bess were promptly married, as it happened, on the day that the peace treaty at last was signed in Paris.

Harry Truman had been almost exactly one year in France, a small part of it in combat, the rest of it waiting to be trained, being trained, and training others, or waiting to return home. He could say at the end what he wrote to Bess at the beginning: "I have been touring France quite extensively at the expense of the American Government" and that he had "seen France as no civilian tour could possibly see it."

Meanwhile, Dwight Eisenhower's hopes that he might see France had been aroused by his next assignment—to Camp Meade, in Maryland, to join a tank battalion that was slated to go overseas that spring. He excelled in his role and was informed that he would be the commander of the battalion and that it would soon embark. He went to New York to be sure everything was ready, then returned to Camp Meade, only to learn that his orders had been changed. He had proved to be such a good organizer that he was given command—the only command he would ever hold until his abrupt ascension in World War II—of a new tank corps, to be trained at Camp Colt, in Gettysburg, Pennsylvania.

Thus, while the future supreme commander in Europe was commanding a tank corps (without any tanks) on the site of a great battle in another war on another continent, the future prime mover of the Marshall Plan and NATO was touring Europe in the midst of this war.

Harry Truman did include in his letters to his lady love back in Missouri, along with efforts to make his cultural and military adventures interesting ("I'll try to write a better letter tomorrow"), certain mild attempts to emulate Mark Twain. He wrote, for example:

> You can always tell a French village by day or night, even if you can't see anything. They are very beautiful to stand off and look at, nestling down in pretty little valleys, as they always do, with red roofs and a church spire. But when you arrive there are narrow dirty streets and a malodorous atmosphere that makes you want to go back to the hill and take out your visit in scenery.

Two of the little towns with French names too hard for Americans to pronounce were honored by being called "Stinktown" and "Manure Town" (Harry probably cleaned these up before passing them on to Bess). Of course he made the comparisons, put-downs, and jokes that Americans, particularly from the hinterland (like Mark Twain), have been known to make about Europe. (Are they mocking things European, the stuffy old ways, or are they mocking themselves for not knowing this higher European culture?)

But there isn't as much of this standard middle-American derogation of Europe in the letters of this innocent abroad as one might have expected. He was not as good a humorist as Mark Twain, and often he did not try to be; although he was trying hard to be entertaining to his girl, much of what he wrote is straightforward and appreciative, and reflects a rapidly expanding understanding. He was not defensive and insecure, and he also was not aggressive or pseudosuperior. Once when he did write that "I wouldn't trade any of the U.S. for any part of France," he finished with the more significant part of the sentence: "but if I had to give up being a Missourian I'd be a citizen of France by second choice." Although it startled him that boundary lines run in "every which direction" and not straight and square like those on the American plains, he appreciated the beauty: " . . . if I were a painter I'd surely want to go to work on the scenery right away." There is much praise for the landscape, not just in its natural beauty but also precisely in the layers of improvement long years of human culture had laid upon it. "The French know how to build roads and also how to keep them up," this future county-road builder would observe. "They are just like a billiard table and every twenty meters there are trees on each side." When he would rebuild the roads of Jackson County a decade later, he would, in emulation of the French, get trees planted alongside them, although the Missouri farmers would soon cut the seedlings down.

While he did make some mild jokes about the language, he never went at it full whistle the way Mark Twain did with German, and in a more serious mode he simply regretted that he did not have time to learn it. Although he went with companions to the standard tourist places in Paris, he did not mock the high culture of Europe, unlike Twain (who said he understood that Wagner's music is better than it sounds). His typical report (at least to the girl back home he was trying to impress) was unusual for an American soldier roaming France. "Saw the opera *Mignon* in Brest, went to *Thaïs* in Paris, got off the train in Orléans because of Joan of Arc and the cathedral." He wrote that he appreciated "a master at the [organ] keyboard in Bar-le-Duc [*sic*] who played a most beautiful offertory from Bach," and "a grand soprano voice sang a part of the Mass." No painting could do justice to the "simply magnificent view" from his room in Nice: "There is no blue like the Mediterranean blue and when it is backed by hills and a promontory with a lighthouse on it and a few little sailing ships it makes you think of Von Weber's *Polacca Brilliante*, which I am told was composed here."

Harry Truman from the small-town Middle West was certainly capable of standard cornball provincialism and ethnic stereotype. His letters from New York City, where the regiment had stopped briefly on the way to embarkation, said that New York's alleged attractions were disappointing and inferior to those in Kansas City, and that the town was filled with "wops" and "kikes." In his letters after the armistice, discussing the regular army officers, he made the standard hinterland sneers at "Dea' old Yale or

Ha'va'd don't ya know." He almost always called the enemy the "Hun" or "Heinie." But perhaps it is a sign of that capacity for growth that his aides would note when he was president that his more extended exposure to the French, seen of course through the lens of companionship in battle, led him to have considerable admiration. He had no habitual epithet for them. "I'm for the French more and more," he wrote after hearing about some horrendous French losses. "They are the bravest of the brave. If only there were millions more."

But to be sure, Harry Truman was not in France for a cultural tour.

Dwight Eisenhower and Harry Truman received their first command positions in the United States Army on separate continents, within a few months of each other in 1918, Eisenhower in March, Truman in July. These were to be the only commands either of them would hold until another war, when Eisenhower the soldier would rise to be supreme commander and Truman the civilian to be commander in chief.

In March 1918, Eisenhower was made a major (temporarily), and given command of (eventually) 10,000 men and 600 officers in training for tank warfare at Camp Colt in Gettysburg, Pennsylvania. On July 11, 1918, Harry Truman was made captain of Battery D in the 129th Field Artillery, composed of 194 men, with 4 French 75mm cannons, 2 machine guns, and 220 Colt six-shooters, which he would lead in the climactic Meuse-Argonne offensive in the closing stages of the Great War.

Both men would make a success of their commands. Dwight Eisenhower, only twenty-seven years old, had a complex responsibility beyond anything he had had before, and beyond anything he would have again for more than two decades. He had the ultimate executive authority for everything in the rebuilding and the operation of a major military training facility preparing to use the major innovation in ground warfare, the tank.

But Eisenhower was trained for military command. How was it that the farmer and bank clerk, the one-day haberdasher and county politician, Harry Truman, was also a success in his military command, so much smaller in one way but so much more exacting in another? The battery of which he was made captain was notorious, "obstreperous," "rough," "tough," "bad," to use words that Harry himself would use when describing its reputation. The members of Battery D had been recruited in Kansas City, in the tough neighborhood of Rockhurst College, a Jesuit high school, and were mostly Irish and German Catholics. There was the further spice, not noted in other biographies but mentioned by Richard Miller, of some tough scabs from the Bowery in New York, who had been shipped into Kansas City to break a streetcar strike but had then been kept off the streetcars by the union and were turned over to the battery recruiters.

How could Harry Truman lead that bunch? How could this piano-playing, book-reading small-town Baptist sissy with thick glasses, who didn't fight and disliked guns, a farmer who was a Thirty-second Degree Mason, become the much-commended and much-beloved commander, under lethal fire, of a very urban, "obstreperous" 194-man gun-shooting unit composed of "wild Irish and German Catholics," which had already gone through three commanders? It is not surprising that he would write that he had been "more frightened" on the morning he faced the battery as their captain for the first time than he had been under fire. He wrote to Bess at the time, "Can you imagine me being a hard-boiled captain of a tough Irish battery?"

Truman's success in that demanding role is the first of three impressive prepresidential performances demonstrating this apparently ordinary man could have some extraordinary qualities. The second performance would be his exceptional road building as county judge from 1928 to 1932, the third his noteworthy chairmanship of the Senate Committee investigating defense production in World War II, from 1941 to 1945.

Truman succeeded, as Eisenhower was succeeding in his larger but also lesser task, by taking it seriously and giving it all that there was in him. Truman wrote to Bess about it on July 14, just after being made captain: "[N]ow I have attained my one ambition, to be a battery commander. If only I can make good at it, I can hold my head up anyway the rest of my days." Harry Truman did make good at it, and did hold his head up the rest of his days. His service as a captain in the field artillery in France would be the making of him.

He wrote to Bess on July 22, "They gave me a battery that was always in trouble and bad, but we carried off all credits this week. It is the Irish battery. . . . They seem to want to soldier for me and if I can get them to do it, I shall consider that I have made the greatest success there is to be made."

Harry Truman's spontaneous principles of leadership might be approved even by a trained commander like Dwight Eisenhower. Truman "started things in tough-cookie fashion," as he put it to Bess; more formally, one might say that he established his authority immediately. When the obstreperous battery, which had greeted his first knee-knocking appearance before them with a Bronx cheer, entertained themselves further that night by stampeding the horses and holding a small riot in the barracks, Captain Harry, the farmer and son of a mule trader who was not unsettled by stampedes, calmly told them now they would have to round up the horses. The next morning, he posted a notice "busting" about "half the non-coms and most of the first-class privates." As one of the men recalled in his oral history, "And then we knew that we had a different 'cat' to do business with. He didn't hesitate at all." The new captain then called the remaining corporals and sergeants together and told them that he was in charge (it was not his job to get along with them, but theirs to get along with him) and that they would enforce discipline (if there were any who couldn't, they should speak up and he'd bust them back right now).

After their first experience of combat in the Vosges Mountains, Truman would write to Bess, perhaps a little smugly, on September 12, "I sit back and inform them [the lieutenants] and my sergeants what I want done, and it is. My noncoms, now, are whizzes. I sorted 'em over, busted a lot and made a lot."

And so there was the "tough-cookie" corollary: the principle of "bust a lot, make a lot," or, more formally, of enforced subordinate responsibility. The other side of the threat of reduction in rank was the *backing* of the noncoms by their captain in discipline.

But "tough-cookie fashion" and "bust a lot" represented only one side of Captain Harry. There are plenty of martinets and rigid disciplinarians in any army; the colonel of their regiment, a man with a name a novelist might have chosen for a military villain, Col. Karl D. Klemm (the three successive *k* sounds, the curt one-syllable names), was such a man, and he would come to be cordially hated by the men in Battery D. But the response to Captain Harry was totally different. The bond of affection and respect was to last not only through the fighting but all their lives.

Like the best of leaders (like Dwight Eisenhower, with his larger commands), Captain Harry, with his 194 men, was careful to bestow credit. "My battery was examined by the chief ordinance officer . . . and he said it was in the best condition of *any in Europe*. . . . I was somewhat swelled up but the chief mechanic deserves the credit. His name is McKinley Wooden and he is the straightest, stiffest soldier I have. It almost hurts me when he stands at attention to talk to me." On the night before the battery's first extensive combat in the Meuse-Argonne offensive, Truman said to the cook as they stood in line for supper (according to Wooden, in his oral history sixty-nine years later), "Feed McKinley Wooden good. He's one of our best soldiers." When afterward Truman himself was commended for having the best-conditioned guns, he wrote to Bess, "As usual in such cases, the C. Op. [meaning, of course, Truman] gets the credit. I think I shall put an endorsement on the letter stating the ability of my chief mechanic [meaning Wooden] and stick it in the files."

Captain Harry got them to take pride in their performance, and to be good at what they did. What they did was fire explosives from those 75mm French cannons at targets carefully calculated with all the "trigs and logs" crammed into Harry's head, and, as Danford had told him long ago in Oklahoma, make the projectile hit the target.

The commander who would one day in a later war order the single most destructive bombing in the history of mankind would in this one write, with an artilleryman's pride (usually he was deferential to the infantry, but not this time), "Talk about your infantryman, why he can only shoot one little old bullet at a time at the Hun. I can give the command to my battery and send 862 on the way in one round and as many every three seconds until I say stop."

After the first days of serious bombardment and rolling barrages, on a day when the regiment had pulled back for a rest, Truman wrote Bess, "I've had a university education and then some in the last year. Being a battery commander is an education in itself."

After the last weeks of intense fighting in the Meuse-Argonne, and the great relief of the armistice, Captain Harry wrote Bess reflectively about his role:

> Personally I'd rather be a battery commander than a brigadier general. I am virtually the dictator of the actions of 194 men and if I succeed in making them work as one, keep them healthy morally and physically, make 'em write to their mammas and sweethearts, and bring 'em all home, I shall be as nearly pleased with myself as I ever expect to be.

Captain Harry did bring all but one of his 194 boys home (one died of influenza in the war's aftermath), and he was "nearly as pleased with himself" as one could be.

Dwight Eisenhower could not be as pleased with himself, not because of any personal failing, but because what fell to him to do did not coincide with his own expectations and desires. Fulfillment and satisfaction depend upon a coinciding of one's own purposes with what the world provides. And often the world, chance, time, and history do not afford the conditions for fulfilling one's desires. Sages of Eastern religions and stoics in Western philosophy counsel the disciplining of desire, aligning one's will submissively with fate or fortune or God's will—with the course of events governed by powers beyond one's own. But that is not exactly what one is trained to do in Kansas, or at West Point, either.

In the autumn of 1918, Harry Truman and Dwight Eisenhower faced

different problems: Truman, high explosives; Eisenhower, frustrated anticipation. During the heaviest fighting in which Americans had been
involved, Capt. Harry Truman was bivouacked "somewhere in France,"
under bombardment with his men; Col. Dwight Eisenhower was living
with his wife and his new son in a large rented fraternity house on the
campus of Gettysburg College, in Pennsylvania, commander of a military camp, foiled, thwarted, confounded, and balked. He had been reprimanded for applying for overseas duty so persistently.

But on October 14, 1918, his twenty-eighth birthday, Eisenhower got
some good news at last: Not only was he promoted to lieutenant colonel
(temporary); he was ordered to embark for France, there to take command
of an armored-tank unit. The date of the embarkation was to be November 18, 1918.

"We stopped firing all along the line at eleven o'clock, November 11,
1918," Truman would later write. "It was so quiet it made your head ache."
Eisenhower's head may have ached that morning for a different reason.
The captain who was sitting in Eisenhower's office at Camp Colt in Pennsylvania when the report of the armistice came quoted Eisenhower as saying, "I suppose we'll spend the rest of our lives explaining why we didn't
get into this war."

II

THE GREAT WAR was one of those huge events that generate an immense
kaleidoscope of changing, varying, multicolored memories. The United
States Congress itself would start doing some official remembering of the
American battles in the Great War in May 1923 by establishing a Battle
Monuments Commission, with the general who had commanded the
American Expeditionary Force in that war, John J. "Black Jack" Pershing,
as its head. The commission was to erect suitable monuments in Europe,
and to "beautify" (General Pershing's word) the eight American cemeteries
left among the other achingly beautiful "cities of the dead," in those Flanders Fields, where poppies grow, and at those disputed barricades, where
some ten million men had their rendezvous with death. The commission
was also to prepare, as its own first edition put it, "an accurate guide to the
American battlefields in Europe." This guidebook, intended for Americans making their individual trips of memory, was to be prepared under
the direction of Maj. Dwight D. Eisenhower.

In the languors of those peacetime years, Eisenhower would be rescued
from coaching football at Fort Benning by his mentor from days in Pan

ama from 1922 to 1924, Fox Conner, who would propose his name to Pershing. Pershing set Ike to work scissors-and-pasting a guidebook, under pressure, in six months, before the fall tourist season in 1927. After his reward—a stint in the Army War College—Ike had a choice: the general staff in Washington, or Paris? Mamie wanted Paris. The job, not arduous, was to oversee the expanding of that guidebook. So there he would be, ten years after the war, at last serving under General Pershing, at last overseas, at last visiting the battlefields . . . after the battles were long over, and the job was not fighting, but memorializing the fighting of others.

The guidebook was anonymous, and in its second, enlarged edition, a group product. Eisenhower was the head of a small staff of four or five captains and lieutenants who visited the battlefields, checked the endless details, and wrote the guidebook's prose. When the stint was drawing to a close, the members of the writing-researching team would produce one of those allegedly humorous end-of-the-job productions affectionately honoring their chief, in which many years later one can read between the lines something of what the task entailed and something of the affection in which the chief was held. Their horseplay of 1928 would be preserved across the years.

KNOW ALL MEN BY THESE PRESENTS:

That we, the . . . Amalgamated Authors and Coauthors; Scribes and Pharisees; Paperhangers; . . . Eraser Benders; Printer's Devils; Messenger Boys; Book and Spell-Binders; Copy Readers; Pencil Chewers; . . . unanimously vote hereby to confer

THE DISGUSTED SERVICE MEDAL

on the following named beneficiary:

IKE D. EISENHOWER

farmer, soldier, author, cutter, copier, reviser, writer and long-distance rewriter.

For extraordinary stoicism or inaction with the Second American Unexpurgated Editionary Farce at or near Paris, France, Rue Molitor, Vingt, from August 1927 to June 1962 inclusive.

When the jokesters put down their comically remote terminal date—June 1962—they could not have imagined, nor could the object of their affectionate mocking, that when that far-off date would at last actually be reached, the winner of their Disgusted Service Medal from the Second American Unexpurgated Editionary Farce would have been supreme commander of Allied forces in Europe in the greatest war ever fought, and chief executive of the mightiest military power the world had ever seen.

Back in 1928, the anonymous humorists made the established travel guides the enemy: "The company to which he belonged having been assigned the . . . difficult mission of capturing the ground strongly entrenched, held and dominated by Michelin, Taride and Baedeker . . ."

They had the citations for battle medals ready at hand for parody:

> Ike assaulted the waste-baskets, rifled files, collected scattered documents, intrenched himself behind mahogany desks. . . . Ruthlessly he struck out commas; without mercy he slaughtered periods. . . . He strangled sentences, scrambled paragraphs, defied stenographers, and cussed draftsmen and messengers in utter abandon. Without respite, and without regard for his personal danger or infringement of copyright, he wrote, unwrote, halfwrote and rewrote above and beyond the call of beauty until stricken with writer's cramp.

They concluded, presenting all this to their chief presumably at some bibulous closing ceremony in 1928 in Paris, "For these meritorious acts he . . . gained the admiration of his fellow citizens and won the immortal title of GUIDE-BOOK IKE."

The quotations from the guidebook produced by Guidebook Ike and his fellow scribblers and eraser-benders in the account below are printed in italics.

One theme recurs in that guidebook: that the Allied forces in Europe in this first war did not include the United States. The United States had not since its founding had any allies; indeed, it had characteristically abominated "alliances," usually characterized by George Washington's modifier, "entangling." The United States had never been entangled. President Wilson, as we have seen, had made the strong point that America had a different purpose (no *selfish, imperialistic* intentions) from the European powers—"associates" merely—that were also fighting Germany. They were colonial powers seeking the restoration of territory, the correction of the balances of power, making secret agreements, as old Europe had always done; America, on the other hand, fought openly and unselfishly to make the world safe for democracy. Although President Wilson left military planning to General Pershing, Secretary of War Newton Baker did tell Pershing that "the forces of the United States are a separate and distinct unit . . . the identity of which must be preserved." For that reason, and also because the American military believed in more mobile and offensive tactics than were displayed in the static, defensive trench warfare of the war's terrible first years, a persistent attempt was made to gather the American forces in Europe into separate armies to fight in separate engagements. In a section called "Interesting Facts," Guidebook Ike and his colleagues wrote:

The United States and the Allies

When the United States entered the World War it did not unite itself to any other nation by a treaty of alliance but merely associated itself with the Allies in their effort to defeat the Central Powers. Such being the case, the United States was not one of the Allies and is not included when that term is used alone.

But when the United States had declared its separate war, it had been unprepared. It took yet another year before American forces were present in strength in France. Harry Truman arrived in France, as part of an advance group of trainees, as we have seen, in April 1918, almost exactly a year after Wilson's war speech and the American declaration of war. Even then he would receive yet more training in France, and not go into combat until late August.

And just as the Yanks were coming in numbers in the spring of 1918, the newly Bolshevik Russia's peace with Germany freed German forces for transfer from the eastern to the western front and resulted in dangerous German offensives on Paris, intended to win the war before America brought her full force to bear.

This crisis interrupted the formation of an American army as the succession of German drives in the spring of 1918 required the use of every available American and Allied division if defeat was to be avoided. It was at this time that General Pershing went to General Foch and freely offered him the use of every American man and gun in France.

Some Americans therefore *did* serve under non-American command—under the nearest equivalent in the first war to Dwight Eisenhower in the second, the Frenchman Marshal Ferdinand Foch. Americans served in the famous battles of Belleau Wood, and Château-Thierry—celebrated, of course, in the guidebook—which turned back the German assault.

When the American divisions had completed their part in the emergency and had assisted in the subsequent counter-offensive which turned the tide in favor of the Allies, the American Commander-in-Chief, despite renewed opposition on the part of the Allies, again insisted upon their assembly into one force, and soon thereafter this was resumed.

The Thirty-fifth Division, and therefore the 129th Field Artillery and Harry Truman, had not been among the American troops that fought, temporarily, under French command in those famous engagements; they continued to train for the later, as it were, all-American offensive.

American Operations on the Vosges Front

The Western Front, extending for more than 400 miles from Switzerland to the North Sea, was so long that neither the Allies nor the Germans could obtain sufficient men to undertake operations on a large scale throughout its entire length.

The southern end of this long front lay in mountainous territory. "The rugged terrain in the Vosges Mountains, north of the Swiss border, was a serious obstacle to major operations in that region. . . . This front, commonly known to the Americans as the 'Vosges Front,' was used by many American divisions for training purposes." The Thirty-fifth, like eleven other divisions of the U.S. Army named in the guide, had its first "sector service" at that front.

> For considerable periods the daily life of the front-line troops would be comparatively uneventful, disturbed only by routine patrolling and desultory shelling. At intervals, however, this comparative quiet was shattered by hard-fought local operations and raids.
> The natural enthusiasm of the American troops and their inherent desire to start active operations as quickly as possible usually produced a marked increase in the fighting in these normally quiet sectors. The Vosges region holds vivid memories for many American soldiers as it was there that so many of them, after arduous months of training in the rear areas, had their first experience with trench life and their first contact with the enemy.

Battery D and Harry Truman had their first contact with the enemy in that place. Every soldier who was there would have memories different in some degree from every other, and as the years would go by these would settle and shift and subtly change, and when one day in the distant future their captain would become a figure of worldwide interest, they would tell, in many different sizes, shapes, and hues, their stories, and biographers and historians could then combine them in kaleidoscopic variations. Among the vivid memories from the Vosges region held by the men of Battery D were those of their captain, who, on the occasion they humorously dubbed "The Battle of Who Run," showed courage, calmness, resolute command, and a profane vocabulary they did not know he possessed, all attributes that they admired.

Captain Harry had located their place on the side of a mountain with great effort, and they had arduously hauled their four guns up there, and they had fired their first serious barrage. Just as return fire began, a sergeant shouted, "Run, fellers, run. They've got a bracket on us!" And some did run.

The chief danger to a field artillery unit was that once it fired its guns, the enemy would of course be eager to plot the location of the battery—to "bracket" it and, before it could move, to wipe it out. As chief mechanic McKinley Wooden would put it many years later, "Of course, the main thing of the artillery is getting the location. You locate them, and it's just about dead duck. Now that's all there is to it." So it was important not only to choose your place carefully but also to move expeditiously after a certain amount of firing. One of the reasons for his battery mates' great regard for Captain Harry, after this was all over, was that he located them well, moved them expeditiously, and brought them home alive.

How many ran at that first encounter, and who they were, would be the subject of much joshing and arguing, to the accompaniment of the tinkle of ice in glasses, during the exchange of memories at reunions of Battery D in later years. But there was always agreement that the captain did not run. Moreover, his spectacular swearing at those who did run brought them back, and would be remembered forever after. The chaplain, Truman's thereafter lifelong friend Father Curtis Tiernan, said, "It took the skin off the ears of those boys. It turned those boys right around."

Harry Truman, it seems, did not have with these men the reputation for swearing that he would later acquire, or have imputed to him, as president, a reputation a young California politician named Richard Nixon, running for vice president, would attempt to exploit in the 1952 presidential elections. Nixon, these many years later, would try to compare the then Republican candidate's dignified and presumably unprofane bearing with the alleged conduct of the then incumbent Democratic president, Harry Truman. Wouldn't it be wonderful to have a president whose language and dignity we can respect? he asked. But the attempt backfired. There were journalists from the second war who remembered private performances by that Republican candidate when he was a general. With Nixon's provocation, they decided to let the world know: Dwight Eisenhower, after years of training in army barracks, could, and did, swear magnificently, regularly featuring the loud exclamation "Jeeee—sus Chri—ist!" echoing through his various posts. The issue was abruptly dropped. After history had taken another turn, the Watergate tapes, released in 1974, would make Mr. Nixon's phonily scrupulous effort appear ridiculous beyond imagining.

But in August 1918, all that was long in the future. The point then was that the men of Battery D, who may have had very high swearing standards, thought their captain was not up to the mark. Richard Miller quotes one of the men as having recalled, "We had a story going around about the way he bawled out two soldiers who went AWOL. 'You, you!' he shouted. 'You spoiled our record, you nasty things, you!'" So his outstanding cursing at the Battle of Who Run had shock value.

Captain Harry's not running, at this first experience of incoming fire, established a point to himself. His letters to Bess before he had gone to the front reveal not the bravado a young soldier might be expected to display, on paper, to his beloved back home, but a certain self-questioning. He made use of a jocular trope not, this time, from Mark Twain, but from Twain's competitor as an outstanding midwestern nineteenth-century American humorist, Abraham Lincoln. Lincoln, in discussing his pardons, would mention his "leg cases": young soldiers whose hearts and minds were brave but whose legs were not, and which took them rapidly away from the shooting. On July 31, from "somewhere in France," Truman wrote to Bess, "I have my doubts about my bravery when heavy-explosive shells and gas attacks begin. I am like a fellow Uncle Harry used to tell about. I have the bravest kind of head and body but my legs won't stand." Then on September 1 (from "somewhere in *Parley-vous*"), after that first exchange in the Vosges Mountains, he wrote that he had "accomplished my greatest wish. Have fired five hundred rounds at the Germans at my command, been shelled, didn't run away thank the Lord and never lost a man." And later in the same letter: "My greatest satisfaction is that my legs didn't succeed in carrying me away although they were anxious to do it."

Meanwhile, at that much higher level at which generals deal in their big pictures, the plans for that first all-American action at Saint-Mihiel were being formed.

American Operations in the St. Mihiel Sector

The plan to develop an army near St. Mihiel when sufficient troops were available, and to reduce the salient there, was proposed by General Pershing and was agreed to by General Pétain at the first conference between them shortly after the arrival of the American Headquarters in France.

Pétain was a name that Guidebook Ike, scribbling it then on the page, would encounter again, in another role, in another war. Dwight Eisenhower would be the commander of the operation in North Africa and the now-aged Marshal Pétain would be the head of Vichy France, and would give him occasions to display his impressive powers of cursing. But now in this war, when the German drives on Paris had been stopped, the American insistence on separate organization and separate engagement revived.

> General Pershing pointed out to the Allied Commander-in-Chief that the improved situation made possible the concentration of American units, and insisted that the formation of an American Army be resumed. Although the French but more especially the British urged that American units be left with their forces, an understanding was reached that most of these units should soon be assembled into an independent army in the neighborhood of St. Mihiel.

The second war that would grow out of the aftermath of the first would have many parallels: many of the same opponents, much of the same territory. This time, the United States would become an ally, and would become the first among the Allies. But when at the moment of climax before the invasion of Germany the American supreme commander, Dwight Eisenhower, would take over active command of the land armies, some British officers would remember how it had been in the first war: Pershing and the Americans insisting on a separate U.S. Army with distinct engagements.

> The American First Army Headquarters began to function on August 10 and on that day started vigorous preparations for the reduction of the St. Mihiel salient . . . a triangle . . . 25 miles wide at its base, extended 16 miles into the Allied lines and had remained almost unchanged in shape for four years. . . . The salient was a veritable field fortress against which the French in the preceding years had made a number of unsuccessful attacks. The value of the salient to Germany lay in the fact that it protected strategic centers. . . . Its reduction was imperative before any great Allied offensive could be launched.

But then the generals, as generals must, changed their plans.

> The preparations for the attack against the salient were well along when, on August 30, the Allied Commander-in-Chief suggested to General Pershing that the offensive be reduced greatly in scope, that most of the American divisions be used for an attack about September 15 between Verdun and Reims and that in the new attack some of the American divisions be assigned to operate under certain of the higher French commands.

So the generals began disputing again, and finally altered the plan somewhat:

> General Pershing felt that the St. Mihiel offensive should be carried out as planned and definitely stated that the American divisions would fight in the future only as part of an independent American Army.

After a series of conferences with Marshal Foch it was finally agreed, on September 2, that the St. Mihiel attack would be carried out, but that its objectives would be strictly limited so that the American Army could undertake another major offensive about ten days later on the front between the Meuse River and the Argonne Forest.

One American president's moralistic combination of an internationalism that turned out to be nationalism set the background for the military decisions described in a future American president's guidebook, which meant, for another future American president, down at the lowly artilleryman's level, a great deal of moving, mostly on foot, mostly at night, through the mud, dead tired.

This agreement put a great burden upon the American First Army as under it the Army was called upon to carry to a conclusion the important offensive at St. Mihiel which was scheduled to start on September 12, to concentrate an enormous force on the Meuse-Argonne front, and to initiate a still greater operation there, all within the brief space of two weeks. In other words, at the time the agreement with the Allied Commander-in-Chief was made the American Army undertook the mission of launching within the next 23 days two great offensives on battlefields 40 miles apart. Never before on the Western Front had a single army attempted such a colossal task, and its successful accomplishment reflects great credit on all those concerned.

The role of the Thirty-fifth Division, and therefore of Battery D in the 129th Field Artillery, in the first of these offensives, at the Saint-Mihiel salient, was to go by train and then arduously on foot to their assigned spot, and to be held in reserve. Then they were to march even more arduously to their new spot for the even greater offensive that would follow it.

When the decision was made to attack in the Meuse-Argonne region the American First Army was busily engaged in preparations for the St. Mihiel offensive, planned for September 12. However, because of the limited time available, the assembly of American divisions not scheduled for the St. Mihiel attack was begun immediately. . . . American units were sent to the region and secretly concentrated. . . .

The movement of men and material was made entirely under cover of darkness, all activity being suspended and the men kept in concealment during daylight hours. Consequently, at night the roads leading into the area were the scenes of great activity as troops and artillery, ammunition and supplies moved steadily forward.

The Thirty-fifth, and therefore Harry Truman and his battery, were part of this enormous nighttime influx of troops. He would later (on

November 2) write to Bess, by way of apologizing for not having written, that "there have been times, and there will be again, when I couldn't possibly write. I have gone as much as sixty hours without any sleep and for twenty-two days straight I marched every night."

> In all, about 220,000 Allied soldiers were moved out of the area and approximately 600,000 Americans were moved into it. The planning and execution of this gigantic movement of concentration was an intricate and arduous task. The fact that it was done with smoothness and precision, and without the knowledge of the enemy, is in itself a striking tribute to the ability of the American Army and to the skill of its staffs.

"Smoothness and precision" may be the interpretation of top commanders and official reports and guidebooks; artillerymen trudging (or, worse, double-timing) in the middle of the night through muddy roads in Lorraine may have had a different view. Not riding: That was verboten. The horses were too tired; many died. One of the deeds of Captain Harry that endeared him to his men was his insisting, against Col. Karl D. Klemm's order, that a man with a painful ankle injury continue to ride on his—that is, Harry's—horse. "You can take these bars off my shoulders," Battery D's supply sergeant remembered Captain Harry saying, "but as long as I'm in charge of this battery the man's going to stay on that horse." His men also remembered his rejecting Klemm's proposal, during that series of marches in the night, that Truman punish infractions by double-timing the bone-tired men. When after a double time up a hill Truman took the men off the road and let them sleep in a ditch, and Colonel Klemm found them and asked what they were doing, Captain Harry is reported to have said, to his men's delight, "Carrying out orders, sir!"

According to the guidebook, "The St. Mihiel offensive which began on September 12, 1918, was the first operation in the World War carried out by a complete American army under the separate and independent control of the American Commander-in-Chief."

On the night of September 12, Harry and his men had come to a halt in the dark streets of the town of Nancy, when, exactly at 1:00 a.m. (according to one of them, a bit of a poet), "the whole front to our north broke out in flame, and a tremendous, continuous and awe-inspiring roar of artillery began; while huge searchlights, interspersed with many-starred signal rockets, shot their shafts like the Northern Lights constantly across the sky. We had heard or seen nothing in our experience like it . . . we realized with a sombre enthusiasm that an event big with importance, in which we might be called upon to participate, was taking place." This was the very first display in the Old World of that awesome power that in this century would develop in the New (except that, this first time, the guns the New World used were French).

The Thirty-fifth Division (therefore Battery D) was not called upon to participate. It was held in reserve for three days, and then, as a result of those new plans by the generals, set to marching at night once more, under even more pressure, to its new assignment for the big offensive in the Argonne Forest.

Meanwhile, the action at Saint-Mihiel that they were leaving behind was, in the American guidebook view (written in part by Eisenhower), a complete, and a quick, success. (Others, more objectively, noted that German troops had already begun withdrawing when it started.)

> The complete success of the American Army in its first offensive greatly stimulated the morale of the Allies and depressed that of the Germans. The railroads in the vicinity of St. Mihiel had been freed for Allied use, the threat of the salient against the surrounding country had been removed and one of the most important obstacles to an advance toward . . . Sedan had been overcome. American staffs had shown their ability to maneuver and control large masses, and the whole Army had developed added self-confidence and a sense of power which was to be of great value in helping it to surmount the difficult tasks ahead.

Among those who participated valiantly in that successful American offensive at Saint-Mihiel were two rising stars who perhaps did not need any added self-confidence and sense of power: the former chief of staff of the Forty-second Division—the famous Rainbow Division—Col. Douglas MacArthur, now promoted to brigadier general and put in command of an infantry brigade; and Maj. George Patton, the first American true believer in tank warfare, in his first tank command in battle. Both of them were far more important than a major (temporary) commanding a camp back in Gettysburg, Pennsylvania, or a mere artillery captain, far down the ranks, waiting in reserve for his orders.

"The transfer of American units to the Meuse-Argonne region, their next great battlefield, was begun even before the completion of the St. Mihiel offensive," the guidebook stated. That was the role of the Thirty-fifth Division in the Saint-Mihiel offensive: to march to it, to wait in reserve as it began, and then to march away from it. They also serve who only stand and wait, and then are transferred.

American Operations in the Meuse Argonne Region

One of the most far-reaching effects of the rapid increase of American troops in Europe, and the resulting Allied and American successes during the summer of 1918, was that it became possible to undertake in September a gigantic convergent offensive movement against the German forces.

This "gigantic convergent movement" was the Meuse-Argonne offensive: history's greatest military campaign up to that point. "The First Army [until very late, the only American Army] which reached a strength in early October of about 900,000 Americans . . . was approximately eight times the size of the army with which General Grant opposed General Lee at the end of the American Civil War." The first edition of the guide, which Ike had done two years before in Washington, had said the First Army was ten times the size of Grant's. The pencil-chewers must have checked and revised.

"The significance of the American Army's part in the general plan lay in the fact that its attack was to be directed against a most vital point of the German system of railroad communications." The railroad center of Sedan was the great prize.

> It was apparent that an Allied attack in the vicinity of the Meuse River, if carried far enough to gain control of the lateral railways, would divide the German Armies . . . the capture or defeat of the German northern armies would be practically certain. . . . In view of the strength of the German positions, the stubborn opposition that would undoubtedly be met with at that point and the vital importance of the front, the American Army could well feel that in the coming combined Allied offensive it had been given the place of honor.

Battery D arrived at its place of honor there after forced marches, together with the rest of the 129th Field Artillery, exhausted, on the night of September 22. Harry then flopped and slept in the woods, got up before dawn to go back to the battery, and saw German artillery blast the spot where he had been—one of those near misses that figure vividly in the soldier's personal store of memories, in this case also a history-altering miss.

In the little sketch in the Eisenhower guidebook, the Argonne Forest is on the left, with the French Fourth Army still farther left, on the west side of the forest. On the right, or east, side, there is first the American

Twenty-eighth Division (from Pennsylvania—a point that will be important in Harry Truman history), which extends into the edge of the forest,
then the Thirty-fifth Division, which came from Missouri and Kansas,
and then several other American divisions over to the Meuse River, where
the French Seventeenth Corps picked up the line again.

"The general plans provided first for an advance . . . which would . . .
force the Germans to give up the Argonne Forest. This was to be followed
by a further penetration . . . which would outflank their defenses . . . and
thus open the way toward Sedan." So now a major action was about to
begin—for the U.S. Army, and for Harry Truman and his men.

"Finally, on the night of September 25–26 the First Army stood on its
new front ready for the momentous battle that was to begin at dawn the
next day." On that night, Captain Harry gave a little talk to his men, and
in it one might almost hear a homely echo of the most famous of all pre-
battle talks, that of the other Harry, the night before Agincourt. "It wasn't
what you'd call a speech," a private present with this Captain Harry on
that night would remember, "just a quiet talk like an older brother sometimes has with a younger boy. A few things that Harry Truman said that
night still stick in my mind: I want to tell you this, too, fellows. Right now
I'm where I want to be—in command of this battery. I'd rather be right
here than be President of the United States. You boys are my kind. Now
let's go in!" We happy few, we band of brothers. Years later, Dean Acheson
would apply another of Shakespeare's phrases about that first Harry now
to the second: "A touch of Harry in the night."

"The artillery preparation for the attack began in full force at 2:30 on
the morning of September 26. Two thousand seven hundred guns kept up
an intense bombardment of the hostile positions until 5:30 a.m., at which
time the assaulting infantry jumped off, protected by a rolling barrage."

Battery D's guns were 4 of those 2,700, the firing of which lit up the
sky and shook the earth and made the gun barrels so hot, they poured
water down them. That stunning first barrage in the early morning of
September 26 went, according to a corporal, "like clockwork." Nothing
else would.

> Five hours before the infantry assault . . . a heavy concentration of
> artillery fire, including gas and smoke shells . . . forced the German
> troops . . . to remain in their bombproof shelters and so blinded their
> observers that when the attack took place the 35th Division was able to
> make rapid progress in the valleys. . . . Those advances isolated the hill
> which then cleared of the enemy. . . . After severe fighting the divi-
> sion front line was established that night about 1 mile beyond Cheppy.

It sounds much smoother in the guide than in the accounts and memories of those who were closer to the confusion on the ground. Battery D was the first "75 unit" of the regiment's four to move up. Mud. A swarm of bees over Harry's head—no, not bees, German bullets. A German dud landed between a private's legs. Mud. A bridge out. Men fell asleep standing up.

The guidebook composed a decade later would take American visitors carefully, by the fractions of kilometers, on tours of the battleground where each American division had fought.

En Route to Mountefaçon to Vauquois

The 35th Division, which jumped off from near Vauquois, reached the German main line of resistance on top of the hill to the left of this road about 8:30 a.m. There a severe struggle took place and it was not until 12:30 p.m. that, with the assistance of tanks, the strong enemy positions on that hill were captured.

(23.1 m 37.2 km) In the next village, Cheppy, the troops who had stormed the powerful main line of resistance of the German first position near here assembled and reorganized before renewing their attacks at 3:30 p.m.

The name of the French village of Cheppy would reverberate in the memories of the men of Battery D.

The guidebook, in its revised, enlarged Paris version, is full of individual cases of heroism of the sort that the eraser-benders had parodied in their award of the Disgusted Service Medal:

It was during the fighting in this vicinity that Captain Alexander R. Skinker, 35th Division, won the Congressional Medal of Honor. When his company was held up by terrific machine-gun fire from "pillboxes" in a strong German position, he personally led an automatic rifleman and a carrier in an attack on the guns. The carrier was killed instantly, but Captain Skinker seized the ammunition and continued through an opening in the barbed wire, feeding the automatic rifle until he, too, was killed.

At Eastertime in 1971, when Harry Truman would be an eighty-seven-year-old ex-president in retirement in Independence, a congressman from Missouri named William J. Randall would go to see him about a proposal to give Truman the Congressional Medal of Honor. Truman told Randall that he would not accept it. First, he said modestly, he did not consider that he had done anything that could be the reason for any award, congressional or otherwise. But then, as one who knew the kinds of things that had been done by those, like Captain Skinker, who had earned that particular medal, Truman wrote that "the Congressional medal of Honor was instituted for combat service. This is as it should be and to deviate by giving it for any other reason lessens and dilutes its true significance. . . . I do appreciate the kind of things that have been said . . . but I will not accept a Congressional Medal of Honor."

The Eisenhower guidebook notes, with a picture, this monument near the village of Cheppy: "A monument erected by the State of Missouri in honor of her sons who died in the World War is located at the road junction beyond town. Many Missourians served in the 35th Division, which had very hard fighting near here." Although Harry Truman would make two retirement sightseeing trips to Europe as ex-president, in addition to his official trip to Potsdam soon after he became president, he never went to see this monument, or to any other scenes of these battles of his youth.

The guidebook intersperses occasional notes from still deeper layers of memory:

> (29.7 m 47.8) Varennes is famous in French history as the place where Louis XVI and Marie Antoinette were captured in their attempt to escape into Belgium at the beginning of the French Revolution. . . . This part of Varennes was captured by the 28th Division about noon on September 26, shortly before the troops of the 35th Division captured that part of the village on the other side of the river.

But the fighting did not go as smoothly as the book makes it sound. There were confused communications among those at the top of the Thirty-fifth Division. As a result, there were conflicting orders about when to start firing on September 27. Harry was awakened at 3:00 a.m. and told to start firing in ten minutes. He said it was impossible and to go to hell. They began firing a half an hour after the attack had begun. After an 11:00 a.m. breakfast, they moved up again. Outside Cheppy, a terrible, twisted pile of American soldiers lay dead, shot by enemy machine gunners. Chattering Battery D men suddenly grew silent—as quiet as a church. The early-afternoon position was in an orchard outside Cheppy, an orchard that would become famous in Battery D lore. The guns were trained on Charpentry, a German-held town. Harry went ahead to the observation post, called back corrections to guns, and was startled to be told he was no longer in American-held territory, but in no-man's-land. The men promptly dropped back. Shells were fired and they were strafed by German planes. Orders came to lay a barrage for renewed attack. A flare dropped by an American plane lit up a German artillery battery getting into position on Battery D's left. (This was a story told and retold by the men of Battery D.) Harry saw that German artillery. What a chance! He waited—the men were impressed by the fact that he didn't start firing right away—until they were set up and the horses were sent back, and then, with the firing data carefully lined up, he ordered the guns to fire and wiped out the German battery. *But*—this impressed the men most of all—that battery was across the Aire River, as Harry knew, *and therefore in the sector not of the Thirty-fifth but of the Twenty-eighth Division.* One was not supposed to fire outside one's sector. Col. Karl D. Klemm called Truman and chewed him out, even threatening him with a court-martial. "I'll never pass up a chance like that," the men remember Truman saying. "We plastered 'em."

Thirty years later, in October 1948, when President Harry S Truman was campaigning for reelection in Wilkes-Barre, Pennsylvania, Congressman Daniel J. Flood told the story to a Pennsylvania audience, assuring them that Truman's action saved a lot of lives in Pennsylvania's Twenty-eighth Division. And some years after that, ex-president Harry S Truman, writing about this episode, said, "I saved some men in the 28th Division on our left and they were grateful in 1948."

McKinley Wooden would tell about another episode from that day in the orchard outside Cheppy (in Wooden's case, to an interviewer in 1986):

> [I]t was just a little before sundown when a German plane came right over, right over our position. By God, you know what Harry did? He moved us back about 100 yards, and to our right about 200 yards, right in a little cut in the road.
>
> It wasn't fifteen minutes until they just shot that orchard all to hell. If he hadn't done that there might not have been a one of us left. . . . He probably saved the whole damn battery's life right there.

"(32.5 m 52.3 km) After passing Montblainville, the village seen on the hill down the road is Baulny, taken soon after dark on September 27 by troops of the 35th Division," the guidebook noted.

On the morning of September 28, Harry sent sixty-four shells into a German observation post he had seen; presumably, this is the "shot up his big observation post" he would refer to in his first letter to Bess after the battle. And a half hour later, he saw an enemy battery leaving position, shelled them, and was told later that "you got 'em all right." A Twenty-eighth Division colonel found six abandoned guns by the road.

> By noon of September 28, after having repulsed a German counterattack that morning, the 35th Division had captured Charpentry, the first village beyond Cheppy; Baulny, the village immediately to the left

of Charpentry; and the large wooded area called Montrebeau . . . 5 1/2 miles away. That night it dug in on the far edge of that wood.

The next day, they started their protective barrage for the infantry, doing their part, but the Thirty-fifth Division as a whole (which the guide-book, of course, didn't mention) was coming apart. The guidebook hinted at an aspect of it by emphasizing the "vicious" German counterattack.

> The next day the division attacked twice and had made further sub-stantial gains when a vicious German counterattack by fresh troops, supported by large artillery concentrations from the Argonne Forest, forced it back to Baulny.
> Neuville-le-Comte Farm, 112 mile[s] east of Exermont. Captured by the 35th Division on September 29, in an attack made under severe artillery fire, but not held due to a heavy German counterattack launched that noon.

One may read between the lines of the following summary describing the heavy hostile fire and the fact that the division's units were being forced back.

> Montrebeau, the large timbered area . . . was captured on Septem-ber 28 by troops of the 35th Division.
> On September 29 the division attacked from the edge of Montre-beau under extremely heavy hostile fire and succeeded in occupying Beauregard Farm and the southern slope of Montrefagne as well as Exermont. . . . A severe counterattack on that afternoon by fresh Ger-man troops, supported by a heavy and well-directed artillery fire from the Argonne Forest, forced the units of the 35th Division back again to a position the other side of Montrebeau.

Richard Miller, who exhumed the cable traffic—a quite different sort of memory—reported this message, sent at 11:15 a.m. on September 29 from the Thirty-fifth Division's commanding officer to the commander of the First Corps: "Regret to report this Division cannot advance. . . . It is thoroughly disorganized, through loss of officers and many casualties, for which we cannot give estimate, owing to intermingling of units. Recom-mend it be withdrawn for reorganization and be replaced promptly."

None of this was Harry Truman's fault, nor was it the fault of the vil-lain to whom his men might want to assign it, Col. Karl D. Klemm. The primary fault for the disorganization of the Thirty-fifth Division rested higher up, with the division commander and the brigade commander, and with their inexperience and that of the Americans in general—and, to be sure, with the fierce German counterattack.

As American infantrymen of the Thirty-fifth struggled back from the front in growing numbers, as some artillerymen in other batteries were killed by direct hits, as the Germans were expected to advance on them, and as a French officer yelled for Battery D to retreat, Harry's Battery had its most severe testing moment, which Miller described: "Maj. John Miles ordered preparation for direct fire, perhaps the most chilling command an artilleryman can hear." "Direct fire" meant stay by your guns, keep firing, and die or be captured. Miller continued: "But the enemy never came. Unknown to Harry's regiment, the 110th Engineers had abandoned their tools and gone into action as infantrymen. They saved the situation. Their commander was the man Colonel Klemm had defeated in the National Guard elections back at Kansas City, Maj. E. M. Stayton."

Thus, even at as exigent a moment as the one just described, the home politics of the National Guard divisions in World War I might be remembered. They reflected the politics that preceded their formation, and would be reflected in politics after the war. The one Republican Harry Truman is known to have supported for public office in the years to come would be John Miles, a comrade in arms in the 129th, the major who gave the chilling order above. And Major Stayton would become an engineer building roads in Jackson County for Judge Truman, who would become his good friend.

"After repulsing a German counterattack on the 30th, the 35th Division, which in four days had fought its way forward approximately six miles, was relieved from the line on October 1 by the 1st Division." That six miles was the primary contribution of the Thirty-fifth Division to the Great War.

The guide's more general summary of the whole First Army's fighting in the first days of the Meuse-Argonne offensive hinted, in slightly defensive touches about the bitter fighting, the rapid advance, and the normality of the pause after October 1, that the course of battle was not altogether smooth—something that the men of the Thirty-fifth Division, in the midst of it, knew very well.

This fighting was exceptionally bitter, the Germans making many severe counterattacks and concentrated artillery bombardments. During the day, the ground gained and lost on this front by both sides was about equal.

> The First Army troops in the line were worn out by four days of terrific fighting and the advance had been so rapid that much of the heavy artillery and many of the supplies could not be brought up until the roads were rebuilt. During this pause, which was normal in every general attack, the 35th, 37th and 79th Divisions were replaced. . . . In all,

a movement of more than 125,000 officers and men in and out of the line was made. As the roads and transportation facilities on the newly captured ground were improved, the wounded were taken to hospitals in the rear.

This was not like Saint-Mihiel; this combat was very costly. The Thirty-fifth Division, like some others, had heavy casualties. Out of its paper strength of 28,000, there were 6,006 killed and wounded, according to a chart in the guide, in the six days of their participation in the Meuse-Argonne offensive. No other division suffered more casualties in those six days. Most casualties were in the infantry. "The real heroes are in the infantry," artilleryman Harry would write to Bess. But despite the heavy losses and the disorganization and inexperience, the sheer numbers of fresh troops the Americans provided helped to cause—rather suddenly—German capitulation.

> The progress on this front threw consternation into the German High Command, who realized that the American Army here could not long be held in check. It urged its Government, therefore, to make peace at once before disaster overcame the German forces in the field.
> When the American Army, in spite of increasing enemy reinforcements and a well-nigh impregnable hostile defensive system, had driven forward to a position dominating the German railroad communications in the vicinity of Sedan, the termination of the war in 1918 was assured.

The rather abrupt collapse of the Germans in the first war would have an echo in the second, when in late 1944, before the Battle of the Bulge, some British and American officers who had been there in the first war thought there might be a similar collapse, without an invasion of Germany. But that was not to be.

The climactic Meuse-Argonne offensive in the first war, according to Major Eisenhower and his scribblers, lasted from September 26 until the armistice on November 11. The armistice ended "the Meuse-Argonne battle, the greatest one in American history." Major Eisenhower would one day see greater ones.

According to a chart summarizing "combat service" in the Meuse-Argonne region, the Thirty-fifth Division, to which the 194 men under the command of Capt. Harry Truman were attached, was in *battle* from September 26 to October 1, near the towns of Cheppy and Baulny. That—not counting mud, midnight marches, desultory exchanges in sector action before and after—was their war: the last week of September 1918.

Six days, six miles: Combat snobs from other battles and particularly from the later (Ike's own) war might deprecate that short time, those short miles, but it turned out that, as part of the larger effort of the American First Army, those were important days, and important miles.

In their efforts to stop the progress of the American units, the Germans quickly began drawing reinforcements from other parts of the Western Front to strengthen their forces in the Meuse-Argonne region and by the end of the fifth day seven more German divisions had been rushed to this crucial region and had entered the battle.

The great progress of the First Army attack and Allied pressure on other parts of the front caused the German High Command on September 29 to urge its Government to forward immediately an offer of peace to the Allied Governments and this was done on October 6.

Harry Truman, unable to write to Bess from September 15 until October 6, finally was able to write a letter that both explained that delay and rejoiced a bit in what he and his men had done.

[*Somewhere in France*]

Dear Bess:
 . . . [T]hings have happened to me so rapidly I couldn't write. There was no chance to mail them if I could have. The great drive has taken place and I had apart in it, a very small one but nevertheless a part. . . . The papers are in the street now saying that the Central Powers have asked for peace, and I was in the drive that did it! I shot out a German Battery, shot up his big observation post, and ruined another Battery when it was moving down the road. . . . I brought my Battery forward under fire and never lost a horse nor a man.

Summarizing the fighting of the American First Army in the great battle of the Meuse-Argonne, the Ike guidebook said, "Its total losses from all causes . . . were about 117,000." But there were no losses in Battery D of the 129th Field Artillery attached to the Thirty-fifth Division. "I brought my Battery forward under fire and never lost a horse or a man."

On October 4, other divisions renewed the offensive, but the Thirty-fifth Division was held in reserve near the battered town of Verdun, where it dug in and fired barrages in support of the infantry until the armistice.

Harry did not say much in his letters to Bess about the horrors of war, and the guidebook certainly did not as an official production for tourists. But there were such horrors. In the comparative calm of camp near Verdun, Harry would write not to his girlfriend, but to his cousins:

I am now in front of the most famous, and hardest fought for city in France. . . . It sure looks like it, too. There are Frenchmen buried in my front yard and Dutchmen buried in my back yard and gobs of both scattered over the whole landscape. . . . There's one field over west of me here a short distance where every time a shell lights it plows up a piece of someone.

The grisly battle for Verdun had lasted for ten static, bloody months in 1916. The arrival of the 1,200,000 Americans, even with their lack of training at the beginning, and their insistence (not altogether carried out) to fight in separate American armies, had turned the tides of war. At least that is the way the Americans would view it. That there was another view, one that would have an effect in the future particularly on Dwight Eisenhower, is captured well in this sentence from a book called *Monty*, written by Bernard Montgomery's biographer. It reflects the attitude of many of the British military—particularly "the Montgomerys and the Brookes"—toward the American role in the first war: "The Americans had come in at the end of the war, when most of the hard fighting had been done, had grabbed the laurels of victory, then run off home again, into the comforts of isolationism, abandoning Europe in a worse mess than it had been in before."

Needless to say, that was not the view of the scribblers working on Eisenhower's guidebook, who wrote, "The American First Army in 47 days of continuous fighting had advanced steadily in spite of all obstacles, amid the most desperate resistance, and had played a vital part in bringing the war to a successful conclusion."

And Harry Truman wrote, "I had apart in it. . . . I was in the drive that did it!"

CHAPTER THREE
Between the Wars

I

THERE THEY WERE AT THE END of 1918, two able and conscientious young men from the lower rungs of the social ladder in small towns in the American heartland, deciding what to do now that the Great War was over. Harry Truman, the civilian, was offered a chance to stay in the army, but he turned that down. Dwight Eisenhower, the army man, was offered chances to go out into the civilian world, but he turned them down.

In the postwar winter of 1918–1919 Dwight Eisenhower was still in camp in Pennsylvania, impatiently waiting to get on with his life, having experiences that sharpened his sectarian Kansas small town–West Point prejudice against politicians. Harry Truman was still in camp in France, impatiently waiting to go home, having experiences that sharpened his Missouri farmer–Jacksonian common man–common soldier dislike of the officers of the regular army.

A hotel owner in Gettysburg sold liquor against orders to soldiers in Eisenhower's command, and when Eisenhower sought to stop him, he brought his congressman to threaten Eisenhower, confirming Ike's impression of the rascality of politicians. That encounter and another with a congressman trying to get him to reinstate an officer caught cheating at cards were so solidly stuck in his memory that he would spread the stories of these two obnoxiously interfering congressmen across three pages of his brief book of autobiographical anecdotes written forty-eight years later.[*]

On December 31, 1918, encamped with his men near Verdun, Harry Truman, who himself promptly chose an "F & I" (full and immediate separation from the army), wrote to Bess about those who chose to stay in the army: "I can't see what on earth any man with initiative and a mind of his own wants to be in the army in peacetime for. You've always got some old fossil above you whose slightest whim is law and who generally hasn't a grain of horse sense. For my part I want to be where I can cuss 'em all I please when I please." He also noted how much attitudes changed when

---

[*] *At Ease*, pp. 142–45.

there was no more chance of promotion—"It's right laughable sometimes"—and said, "I'd give my right arm to be on the Military Affairs
Committee of the House."

> We just live from one inspection to the next. You know these regular
> army colonels and lieutenant colonels who've had their feet on the
> desk ever since the argument started are hellbent for inspections. Some
> of 'em haven't been over here but a month or two but they can come
> around and tell us who went through it exactly and how we did not
> win the war. . . . This peacetime soldiering is an awful bore and any-
> body who wants to do it is certainly off in his upper works.

On July 4, 1917, after the American troops had landed in France, an
American colonel had made a gallant statement, instantly famous, at the
tomb of the French aristocrat who was celebrated for his aid to the American Revolution: "Lafayette, we are here!" On January 27, 1919, with his
men being put through maneuvers in France even though the war had
been over for more than two months, Capt. Harry Truman passed on to
Bess the soldiers' wisecrack: "Lafayette, we are *still* here!"

> I guess they give us those things to do to keep us from going dingy and
> also to have some legitimate employment for the oceans of staff offi-
> cers running loose. Staff officers, you know, are purely ornamental and
> utterly useless as far as I can see. They are mostly lieutenant colonels
> and majors and fresh young captains. They sit close to the throne and
> promotion comes easy to 'em whether they know much or whether
> they don't, and mostly they don't.

Finally, on April 9, 1919, Harry and the 129th Field Artillery sailed for
New York on the former German liner *Zeppelin.*

Dwight Eisenhower, who had expected to sail with his men in the
opposite direction the previous fall, was, to his dismay, assigned instead to
another home-side job at Camp Meade, Maryland.

In the shrinking peacetime army, he was reduced to the permanent
rank of captain, after which he was promoted to major, a rank at which he
would remain for sixteen years.

II

HISTORY DOES NOT always arrange itself so that it breaks into convenient
units corresponding to the decades of the calendar, but in the 1920s and
1930s it almost perfectly did, and emphatically. The twenties ran from
the end of the Great War to the stock market crash, and the thirties from
the crash to the outbreak of World War II, and each of these pungent

decades had a quite distinct atmosphere, and is sharply distinguished from the other. The events that brought their beginning and their ending were world-altering events that cast their effects over the years that followed. The deep experiences of those years had a profound effect on America's political education.

Harry Truman, between the wars, was fully engaged in the shared American public experience; Dwight Eisenhower, in the shrunken and marginalized peacetime army, was, to a remarkable degree, insulated from it.

The months after the end of the Great War in Europe and the last phases of the presidency of Woodrow Wilson were crammed with portentous events. The Treaty of Versailles carried the seeds of the war that would make Dwight Eisenhower and Harry Truman into world figures. In the tremendous struggle over the League of Nations, the American public for the first time confronted the worldwide pattern of American responsibility that Harry Truman and Dwight Eisenhower would one day epitomize. A little later, on the much smaller scale of domestic preoccupations, there were the "Palmer raids" and the "Red Scare," which would anticipate the ugly underside of American public opinion, the worst recrudescence of which Dwight Eisenhower and Harry Truman would one day have to cope with. But so far as his biographers can tell, the shared public event that most engaged the young Dwight Eisenhower in those months— he was twenty-eight when the war ended—was the "Black Sox scandal," the alleged throwing of the World Series of 1919 by eight members of the Chicago White Sox.

Stephen Ambrose wrote of Eisenhower in the interwar years:

> He was to remain a major for sixteen years. As the American economy boomed, as fortunes were made, as his own brothers forged ahead in their varied careers, Eisenhower stayed in place. During the [First World] War, although he had not been where he wanted to be, he at least had important responsibilities; in the 1920's and 1930's, save as a football coach, he had none. He made almost no decisions between his twenty-eighth and his fifty-first birthdays, except to stay in the miniscule army and do his best.

Harry Truman stayed in civilian life and did his best, making many decisions about both public affairs and the shifts and chances of his own life. He knew what it was to be a bank clerk, a farmer, and a civilian turned soldier overseas. After the war, he risked all the funds he had, and went broke, with his shirt store. At first, the store did well, so that he had a brief taste of the decade's prosperity. But then in the "Republican recession," as he called it, in 1920–1921, the store failed. He knew what it is to start his own business—and, through no fault of his own (at least as he saw it), to see that business flop. He incurred a debt that he had to keep paying on into the thirties.

Truman then entered into a political career, and engaged in politics in a particularly elemental form—the politics of Kansas City and Jackson County, Missouri, in the days of Boss Pendergast. He toured Jackson County repeatedly, making political speeches, shaking hands, asking for votes, learning what was on the minds of the public. He knew what it is to win—and he knew what it is to lose. After his one two-year term as the judge from the eastern part of the county, he was defeated for reelection in 1924. He knew what it was to have to find another job (selling membership in the Kansas City Automobile Club, as it turned out) when he lost that race for political office. He then experienced some more winning, being elected presiding judge, which carried a four-year term, in 1926 and again in 1930.

In 1933, at the time of the Great Depression and the coming of the New Deal, Truman, while still serving as presiding judge, was appointed the director of the Federal Reemployment program in Missouri, for which he was paid one dollar a year, plus expenses; in this post, he had another encounter with what the general populace was experiencing at this time, registering and attempting to find jobs for the jobless, in anticipation of the huge work relief programs of the New Deal. Twice he went to Washington for conferences, met Harry Hopkins, whom he admired, and saw something of a national administration under stress.

And then, after a disappointment when he wanted to run for governor, he was nominated for and elected to the United States Senate in 1934 and reelected (very narrowly) in 1940. He never again experienced losing, but the scare in 1940, when he might have lost, was instructive, too.

The reason for Ike's contrasting insulation was his line of work. You can write a history of American life and culture in the twenties and never mention the army—indeed, *Harper's Magazine* editor Frederick Lewis Allen did just that in a once widely popular book called *Only Yesterday*, written right at the height of the time he was describing and therefore doubly revealing of his subject. And you could also write a book about American life and culture in the radically different decade of the thirties, and again there would not be any passages about the army. And Frederick Lewis Allen wrote that one, too, a parallel book entitled *Since Yesterday*, and once again there was no mention of the nation's military institutions. But with the forties, that striking omission would come to an end: No institution was more central to the forties than the army.

The United States Army at its wartime peak had been a gigantic force of 3.7 million men, 2 million of them in Europe. But once they had been packed into transports at Brest, had their ticker-tape and victory parades, and were mustered out, like Harry Truman, they got married, looked for jobs, joined the civilian population, and disappeared from the story as *soldiers.*

The reductions in the armed forces were sudden and severe. The United States Army, just yesterday that huge force of 3.7 million, was reduced by actions of Congress in 1920 to 300,000; in January 1921, to 175,000; in June 1921, to 150,000; and a year later, to 125,000 enlisted men, where it would remain until the late thirties. Insofar as one considered national defense at all, the navy was thought to be the first line. The peace-time army had been shoved clear over to the periphery of the nation's consciousness, and it shrank almost into oblivion. The United States had become a major economic power among the nations of the world, and was still growing, but its standing army shriveled down to seventeenth among the nations with standing armies. So it did not matter whether Dwight Eisenhower coached football, as the army seemed to keep trying to make him do, or whether he worked with tanks, which the army itself did not much believe in. The army, in any event, was not where the action was.

Commanding a tank corps without any tanks; building a new tank corps training facility (Camp Colt) with only, belatedly, a few French tanks; experimenting with this new instrument of warfare with a new friend, George Patton; writing an article about tank warfare—all this would be about as far outside the interests of the broad public at the time as it was possible to be. The war was *over.* Not only was the Great War over, but *all* war was supposed to be over. President Wilson had said that this was to be a war to end all wars. He was just now, while Eisenhower and Patton were puzzling about how to fight a war with tanks, trying to build a world of peace and of law where there would be no warfare with or without tanks.

And no one in the upper echelons of the army wanted to hear about tanks, either. The tank turned swiftly from novelty in 1916 to anachronism by 1920. Ike's specialty was irrelevant not only to civilian life but to army life, as well. Eisenhower and Patton were told to stop writing about that aberration in warfare. It is a little hard to credit the report, but Dwight Eisenhower was threatened with a court-martial in the autumn of 1920 by the major who was chief of the infantry if he did not stop publishing tank-dominated ideas that were incompatible with solid infantry doctrine. The generals in the cavalry wanted horses, not tanks, and those in the infantry wanted the tank only as an adjunct to the infantry, not as an independent force. The top brass of a rapidly shrinking peacetime army were not oversupplied with nimble imaginations.

For three long stretches, Eisenhower was out of the country, remote from its politics: among the bats and lizards of the Panama Canal Zone from early 1922 to late 1924; in Paris, rewriting the guide to battle monuments, as we have seen, for thirteen months in 1928–1929; and in the Philippines, from 1935 to 1939, coping with the theatrics of Douglas MacArthur. Before this last absence, though, there was a period in which he was not at all removed geographically or physically from American political currents; rather, he was smack in the middle of great events, working in the nation's capital. He spent more than five years in Washington, toiling in the War Department from November 1929 (just after the crash) until late in 1935, experiencing the onset of the Great Depression, the struggles of the Hoover administration in its last throes; the momentous election of 1932; and the coming of Franklin Roosevelt, the famous hundred days, and the New Deal—one of the most gripping periods in American political history. But Eisenhower was not gripped. Working in the peacetime army on plans for a future war that no one believed was coming, and serving an army boss whom political Washington viewed as something between a menace, an irrelevance, and a joke (Douglas MacArthur), he was effectively separated from the New Deal excitement. While his countrymen were recovering from, and recoiling in revulsion against, the Great War; hunting out "Reds" in the Red Scare (some hunting, some others deploring the hunting); coping with the postwar spread of the Ku Klux Klan, even into sections of the North; enacting, and violating, the Volstead Act; participating to whatever degree in the common symbols of the twenties, the Jazz Age, the flapper era, the speakeasy; supporting, or attacking, Sacco and Vanzetti; being driven to jump off skyscrapers by the great crash, and to sell apples and pencils on street corners and to live in Hoovervilles, by the Great Depression; learning in the depths of the Depression that we have nothing to fear but fear itself; pasting the blue eagles of the National Recovery Administration (NRA) in the store windows, and restricting their planting for the Agricultural Adjustment Administration (AAA); learning a string of initials for the new agencies in Washington; feeling more secure because of, or attacking as the ultimate in socialism, the Social Security program; blocking access to factories in sitdown strikes, or condemning others doing so; and enacting into law the fullest body of social legislation in the history of the nation. During all these and the other great shaping events of the interwar period, Dwight Eisenhower was set apart in the monastic world of the peacetime army.

Eisenhower had a salary that, although not particularly generous, was regular and certain. He had an institutional home, and even though much of the time this must have seemed like obscurity, it also provided security. It is a cliché of the Eisenhower biographies to say that through all these years the Eisenhowers never owned their own home—not, in fact, until they retired to Gettysburg—and that they moved seventeen times. But their peripatetic and apparently homeless life actually had a secure institutional underpinning not so common in American lives in the twenties and thirties. Their "homes," although temporary and not their own property, were provided. Their medical care was provided. When in the darkest moments of the young Eisenhowers' lives their first son "Icky" contracted scarlet fever and died while they were at Camp Meade, the anxiety of paying the medical bills was not added to their sorrow. Ike did not need to plan his own retirement benefits as, in the days before Social Security, millions of Americans did. The Great Depression had a shaping effect upon the political mind of millions of Americans of Eisenhower's generation, but not to any comparable degree on Eisenhower himself. If you read his biographies in parallel with historical accounts of the years in which he lived, you are struck repeatedly by a dissonance, a separation, a counterpoint.

What happened to him when the crash came in 1929 and during the Great Depression? The Eisenhowers were in Paris at the actual moment of the crash, in late October 1929; they were spending a pleasant but uneventful fifteen months there, at Mamie's behest. Ike was rewriting the guidebook to battle monuments in Europe, portions of which were quoted in the previous chapter. They returned to the States in November 1929, and Eisenhower was assigned to the office of the assistant secretary of war in Washington. That office had the task, under the National Defense Act of 1920, of developing an industrial-organization plan for use in the event of war, and Ike's task was to develop such a plan. An act that had been passed in the immediate aftermath of the Great War required that in the event of another war, there should be in the files of the War Department a plan to mobilize American industry, to avoid the delays, misallocations, and, to use an acronym that would not come to be employed until the next war, snafus that had bedeviled efforts in the past war. Ten years had passed since the law had been enacted, and here was the forty-year-old major, in the shrunken army of a weak and half-isolationist nation descending into economic depression, planning for industrial mobilization in another, unanticipated, war. Kenneth Davis, writing in 1944, in the midst of the war that *had* come, put it this way:

> It was strange to be planning for plant expansion—to be thinking in terms of material and power shortages—when all around you plants were shutting down, products were begging for non-existent buyers, and ten million men were unemployed. Strange, too, to be planning in terms of unlimited government expenditures during an adminis-tration whose principal answer to the Depression was a *reduction* in government expenditures. Stranger still to be basing the whole of one's work on the assumption that the government had emergency powers which the government itself, at that particular moment, was denying it possessed.

Stephen Ambrose, viewing this period from a much greater distance, wrote, "A job more out of joint with the times could hardly be imagined."

Eisenhower's job lasted straight through the worst of the Depression. Although he did suffer a small pay cut, his job was secure; prices were fall-ing, and so he came out ahead; and he lived in the one place, the nation's capital, that was not depressed, but, because of government activity to combat the Depression, thriving. He and his circle of army friends had secure positions—not a small point in shaping the political mind of a member of his generation.

Harry Truman had no such security and no such isolation.

III

HARRY TRUMAN would become, in the years between the wars, a lifelong practicing politician; Dwight Eisenhower would have reinforced, in those same years, his lifelong disdain for practicing politicians.

Harry Truman's mother and father were Democrats; their parents were Democrats; the Scots-Irish ancestors who, as Democrats, had made the nineteenth-century trek from Kentucky to Missouri had named their new county *Jackson* County, after the great original leader of the Democratic party, Andrew Jackson. When George Allan told Harry Truman's mother that, growing up in Mississippi, he had not met a Republican until he was twelve, she is said to have replied, "George, you ain't missed much."

Dwight Eisenhower's mother and father were members of the River Brethren; his uncles were River Brethren preachers; his paternal grandfather was a River Brethren preacher-patriarch. When this grandfather and his family made the nineteenth-century trek from Pennsylvania to Kansas, they did so as part of a planned communal move by the River Brethren.

Harry Truman's father, the mule trader John Truman, got a job, through political connections, as overseer of the roads in Jackson County. Dwight Eisenhower's father, the mechanic David Eisenhower, got a job, through River Brethren connections, with the Belle Springs Creamery, which resulted in the family's moving back to Abilene from Texas.

Harry Truman, age eight and a half, went off to grade school in Independence in 1892 wearing a cap that said GROVER CLEVELAND FOR PRESIDENT, ADLAI STEVENSON FOR VICE PRESIDENT—the Democratic ticket for that year. He remembered his father riding a gray horse in the Democrats' victory parade, and, in his partisan enthusiasm, climbing up on their roof to attach a bunting, which he proclaimed would stay there as long as Democrats ran the government. In 1900, sixteen-year-old Harry Truman served as a page at the Democratic party's convention in Kansas City, where, for the second time, the Great Commoner, William Jennings Bryan, was nominated.

In 1912, as was noted earlier, when his father and other Missouri Democrats supported Missouri senator Champ Clark for the Democratic presidential nomination, the twenty-eight-year-old Harry Truman supported the idealistic governor of New Jersey, Woodrow Wilson. After interrupting his plowing, he learned from the telegraphed results that Wilson had been nominated, and he was thrilled again when Wilson was elected.

Harry Truman, after first the success and then the failure of his shirt shop, would go on to a thirty-one-year career as an active politician in a very political county and a very political state.

Eisenhower would have a thirty-seven-year insulating career in the army, most of it—until he was past fifty—in the peacetime army of a country that thought it had repudiated war. That career seems both to have preserved, as under glass, and to have reinforced the separation from, and the disdain for, "politics" that was endemic to his small town–Kansas Protestant beginnings.

Eisenhower went from a small town in Kansas where politics were muted to an education at West Point, where politics were eschewed and disdained. "West Point had . . . repeatedly instilled in young Eisenhower and his classmates," wrote Carlo D'Este in the best Eisenhower biography, "a thorough distrust of politics and politicians. The cadets were inculcated with, and readily came to accept, the premise that politicians in general, and Congress in particular, were a contemptible dishonest lot."

His disdain for politicians was reinforced when he spent that period in Washington toiling in the War Department while Hoover tried to cope with the Depression and Roosevelt unfolded the New Deal. In those years, D'Este wrote, "his aversion to politicians would harden."

And working under MacArthur, at first in Washington and then for long years six thousand miles away in Manila, would harden his aversion in another way, by providing daily encounters with a blatant example of the political general at its worst.

Harry Truman had been a Democrat, so to speak, since before he was born. He was a voter and a worker in every election of his lifetime, and a candidate eight times, in elections at every level: the county, the state, and the nation. And for good measure, he had once (in 1916) run for a town office: committeeman.

Eisenhower, by contrast, ran for no office, rang no doorbells, made no political speeches, and, so far as we know, did not even cast a vote in any election until he was nearly sixty years old and had himself become a major figure, willy-nilly, in world politics. Furthermore, neither the public nor close associates were certain to which of the great American political parties he might attach himself. Members of both parties could urge his candidacy. His entry into political life would take the quite curious form, for a man past sixty years old, of an enormously belated indication of the political party he preferred.

Eisenhower's not voting and not favoring a party was not at all peculiar to him; it was part of the ethos of his world. Carlo D'Este, himself a retired U.S. Army lieutenant colonel, would write, "As a body the officer corps avoided politics to the point that fewer than one in five hundred even bothered to register as a member of a political party or vote in an election." Ike internalized and embodied that tradition of the army's officer class.

From the moment that Jim Pendergast and Mike Pendergast walked into his shirt shop one day in July or August of 1921 and asked him to run for eastern judge in Jackson County, Harry Truman was engaged in the sort of politics that Dwight Eisenhower would learn to abominate. Agreeing to run, Truman became the candidate supported by—as it would be seen with the eyes of Abilene and West Point—the nefarious Kansas City machine.

The Pendergasts did not ask Harry to run either because he represented some national good they wanted to promote or because they were impressed with his virtue or talent as a statesman (although Jim Pendergast had a high regard for Captain Harry, having served with him in the war); they wanted him to run because they needed a candidate with his characteristics to advance the machine's power in the county.

The post for which Truman was to run, although called "judge," was not a judicial office, but an executive office. The county court had three judges—a western judge for the Kansas City area, an eastern judge for Independence and the county outside Kansas City, and a presiding judge—and controlled county budgets, county institutions, and, most important, county roads. It controlled all the jobs connected with those county activities. The Pendergast organization, not yet as dominant as it would later become, was engaged in battle with an opposing faction within the Democratic party and needed a candidate for this non-urban section of the county, and Harry Truman fit the bill: He was a Baptist, to balance Catholic Pendergast Kansas City; he was a veteran, popular with the men he had led and other veterans; he and his family were active Democrats; he had been a farmer and then an honest businessman; his family was well known in the relevant territory. He was what the Pendergasts needed to run for that office. Was the office also what he needed to support his family? One of his biographers—Richard Miller—contradicting other accounts, insisted that "Truman did not turn to politics in desperation after the haberdashery failed. . . . Truman wasn't a supplicant seeking Pendergast faction backing. . . . The Pendergasts sought him." But they sought him at a convenient point in his life.

And did Truman accept because he had an ardent wish to be of service to the common good? Truman did have, mingled with his other motives, more of such a purpose than might appear to the eyes of Abilene or West Point—when he gained power as presiding judge he would demonstrate that worthy purpose—but it was also true that in 1922 he needed an income to support his family.

The decisive battles in this political universe, unless some Democratic faction defected to the Republicans, came in the Democratic party's primary. In complicated factional fighting, Truman barely won in 1922, and in even more complicated factionalism, with the opposing Democratic Shannon faction defecting to the Republicans, in 1924 he narrowly lost, his only defeat in a general election in his political career.

He was in a strong position, however, to run again, and the Pendergast organization also was stronger when he ran in 1926 for the more powerful position of presiding judge, which was for a four-year term. He would fill that more powerful office for two terms, from January 1, 1927, until January 1, 1935. That is what he was doing while Dwight Eisenhower was in the War Department planning for an imaginary war.

A Pendergast man was elected to the court with Truman, so that he was able to dominate the court and county government, build roads and a new courthouse, and, in some defiance of his boss, or ally, Tom Pendergast, keep it all honest—at least mostly so.

The Pendergast contribution to Truman's election to the Senate in 1934 would not have improved his reputation in the eyes of the River Brethren, or of Abilene or West Point, or of the peacetime army, or, in some regards at least, of almost anyone else. He was not chosen because the people of Missouri wanted him to speak for them in the corridors of power; he was chosen instead because the Kansas City machine needed somebody to fill that office. But he was not Tom Pendergast's first choice for that purpose.

Did Truman benefit from their ghost votes and repeat votes and riders and sleepers? The fraudulent voting practices of the Pendergast machine in the 1936 election were shown, by investigations after Pendergast's fall, to have been gargantuan. In his biography of Truman, Robert Ferrell has reported that a single house at 912 Tracy Street managed to produce 141 voters, and a vacant lot at 700 Main Street yielded 112 voters. The Second District, with a population of 18,478, brought in 19,202 votes for Pendergast's ticket, to 12 (who could they have been?) for the opposition. The total Kansas City vote would have been possible legitimately only if the city had had 200,000 more adults than its actual population. Indeed, everything was up-to-date in Kansas City; they had gone about as far as they could go.

That was in 1936, when the machine reached its apogee of power and seems to have lathered itself in heedless arrogance. Had it been true also in 1934, when Harry Truman was making his first bid for the Senate? Perhaps not on the grandiose scale of two years later, but Ferrell has reported that that dependable Second District gave him 15,145 votes, to 24 for his opponent, and that when that district is joined to two other equally lopsided Kansas City districts, one can account for the entire margin by which Truman carried the state. His "realistic" defense of his link to Pendergast's Kansas City organization might not win over every critic: that "any politician" who could do so would ally himself with an organization that controlled 100,000 votes.

In the years that Truman was preparing to run for the Senate, Kansas City would come to the attention of the nation and the world because of the spectacular outrages committed by its underworld figures. One of the most notorious episodes in the colorful history of Depression gangland warfare took place right in downtown Kansas City—at Union Station, in fact, in broad daylight on the morning of June 17, 1933: the Kansas City Massacre. A convict who had escaped was being transferred to Leavenworth, via Kansas City. Friends of his in the outlaw business, perhaps including the colorful scoundrel "Pretty Boy" Floyd, learned the time of the transfer, and in their attempt to free him three policemen and an FBI agent were killed, as well as the prisoner.

Still worse was another outrage the following year, directly tied to the political machine. *Time* magazine, on April 9, 1934, gave the following report on the municipal election in the city from which Harry Truman received his pivotal support, in the year in which he was elected senator:

> Sprawled across the sidewalk in front of a Kansas City polling place lay the body of William Findley, Negro election worker, blood on his face, a bullet in his brain. . . .
>
> Slumped in a heap lay Lee Flacy, deputy sheriff, pumped full of buckshot. . . .
>
> A mortal head wound crumpled Larry Cappo, sleek little gangster . . . in the back of a wrecked sedan.
>
> A few doors away Pascal Oldham, 78, hardware merchant, was locking up his store when he turned to see a car flash by, to hear guns crackle. A stray bullet drilled clean through his head. . . .
>
> Slugged and beaten with blackjacks, brass knuckles, gun-butts and baseball bats were a housewife, a Kansas City Star newshawk, a candidate for the City Council, a chauffeur, a policeman, and five other persons.
>
> Such was last week's score in Kansas City's municipal election. When blackjacks were pocketed and votes were counted, Kansas Citizens knew the worst: The Fusion attempt to break the rule of Boss Thomas Joseph ("Big Tom") Pendergast's Democratic machine had failed. Re-elected by a 59,566 plurality was Boss-backed Mayor Bryce Byram Smith, a mild-mannered baking company official in his spare time. Defeated was Dr. Albert Ross Hill, 64, anti-Boss Democrat, one-time (1908–20) president of the University of Missouri. . . .
>
> Thus ended Kansas City's hope of a municipal New Deal, as represented by the Citizens-Fusion ticket put forth by the National Youth Movement. Founded a year ago by a small group of young, public-spirited citizens, the National Youth Movement aimed to

depose the Pendergast machine as Tammany had been deposed in New York.*

But in a hail of bullets, they did not succeed. And so it would not be surprising that when the candidate supported by that machine was elected in statewide elections the following November, and arrived in Washington at the start of the new year to take his place in the Senate, his fellow senators would look at him warily.

When Truman arrived in the Senate in 1935 and was dubbed in the press and by some of his fellow senators "the Senator from Pendergast," his response was defiantly to display a picture of Tom Pendergast on his office wall.

When Harry Truman came to the nation's capital to be sworn in as a United States Senator on January 3, 1935, Dwight Eisenhower was already in town, working as the principal assistant to the Army Chief of Staff, Gen. Douglas MacArthur, in the old War Department building next to the White House (now the *Eisenhower* Executive Office Building). Eisenhower worked hard in a tiny office next to MacArthur's large one; MacArthur would summon him by lung power.

Ike and Mamie and son John lived in the Wyoming Apartments, where they had lived on their previous stint in Washington; MacArthur was grandly driven around town in a chauffeured limousine but never offered Ike a ride or use of the car. When Ike traveled to Capitol Hill, as he did frequently, he had to take a streetcar or a taxi and fill out a form to get his quarters and dollars back.

The Trumans, newly arrived, found an apartment in Tilden Gardens, from which he would often walk, at the army clip of 120 paces a minute, the several miles to the Capitol. But sometimes he took the streetcar down Connecticut Avenue, past the White House on Pennsylvania Avenue, and then on up to the Capitol.

The two men and their families would both be there in New Deal Washington from January 3 to October 1, 1935, when Ike left from Union Station with MacArthur and his entourage on the first leg of the journey to Manila, where Ike would serve as MacArthur's sidekick in the Philippines for four years.

But meanwhile, back in those ten months when they were both in

---

* Several sentences in this extract show the stylistic fancy of the early *Time* magazine, of which Woolcott Gibbs wrote an immortal parody in *The New Yorker:* "Backward run sentences until reels the mind"; Gibbs concluded, "Where it will end, knows God."

town, might Ike and Harry have crossed paths? It is not likely they would have encountered each other in the line of business. Although the freshman senator wanted to be assigned to the Military Affairs Committee, he did not succeed, and was assigned instead to Commerce. And Ike at that stage was not a major player, but a flunky. Perhaps one can imagine, just for the poetry of it, that on one of the days between January 3 and October 1, 1935, they would both have ridden on the same trolley. If they had met in those months, in the Capitol, on the trolley, or in a Hot Shoppe, Ike surely would have been disdainful of this raw politician—this newly minted "Senator from Pendergast." And Truman would have been dismissive of this deskbound army officer who had never seen combat and was serving as a paper-shuffling army bureaucrat.

When Senator Truman's term was running out after six years, he faced the problem of being a boss's candidate for a different reason. In 1939, as Truman neared the end of his senatorial term, Tom Pendergast, back home in Kansas City, was indicted for tax evasion, pleaded guilty, and was sent to the federal prison in Leavenworth. Pendergast was now widely denounced, but Truman did not do any of the denouncing. The well-heeled Democratic governor of the state, a wealthy apple grower named Lloyd Stark, barred by law from another term, eyed the Senate seat held by Harry Truman, and presented himself as a reformer in the Democratic primary. He was making sounds that indicated that he would try to displace Truman as senator in the election of 1940. Stark was separating himself from Pendergast, whose support he had once sought and accepted. Stark was now presenting himself, and being presented by some of the press in Missouri and nationwide, as an honest man, a "moral leader" in the swamp of Missouri politics, in implicit contrast to Harry Truman, Boss Pendergast's man.

If Maj. Dwight Eisenhower, just returned from the Philippines and serving in army maneuvers in the West, had paid any attention to a Senate race in Missouri—surely he did not—and if he had had political preferences—which, like his fellow officers, he avoided—and if realism had forced him to have preferred not the Republican candidate, who had no chance, but one of the contestants in the Democratic primary—then we may surely guess that he would have hoped that Governor Stark would defeat Senator Truman. But Stark didn't. Truman managed to win that 1940 Democratic primary, defeating Stark, although very narrowly. He succeeded in this, the hardest race of his life, mainly because of his extraordinary campaigning, which took him into 85 of Missouri's 114 counties—in his own automobile. Truman won the nomination with a margin of barely more than 1 percent of the votes cast, and, a successful politician, returned to the Senate for his second term.

IV

TRUMAN AND EISENHOWER, however much they differed in other ways, were alike in some of their responses to the culture of the twenties. They did not overindulge when it came to the movies, radio, or dancing, and although they both drank some alcohol in the decade of Prohibition, they did not overdo that, either. They played poker and bridge, not mah-jongg; Ike was a superb poker player and, as he explained in *At Ease,* learned early to play the percentages. They did not dance the night away with flappers: Bess Truman was no flapper, and although given a chance Mamie might have become one, she was stuck for most of the twenties as an army wife in stodgy military camps. These two couples certainly were not bloated with the decade's vaunted prosperity: Ike supported his wife and son on the severe pay of a major in the peacetime army; Truman supported his wife and daughter—Margaret was born in 1924—while coping with the debts from his shirt store and the chancy contingency of a lowly political office.

But there was one arena in which they were both completely in tune with the times: Both of these men loved automobiles. Both of them also cared about the roads cars were driven on. Both of them, when they acquired the power to do so, built roads.

The two presidents were shaped by turn-of-the-century America, when the country was still feeling its way from the farm to the city and from the horse to the automobile. They were old enough to remember when cars, movies, and the radio did not exist, but their adult lives unfolded at a time when each of these were dominant aspects of life. They began to have dealings with motor travel while they were still young enough for it to become an integral part of their lives. The great technological novelties that come into our lives in our mature years are perhaps always a little strange, and those that were already fully developed before we were born are taken for granted. But those that come into general use when we are young, supplanting something we have known and used, are likely to be, in a distinct way, a part of us. Harry and Ike were born and spent their first years in a world of horses, but with the development in their early years of the horseless carriage they became automobile people—or perhaps one should say, thinking of Eisenhower, motor-travel people (the internal combustion engines in his world importantly included those in tanks and trucks).

Young Harry Truman's romance with automobiles began before he went off to war. When in 1913 he got a little money from the settlement of a family lawsuit, he purchased a five-passenger automobile—one of those early, now-forgotten makes, a Stafford. This Stafford was not just another automobile of the sort that millions would buy and drive in later years; it was, instead, one of the rare and early makes, and would later become an object of endless fascination to automobile buffs like Harry Truman himself. In the Truman Library, there are many old articles and letters dealing with this car, including letters written in retirement by Truman himself.

Truman had known the maker of this car, one Terry Stafford, and reported that he had at first made the cars in Topeka, then moved the business to Kansas City. Truman said that Stafford made a grand total of only 315 of these vehicles, the last, probably in 1915, for himself. The publisher of a magazine about cars who corresponded with Truman about his Stafford visited him in Independence and reported, "Mr. Truman had a remarkable knowledge of the mechanical features of the car"—this in 1953, when Truman was sixty-nine years old, thirty-five years after he had sold the car, and after his having been senator, vice president, and president of the United States.

Young Truman proudly drove this car around the Middle West and used it to go calling on Bess. He kept it through the years, and in the wartime army in Oklahoma, used it to carry ice and other items that the men of Battery D needed. He finally sold it when he went overseas in 1918.

Home from the war, married to Bess, needing transportation to the haberdashery in Kansas City while living in Independence, he bought the first in a series of Dodges. An "owner endorsement" of a "used vehicle" offered for sale by ex-president Harry Truman in Independence in 1955 carries these testimonies: "This is a 1st choice car in every detail" and "I have driven Dodges since 1919." The string of Dodges (together with some Chryslers) that the Trumans would own would take Harry from one end of the country to the other.

When back in 1924 he was defeated for reelection as eastern judge—the one hiatus in his political career—what he did to support his family was to sell memberships in the Automobile Club of Kansas City.

Again and again when he was faced with an issue, he would go not to the library or to the experts, but to his car. He would hit the road, driving around the country pursuing an answer. When as presiding judge of Jack-

son County he successfully promoted bond issues to build a new courthouse in Kansas City and to renovate the courthouse in Independence,
and he needed an answer to the question of their design, he got in his car
and drove around the country to look at public buildings.

> Then I took my private car—not a county one—and drove to Shreve-
> port, Denver, Houston, Racine, Milwaukee, Buffalo, Brooklyn, Lin-
> coln, Baton Rouge and several other places and looked at the new
> public buildings, met the architects and contractors, inspected the
> buildings and finally decided to employ the architect of the Court
> House at Shreveport as consulting architect for our county buildings.

Determined to have a statue of Andrew Jackson at the center of Jackson
County, he drove to Charlottesville, Virginia, to see the statue of another
Jackson—Stonewall—and hired the sculptor. He also drove around the
county during his county campaigns, and around the state in his Senate
campaigns.

Reelected to the Senate as war came, and hearing about wickedness in
the construction of new army camps, he got in his car and made a tremendous tour, looking into the preparation for war. He himself would say that
he drove thirty thousand miles, which is plainly what Huck Finn would
call a stretcher, but he did drive a long way—perhaps ten thousand miles:
down to Florida, back up into the Midwest, and up into Wisconsin and
Michigan, stopping at army installations and defense plants, laying the
groundwork for the investigation of military preparedness by the Senate
Committee.

After he was nominated for vice president in Chicago in 1944, he drove
Bess and Margaret back to Independence. Bess had not wanted him to
accept the nomination, so that trip was marked by frosty silence.

His driving would then be interrupted by service as vice president and
president of the United States, but in retirement he started driving again.

Because Eisenhower went to West Point in 1911 and stayed in the army
thereafter for much of his life, his relationship to motor travel would have
a different angle. Although his father-in-law would give him and Mamie
a car (another forgotten make, a Pullman) after he was married in 1916,
the great impact on him would be not the private automobile (for a large
part of his life somebody else would drive his car—in World War II, noto-
riously, Kay Summersby), but the use of motor vehicles in warfare. He
would be an advocate of greater mobility, and after having trained men
for tank warfare in the last months of the Great War, he became after the
war, along with his new friend George Patton, an expert on mobile motor-

ized warfare, featuring the tank. Writing about Ike and Patton, Michael Korda said, "Without drawing too much attention to themselves, they experimented with tanks, and spent their spare time taking a tank completely to pieces like a pair of shade-tree mechanics, right down to the last nut and bolt, then painstakingly reassembled it to understand how each component worked. Ike's fascination with the internal combustion engine and the automobile was certainly a factor in his enthusiasm for the tank."*

That enthusiasm was not in tune with the interest either of the public or of the army at the time.

When the time would come for D-Day, in Sicily as well as in Normandy, the romantic leader from a different age, an age of horses and sabers, perhaps, Winston Churchill, would have a hard time believing that so huge a fraction of the immense supply chain would consist of unarmored motorized transport vehicles—in other words, *trucks* (or, if you are British, lorries).†

Because Truman and Eisenhower cared about cars and trucks, both of these American prairie boys in the automobile age cared also about roads. When Harry Truman was elected presiding judge, the chief county official of Jackson County, and served from 1926 to 1935, his primary focus was roads. The "pie crust" roads that existed were not adequate to the rapidly expanding needs of the automobile. Truman announced that no county taxpayer would be more than two miles from a good cement road. He rebuilt the roads of his county so well and so completely that it was said of him, in local celebration, "He took Jackson County out of the mud!"

Dwight Eisenhower had his own experience with the mud when, in July 1919, in the difficult decompression days after the Great War, he accompanied a military truck convoy—a collection of eighty-one assorted army vehicles—across the country, thereby learning about the condition of the nation's roads the hard way. The convoy traveled, according to Carlo D'Este, on the dirt and mud roads of that day, going 3,251 miles, from Washington to San Francisco, in sixty-two days. They experienced breakdowns, impasses, interruptions, mud, quicksand, 230 road accidents, averaging fifty-eight miles a day, at an average speed of six miles per hour. When after one more war, and a look at the *Autobahnen* of Germany, Eisenhower became president of the United States, the most expensive

---

* Michael Korda, *Ike: An American Hero* (HarperCollins, 2007), p. 151.

† Churchill would be still more astonished that the provisions taken across the Channel into Normandy, along with five divisions of soldiers, would include several dentist chairs.

positive new program of the federal government proposed during his two terms was the Interstate Highway System, and it was a program, unlike some others in the administration's list, that Eisenhower himself really believed in and fought for, and compromised on the financing of it enough to get it through. In his presidential memoirs, *Mandate for Change,* he described the system as a "true concrete and macadam lifeline" and celebrated the result, without apparent irony, in the following way: "The total pavement of the system would make a parking lot big enough to hold two-thirds of all the automobiles in the United States. The amount of concrete poured to form these roadways would build eight Hoover Dams or six sidewalks to the moon. To build them, bulldozers and shovels would move enough dirt and rock to bury all of Connecticut two feet deep."

V

THERE WAS ONE notorious public event in the interwar period in which Eisenhower *did* participate—but, as one might put it, on the wrong side, and against his will. This was the suppression of the famous Bonus Army that marched on Washington and was forcibly dispersed in July 1932.

The Depression left millions of men unemployed, impoverished, even homeless; the new president elected in that year would later refer to "one-third of a nation ill-housed, ill-clad, ill-nourished." Thousands of these desperate men had served in the army in the Great War. In 1924, Congress had passed the Adjusted Compensation Act, but full payment to veterans was to be made twenty years hence—in 1945. Because of the Depression, there was great pressure on the government to make that payment sooner—in fact, to make the payment now. President Hoover vetoed one bill. Around the nation, the idea arose of a great march on Washington—a petitioning of Congress by great numbers of hungry men (and some women and children, as well) who arrived on its doorstep.

The ragged troops of the unemployed camped out in makeshift huts and shanties. The "Hooverville" encampment in the Anacostia Flats grew to perhaps twenty thousand hungry people. The conservative Hoover administration, and many others, were, or said they were, frightened; there was much talk of radicalism, communism, anarchism—a mob. But the marchers and squatters were by and large not radicals, certainly not revolutionaries, and not a mob. As onetime soldiers, they disciplined themselves, and called themselves—in a pathetic echo of the name they had once proudly borne—the "Bonus Expeditionary Force," or BEF, left over from the great American Expeditionary Force (AEF) of the war.

Given one or two turns of bad luck, Capt. Harry Truman might have been a part of this BEF.

In its last beleaguered months, the Hoover administration considered them to be the menace of Bolshevism. MacArthur, now chief of staff of the army, saw them to be infiltrated with "Reds" and the first wave of revolution. Eisenhower shared none of his chief's beliefs on that point, nor did he approve of the actions that followed, in which he was required to participate. Even though MacArthur's efforts to identify Communists in the marcher's midst were fruitless, the Hoover administration ordered the Washington police to evict the marchers.

The police chief of the District of Columbia, a veteran himself, dealt sympathetically with the marchers, but Washington, as the nation's capital, was subject to federal control—therefore, the prohibition on the use of the army for police work did not apply. So the army *was* used for police work, and with a vengeance. President Hoover was unsympathetic to the Bonus Army; the archconservative secretary of war, Patrick Hurley, was even less sympathetic; and the opinionated army chief of staff, Douglas MacArthur, saw in the unkempt shantytown an incipient revolution, a veritable threat to the nation's institutions.

Eisenhower was ordered by MacArthur to put on his uniform and join him in this repugnant escapade. Eisenhower, who looks unhappy in pictures of the event, wore no decorations, and expressed strong disapproval of MacArthur in his diary. Hoover ordered the army to cooperate with the police to clear the area of public buildings near the Capitol. Hurley heightened the order to call for the army to clear the entire city, and MacArthur took it upon himself to lead the troops in that endeavor. He deliberately declined to receive a messenger from President Hoover ordering him not to cross the bridge into the shantytown in the Anacostia Flats, and he did cross the bridge, and the shantytown went up in flames.

Someone started a fire—each side blamed the other—and the shantytown was burned and the marchers routed. The tattered marchers, unarmed, attacked by the army in which they once had served, lined the roads around Washington, shuffling back into the great anonymous ranks of the unemployed.

Ike did not think MacArthur should have led this venture himself—the army chief of staff, a four-star general, leading the little posse of eight hundred or so to disperse a band of unarmed civilians. On horseback? In full uniform? MacArthur not only put on his own uniform with five rows of medals but also ordered Eisenhower, to his great disgust, to go home and put on his uniform, too, to accompany his chief into battle.

The force led by these notable generals was to include yet another general who would distinguish himself later in more honorable combat, George S. Patton, commanding the Third Cavalry, brought in for this task from Fort Myer. So among the eight hundred or so men engaged in the one-sided "Battle of Anacostia Flats," there were two hundred cavalry troopers on horseback. They rode down Pennsylvania Avenue wearing steel helmets, dressed in full battle gear, equipped with gas masks, and with their sabers drawn. And they were accompanied by six lumbering tanks. (So this was what tank warfare had come to, that new mobile warfare that Eisenhower and Patton had practiced, argued about, written articles about, and been told to abandon. Now the last few tanks in the U.S. Army rolled through the city to disperse a band of wretched civilians, and the tanks broke down.)

There is a memorable photograph from this episode showing a strutting, somber MacArthur, mounted and in full dress, proudly facing the camera, while in the background an embarrassed Eisenhower, wearing no medals, looking glum, clearly appears to wish he were somewhere else. Entries from his diary show that he disapproved of MacArthur's role; Stephen Ambrose even claimed to have extracted from him, many years later, a startling condemnation of MacArthur: "I told that dumb son of a bitch he had no business going down there. I told him it was no place for a chief of staff."* But he did write the report for MacArthur, justifying the action, and his rare public references to the event, as in his book *At Ease,* include no criticism of MacArthur or of the army's action.

In retrospect, almost everyone regarded the whole episode as a shameful example of something Americans could not believe would happen in their country: armed forces, with a general strutting at their head, attacking unarmed, peacefully protesting civilians. The *Washington News* expressed this view: "What a pitiful spectacle is that of the great American government, mightiest in the world, chasing unarmed men, women, and children with Army tanks. . . . If the Army might be called out to make war on unarmed citizens, this is no longer America."

While a great many Americans, chagrined and disturbed, held a similar view, MacArthur did not. He continued to say that "the mob" was "animated by the essence of revolution," and claimed that the bad publicity was the doing of Communists.

The new president, Franklin Roosevelt, also did not want to take the huge hit to the federal budget that paying the bonus would represent, but

* D'Este, quoting Ambrose, p. 224.

he handled the returning Bonus Marchers, when they marched again the following year, with much more sensitivity than Hoover had. When in 1933 frustrated veterans again turned up in Washington, he ordered the Veterans Administration to set up a camp "with electric lights and running water, including showers." FDR rode through the camp, flashing his soon-to-be-famous smile and giving a wave, and he sent his wife to serve coffee and talk to the men. Jonathan Alter, telling this tale, quotes a veteran: "Hoover sent the army, but Roosevelt sent his wife." But more than that was needed. Roosevelt, therefore, offered the veterans jobs in his new Civilian Conservation Corps (CCC), one of the most successful of New Deal programs. This required raising the age limit—the CCC was supposed to be for men under twenty-five—but when that was done, many veterans did sign up and were put to work, particularly on the Intracoastal Waterway in the Florida Keys. When in 1935 the death of some in a hurricane dramatized their continuing plight, Congress did pass a bonus bill, which Roosevelt then vetoed. The only vote cast against the wishes of Roosevelt in the president's first term by the Senator from Missouri, Harry Truman, was his vote to override the veto of the veterans' bonus.

VI

BOTH TRUMAN AND EISENHOWER built the foundation for their later ascent by working hard in the posts they held in the years between the wars—relatively lowly posts, except for Truman's position as a United States senator. Truman said he tried to do each of his jobs better than they had ever been done before, and something like that could have been said by Ike, as well. Whereas Eisenhower had graduated from West Point in 1915, in a class of 164, ranked 61st in academic performance and 125th in discipline—he graduated first in his class from the more demanding Command and General Staff School in Leavenworth in 1926. What had intervened between the two performances was, first, his disappointment at not holding a command overseas during the war and, second, his immensely fertile service in the mud of Panama with the military intellectual Gen. Fox Conner from 1922 to 1924.

Harry Truman's great benefactor in the twenties was the machine politician Tom Pendergast. Dwight Eisenhower's great benefactor in the twenties was the military intellectual Fox Conner.

Brig. Gen. Fox Conner, always described as a brilliant military mind, had been General Pershing's operations chief in the Great War. Conner had met Eisenhower, a former lieutenant colonel just reduced to captain by the war's end, at George Patton's house, and he asked that Eisenhower be assigned to him as his executive assistant in his new command in Panama. And so while the twenties roared in the United States, the Eisenhowers fought bats, snakes, lizards, mosquitoes, and mud in the Panama Canal Zone.

Conner had experienced an abrupt postwar deflation also, descending from his central role in creating the AEF, the mightiest military force in American history, in 1918 to commanding just one infantry regiment of Puerto Rican soldiers in the Panama Canal Zone in 1922. He spent his time educating young Eisenhower, assigning him readings. If you had asked in 1924 what young American in public life would be a top national leader in the years to come, you would have named Franklin Roosevelt of New York, whose sparkling speech nominating the "Happy Warrior," Al Smith, had been the only bright spot in the dreary Democratic National Convention that year. You would not have named the obscure Missouri politician Harry Truman, who had just been defeated in his effort to be reelected as eastern judge—one of three administrators—in a scandal-plagued county government in western Missouri. Still less would you have named the unknown army captain Dwight Eisenhower, who had enough time in his army service in the unpleasant remoteness of the Panama Canal Zone to train a horse named Blackie not only to respond to commands but also to do enough tricks to win a third-place yellow ribbon at a horsemanship event.

According to Eisenhower's biographers, Fox Conner seems to have treated this soldier, who was under his command for three years, like a graduate student in a seminar. He loaned Eisenhower books from his own library, almost as if assigning them, and gave quizzes on them, covering the battles and warriors of the classic past, the American past. And accompanying that reading and study were Fox Conner's interpretations of the years ahead. Although the treaty the victorious Allies made at Versailles had been intended—by the American president Woodrow Wilson in particular—to establish the peace, Fox Conner saw that it held the seeds of war. A war was coming, he taught Ike, and that war would be fought with allies.

Apparently, the command of the small American force in the Canal Zone was not terribly demanding; Conner and Eisenhower are reported to have spent most of their time together—it was a bad period for Mamie and for the marriage—and Conner was not only Ike's most important teacher, setting him to read Clausewitz (three times, we are told) and, among others (according to Ike's *At Ease*), Nietzsche, but also quizzing him about why Lee invaded the North the second time and what Napoléon should have done at Waterloo. The relationship to Conner was by all accounts—Ike's own and those of his biographers—essential to his later ascent and achievement. One part of it was the reading and conversing— the informal seminar in what a general needs to know. But the other way Conner was essential was in the boosts and introductions he gave to his pupil. Conner pulled strings to get Ike into the Command and General Staff School, and suggested that he meet George Marshall.

There are a couple of intriguing passages about the way one gets ahead in the army in Carlo D'Este's outstanding and generally appreciative biography, *Eisenhower: A Soldier's Life,* which passages gain value from the fact that D'Este himself is a retired lieutenant colonel in the U.S. Army and presumably knows whereof he speaks. These passages appear as D'Este describes Ike's close tie to Conner. D'Este remarks in passing that "Conner's mentoring of Eisenhower provides a classic example of the unofficial ways in which the military functions. For an officer to enjoy a successful career (then and now) and attain generalship, it was absolutely essential to impress at least one senior officer, who would act then as a mentor." He goes on to observe that "even Mamie . . . scoffed at her husband's claims to have succeeded on his own." He then quotes from an interview with Mamie Eisenhower: "Ike used to have a favorite expression that he was a self-made man . . . [but] nobody can make it . . . without the help of somebody else. Ike had a lot of help from different officers." D'Este lists not only Fox Conner, George Marshall, and Douglas MacArthur but also three others who at key points advanced Ike's career.

D'Este goes on to describe an exchange between Eisenhower and Maj. Bradford G. Chynoweth, a West Pointer who served with Ike under Fox Conner in Panama.

> Chynoweth detected disturbing signs that, in his opinion, marked Eisenhower as something of a yes-man. After a tense meeting with Conner over regulations for marksmanship training during which Chynoweth and the other battalion commanders won their point, he and Eisenhower walked home together. Chynoweth angrily challenged Eisenhower's failure to support them. "Ike you are an infantryman. You know that we were right. Yet you never said a word to support us." Eisenhower replied, "Well, Chen, I'll tell you my guiding philosophy. When I go to a new station I look to see who is the strongest and ablest man on the post. I forget my own ideas and do everything in my power to promote what he says is right." In his post-presidential memoir, *Mandate for Change,* Eisenhower signaled that he had not forgotten their fiery encounters forty years earlier, noting that he and

Chynoweth had engaged in a "very fine and hot argument" in Panama. Nor was he ever apologetic over his maxim that, to be successful, one had to learn from and profit by an association with those wiser, more experienced, and of higher rank.

Of higher rank? Surely that is a different consideration from wisdom and experience.

In his book *At Ease,* Ike would draw back from the anecdotal narrative to pass on, explicitly, to "any young person who reads these words" the avuncular advice he had expressed back then:

> Always try to associate yourself closely with and learn as much as you can from those who know more than you, who do better than you, who see more clearly than you. Don't be afraid to reach upward. Apart from the rewards of friendship, the association might pay off at some unforeseen time—that is only an accidental by-product. The important thing is that the learning will make you a better person.

One may have a slight reservation about this generally sound advice in the mildly troubling aspect that the direction in which it is recommended that an aspiring youth reach is "upward" and to those of "higher rank," and that this reaching may "pay off"—an admission that is then quickly covered by the claim that of course the important result is becoming a better person. In all realms of collective life, one may observe not altogether favorably those who rise through careers of advancement by flattering attention to well-chosen superiors. On the other hand, there are those who, almost perversely, decline to polish any apples. There is no doubt that the sponsorship of Fox Conner and George Marshall would be absolutely essential to Eisenhower's career, with its sudden spectacular advancement. D'Este notes that Chynoweth was "a brilliant, outspoken, often acerbic maverick" and, by contrast to Eisenhower, "was never afraid to criticize his superiors to their faces by telling them the truth as he saw it (rather than what they wanted to hear)," and he adds that in the prewar army there were others like that—namely, George Patton and "Vinegar Joe" Stillwell. But Dwight Eisenhower was not like that.

And Harry Truman? Truman functioned in the much different environment of civilian politics, in which there was no chain of command, so it is difficult to make comparisons between him and others. But there certainly was a field of power. Was he, in his civilian role, like Chynoweth and Stillwell? Or more like the more ingratiating Eisenhower? One might say, on the subject of yes-men, that what Truman gave Tom Pendergast was not the subtle yes of an ingratiating intellectual subservience, but the great big Yes of political subordination. And yet that is not quite right. Truman certainly was dependent on the Pendergasts—first on Mike and then on Tom—at key turning points, and certainly he was loyal, not breaking with Tom Pendergast even after the boss was sent to prison, and shocking many by going to his funeral. But at the same time, Truman exhibited a kind of independence from the start.

One might say, despite one's slight reservations about this trait in Ike, that it would have great benefit in the peak moments of the war, when it surely played a role in his securing a relationship to Winston Churchill. Ike did not win over Montgomery, and he did not win over Lord Alanbrooke, but he did not need to win them over; he did gain favor with the prime minister, and that was a key to the leadership of World War II. Ike's friend the non-apple-polishing George Patton even accused his friend Ike of having become too favorable to the British.

Having received an enormous boost from Fox Conner, Ike then received another, eventually, from an officer Fox Conner told him to seek out: George C. Marshall. He was helped, as well, by his service with General Pershing, and, perhaps one can say by his service under Douglas MacArthur—these last two the highest-ranking figures in the interwar army.

All of this went on below the radar of public attention during the period between the wars. But in 1940–1941, it would rise abruptly into public view.

At each of the pivotal points in Ike's rise, it was George Marshall who made the decision, until the climactic decision was made by Franklin Roosevelt.

VII

TRUMAN, as we have seen earlier, faced a most compelling sample of life in the real world when he ran for reelection as senator from Missouri in 1940. He was fifty-six years old. The Pendergast machine, which had been his mainstay, had emulated the one-horse shay in its abrupt and total collapse. The successful Democratic governor of the state, Lloyd Stark, who was constitutionally prohibited from seeking another term as governor, wanted to win that Senate seat, and he had deep pockets and wide support. Truman was opposed to a precedent-breaking third term for President Roosevelt, and Roosevelt did not give Senator Truman his clear-cut support. Truman did not have much money. The state's major newspapers all opposed him. To many, it appeared that Truman would lose to Stark in the Democratic primary. But he did not lose. Truman won by the dazzling statewide margin of 7,926 votes out of 665,000 votes cast.

In contrast to the election-night scene eight years later, Truman went to bed thinking he had lost. When a midnight call came with contrary news, Bess slammed down the phone, thinking it was a bad joke. But it was no joke. And—to be sure—although he ran slightly behind FDR statewide, he did defeat the Republican Senate candidate by winning 51.2 percent of the vote in the general election.

How did he squeak through? Of course, he tirelessly crisscrossed the state in his car; his speech making was not good, but his appearance won votes anyway. There was a third candidate in the race, Maurice Milligan, who split the anti-Truman vote. Stark, insisting that his chauffeur salute him, exhibited some traits that were not appealing. Truman had successfully courted the black vote—a harbinger of events to come. And—a feature to note, even if it did not mean a big gain in votes in Missouri—a larger number of his fellow senators than one might have expected went out of their way to give him more help than the usual. When he won and returned to the Senate floor, they interrupted business and gathered in an unusual congratulatory huddle. He had indeed won the respect of his fellow senators, which would be a big help in the larger undertaking on which he would now embark.

VIII

WHEN THE EISENHOWERS LEFT Manila on December 13, 1939, Ike's radical insulation from the politics of his time was about to end. The war in Europe had already been going on for more than three months. Hitler had invaded Poland on September 1; England and France had declared war on September 3, Canada on September 8. Germany had overrun Poland and divided it with the Soviet Union. On November 30, the USSR had attacked Finland.

The Eisenhowers arrived in San Francisco on January 5, 1940. Ike was ordered, at first, to the headquarters of the Fourth Army there in San Francisco, where he was assigned another staff job. From February to May 1940, he led training exercises at Fort Lewis, in Washington State.

In May 1940, the so-called Phony War ended in Europe when Germany invaded France and swept across the Low Countries. The speeding tanks of Hitler's blitzkrieg made tank warfare suddenly inescapable.

Starting on May 27, the British turned devastating defeat into a kind of moral victory by the miracle of their extraordinary evacuation of their troops from the Continent. Over a third of a million men were evacuated at Dunkirk and taken across the Channel in a bizarre fleet of little ships of all kinds, including motorboats, fishing smacks, trawlers, lifeboats, and paddle steamers. The escape captured the minds and hearts of the British people at a time when it looked probable that they would be invaded. In June, Paris fell.

In that month of terrifying portent, Eisenhower was appointed chief of staff to Gen. Walter Krueger, commander of the Third Army, at Fort Sam Houston, located in San Antonio, Texas. General Krueger, a respected military leader, would be another in the series of mentors and sponsors who would enable Ike's career. From his vantage point in the Third Army, Eisenhower studied the problems of the expanding army and of the citizen-soldier force he was helping to build.

The culmination of Ike's prewar training came in the Louisiana maneuvers of August and September 1941, which saw more than a half million men in nineteen divisions engaged in simulated combat. It was the largest and most realistic military exercise ever held in the United States.

The wide-ranging war games got national publicity, and when Eisenhower was credited with devising the Third Army's plan of battle, he began to receive his first public notice. His prominence as a strategist and organizer during the army's Louisiana maneuvers earned him not only some national attention but also his first star; he now was a brigadier general.

The twenties and the thirties were over, and the significance of the roles Truman and Eisenhower played was radically redefined. Ike's apparent irrelevance was over.

If Ike, in contrast to Truman, had been separated, even insulated, from the main currents of political and economic life in the years between the wars, he nevertheless had experiences that would abruptly have a tremendous relevance when war came again. What Eisenhower had been involved with was disconnected from the twenties and thirties, but it would suddenly come to have the most crucial connection to the forties. If he was radically disengaged from the present, he was, without knowing it, fully engaged in the future.

As it was with his venture into the new field of tank warfare, and his seminar in military history and practice with Fox Conner in Panama, so also it would be with each of Ike's other apparently irrelevant activities during the unmilitary years of the prosperous twenties and the depressed thirties. Attendance at the prestigious Command and General Staff School at Fort Leavenworth (1925–1926)—without which one could not expect to attain a high command—made no sense at a time when no one aspired to any such high command, or cared who attained it. But in 1940–1941, suddenly it was a prime national asset. To remember working under the most famous general of the last war (John G. Pershing) and writing that guidebook to the battles of that past war was to participate in an exercise of total national nostalgia—except when warfare would once again be fought on those same Flanders Fields. Serving as a staff officer in the dusty halls of the War Department, writing a mandated study of industrial mobilization for a war that nobody believed would ever happen, was clearly out of joint with the times—until it *did* happen and that plan would be dusted off after all. Putting up with the idiosyncrasies of General MacArthur and the struggles of the Filipinos to build an army would seem pretty distant from the main events of history—until history took another turn and the actions of generals and the building of armies again became main events.

CHAPTER FOUR

Two Warriors, Second War

I

HARRY TRUMAN AND DWIGHT EISENHOWER were both caught napping, literally but not figuratively, by the attack on Pearl Harbor. Neither was surprised that war came; both were surprised by the way it came. Both had been on the side of "preparedness," opposed to isolationism, alert to the growing threat of the Axis powers, in the prewar debates. But on the afternoon of Sunday, December 7, 1941, they both needed a nap.

The Japanese, in fact, planned the attack for that day of rest, and somewhat to their own surprise caught even the Pacific Fleet napping.

Senator Truman, on an arduous political trip to his home state, had gone back to bed after Sunday breakfast in the Pennant Hotel in Columbia, Missouri. A young deputy marshal awakened him with stunning news; Bess, on the phone from Washington, told him that the secretary of the Senate had called to say that he should be there for a joint session on Monday. He called the little airport, took a small plane to St. Louis, tried to go through Memphis, then attempted to go through Chicago, "and finally I think TWA dumped somebody off and I got on the II pm plane for Pittsburgh." Truman sat up into the night in Pittsburgh, met other senators on the same errand, finally arrived in Washington at 5:30 a.m., got home and went to bed again at six, got up at ten and went to the Senate to hear President Roosevelt say that December 7 was a day that would "live in infamy," and to vote for war with Japan.

Brigadier General (temporary) Eisenhower, chief of staff to the commander of the Third Army at Fort Houston, San Antonio, exhausted by maneuvers, left strict orders with his assistant, "Tex" Lee, that he was not to be disturbed, and, too tired to take his shoes off, he collapsed on his bed and went to sleep. Notwithstanding the orders, an hour later he was awakened with the news. Orders poured in immediately to shift men and guns to protect the West Coast, the borders, industrial plants, and ports against (phantom) bombers, (nonexistent) sabotage, (imagined) attacks by the Japanese. After five days of intense activity almost around the clock, early on the morning of December 12, 1941, Ike received a phone call from destiny—represented by the direct line to the War Department and by Col. Walter Bedell "Beetle" Smith, secretary of that department's general staff, in which he was told, "The Chief says for you to hop a plane and get here right away." Early on the morning of Sunday, December 14, he reported to the chief of staff, Gen. George C. Marshall, in the old War Department building in Washington "and for the first time in my life talked to him for more than two minutes." Marshall put him to work immediately planning the general line of action in the western Pacific.

Both Truman and Eisenhower, summoned to Washington, plunged into the wartime frenzy. The war lifted Eisenhower into an accelerating whirlwind of war planning; it stirred Truman into an intense round of investigating "defense," which now became "war" preparation. Eisenhower rose in wartime Washington because he was good at making war plans, and army chief of staff George C. Marshall recognized his ability. Harry Truman rose in wartime Washington because he took an important initiative, proved to be a good committee chairman and investigator, and his ability came to be appreciated by his fellow senators and the press.

Eisenhower rose in wartime like a meteor, shooting abruptly upward from obscurity to the beginnings of fame in less than a year. *Time* magazine would feature on its cover for November 16, 1942, the new supreme commander of American forces in England, Dwight Eisenhower—the first of what would be eighteen *Time* covers for him. Harry Truman rose in wartime like an escalator, moving steadily upward in public visibility and reputation. *Time*'s cover on March 8, 1943, would be of Senator Harry Truman, chairman of the Senate Special Committee to Investigate the National Defense Program—the first of nine Truman covers.

During the intense first six months of wartime in Washington, Eisenhower made war plans, won General Marshall's favor, joined in the first Allied war conference with British military chiefs, was chosen by Marshall in February to succeed his friend General Gerow as head of the war-plans division, spent ten days in England examining the defects of the American military presence, planned for a big buildup of American forces in Great Britain, and was himself chosen by Marshall to command that force. He left for England on June 23, 1942.

Harry Truman's wartime ascent had begun before Pearl Harbor. Immediately upon his taking his seat for a second term as senator from Missouri, in January 1941, he had received letters complaining about the crookedness in contracts for building Fort Leonard Wood, in Rolla, Missouri, one of the new army camps being rapidly constructed by a nation preparing for war. Truman thought—rightly, as it turned out—that the malfeasance there was probably true of other of the rapidly expanding army camps. As was noted when pointing out his attachment to automobiles, this automobile man did his research on this point in his way: not by mail or phone or reading or assignment to an assistant, but by getting in his car and making his own tour of the country's army camps, traveling down into the South, then back through Arkansas, Oklahoma, and Missouri.

On February 10, 1941, Senator Harry Truman gave a speech on the Senate floor, with only sixteen senators present, proposing an investigation of the national defense buildup. Loaded with horror stories, his speech offered a resolution to establish a Senate committee empowered to investigate all aspects of the defense program. He became its chairman; selected—upon the advice of Attorney General Robert Jackson—an able investigator, Hugh Fulton; finagled membership on the committee for seven able workhorse senators from both parties; and set to work investigating, first, camp construction. In April 1942, he took on an investigation of a coal mine strike, making clear that the committee investigations would not be confined solely to abuse in war production by business, but would include interference with national defense by others—including labor unions—as well.

In June 1942, as Eisenhower was headed for England to command American forces, the Truman committee took up the serious shortage of aluminum, needed for airplanes, and would later claim credit for heavy federal support for a competitor with powerful Alcoa, the Reynolds Metals Company, producers of aluminum.

Once more the two men would be in Washington at the same time, from December 14, 1941, when Ike arrived from San Antonio, until June 23, 1942, when he left for England; at least they would be based in the same city. Through that first winter of American involvement in the war, Eisenhower lived for a time with his brother Milton and his wife, Helen, in Falls Church and, he said, worked such long hours in General Marshall's planning shop that he never saw the house in daylight. Then when Mamie joined him, they lived at the Wardman Towers, not far from the War Department, which in those pre-Pentagon days was located in the old munitions building on Constitution Avenue.

After constant moving during his first term, the Trumans had, at the start of his second term, in 1941, rented an apartment in a building at 4701 Connecticut Avenue, with room for Margaret's piano. They would stay there until suddenly having to move to another residence in April 1945. When Bess and Margaret went to Independence in the summer, Truman lived in that apartment alone, sometimes dusting the furniture himself. But subcommittee hearings often took him on the road.

When war came with Pearl Harbor, two men with whom Eisenhower had connections, Under Secretary of War Robert Patterson and, particularly, Quartermaster General Brehon Somervell, proposed that now that the United States was in the war, the Senate Special Committee to Investigate National Defense Program—the Truman committee—be abolished; it was no longer needed, these critics said, and, indeed, might become a pest. American history furnished a redolent example of what they feared: the obnoxious Joint Committee on the Conduct of the War, which during the Civil War created severe difficulties for President Lincoln and for Union generals, with repeated leaks to the press and half-baked interference in military strategy. Truman tried, with a speech on December 10, to head off executive-branch proposals that his committee be abolished; as a knowledgeable reader of history, he specifically referred to that Civil War committee as an example of what his committee was *not* going to be. Truman insisted that his committee would not interfere with generals and admirals or with military policy—but only with crooked contractors and inefficient business practices and blockages to war production. In the event, the Truman committee did acquire a reputation contrary to, and vastly superior to, that of the Civil War committee.

II

DURING HIS STAY in Washington in the first half of 1942, Ike almost certainly never met, and probably never saw, the senator from Missouri, but he certainly saw his own brother Milton, a high-level federal bureaucrat based in the Agriculture Department; for a brief time, as noted earlier, Dwight stayed at the home of Milton and Helen in Falls Church. And so the question arises: Did they talk about what Milton was doing, after the president gave him a new assignment in March?

Of course what Dwight was doing, planning the war, was of the most intense interest and importance, but did the two brothers have occasion to talk also about Milton's task—the relocation? While his brother was furiously planning the American role in the war against a virulently racist enemy, the United States was carrying out its most disgraceful wartime action, the forcible mass evacuation of Japanese and Japanese-Americans from the Pacific coast on racial grounds alone—and Milton was playing an uncomfortable role in that disgrace. He was asked to do it, on March 10 or 11, by President Roosevelt himself. He was summoned into the Oval Office and told that his "war job," starting immediately, was "to set up a War Relocation Authority to move Japanese-Americans off the Pacific coast." The President said he had signed the executive order giving full authority to carry out this stunning project, and he insisted that great speed was essential. Roosevelt indulged in none of his usual bantering pleasantries, as Milton related the story of the interview in his book, but was grimly authoritative; Milton felt he had no chance to question, and certainly no room to decline. Milton clearly was troubled by what he had to do; but he does not come off as badly, in retrospect, in this sorry episode as do many others—including some great liberals, starting with President Roosevelt himself and California governor Earl Warren. Milton told the story in a rueful chapter of his book about his service to several presidents.

There was a strain of anti-Japanese racism already present in American attitudes, especially on the Pacific coast. Then Pearl Harbor frightened people, giving that bigotry a huge jolt. A government report on Pearl Harbor alleged (falsely) that Hawaii-based Japanese-Americans had abetted the attack. Hysterical racial rumors led the general who headed the Western Defense Command to recommend to the president that those of Japanese ancestry be forcibly removed from the Pacific coast area. The general who held the Western Defense Command was a man Ike knew and indeed had served under at Fort Lewis in the state of Washington on his return from Manila in 1939, Gen. John L. DeWitt. General DeWitt said, in response to the fact that two-thirds of the 120,000 evacuees were American citizens, "A Jap is a Jap." He reported to President Roosevelt that no sabotage by Japanese-Americans had as yet been confirmed, but he commented, in a circular response that itself has lived in infamy, that this fact only proved "a disturbing and confirming indication that such action *will* be taken." One learns from Milton's book that General DeWitt was not the only one to make this astounding argument; the nation's most distinguished political columnist, Walter Lippmann, favoring mass evacuation, wrote that the absence of sabotage by Japanese-Americans "was an indication that they were lying low and waiting for a signal from Tokyo." California's attorney general, Earl Warren, testified that the absence of sabotage was "the most ominous sign in our whole situation . . . we are being lulled into a false sense of security."

Roosevelt allowed himself to be persuaded, by fears and threats and rumors, that people of Japanese ancestry had committed, or were about to commit, or might someday commit, acts of sabotage; he therefore signed Executive Order 9066, ordering their forcible removal from the

Pacific coast. This he did in spite of the total absence of any sabotage, or any evident threat; in this case, indeed the only thing we had to fear was fear itself. In February, President Roosevelt signed Executive Order 9066, which established the War Relocation Authority, the agency that did the moving and the relocating. Roosevelt then asked Milton to be its head.

Again, one may wonder whether the two busy brothers ever talked about Milton's job, and what Ike thought of it. Milton served in that post only from March until late June of 1942, when he moved to the War Information Board, but that spring of 1942 was when the forced removals began and when most of the camps were set up. Ike was staying with Milton and Helen Eisenhower during those months, although working so hard, he scarcely saw them.

To look ahead: Harry Truman appears at the other end of this sorry story, doing what President Roosevelt should have done but didn't. When President Truman learned in December 1945 of the discrimination and violent resistance facing returning Japanese-American internees in California, he was outraged, and he immediately ordered his attorney general to investigate whether there was any way that the federal government could either legally intervene or pressure state authorities into doing their duty to enforce the law. Told of the disgraceful conduct of the Californians, he snapped, "[A]lmost make[s] you believe that a lot of our Americans have a streak of Nazi in them." In 1946, Truman invited to the White House the 442nd Regimental Combat Team—the most highly decorated military unit in the history of the American armed forces, composed mainly of Japanese-Americans, many of whom had relatives in the relocation camps. President Truman told the Nisei soldiers, "You fought not only the enemy, but you fought prejudice—and you have won." He also privately lobbied congressional leaders during 1946 to pass a bill to compensate the internees for losses. When Congress failed to act, Truman made a public appeal for evacuation-claims legislation as part of the civil rights program he submitted to Congress in 1948, and he signed the bill into law that August.

III

WHILE MILTON was administering the Japanese-American relocation, his brother was planning the American role in the war.

The first collaborative planning after the Americans were in the war took place at a conference code-named Arcadia—every action would now have a code name—held in Washington in December 1941, just two weeks after Pearl Harbor, with an immensely relieved Winston Churchill coming to the United States to confer with his new ally. (Churchill said that when he heard of Pearl Harbor, he knew the Allies would win the war.) The conference in December 1941 and January 1942 put in place commitments by the United States and the UK that would persist under many strains and countercurrents through the following years of war and emerge in the end as the core of victory.

Ike was particularly conscious that there was another ally, in addition to these friendly English-speaking folks, and that this other ally was the most important, without whom perhaps the English-speaking Allies could not have prevailed: the Soviet Union. The alliance with the USSR, however, was external and hugely tentative; there was nothing like the combined staffs and joint action of the English-speaking Allies. The Russians demanded much, and shared almost nothing—except, of course, that their armies and their people bore the heaviest burden of all. It might be said of the whole war what Chester Wilmot said in his classic *The Struggle for Europe* about the climactic event: "The cross-Channel assault of 1944 would certainly have been defeated if the Germans had not been fighting with the Russians on their backs."

As to Great Britain and the United States: In the first place, the Arcadia Conference would create, or confirm from earlier beginnings, the shape of their close-knit collaboration, the Combined Chiefs of Staff, or CCOS, through which the two nations joined in combined planning and command. The signal accomplishment of the alliance was that the Allies, for all the strains and difficulties, did indeed remain allied—history's most successful alliance. The role of the CCOS in World War II may be history's best refutation of the lazy cynicism that says that committees never accomplish anything. This committee would be of utmost importance to Dwight Eisenhower as this story played out; it was his boss.

A second principle—unity of command—both gave that central commitment a realistic embodiment and put it under enormous strain. This principle, approved at the Arcadia Conference of the British and American chiefs of staff in December 1941, held that there should be one person with supreme command in each theater of operations; he should command—the directive achieved a certain poetry—"all armed forces, afloat, ashore, and in the air." It was a principle easier to state than to hold in place in the vicissitudes of a giant collaborative war effort. Within one nation's forces, it meant that the forces "afloat and ashore"—the navy and the army—would have to obey a commander from one service or the other. That was difficult enough, with the U.S. Navy in particular suffering from the attack on Pearl Harbor. But then the principle became vastly more difficult when two nations collaborated and any commander coming from one of them commanded soldiers and sailors from the other. And the force "in the air," although not yet an independent branch in the U.S. armed services, might be the most difficult of all—in preparing for Operation Overlord, Eisenhower would have the major task coordinating control of the strategic air forces.

Unity of command meant, to cite perhaps the most difficult application in the war that followed, that in the climactic battles on the Continent, as the Allies approached the German heartland, the English hero Bernard Montgomery would have to subordinate his command to that of the American Dwight Eisenhower—or rather, to the Supreme Allied Commander Dwight Eisenhower—and not lead British troops triumphantly into Berlin.

The initial Allied planning would also decide two overarching principles of the allied effort:

1. Germany first
2. By means of a cross-Channel invasion.

Germany first: The decision to concentrate the Allied force in Europe and the Atlantic—against Germany first—would run counter to a strong current of American popular opinion, since for the Americans, in contrast to the English, the war had begun in the Pacific with an attack by Japan. And the United States Navy had a strong preference for war in the Pacific against Japan. Japan had attacked the navy and had sunk a major portion of its Pacific Fleet. American admirals could not help but be aware that war against Japan would be a war featuring the navy, while to an extent a war in Europe would not be. And by far the most prestigious American army leader, Douglas MacArthur, held his command in the Pacific. Nevertheless, Churchill, to his great relief, found that the key Americans making the planning decisions—-Franklin Roosevelt and George Marshall—were committed from the beginning to defeat Nazi Germany first. Together with their staffs (which in the spring of 1942 came to include Dwight Eisenhower, as top army war planner under Marshall), they made a commitment to the priority of the European war right from the start, and they held to it without much wavering throughout all the vicissitudes from Pearl Harbor to D-Day to the German surrender in May 1945.

The reasons for focusing initially on the defeat of Hitler were these:

First of all, from the American point of view in 1941–1942, that there were two Allied nations already engaged in that fight—England for more than two years and Russia since June 1941—and that it was of pivotal importance to keep both of them in it. Second, it was much wiser strategically to defeat the stronger enemy before the weaker. Third, practically, the supply route to Australia, the Allied base in the Pacific, was three to four times as long as the North Atlantic route to supply England, which provided the base from which to attack German-held Europe. The longer Pacific route was much more susceptible to attack by enemy warships and submarines. And there was no base in the Pacific remotely comparable to the Allied base in Europe—the British Isles.

In the war years to follow, in perhaps two instances, British foot dragging about an invasion of northwest France led the Americans to hint that they might shift focus altogether to the Pacific, but it was an empty threat.

There were two other reasons, at altogether another level, for putting the war against Hitler's Germany in first place: The ties of sympathy and affection to England surpassed all others, and the threat of the domination of Europe by Nazism and Hitler was a unique evil, requiring opposition as the highest priority.

This last point may be illustrated by a response from Eisenhower when, after Tunisia fell to Allied forces in the spring of 1943, some of the Allied staff felt that the defeated German general should be allowed, as was ancient custom, to call upon him. Ike said no. "The tradition that all professional soldiers are really comrades in arms has, in tattered form, persisted to this day." But he said it did not apply to those fighting for Nazi Germany. "For me World War II was far too personal a thing," wrote Eisenhower, "to entertain such feelings. . . . [T]here grew within me the conviction that as never before in a war . . . the forces that stood for human good and men's rights were . . . confronted by a completely evil conspiracy."*

For the Anglo-American alliance, World War II was going to be, first of all, a crusade in Europe, not a crusade in Asia.†

The commitment to fight that crusade by an invasion of northwest France across the English Channel was also part of the original plan, but it would be interrupted and postponed by detours and buffeted by conflicting

* *Crusade in Europe,* p. 157.
† "The United States devoted only 15 percent of its war effort to the war with Japan. The other 85 percent was expended in the defeat of Germany." (See Overby, p. 394.)

opinions before finally coming into place as the climax of the story. Its fortunate realization, pressed particularly by the Americans, would, fortunately, be delayed, pressed particularly by the English.

The Americans, in the person of George Marshall, were immediately and consistently in favor of this forthright method of beating the Nazis: by landing an invading force right up under their chins on the continent they had come to dominate. They would do that by the shortest route—across the English Channel—using as a base for preparation the remarkable advantage of the island nation of England itself. The British agreed with that method in the first planning meetings, and they did in the end keep that agreement, but the British in general and Churchill in particular had reservations and qualifications that would deflect their commitment, which was not as clear-cut and unqualified as that of the Americans. The British agreed to—indeed, welcomed—the buildup of American forces in England, code-named Bolero. The Americans could load in men and material until it was said that the island might sink from the weight of the Yankees, or that it would need balloons to keep from sinking. But the British did not agree to an early invasion across the Channel.

Marshall, and Eisenhower, in fact, were already urging invasion in 1942, and the idea went far enough to acquire one of the more belligerent of those ubiquitous code names that sprinkle the story of World War II: Sledgehammer. The Americans argued for Operation Sledgehammer not only because they were go-getters and can-doers ready to take the direct path to the desired result, but for a much different reason, as Eisenhower expressed it: to keep eight million Russians in the war. A 1942 invasion, with little hope of lasting success—some used the word *suicide* to describe it—nevertheless should draw German forces from the eastern front and reassure the Russians that a second front was coming. But the wiser and more experienced British were adamantly opposed to Sledgehammer; and on July 22, 1942, the decision of the combined staffs went against it, to Eisenhower's severe but temporary dismay.

The British knew what it meant to be defeated, and they knew what it meant to be bogged down in Europe; they remembered Passchendaele from one war and Dunkirk from another, as the Americans did not. The British, more realistic, had been fighting the fiercely competent German Army for two years before the Americans even entered the war. They knew that the Allied forces were not ready to invade the Continent in 1942. Surely it was better that the Americans did not prevail in this first dispute; on the other hand, surely it was also better that they did prevail in the end—that the Allied effort did not keep expanding efforts in the Mediterranean, chipping around the edges of Nazi-dominated Europe and coming up only through the "soft underbelly" (which Americans sometimes took to be the proposed scheme at least of Churchill, if not of the British in general), but did in the end mount a major head-on cross-Channel attack.

It seems fortunate that British wisdom derived from experience prevented the premature effort to land in France; but then, it also seems fortunate that American practicality, derived from a different experience, caused the cross-Channel invasion to happen when the time was finally ripe.

So Operation Sledgehammer—the proposed invasion of the Continent in 1942—was decisively voted down by the chiefs; the invasion, now called Operation Roundup, was pushed forward to 1943. But what, then, should the growing Allied armies be doing? The strong desire on the part of the American president, Franklin Roosevelt, that American forces be engaged with the enemy *somewhere* in 1942 gave Churchill and the British (who had throughout a penchant for Allied action in the Mediterranean) the leverage to get a commitment to invade North Africa, an operation once called Gymnast and now called Torch. This would be the operation in which American forces would see their first combat, and the Allies would fight side by side for the first time, and Dwight Eisenhower would command men in battle for the first time.

While Ike was planning and then commanding, Harry Truman was investigating. While Ike was preparing to lead remarkably well-equipped armies—probably the best equipped in the history of the world—into battle abroad, Senator Harry Truman was diligently investigating the supply of that equipment at home.

The conversion of the American economy to wartime production, and the gargantuan output that followed, was a stunning central fact of the war—one of the reasons for the Allied victory. An excellent analysis of why they did win, called precisely *Why the Allies Won*, points to the discrepancy in the noncombat aspects of war—"procurement, logistics, military services" between the Allied and the Axis powers. "In the Pacific war there were eighteen American personnel for every service man on the front. The ratio in the Japanese forces was one to one. . . . In the German army in Europe there were roughly two combatants for every non-combatant; but the American army had a ratio almost exactly the reverse. . . . The American backup for combat troops was formidable."*

---

* Ibid., p. 392.

Sheer superiority in terms of matériel alone is not enough to explain victory, in this war or in others. But when combined with the practical energy and will to win that the Allies had in World War II, it is certainly a key to victory. Dwight Eisenhower's *Crusade in Europe* repeatedly celebrates the service of supply, the prodigies of production and delivery, that fueled the Allied victory.

Dwight Eisenhower was the son of a man who loved mechanics, the grandson and great-grandson and nephew of farmers, and would himself be the commander of Operation Overlord, which would be, along with everything else it was, a prodigious physical feat, the biggest amphibious assault human beings ever carried out, or, we may venture to say, ever will carry out. It involved such an immense array of physical equipment as to require pages just to enumerate the kinds. Eisenhower himself told a story in *Crusade in Europe* about a moment back in the planning not of Overlord but of the earlier invasion of Sicily, called Operation Husky, that dramatized the "amazement" (his word) that American practicality and mass-production methods could evoke in citizens of other lands less imbued with American know-how. British engineers had given up any hope of building a landing field on a little island called Gozo, near Malta, in time for use in the campaign in Sicily, but then an American specialist in building airfields visited the British air marshal who had command of the air forces of the island. The reader can guess the dialogue that followed; it was right out of the file of folklore marked "American Know-How That Won the War." The marshal asked the American how long it would take to build an operational airfield on this impossibly difficult terrain. "About ten days" was the "nonchalant" (Eisenhower's word) reply. The marshal thought the American specialist was kidding. But he did ask, "When can you start?" "As soon as my equipment gets here, which should take several days," the specialist replied. The reader will know the outcome of this little tale. "The upshot was that messages began to fly through the air," wrote Eisenhower, "and thirteen days from the time the first American construction unit stepped on the island the first fighter plane was taking off from the strip." Eisenhower commented, "This story was told to me over and over again by British officers on the island whose admiration for the American engineers was little short of awe."

When one turns from reading Eisenhower's account of the marvelous flow of support that came from the United States to the Allied forces in Europe to reading the Truman committee's examination of the cheating and corruption that accompanied its production on the home front, one finds oneself suddenly flipped into a radically contrasting universe.

Truman and his senators did appreciate the central miracles of American wartime productivity—exemplified by Henry J. Kaiser and his Liberty ships built in ninety days, for example, or by Reynolds with his aluminum, or by Andrew Higgins, whose role in providing the right kind of landing craft will be described shortly. But alongside these and many other instances of superbly efficient productivity, there were many other stories of various sorts of wickedness and abuse that Truman had made it the business of his committee to investigate and expose.

The contrasting perspectives of Dwight Eisenhower and Harry Truman on the American war effort may be illustrated by their respective dealings with Gen. Brehon Somervell, the officer in charge of the services of supply during World War II and the builder of the Pentagon, among many other things. Looked at from Eisenhower's perspective, from Europe, Somervell was a hero of logistics; looked at from Truman's point of view, and from investigations in the United States, there was another story.

Somervell was a friend and colleague of Eisenhower; when Ike flew to Washington after Pearl Harbor and Marshall gave him his first assignment—to discover what should be done about the Philippines—his partner, with whom he went to work on the problem, was, Eisenhower wrote, "Brigadier General, later General, Brehon Somervell," already chief of the War Department's supply and procurement. Then when Ike was overseas, he would refer, always favorably, to Somervell in connection with the miracles of supply.

Usually, Somervell was back in the States, priming the pump, but on one occasion just after the Kasserine Pass battle in North Africa—the Americans' first battle and first defeat—Somervell happened to be visiting Allied headquarters, and Ike told him about their desperate need, in muddy North Africa, of more trucks. Somervell said the 5,400 trucks Ike needed could be loaded out of American ports in three days if the navy could furnish escorts. The navy said, "Yes, we can." (According to Eisenhower, he told the story partly "to give pause to those people who picture the War and Navy Departments as a mass of entangling red tape.") The trucks began arriving in less than three weeks. Somervell was still at headquarters when the last trucks were delivered. The telegram from Somervell's assistant told of the hours of intense work required to make the delivery happen, and then closed on a note that Eisenhower called "plaintive" but that one might instead call bravado: "If you should happen to want the Pentagon shipped over there, please try to give us about a week's notice."

Senator Truman and his committee saw rather a different side of Somervell—the bravado but not the delivery. The relationship did not begin on the best footing, in that Somervell, as noted earlier, had tried, right after Pearl Harbor, to get the Truman committee abolished.

The first projects the Truman committee looked at, the construction of the new army camps, at first fell under General Somervell's authority, and he did not look kindly on the committee's intrusive investigations into the huge cost overruns in the building of the camps. The committee criticized "cost-plus" contracts (invitations to profiteering) and "dollar-a-year" men (invitations to conflicts of interest). The construction of the army camps was loaded with inefficiency and profiteering. The prodding of the Truman committee helped to persuade the army to transfer the construction of the camps from the Quartermaster Corps—Somervell—to the Engineering Corps.

Somervell kept saying that in wartime one could not worry about money or count the cost. Truman and his lead investigator, Hugh Fulton, kept trying to get them to understand that money was the measure of finite materials and that therefore one had to count the cost, even in, or perhaps especially in, wartime. Yes, one should worry because the cost stood for materials and resources that could be used elsewhere and were in dire need in wartime.

Somervell, the efficient martinet, liked to quote the lines "The difficult we do right away; the impossible takes a little longer" more often than Truman or Fulton, or the other senators on the committee, cared to hear them. (The assistant who sent that telegram to Ike about the delivery of the trucks clearly had caught the tune that one was supposed to sing.)

The most flagrant example of Somervell's performance, as seen from the Truman committee's point of view, was the ill-conceived Canol project, which Somervell launched with almost no coordination or consultation, merely on a nod and a scrap of paper. The project entailed transporting oil twelve hundred miles across Canada to Alaska (hence Canol, Canadian oil) through a four-inch pipeline. The committee's relentless questioning brought out the staggering neglect of relevant facts and Somervell's failure to consult almost anybody. Of the skeleton memorandum upon which the project was based, one scholarly study observed:

> No reasons or supporting evidence of any kind were included in the memorandum; it was a set of bare recommendations as simple as

though [the writer] had recommended: "Build a bridge from New York to London" (and in view of the specified schedule, almost as fantastic). Somervell approved the memorandum the same day and the next day directed the Chief of the Engineers to take the necessary steps.*

The Truman committee started investigating this gargoyle in the summer of 1943 and issued a report in January 1944 that stated, "Instead of making a contribution to the war effort, the project was a drain on our resources in 1942 and 1943."† The two arguments for the project were "military necessity"—unexplained—and the fact that so much money had been spent on it that it had to be finished to justify that cost. The pipeline finally did open in 1944, then closed down in just nine months, in 1945. Senator Kilgore of the Truman committee said that the effort wasted $100 million, which was a lot of money in those days.

The impossible did indeed take a little longer, cost a great deal of money, and was not worth it.

IV

THE LARGER STORY of American war production, as the Truman committee recognized, was a triumph, but there were many smaller stories within it that were not triumphs. And there were stories that were decidedly mixed, like that concerning landing craft.

If one has not read much about World War II and then reads about it extensively, one is astonished to discover the remarkable importance throughout the whole story of the smaller ships and boats that carried men, artillery, supplies from the larger ships up onto a shore—usually a hostile shore: landing craft.

Dwight Eisenhower played a central role not only in the main drama of the mighty Allied effort in World War II but also in the irksome subplot winding around inside the main one, that story of landing craft. And in that smaller, inside drama, a bit part was played by Harry Truman.

"He [Eisenhower] was one of the first on the General Staff to sense the importance of landing craft, and his papers during the months he headed the Ops Division are filled with indications of his strong feeling that not enough was being done to produce them."‡ That means he had already perceived that importance in the first spring of his active encounter with war planning, in 1942. The story of landing craft would continue through-

---

* Donald H. Riddle, *The Truman Committee* (Rutgers University Press, 1964), p. 103.
† Ibid., p. 115.
‡ Larrabee, p. 415.

out the war, stretching into all the theaters of operation, and winding through the relationship among the Allies and particularly between the branches of the service. Using the designation for one kind of landing craft, Winston Churchill is quoted as having said, in dismay, as the great effort reached its European climax in 1944, that "the destinies of two great empires . . . seem to be tied up in some goddamned things called LSTs."

Eisenhower's friend Harry Butcher quoted Ike as having said that when he was "buried his coffin should be in the form of a landing craft, as they are practically killing him with worry."

The Allied effort in World War II was to a quite unusual degree—far more than in World War I or any previous American war—an *amphibious* war effort. In the past, armies had fought armies on land, and navies had fought navies at sea. Or if forces had landed from ships to fight, there had not been an expectation that depositing the men and the equipment of warfare on some foreign shore would require any specialized kind of a vessel. But the emergence of the tank at the end of the Great War indicated to the British—who at first were more attuned to the matter than the Americans—that a new boat was needed to transport these tanks to battles on foreign shores—in rough weather, on beaches where there was no harbor, under fire from modern weaponry. They began to produce early versions of the landing craft that, when elaborated upon, would be described by an alphabet soup of names beginning with the letter *L*, for landing, then *C*, for craft (or, for larger vessels, *S*, for ship), followed by one or more letters indicating the primary cargo—first of all *T*, for tank. There were also the LCM (landing craft, mechanized) and the LCI (landing craft, infantry) and the LCA (landing craft, assault), among many others. One of the most successful craft was a LCPV—landing craft, personnel and vehicles. Once war came in 1939, the tremendous pressure on British shipyards meant that the primary task of producing further landing craft, like much of war production in general, would fall to the United States.

The war in the Pacific, taking place in an immense ocean with myriad islands, would, of course, feature a long series of amphibious landings, but World War II in Europe in the American experience (decidedly not the Russian) would also feature one amphibious landing after another: in North Africa (three places); on the small Mediterranean island of Pantelleria; in Sicily (the second-largest amphibious landing of the war, measured by the number of men landed and the frontage); in mainland Italy (at three different places); and, famously, in Normandy—all commanded by Eisenhower. Operation Anvil (later renamed Dragoon), the invasion of the south of France after Operation Overlord, would then be another huge amphibious undertaking.

When in 1942 the United States had joined the war and Eisenhower became a war planner, he saw—looking ahead to the day when the Allies would go on the offense—that the biggest problem of procurement was for landing craft, required for every amphibious activity. Eisenhower wrote in his diary in May 1942 that the members of the joint landing-craft committee were still haggling over "questions on which I begged the answers last February: (1) Who is responsible for building landing craft? (2) What types are they building? (3) Are they suitable for cross-Channel work? (4) Will the number of each type be sufficient, etc. how in hell can we win this war unless we crack some heads?"

The heads that stood most evidently in need of cracking were to be found in the United States Navy; some of the cracking would be provided by Senator Harry S Truman.

The production, the allocation, and the design of the assault landing craft—which were ships, after all—were under the iron control of the navy. The hard-bitten, irascible Adm. Ernest J. King, chief of naval operations, and the service that he headed were—not surprisingly—fervent advocates of sea power. They favored a Pacific-first strategy for the Allies and, having been hit hard at Pearl Harbor, were understandably focused on defensive rather than on offensive warfare, which would require those landing craft. Key elements of the war required ships—the immensely important Battle of the Atlantic required not only carriers but also escorts. The war in the Pacific would be fought in large part not only with battleships but with aircraft carriers. Yet war planner Eisenhower saw that the day would come when the Allies would take the offensive and would need, in addition to all the other sorts of ships, most of them larger and more glamorous, more and better landing craft.

He tried to talk to King about it, to no avail. The navy's Bureau of Ships had its own ideas about the design and production of seacraft, including landing craft.

One reason that Operation Sledgehammer had to be jettisoned was that there were landing craft available for only four to six divisions, which would have faced twenty-five German divisions. Operation Torch, which FDR agreed to in July 1942, had to be postponed until landing craft would become available in November. When the capture of Tunis meant the success of Operation Torch, the next step—the invasion of Sicily (Operation

Husky)—had to be postponed until July 1943, largely because the necessary landing craft would not be available until then. Operation Husky competed for landing craft with Operation Roundup—the 1943 name for a projected Normandy invasion.* When Operation Husky succeeded, the issue arose yet again: Should the bulk of the LSTs and LCMs be sent to England (for Operation Overlord—the 1944 name for the Normandy invasion)—or kept in the Mediterranean for an Italian campaign?

The "goddamned things called LSTs" would be a bottleneck, impeding plans for an invasion of France in 1942, or in 1943. The navy shipyards would concentrate on building merchant ships that could transport an invasion force—but they would be of no use, said Eisenhower, if there were not the landing craft to take that force the last stretch across the Channel. The navy wanted also to rebuild its fleet after the devastation at Pearl Harbor—understandable, although that would cut into the production of LSTs and LCMs.

When the time came at last for Operation Overlord, in 1944, the worldwide shortage of landing craft had two large effects: It figured centrally in the postponing of the invasion from May 1 until June, so that there could be another month to produce landing craft, and it was also a main reason that Operation Anvil—the invasion of France from the south—could not be simultaneous but had to be moved back a month.

Eisenhower's biographer Carlo D'Este gave a summary: "The shortage of landing craft was to prove the single greatest impediment to Allied operations in the Mediterranean and northwestern Europe. There were never enough, and with priorities split between Europe and the Pacific it became a constant struggle."

Why were there never enough? Because the United States Navy had other priorities. Because key leaders—FDR, for one—did not at first share Ike's perception of their importance. Because other larger and more glamorous ships dominated the field. Because their allocation was continually caught in the tugs-of-war between Britain and the United States, between the Mediterranean and the cross-Channel invasion, between Europe and the Pacific.

Occasionally when in these later years one reads through the materials on World War II, one suddenly feels the sharp sting of resentments still

---

* Lord Alan Brooke, not one to miss any error by an American decision maker, noted with contemptuous amusement that the seventy-four-year-old secretary of war, Henry Stimson, would crunch together the code names of the 1942 Normandy invasion, Sledgehammer, and the 1943 invasion, Roundup, and speak of "Roundhammer."

not buried. One of these stinging remarks outside the boundaries of normal dispute comes from the diary of the constantly exasperated chief of the Imperial General Staff, Alan Brooke (the British equivalent of George Marshall), in the arguments over Mediterranean strategy in April 1943. Ike and the Americans wanted Operation Anvil to begin sooner, to accompany Operation Overlord; the British wanted the Allied force in the Mediterranean not to be interrupted by Anvil but to continue to exploit what they saw to be the golden possibilities of the war in Italy and the eastern Mediterranean. After a contentious meeting on April 8, Brooke wrote in his diary:

> They [the Americans] have at last agreed to our policy but withdrawn their offer of landing craft from the Pacific. This is typical of their methods of running strategy. Although we have agreed that the European theatre must take precedence over the Pacific, yet they use some of their available landing-craft as bargaining counters in trying to get their false strategy followed.

Then, on April 19, reporting that "our troubles about Anvil are over" and "We have got the Americans to agree," he added, "but have lost the additional landing craft they were prepared to provide." And then comes the shocking passage: "History will never forgive them for bargaining equipment against strategy and trying to blackmail us into agreeing with them by holding the pistol of withdrawing craft at our heads."

When we ask, what, after all, did Dwight Eisenhower, for all his titles, contribute to the winning of World War II, one item high up on the list of answers would be that he saw early and throughout the key role of amphibious warfare, of going on the offense, and he saw the importance of a specialized craft in that activity.

Now we come to the bit part played by Harry Truman.

In New Orleans there was a vigorous and patriotic industrialist named Andrew Jackson Higgins, who had been building shallow-draft boats for the oil industry, which needed them to explore the swamps and bayous. Back in the 1930s, Higgins could see the war coming, and he knew that the "U.S. Navy doesn't know one damn thing about small boats."

When in the spring of 1942, with the United States now in the war, Andrew Higgins realized that the navy's Bureau of Ships was still insisting on producing LCTs of inferior design, he paid a visit in Washington to meet with a figure then becoming more visible on the national scene, who might be of help: Senator Harry Truman of Missouri, the chairman of a special Senate committee dealing with national defense. What Higgins told Truman elicited the senator's vigorous agreement; Truman and Higgins then had two more meetings and became allies.

The newly powerful senator sent a challenge to the navy: Put one of your boats in a head-to-head competition with a Higgins boat and see what happens. Truman, with his committee, now had a power and visibility that made it impossible for the navy to ignore his demand. So the competition was held on May 25, 1942, in Norfolk, Virginia.

One of the observers of that competition—along with a phalanx of navy men, Higgins, and a member of Truman's committee—was Maj. Howard W. Quinn of the U.S. Army's Quartermaster Corps, which had its own distinct interest in safe and efficient landing craft. On the day after the competition, Major Quinn sent to his commanding officer this unequivocal summary: "As far as comparisons of characteristics of the types of tank lights [meaning LCTs] are concerned, it may be stated that on May 25 tests there was no comparison. It was clearly demonstrated even to our enlisted men accompanying the tests that the Higgins lighter could get them there in a choppy sea and the other lighter just couldn't make the trip."

The Truman committee would issue a report on August 5, 1942, saying, "It is clear that the Bureau of Ships for reasons known only to itself persisted for five years in clinging to an unworthy tank-lighter of its own design." The committee report included devastating exchanges with officers in the navy's Bureau of Ships that indicated their ignorance of the tests, which had shown not only that the ships of their design would be unable to land men and vehicles in stormy seas and on shallow shores but also that Higgins had developed a design for a landing craft that would perform.

> The committee considers it incredible that the Bureau should have proceeded on a program of such magnitude with a design concerning which no data had been accumulated with respect to its performance in rough water with a tank or equivalent weights aboard. . . . Apparently the Bureau of Ships . . . did not consider the possibility of the design being unseaworthy in choppy or rough water, and therefore did not concern itself with insisting on such tests prior to awarding these contracts.

The navy's bureau had its own design for landing craft, which it kept insisting on building even after its defects had been demonstrated, and even after Higgins had shown that a craft of his design was clearly superior. The Truman committee said: "On the one hand the bureau awarded contracts to a group of builders whose performance was so unsatisfactory that when an emergency arose their services had to be dispensed with entirely. On the other hand, the Bureau failed to award contracts to the only builder who could produce lighters quickly and successfully."

The Truman committee said about the testimony of naval officers that they "deliberately attempted to misinform the committee or were not fully cognizant of the facts surrounding the subject matter under consideration" and that the navy had displayed "flagrant disregard for the facts, if not also for the safety and success of American troops."

The Bureau of Ships had to capitulate. It ordered all shipyards under contract for LCTs to convert to the Higgins design. Higgins (and Truman) had won that point. Once A. J. Higgins got his contract, everything hummed. At the height of production, some thirty thousand workers all over New Orleans were turning out Higgins boats, some from "factories" that were nothing but canvas-covered assembly lines along the hot, humid docks.

How to get a vast invasion army ashore in choppy waters under intense fire on uneven beaches, and have enough troops survive to assault an entrenched enemy dug into bunkers and atop cliffs? Higgins designed the perfect landing craft: not a big target, but a small, light wooden boat with a protected propeller and diesel engine capable of carrying ashore thirty-six men, or a dozen men and a jeep. It could land a whole army a platoon at a time—easy in, easy out, and then back again. The hardest part had not been designing the landing craft, or even turning them out by the thousands. Higgins was a natural at design and production. The hardest part was selling the navy on his boat—which he finally did with the help of the Truman committee.

On June 8, 1942, the Truman committee, holding hearings across the country on soft spots, dubious practices, and wickedness in the booming business of war production, examined particularly the awarding of contracts by the navy's Bureau of Ships. A bevy of navy captains, commanders, rear admirals, and lieutenant commanders attended, and some displayed in their testimony a distinct ignorance about landing craft—which proved to be the committee's chief interest. One army man also testified—Major Quinn, who had been on the Higgins boat in the May 25 competition. And Andrew Higgins also testified. After two days of testimony, the committee decided that its investigators should pursue the subject further.

On August 5, the committee completed its report—like all the others, a unanimous report by all the senators, representing both parties—and sent it to the secretary of the navy, Frank Knox. The report severely criticized the Bureau of Ships. Senator Truman said in his cover letter to Secretary Knox that "he could not condemn too strongly the negligence or willful misconduct . . . of the Bureau of Ships" and that Higgins should have been commended rather than resisted and condemned.

Secretary Knox, understandably, asked the committee to withhold its harsh words for a time, and so for nineteen months the committee sat on its report. When finally, in March 1944, the Truman Committee did publish its report on the navy's Bureau of Ships, it was able to say that starting on August 5, 1942—the date its report was sent to Secretary Knox—the bureau had been reorganized. The committee gave itself credit for that change.

Despite all the turmoil in producing and allocating them, when the most crucial moment came—D-Day for the cross-Channel invasion of the Continent—the needed landing craft at last were there. On June 5, Eisenhower said the first "Let's go," and on the early morning of June 6, when the tremendous fleet headed out in a ten-lane formation stretching twenty miles, there were nestled into transports among the five thousand ships in this great armada more than fifteen hundred Higgins boats, ready to carry men, tanks, trucks, and artillery deep up onto the Normandy shore.

As the Higgins boats made their runs up onto the beach, depositing the troops, tanks, trucks, and supplies in the Normandy sand under German fire, the primary producer of those boats, Andrew Higgins, was giving a speech to a Rotary Club in Chicago. In that speech, he would strongly recommend, for the Democratic party's vice presidential nominee in the convention that would take place in that city a month later, the man to whom he gave primary credit for fixing his connections to the navy so that he could produce those landing ships, Senator Harry S Truman.

The news of D-Day overwhelmed the news coverage of Higgins's speech, but four days later Higgins wrote to Senator Truman that in the speech he had strongly recommended him for the vice presidential nomination at the Democratic National Convention coming up in July. He wrote that "the work of your committee is the most outstanding thing in the war effort." Truman thanked Higgins but said that he liked being a senator and had no ambition to become vice president.

Truman would nevertheless be nominated on July 21, and on July 23 a ceremony in New Orleans would celebrate the ten thousandth boat built by Higgins for the U. S. Navy.

Looking still further ahead, we find that Higgins was in Washington on April 12, 1945, and was scheduled to meet in his hotel suite with several senators and his new friend, now the vice president, Harry Truman. But the events of that day kept Truman from appearing. As the new president, he sent his friend Harry Vaughan to express his regret that he could not keep the appointment. Back at the White House on the next day, Friday, his first full presidential day, Truman, among other duties, accepted the congratulations from Andrew Higgins, the New Orleans hero of landing craft.

By war's end, A. J. Higgins and his hardworking company had turned out some twenty thousand LCVPs, which would carry troops ashore from Normandy to Okinawa, Guadalcanal to Iwo Jima. To quote one historian: "More American fighting men went ashore in Higgins boats than in all other types of landing craft combined."

"If Higgins had not designed and built those LCVPs," Ike recollected after the war, "we never could have landed over an open beach. The whole strategy of the war would have been different."

And if Harry Truman had not investigated their production, Eisenhower might never have had those Higgins boats.

Harry Truman would come to have a well-earned reputation in other contexts for bluntness and vigorous partisanship, but in his chairmanship of the Senate committee, he was widely praised for his even-handed fairness, and for sharing the limelight and the credit. At the outset, there were those in the press and the administration who were wary about an investigating committee, fearing grandstanding and headline seeking of the sort that other congressional investigations have been known to produce, as well as interference in the actual conduct of the war, on the pattern of the Civil War committee. But Truman made sure the committee's work evoked no such bad memories. The initial resistance to the committee was overcome partly by presenting it as a better alternative than the activities of others in Congress who were itching to investigate the war effort, and then partly by making clear throughout that the committee's relationship to the administration was totally nonadversarial: Those on the committee only wanted, said Truman, to help Roosevelt win the war.

Then within the Senate, and within the committee, there was a further conciliatory posture. There were no partisan or sharp ideological differences. It is an important indication of Truman's success that each of the committee's reports during his chairmanship was unanimous—all the Republicans joined all the Democrats in signing every one of the reports.

Truman picked the senators who served on the committee—seven at the start, enlarged to ten—because, in the common senatorial metaphor, they were workhorses, not show horses. The topics the committee took up were not subject to much disagreement: the prodigious waste in constructing camps; the shortage of essential commodities like rubber, magnesium, and aluminum; the protection of the consumer economy; and the expansion of the labor pool. The committee also exposed corruption in war production—the worst example being the faulty engines for military aircraft produced by Curtis-Wright. One major role of the committee was simply to extract and publicize information that a nation at war needed—for example, in its first year, that airplane production was badly lagging.

Truman's own populist sympathy with small business and his suspicion of big eastern business—Alcoa, Dow, Standard Oil, Curtis-Wright, U.S. Steel—flavored the entire undertaking, but that was a bias widely shared by the general public, and even those who did not share the bias still could not fail to support in wartime exposing faulty engines, rubber shortages, and dramatic waste. Truman always claimed, although the figure cannot be substantiated, that his committee saved the embattled nation fifteen billion dollars, which again was real money in those days. The publicity the committee received was generally quite favorable, and Truman's public reputation steadily rose through the war years.

In the late fall of 1943, as Dwight Eisenhower, having commanded the invasion of Italy in September and attended the Cairo Conference in November, was about to be appointed to command Operation Overlord, and thus stood on the cusp of his greatest wartime contribution, Harry Truman, in Washington, was turning with his committee to the future. The converting of the nation's economy to war production was by then largely completed; Truman and the committee turned to the issues of reconversion—of turning that war economy back into a civilian postwar economy. This effort met with much resistance from the military, who feared that too much emphasis on reconversion to civilian status would harm the effort in the war that was still in progress—indeed, just reaching its climax. An ailing President Roosevelt also did not support reconversion. The Truman committee tried to alert the nation to prepare for the wrenching change that would accompany the conversion to a peacetime economy—the sudden shortages, the labor troubles, and inflation—but the warning was in vain. Ironically, the president who would have to cope with the nation's failure to prepare for the postwar troubles that the Truman committee had warned against would turn out to be Roosevelt's successor—Harry Truman himself.

· · ·

Ike's rise began not as Truman's did, by his own initiative and his colleagues' endorsement, but by the judgment about him of two key leaders in the hierarchy above him—George Marshall at the outset, and then Franklin Roosevelt. Marshall had been chosen, in one of Franklin Roosevelt's best decisions, to be chief of staff just as the war had started in Europe and the United States was beginning to rebuild its armed forces.

Roosevelt was wise enough to reach down through the ranks, past 34 senior officers, to choose Marshall, and Marshall was wise enough to reach down through the ranks, past 350 senior officers, to choose Eisenhower.*

Marshall had already a positive impression of Eisenhower; their face-to-face dealings at the very end of 1941 and at the beginning of 1942 confirmed that impression. Marshall made Ike head of planning, and then commander of the American forces being sent to England.

Once he landed in England, Eisenhower confronted the distinct issue that would define his role throughout the war: reconciling the two great English-speaking nations. By all odds, the most important friendship he would make—essential to everything else—would be with Winston Churchill; he dined with the incandescent prime minister every Tuesday, watched him slurp his soup, put up with his late-night habits, endured his romantic extravagance, and created a bond that would last through many severe disagreements. (Harry Truman would later have his own encounters with Churchill, most notably at the Potsdam Conference, after the war, and then on a long train ride across the country, featuring poker and whiskey, when Churchill would give his "Iron Curtain" speech in Missouri in 1946.) Eisenhower would also come to have other British friends, perhaps surprisingly for the lad from the wrong side of the tracks out in small-town Kansas: blue-blooded Adm. Lord Louis "Dickie" Mountbatten and Sir Harold Alexander, the son of an earl. He would have good relationships with key British officers with whom he would work: Air Chief Sir Arthur Tedder, the airman who would later be his deputy in Operation Overlord, and particularly Adm. Andrew Cunningham, among many others. There would, however, be a couple of bumps in the otherwise-

---

* Larrabee referred to FDR reaching down through the ranks to pick Marshall (see p. 96), and explained his doing so (see pp. 106–9). He also explained Marshall's decision to pick Eisenhower (see p. 117); Marshall and James Byrnes managed to get legislation through Congress that made this violation of seniority possible.

smooth road of Ike rolling along with English leaders: the chief of the Imperial General Staff, Alan Brooke, and top general Bernard Montgomery would have their reservations about this American "Ike."

As noted earlier, General Eisenhower, newly in the job of planner, was much distressed when, on July 22, 1942, the British decisively rejected the proposed cross-Channel invasion, code-named Sledgehammer, that he and the planning team had designed; he even burst out, according to his friend Capt. Harry Butcher, with the exclamation that this might be "the blackest day in history." But it was not the blackest day in history; far from it. It was, instead, an early day in the education of Americans about modern warfare. Marshall and Ernest J. King, reacting in American indignation to this British decision, considered shifting altogether to the Pacific, and might have done so had Roosevelt not reaffirmed the principle of Germany first and Churchill made the North African invasion (code-named Torch) sound like a good way to engage the Nazis immediately, as well as a good preliminary to a later cross-Channel invasion. (Churchill wanted the buildup of American troops in England—Operation Bolero— but he did not want those troops to attack the Continent just yet, so, in the language of the code names, it was to be Bolero with no Sledgehammer, or Torch instead.) Roosevelt, who wanted American soldiers engaged in fighting Nazis somewhere in 1942, expressed his desire to do Torch by October. The shortage of landing craft meant that the operation was postponed until November 8—after, not before, the midterm elections, to Roosevelt's regret.

Two experiences that fall showed how right the British had been to scuttle Operation Sledgehammer. A spectacularly unsuccessful raid on the French coast at Dieppe by a largely Canadian force in August 1942, in which 3,369 of the 5,000 Canadians who took part were casualties, showed that the Allies were not ready yet for a direct assault on the Nazi-fortified Continent. And then in the first battles the Americans fought in North Africa, around the Kasserine Pass, these newcomers did not perform well. The German commander "Desert Fox" Erwin Rommel and his troops showed the retreating and defeated Americans that they did not yet have what it took to match the Germans. The experience of heavy losses in men and tanks, and of retreat—a humiliation but not a major defeat—shook American confidence and fed British disdain. Some British soldiers began to say, "How green was my ally," and to refer unkindly to the Americans as "our Italians." All of that would be overcome—or at least modified—by later experience, when the Americans would fight well in Tunisia and Sicily, but the lesson was clear: The inexperienced Americans had not been ready for an all-out, head-on engagement with the best soldiers in the world, the Germans, in 1942, and the British knew it. In his book *Crusade in Europe,* Ike did not quote his statement about the blackest day; instead, he made a rather wordy concession: "Later developments have convinced me that those who held the Sledgehammer operation to be unwise at the moment were correct in their evaluation of the problem."

In Operation Torch—the invasion of North Africa—the British and the Americans joined in a common enterprise for the first time. Eisenhower, already in place as commander of American forces in England, and now known to the British leaders, was first chosen to head the planning for Torch, and then was told by Marshall, who no doubt had recommended him strongly within the Combined Chiefs of Staff, that he would command the operation itself. He was chosen in spite of the fact that at that stage of the war the Americans were green and not yet fully mobilized; that Ike himself had never commanded men in combat; and that the British, who had already been fighting the Axis powers for two years, would still have the larger role in battle. Ike was chosen to command in spite of the fact—or perhaps partly because of the fact—that the Americans had had a certain resistance to the North African operation.

The joint planners of Operation Torch felt that it was wise to feature American leadership for another reason, a delicate political reason that reflects another facet of alliance management: the attitude of another power—in this case, France. There was resentment on the part of the French in North Africa toward actions the British had already taken in the war. Shortly after France fell to the Nazis in June 1940, Churchill had made the utterly realistic wartime decision that his British forces should attack and destroy the French fleet in order to keep it from falling into the hands of the Nazis. French ships had been sunk during the British assault and a thousand Frenchmen killed. Although some Frenchmen might have understood the reason for this action, it still created a deeply awkward atmosphere between the British forces and the French. So the plan was to give the Allied invasion of French North Africa, even though the larger part of the invading force would be British, an American look by having this American general in command. Eisenhower would be acutely conscious that his appointment came about in part for that reason. At that time, it was assumed, in the higher reaches of Allied collaboration, that because an American would command this first joint operation, an Englishman would command the great joint action to come, the cross-Channel invasion of the Continent.

Now with the first joint action came the moment to shape the unified

Allied organization, of which much had been said in theory. The theme of Allied unity had been planted in Eisenhower's mind, as we have seen, by Fox Conner, when they were in Panama in the early 1920s. Ike quoted him in *Crusade in Europe:* "We cannot escape another great war. When we go into that war it will be in company with allies. Systems of single command will have to be worked out. We cannot accept the 'co-ordination' concept under which Foch was compelled to work [in World War I]. We must insist on individual and single responsibility—leaders will have to learn how to overcome nationalistic considerations in the conduct of campaigns."

So now Eisenhower had the occasion to act on Fox Conner's teaching. He would also be acting on the plans made in that first British-American conference after Pearl Harbor—code-named Arcadia—when Churchill and his advisers had traveled to Washington and first put in place the shared agreements that would guide them throughout the war, as has been described earlier.

Now Dwight Eisenhower had the opportunity to apply the principle of Allied unity to his staff for Operation Torch: "In the organization, operation, and composition of my staff we proceeded as though all its members belonged to a single nation."

And again:

> The whole of our higher organization was new. Time and again during the summer old Army friends warned me that the conception of Allied unity which we took as the foundation of our command scheme was impracticable and impossible; that any commander placed in my position was foredoomed to failure and could become nothing but a scapegoat. . . . I was regaled with tales of alleged failure starting with the Greeks, five hundred years before Christ, and coming down through the ages of allied quarrels to the bitter French-British recriminations of 1940. But more than counterbalancing such doleful prophecy was a daily and noticeable growth of co-operation, comradeship, faith, and optimism in Torch headquarters. British and Americans were unconsciously, in their absorption in common problems, shedding their shells of mutual distrust and suspicion.

Ike reported not to a national leader or organ but to the CCOS of the two nations. The staff was deliberately mixed. In Eisenhower's headquarters every major subordinate or staff head of one nationality had a deputy of the other. One could not describe a plan or position as "British" or "American"; all were mixed.

But, of course, that intermingling of staff did not cause national differences to vanish. At the higher levels, there was a tug-of-war about where and when to fight, a conflict that had already arisen with regard to Sledgehammer and Torch. The Americans, with their newness on the world stage, their naïveté perhaps, their immense advantage when it came to resources, and their can-do attitude, wanted to go straight for the prize by the most direct means—the cross-Channel invasion—long before it would have been wise to have undertaken it. Churchill would refer more than once to his horrific vision of the bloody bodies of Allied soldiers floating in the Channel. Churchill and Brooke and the British wisely wanted to postpone the dangerous cross-Channel undertaking against the potent Nazi fortification of the Continent; sometimes American colleagues suspected them of being willing to postpone it indefinitely. But they had a positive as well as a negative inclination to fight in the Mediterranean: Opening the sea-lane for ships through the Mediterranean Sea and Suez Canal to the Indian Ocean was surely something more on the mind of the British than the Americans, and behind that was the long experience of an imperial power. And Britain, with long experience as a prudent world power, and now depleted by two years of war, sometimes seemed to prefer nibbling around the edges of the Nazi-dominated Continent on the chance that the cross-Channel invasion would not even be necessary.

In November 1943, when the three simultaneous landings in the North African invasion were accomplished—the first joint action, the first time Americans fought—the broadcast to the world of that event was accompanied by the name of the commander, with a picture spread on front pages in the United States, in London, and elsewhere. Eisenhower's name, now spelled correctly (on first appearing, there had been some misspelling), was permanently removed from obscurity. From that moment, and for the rest of his life, he would be famous around the world.

The accounts of the three landings in North Africa—one of them, due to American insistence, not within the Mediterranean, but along the Atlantic coast at Casablanca—varied, but in general they were considered successful, and of course brought new problems. In his *Crusade in Europe,* Eisenhower succinctly described the political-military perplexity: "The Allied invasion of Africa was a peculiar venture of armed forces into the field of international politics; we were invading a neutral country to create a friend." And so, would the French resist? Much of France was dominated by the Vichy regime, which collaborated with the Nazis, but what would be the attitude of individual Frenchmen, and the residents of

French colonies in North Africa? Would they regard the Allies coming in from the sea as invaders to be resisted or as friends to be aided? Among those captured at Algiers was Admiral Darlan, commander of the French navy and a high Vichy official, to whom most French officers felt allegiance. And so there arose the "Darlan deal," an agreement worked out with this character that brought some outrage, the latter mainly aimed at Ike. Darlan did order a cease-fire, and the shooting did stop, but in return Darlan was made de facto military governor of North Africa. The arrangement was condemned in England and the United States as an odious deal with a Nazi collaborator, and it left a little nick in Eisenhower's reputation, with the charge that it showed his political naïveté. But those who understood the situation believed he had no realistic alternative. The deal, made in the first instance by Mark Clark and then accepted by Ike when he moved his headquarters to Algiers, did stop the shooting and did settle the control of North Africa. But then fortune helpfully intervened: On Christmas Eve, a young anti-Nazi monarchist assassinated Darlan. Although assassination is generally deplored, in this case there was another response as well: a sigh of relief.

As the war developed, Ike dealt more effectively with the French than did Roosevelt. The president detested, and would not deal with, the difficult but essential Free French leader, Charles de Gaulle. Eisenhower, though, did deal with him, and de Gaulle gave an appeal to the French on D-Day, and in his difficult way did cooperate with the Allies in the final battles on the Continent.

Ike had moved his headquarters from London to Gibraltar as the time for the Torch landings approached. He occupied a dank, dark, dripping quarters inside the rock, presenting the unlikely scene of a Kansas prairie lad commanding this ancient site. Then after the landings in November, he had moved to Algiers to command the campaign in Tunisia.

The objective in North Africa was the capture of Tunis. The larger objective, which Brooke thought the Americans did not clearly understand, was the clearing of the Mediterranean shipping lanes. The Allies were not able to achieve the first goal before Christmas 1942, but when FDR asked Ike at the Casablanca Conference in January when Tunis would be captured, Eisenhower pulled a date out of the air and said May 15—which proved to be exactly right. Montgomery and the Eighth Army, victors in the banner British victory at El Alamein, came from the east and the armies from the landings commanded by American generals from the west.

When Tunis fell and North Africa was cleared of Nazis, it was the first great Allied victory, and on May 20 there was a huge victory parade planned by British generals Alexander and Anderson, with Ike reviewing a full array of marching troops—French troops, the Foreign Legion, Algerian and Moroccan soldiers in colorful garb, for a brief moment a few American GIs, and then regiment after regiment of the British armed forces slow marching with their distinctive music played on the bagpipe. Ike stood in the reviewing stand, with two tanks alongside, saluting each unit, a memorable moment for him.

And to be sure, it was a memorable moment for the British generals standing with him, and for the armed forces of the British Empire. But it was the last such moment there would be. The British would never again be the dominant Allied power. This was the high point of British prestige. In the victories that the Allies would win thereafter, the bumptious junior partner, providing more and more of the troops, would never again be relegated to the inconspicuous place that Bradley and Patton and the Americans occupied, somewhat resentfully, at the victory parade in Tunis. From this moment, the world role of Great Britain would decline, and the United States would increasingly have the larger place.

It was painful for Great Britain to yield, given its long history of world leadership. Something of the problem Ike had in actually commanding the Allied forces is indicated by a report from Alan Brooke, the British chief of staff, made after the conference of leaders at Casablanca in January 1943, while the North African operation was still in progress. Brooke described the agreement that was reached on the command structure in this invidious way: "It was clear that centralized command was essential . . . but who was to be placed in this responsible position? From many points of view it was desirable to hand this Command over to the Americans, but unfortunately up to now Eisenhower . . . had neither the tactical nor strategical experience for such a task."

Brooke gave a distinctly British view of the way to solve that problem:

> By bringing Alexander over from the Middle East and appointing him as Deputy to Eisenhower, we were carrying out a move which could not help flattering and pleasing the Americans in so far as we were placing our senior and experienced commander to function under their commander who had no war experience. . . . We were pushing Eisenhower up into the stratosphere and rarified atmosphere of a Supreme Commander, where he would be free to devote his time to the political and inter-allied problems, whilst we inserted under him one of our own commanders to deal with the military situation and to restore the necessary drive and co-ordination which had been so seriously lacking.

So the Americans were supposed to be pleased that a real British soldier, "our senior and experienced commander," would be driving the military action, while this American nonsoldier was pushed up into the
rarified air to flap around in inter-Allied politics. Needless to say, that is
not the way Generals Eisenhower and Marshall understood the arrangement the leaders had made; Ike said succinctly and matter-of-factly in
Crusade in Europe, "General Alexander was to become the deputy commander of the allied forces."

Brooke would write, developing further the British corrective to the
alleged military inadequacy of Eisenhower and the Americans, "Under the
supreme command of Eisenhower [the final report from Casablanca]
placed the active direction of the land, sea, and air operations to clear the
African coast . . . and to invade Sicily in the hands of three British officers,
Alexander, Cunningham, and Tedder."

Eisenhower and Marshall did not intend that Eisenhower should be
shunted upward, as it were, in the way Brooke's report from Casablanca
indicated; he got on well with all four of the British officers grouped under
and around him by this arrangement, but he did not intend that he should
thereby be shut out of the military action. It happened that a minor possible conquest presented itself, on the way to Sicily and Italy as it were, in
which he could indeed be the commander. The tiny island of Pantelleria,
in the Mediterranean between Tunis and Sicily, was a rocky spot with an
airfield and some guns—those against the attack viewed it as a veritable
Gibraltar bristling with guns. Ike, who wanted to invade and take it over,
made a trip to the coast and was greeted by a couple of inaccurate Italian
batteries. Alexander was strongly against invading this little place, because
failure would be disheartening, a blow to morale, and the other three British officers were at first opposed, as well, so this was Commander Eisenhower's project. He ordered intense bombardment of the little island for
three weeks, and then on its own D-Day the British troops set out to
invade at eleven in the morning, and by noon the word came back to headquarters that Pantelleria's defenders had all surrendered before a single
British soldier had even landed; they were, D'Este says, "eager to surrender." The number of Italian soldiers captured was 11,559. The airfield
proved useful in the taking of Sicily. But the major contribution of the
Pantelleria invasion to the Allied effort in the war was its effect on the
self-confidence of the supreme commander. He confessed in a telegram to
Marshall that he might sound like he was gloating. He was the supreme
conqueror of Pantelleria. Other summaries of World War II barely men-

tion, or don't mention, Pantelleria, but Ike devoted two full pages to it in his book.

But Operation Husky—the invasion of Sicily itself—would be another matter, vastly larger and more difficult. It was the largest landing of an invading force on a hostile shore until that time, second only to the Normandy landing in history. It was a major amphibious and airborne undertaking, in many ways anticipatory of the Normandy invasion itself, with multiple landings by multiple armies, with a D-Day (July 10, 1943), and even with a decision by Ike to go ahead despite the weather. There was a successful deception in this operation, too, as there would be in Overlord—in this case a famous floating dead man with false papers on him.

The campaign in Sicily was in the general view a success, driving the Germans from the island in six weeks, opening the shipping lanes through the Mediterranean, toppling Mussolini, and, after some intrigue and maneuvering in which Ike played a central role, bringing Italy's exit from the war and its alignment with the Allies. But in the closer and more discriminating view, Husky fell short of what might have been. The German armies that might have been trapped and defeated were allowed to escape from the island almost intact, and lived to fight on in Italy.

The command situation is not easy to discern. The two chief ground commanders in Sicily would be two generals who would be particularly celebrated, analyzed, and sometimes deplored again in the later operations, and who would provide distinct perplexities for Supreme Commander Dwight Eisenhower: the unavoidable Bernard Montgomery and the difficult George S. Patton. One history of these events found Monty saying to Patton, when the latter complained about an adverse decision by higher-ups there in Sicily, "Let me give you some advice. If you get an order from Army Groups that you don't like, why just ignore it. That's what I do."

In Operation Husky, these two headstrong generals reported in the first instance to Alexander, who had been given command of the ground forces. Montgomery's assignment was to push toward the key objective, the port of Messina, which controlled the traffic between the island and mainland Italy. As Montgomery's army began to get bogged down, Patton jumped his assignment and pushed to take the island capital, Palermo. Alexander, commanding on the ground, under Ike's nominal overall command, ordered a two-prong assault on Messina; Patton made sure it was his prong that got to Messina first, just after the Axis troops departed and just before Montgomery arrived, so that he could be featured on the cover of *Time* as the liberator of Sicily.

But just at the moment when Patton beat Montgomery into the key city, Messina, General Eisenhower learned that twice in visits to wounded veterans Patton had slapped and denounced wounded men he thought were malingering—this in a day before the traumas of battle were well understood. Ike had to reprove him severely, squeeze an apology out of him, and plead with journalists who knew about it to keep the incident quiet so that Patton's military contribution could be preserved. Serious observers thought Ike handled that episode well, given the value of Patton's continuing as a general; in some other cases, they thought he did not. In North Africa, new at his demanding task, he told his subordinates that they must be ruthless in dismissing those who did not perform, but he himself did not dismiss for far too long a plainly inadequate American general named Lloyd Fredendall, whose persistent denigration of the British, elaborate arrangement for his own spacious headquarters located far from the front, and military inadequacies fed the negative stereotype of the Americans as incompetent fighters that it would take a long time to dispel.

After Operation Husky, the argument between the Allies was the same as it had been before Husky: The Americans wanted no more adventures in the Mediterranean, while the British insisted on the golden opportunities in the next step in the Mediterranean, where the troops were already located. Italy had airfields from which the Nazis could be bombed; fighting in Italy would draw German troops from northwest France or the Russian front. And the fact remained that it was not really possible to mount the cross-Channel invasion in 1943. The specialized amphibious landing craft were not yet available in sufficient numbers, and after midsummer the weather conditions would have made it difficult. So once again the action in the Mediterranean was continued, as the British wanted; Churchill had visions of going beyond an Italian campaign to Allied efforts in the Balkans and the Greek islands. Marshall at last drew the line. In Cairo, when the prime minister was waxing eloquent about one of his projects—an invasion of the island of Rhodes, in the eastern Mediterranean—Marshall burst forth with quite uncharacteristic vehemence: "Not one American soldier is going to die on that goddamned beach."

And not one American did die on that goddamned beach, but there did follow a long, drawn-out, and very difficult campaign in Italy in which

American soldiers did die. That campaign, under the command of the Briton Harold Alexander and the American Mark Clark, would finally arrive with the capture of Rome on June 5, 1944—just in time to have their triumph totally upstaged by the central event of all their planning, the project the Americans had most wanted all along: the direct assault on Nazi domination of the Continent by a cross-Channel invasion.

In November 1943, a commander was chosen for an invasion that would take place the following June.

The British journalist Chester Wilmot, a great admirer of Montgomery, in his classic history of the war, *The Struggle for Europe,* wrote this about Ike: "This welding together of the Allied armies in the field was Eisenhower's unique contribution to victory. He may not have been one of the great captains, but he was a man to whom the great captains of his day gladly paid allegiance." ("Gladly" may in some cases be a stretch.) Wilmot later added this superlative: "Because he remained true to this principle [of non-nationalistic Allied unity] Eisenhower was to become the most successful commander of allied forces in the history of war."

The last rung in the ladder to fame and power was the same for both Harry Truman and Dwight Eisenhower: selection by Franklin Roosevelt. Roosevelt would pick Truman, instead of the other possibilities, for the vice presidential nomination in 1944; Roosevelt would pick Eisenhower, instead of one of the two other possible candidates, as commander of Operation Overlord late in 1943 for action that would take place in 1944.

The two other military leaders who might have become the commander of the Normandy invasion rather than Eisenhower were George Marshall, still a possibility when FDR made his choice, and his English counterpart—the chief of the Imperial General Staff, who has already been quoted in these pages—Alan Brooke, who had at an earlier time been led by Churchill to believe he would be chosen.*

When Ike was given the first Allied command, in North Africa, it was assumed—perhaps even promised—that having an American commander at that stage would then be balanced by having a British commander when the time came for the cross-Channel invasion. Throughout the two books on the war drawn from Alan Brooke's diary by his friend Arthur Bryant, there winds an electric thread of disappointment that that did not happen.

---

* When Alan Brooke's title is affirmed, his name is crunched together in the peculiar English way, and he becomes 1st Viscount Alanbrooke.

Because in 1943 Britain was still militarily the predominant Power and because the Supreme Command in the Mediterranean had been given to an American, many, including the Prime Minister, expected the command of the armies that were to liberate Western Europe would be entrusted to a British soldier. An understanding to this effect had been reached by Roosevelt and Churchill when the latter had agreed to Eisenhower's appointment as Supreme Commander in Africa despite the fact that Britain had at least a dozen divisions there to America's seven. The obvious choice was Brooke.*

On June 15, 1943, Brooke wrote in his diary that Churchill (whom he refers to as the "P.M.") had "called me in before the evening meeting of the war council to tell me that he had been wanting to let me know during the last few days that he wanted me to take Supreme Command of operations from this country across the Channel when the time was suitable. He said many nice things about being full of confidence in me, etc."

Brooke then went on in his diary to say that this appointment "would be the perfect climax to all my struggles to guide the strategy of the war into channels which would ultimately make a re-entry into France possible, to find myself in command of all the Allied forces destined for this liberation." But that was not to be.

After the king had left a dinner party at 10 Downing Street on July 7, the "P.M." took Brooke aside, off into the garden in the dark, "and again told me that he wanted me to take over the Supreme Command. . . . This time he was actually mentioning a suggested date for my take-over, a date only just over half a year ahead. I was too excited to go to sleep."

Brooke, sworn to secrecy, had not even told his wife, but on July 14 the irrepressible Churchill asked her how she liked the idea of his becoming "Supreme Commander of the invasion of France."

All of this was before the invasion of Sicily in the summer of 1943. But then in August, at the time of the conference in Quebec, with a steadily mounting number of Americans in the composition of the Allied force, Brooke had to hear some bad news. Churchill came from a meeting with

* Brooke's account of his wartime experience has an unusual form. He kept a diary, originally for his wife, with many sharp comments. An expanded version of that diary was quoted extensively by his friend and admirer Arthur Bryant, a well-known political writer, in two books he published. Because Brooke is not exactly the author speaking directly to the reader but, rather, a diarist, writing for his private muse, and because it is Bryant who addresses the reader in the surrounding commentary, the books present more pungent statements from these two voices than might have come from a book by Brooke himself.

FDR in Hyde Park and delivered to Brooke the devastating message that the latter described in his diary thus:

> Then Winston [not P.M. now, but Winston] sent for me, asking to see me a quarter of an hour before lunch. He had just returned from being with the President and Harry Hopkins at Hyde Park. Apparently the latter pressed hard for the appointment of Marshall as Supreme Commander for the cross-Channel operations and, as far as I can gather, Winston gave in, in spite of having previously promised me the job. He asked me how I felt about it, and I told him I could not feel otherwise than disappointed.

As he and "Winston" walked on the terrace overlooking the Saint Lawrence River, "all that scenery was swamped by a dark cloud of despair." He remembered that at an earlier stage of the war he had turned down the chance to command the British forces in North Africa before El Alamein because he thought he could serve more usefully staying by Churchill's side—and now that Churchill could spare him, he was to be denied his chance.

> But now when the strategy of the war had been guided to the final stage [guided, it is implied, by Brooke himself above all]—the stage when the real triumph of victory was to be gathered—I felt no longer necessarily tied to Winston and free to assume this Supreme Command which he had already promised me on three separate occasions. It was a crushing blow to hear from him that he was now handing over this appointment to the Americans.

This displacement of Brooke by Eisenhower (as it appeared on the British side) was a symbol of a larger fact: the displacement of England by the United States in the dominant position in the politics of the West. Those who think the issues were only power and international politics, with no personal element, can surely hear otherwise in Brooke's lament that "when the real triumph of victory was to be gathered," it was not to be gathered by him, alas.

In the strictly human story, it did not soften the blow for Brooke to be told that in exchange FDR had agreed to the appointment of Lord Mountbatten as supreme commander for Southeast Asia. Brooke wrote, "Not for one moment did he [Churchill] realize what this meant to me. He offered no sympathy, no regrets at having had to change his mind, and dealt with the matter as if it were one of minor importance."

Eisenhower did not have anything like Brooke's expectation, and perhaps not his ambition, either. He had never been promised the Overlord command, and although he had been a key figure throughout the long planning, one cannot imagine him writing, in the self-dramatizing way that Brooke did in his diary, about the command being "the perfect climax to all my struggles." Ike, an American from a small town on the plains who was never going to be—as Brooke would be—a viscount, knew that the whole thing was a collaborative effort throughout.

What did Brooke, who might have been the supreme commander of Overlord, think of Eisenhower, who did become that commander?

On May 15, 1944, three weeks before D-Day, there was a "final run-over" of plans for the cross-Channel invasion at St. Paul's School, where Montgomery had his headquarters, and Brooke wrote in his diary his appraisal: "The main impression I gathered was that Eisenhower was no real director of thought, plans, energy or direction. Just a co-ordinator, a good mixer, a champion of inter-Allied co-operation and in these respects no one can hold a candle to him. But is that enough?"

Looking at this diary entry in the cool aftermath of the war, Brooke did not take it back at all: "If I was asked to review the opinion I expressed that evening of Eisenhower I should, in the light of all later experience, repeat every word of it. A past master in the handling of allies, entirely impartial and consequently trusted by all. A charming personality and good co-ordinator. But no real commander."

Brooke cited an instance of a "real commander":

> I have seen many similar reviews of impending operations, and especially those run by Monty. Ike might have been a showman calling on various actors to perform their various turns, but he was not the commander of the show who controlled and directed all the actors. A very different performance from Monty's show a few days previously.

And so what did Eisenhower, in his turn, think of Brooke? Eisenhower's book on the war was written for a broad audience, and is therefore not decorated with the sharply etched opinions in which Brooke indulged in his diary. And Ike did not have Brooke's flavoring of the acerb. But he still managed to patronize Brooke almost as thoroughly as Brooke had patronized him: "Impulsive by nature as became his Irish ancestry he was highly intelligent and earnestly devoted to the single purpose of winning the war. When I first met him in 1941 he seemed adroit rather than deep, and shrewd rather than wise."

As Brooke had an alternative figure whom Eisenhower did not match, so Eisenhower had an alternative figure whom Brooke did not match:

But gradually I came to realize that his mannerisms, which seemed strange to me, were merely accidental, that he was sincere, and though he lacked that ability so characteristic of General Marshall to weigh calmly the conflicting factors in a problem and so reach a rocklike decision, I soon found it easy to work with him. . . . He must be classed as a brilliant soldier.

Brooke said that the charming mixer Eisenhower was no Monty; Eisenhower said that the shrewd and adroit Brooke was no Marshall.

But Brooke was certainly a central figure in the story of the war, even if he did not become supreme commander. His account of the war is laced with criticisms of the Americans—of Marshall in particular but of Eisenhower as well, and of Admiral King, Henry Stimson, and the whole American crew. These Americans, Brooke said, did not think *strategically.* I take that to mean that they did not relate the several parts of the vast war to one another, and perhaps that they did not link the military choices to the larger political frame, as Brooke and the British, with years of empire behind them, would do. Brooke had in mind in particular that Marshall did not understand the relationship of the action in the Mediterranean to the larger war—in particular, the importance of freeing the route by sea through the Suez Canal to the Indian Ocean.

With the point settled, that the commander of Overlord should be an American, the choice came down to Marshall or Eisenhower, to be decided by the American president.

The case for Marshall resembled that of Alan Brooke—that he was the chief of staff who had been the architect of the Allied effort—but was even stronger than that of Alan Brooke, in that Marshall had been the most consistent proponent of the cross-Channel invasion, which perhaps he would now command. But in December of 1943, Franklin Roosevelt chose Eisenhower instead of Marshall.

Roosevelt gave as his reason the fact that he could not spare Marshall from Washington, from the chief of staff position and the Joint Chiefs. He wanted Marshall there by his side, overseeing the war. There were others in the administration who agreed that Marshall could not be spared. But there was an additional and perhaps more significant reason for picking Ike. Asked by his son James some time later why he had picked Eisenhower, FDR replied, "Eisenhower is the best politician among the military men. He is a natural leader, who can convince other men to follow him, and this is what we need in his position more than any other quality."

One might elaborate on Roosevelt's point to say that the post required a particular kind of "politician"—one who could act positively in the intricate connections between two sovereign nations (and more) and between military and political requirements. Ike managed to mold in the first place, and to hold together under severe strain in the second, Englishmen and Americans (and Canadians, Frenchmen, Poles, and others) in an enormously exacting common cause. It is not clear that Marshall would have been as good as Ike at that, and it is very clear that Brooke would not have been. Those qualities that his British critics granted to Ike, as a preliminary to disdaining his military or "strategic" limitations—that he was "a past master in the handling of allies, entirely impartial and consequently trusted by all"; "a charming personality and good co-ordinator" and "just a co-ordinator, a good mixer, a champion of inter-Allied co-operation and in these respects no one can hold a candle to him"—stated more positively, were of the essence of the post.

Presumably, Marshall would have liked to command Operation Overlord—the most coveted command in the history of warfare—and could have described his not being chosen in terms like those that Brooke used. But unlike Brooke, he had not indicated his desire (one cannot imagine Marshall doing that), and Roosevelt had made him no promise equivalent to those that Churchill had made to Alan Brooke. But Roosevelt was as insensitive to Marshall's feelings as Churchill had been to Brooke's: He even had Marshall transmit the news of Ike's appointment to Stalin. Marshall, in an act of self-denying generosity, saved the note he was told to send to Stalin and sent it to Eisenhower, along with a note from himself:

> *Dear Eisenhower, I thought you might like to have this as a memento. It was written very hurriedly by me as the final meeting broke up yesterday, the President signing it immediately.*
>
> G. E. M.

The message General Marshall enclosed was this:

> *From the President to Marshal Stalin*
> *The immediate appointment of General Eisenhower to command*
> *of OVERLORD operation has been decided upon*
> *Roosevelt.*
> *Cairo, Dec. 7: 43*

CHAPTER FIVE

Normandy, Nomination, Nagasaki

ENDINGS AND BEGINNINGS

EVENTS IN THE SUMMER OF 1944 would have mammoth importance for Dwight Eisenhower and for Harry Truman.

The supreme moment in Eisenhower's career—beyond anything that would come when he was president—was the occasion in June of that year when he commanded "the greatest amphibious operation in history against the most strongly defended coastline that any force had ever tried to assault."* He gave the order and at dawn on D-Day the sea in every direction, as far as the eye could see, was filled with ships—6,483 vessels crowding the horizon. Wave after wave of Allied soldiers would be deposited by the landing craft under the guns on the hostile shore and the climactic battles of a historic world conflict would follow.

The whole event included not only the landings themselves and the battles that followed to secure the beachheads but the scrupulous preparation for months prior to that day, and the intricate coordination of the vast panorama of ships, supplies, armaments, vehicles, and supplies that made the huge event achieve its purpose. Nothing like it had ever been seen before; nothing like it will ever be seen again.

There was, by contrast, no vast armada flowing from any decision by Harry Truman in that summer; the pivotal moment for him was a decision by others to obtain for him the nomination for vice president of the United States on the Democratic ticket in the presidential election in the fall, replacing Henry Wallace. The evident deterioration of President Roosevelt's health meant that it was all too probable that the vice presidential nominee would become president, and the possibility of the starry-eyed Wallace assuming that office gave responsible old pols the shivers.

In June and July, while Eisenhower commanded the invasion, and while Generals Montgomery and Bradley maneuvered against the Germans in the bocage and hedgerows of northwestern France, seeking a breakout, back in the United States political boss Ed Flynn and Demo-

---

* Chester Wilmot, *The Struggle for Europe* (Konecky and Konecky, 1952), p. 186.

cratic party chairman Bob Hannegan and a clutch of party bosses were maneuvering in the bocage and hedgerows of the Democratic party, seeking a breakout for Harry Truman.

On July 11, Hannegan, Flynn, and other Democratic party bosses had dinner with President Roosevelt in the White House to consider the vice presidential nomination. They all opposed Wallace. Multiple names were mentioned, but in the end Harry Truman was the consensus choice, and FDR almost agreed. After they departed, Hannegan went back to FDR and obtained a note saying Truman was the man.

Or did it? FDR, in this as in other events, was the opposite of straightforward.*

If Harry Truman did not yet have any extraordinary role, Dwight Eisenhower, by contrast, had an enormous and unique responsibility. His D-Day decision had come out of a vast web—layer upon layer, of military, political, and technical governmental apparatus—and followed a plan carefully developed by an excellent body of planners at work since early 1943 under the command of a British officer, Lt. Gen. Frederick E. Morgan. It set in motion the huge, waiting panoply of Allied military might. But when the moment came, it was one man's decision, not referred to higher authority, not submitted to a collective review; it was Dwight Eisenhower who said, "O.K., we'll go." A German officer was astonished that such a decision could be made without any reference to superior authority. In this moment, Dwight Eisenhower was indeed the supreme commander.

He was making essential contributions to the Normandy invasion beyond the central decision to launch. If in examining his commandership in the Mediterranean in 1942 and 1943 one does not get the sense that he decided or directed much of the action, with the British being sure he was surrounded by their officers to make the concrete military decisions (Brooke was quite explicit that they wanted it that way), in Operation Overlord the location of actual command was otherwise: General Eisenhower did indeed make the key decisions, giving the directions that shaped the invasion. Looking at the plans even before being chosen supreme commander, Eisenhower insisted that there be in the first wave a wider, bigger invasion of five divisions, rather than three (partisans of Montgomery wrongly claim that he alone made this point). In that endless scramble

---

* Robert Ferrell told the story of the nomination of Truman in a little book entitled *Choosing Truman* (University of Missouri Press, 1944). The difficulty the active Democrats had in extracting a decision from the devious Roosevelt is a major theme.

for landing craft, it was Ike who obtained enough to enlarge the Normandy attack. He was the prime defender of two further elements of its success: the "transportation plan"—using bombing to destroy railroads, depots, switching yards, and roadways leading to the Normandy coast to impede the response of the German forces; and Operation Anvil—the landing in southern France that Churchill and the British had strongly resisted throughout and that Eisenhower and the Americans had insisted upon. Ike had wanted it to take place simultaneously with Overlord—in the north there would be Overlord, the hammer, and in the south, Anvil—but the latter had to be postponed for a month.

General Eisenhower also had to make specific hard decisions surrounding the invasion. One of them—"soul-racking" was his word for it—was his deciding what to do when his air commander, Leigh-Mallory, came to him, rather late in the process, with the apprehension that if the American 82nd and 101st airborne divisions were indeed dropped behind enemy lines at Utah Beach on the night before the invasion, they would be massacred; he urged cancellation of the airborne landings. But General Bradley insisted that the results of such a cancellation would be dire. This was another one of those terrible cases in which somebody, finally, had to decide. Ike did decide that the drop should proceed as planned. The airborne troops were not massacred, and they contributed an essential element to the establishment of a beachhead.

Eisenhower's most difficult larger struggle within the Allied command leading up to the invasion did not break down along national lines but, rather, along service ones; he believed, in keeping with the doctrine of unified command, and on the basis of his experience in the Mediterranean, that he should have command, for the purpose of the invasion, not only of the tactical air forces but also of the strategic bomber forces. But the barons of the RAF and the USAAF—Arthur "Bomber" Harris and Carl "Tooey" Spaatz—although nominally under his command, were fiercely independent and devoted to their own program of bombing Germany, night and day, which some among the bombers thought would suffice to break the German will. Eisenhower needed bombers for the transportation plan, and with the leverage of appeal to the Combined Chiefs, he finally did prevail.

One picture of Ike's distinct responsibility is that moment in the room at Montgomery's old school, with Allied officials all gathered and the weatherman reporting the slim, ambiguous opportunity—one of the most important weather reports in history—and Ike giving the word. Another picture is of his visiting the waiting troops in the days before, shaking

hands, giving greetings, asking men where they came from, the commander making a human connection.

"On D+1 [June 7] we were five to six miles inland" (General Montgomery).

On June 10, the British on Sword and Juno were joined to the Americans on Omaha Beach. "By D+4 [June 10] the lodgement area was joined
up into one continuous whole; it was sixty miles long and varied in depth
from eight to twelve miles; it was firmly held and all anxiety had passed"
(Montgomery).

On June 13, Omaha and Utah beaches were joined. The Allies were
able to secure the beachhead and build up the Allied force because they
commanded the air and therefore the way by which these troops came:
The Channel was completely under their control, while the German effort
to send reinforcements was severely hampered by the Allied bombing of
the railroads.

By July 4, one million Allied soldiers had been landed on the Normandy beaches.

Given the success of Operation Overlord, it is very hard now, looking
back, to see that the whole thing might have failed—that Churchill's
nightmare of the bloody bodies of Allied troops floating in the Channel might indeed have happened. The raw contingency of the whole
enterprise—the catastrophic stakes—make the decisions upon which it
depended all the more impressive.

On July 17, the Democratic National Convention convened in Chicago,
with the vice presidential nomination the only unsettled point.

On July 20, the day before Truman was nominated, the day that the
convention in Chicago nominated Franklin Roosevelt for his fourth term,
there was an event (or nonevent) in another part of the world that might
have transformed the situation for Eisenhower, for Truman, and for much
of mankind—but didn't. In Hitler's conference room in his East Prussian
hideaway, a German officer innocently pushed a briefcase under the table
away from his feet, moving it behind a table leg, so when the bomb placed
in that briefcase by anti-Hitler conspirators exploded, it did not kill Hitler
but only burst his eardrums. The conspirators were executed and Hitler's
insistence on conformity to his will increased. It became even more dangerous than it had been for German officers to differ with Hitler's fanatical
conduct of the war. So the conduct of the German armies in the last bat-

tles of the war would have an added strand of irrationality that prolonged the war.

In Chicago on the July day when the bomb did not kill Hitler, the Democratic National Convention, which had nominated Franklin Roosevelt, heard his address broadcast from San Diego (he was on his way to Pearl Harbor to confer with General MacArthur and Admiral Nimitz about the Pacific war) and amplified to the convention hall, and headed off an incipient Henry Wallace stampede. They pushed the vice presidential nomination off until the next day.

On July 21, Senator Harry Truman was chosen, on the second ballot, to be the nominee of the Democratic party for vice president. Margaret was thrilled; Bess was not.

Truman himself had always said he was happy being a senator and did not want to be vice president, but FDR's booming insistence over the phone brought him around.

On July 25, the Allied armies in Normandy at last effected a breakout against the German armies—Operation Cobra—which meant they would not be bogged down in trench warfare like that of World War I.

On August 7, Supreme Commander Eisenhower moved his advanced command post from London to a Norman apple orchard.

On August 15, at his first press conference in Normandy, Ike revealed for the first time that George Patton was in France commanding the Third Army. Up until that point, Patton was supposed to be the commander of the imaginary army in the hugely successful deception, code-named Fortitude, which fooled the Germans into thinking the Allies would land at Calais.

Also on August 15 there came the other major Allied invasion, oddly obscured in historical memory, overshadowed, as it were, by Overlord: the landing in southern France—Anvil, later called Dragoon. This was the major complement to the Normandy invasion that Churchill had resisted steadily and Ike had defended equally steadily. The largest force ever to sail in the Mediterranean landed on the coast of the French Riviera on the "other D-Day," providing an Allied force coming up from the south, beginning to do everything Eisenhower and Marshall said it would: It provided a port in Marseille through which supplies could come before the Allies captured Antwerp; it put in place a way for the French to participate in the liberation of their own country; and it drew off German divisions from the north.

On August 18, as the Allies in France fought the decisive engagement of the Battle of Normandy, the Battle of the Falaise Pocket, back in the United States the 1944 Democratic running mates had their first and only personal meeting, a lunch on the south lawn of the White House on a hot day. The new vice presidential nominee, Harry Truman, was shocked to see how President Roosevelt's hand shook when he tried to pour cream in his coffee. At that point, Truman did not have much responsibility beyond drinking his own coffee, but that trembling presidential hand and that spilled cream were omens.

On August 25, Paris was liberated; that event may be said to have marked the end of the Battle of Normandy, the triumphant end of Overlord. Supreme Commander Eisenhower arranged to have French troops lead the parade entering the city.

On August 27, Eisenhower, accompanied by Bradley and a British representative (Montgomery being too busy), paid an official call on Charles de Gaulle, which had the effect of a de facto recognition of de Gaulle as the leader of France—a gesture for which de Gaulle would always be grateful. Ike would have better relations with the difficult de Gaulle than any American leader—certainly better than Roosevelt, who detested de Gaulle.

On September 1, Eisenhower took over from Montgomery the formal command of the ground forces in northwest Europe, a move, though planned from the start, still fraught with controversy. By way of palliation, Churchill announced that he was making Montgomery a field marshal, the highest rank in the British Army.

On September 8, the first of the V-2 rockets landed in England. These dreadful weapons plunged from great heights without warning; they could not be detected or intercepted. These attacks increased the pressure on the Allied armies to reach the launch sites that were thought to be in Holland and Belgium.

From the middle of August until early September, there came a string of Allied advances and German retreats that brought exaggerated expectations—the "victory disease," noted in many wars—in Allied leaders and in the general public. It was widely and confidently expected that the Germans might surrender any day now and the war would be over.

On September 23, making a campaign speech to the Teamsters in Chicago, an ailing President Roosevelt seemed for the moment to recover the magic of his past campaigns, when he made an inspired aside about Republican attacks on his dog: "These Republican leaders have not been content with attacks on me, or my wife, or on my sons. No, not content with that, they now include my little dog, Fala. Well, of course, I don't resent attacks, and my family doesn't resent attacks, but Fala does resent them."

On November 7, the Americans went to the polls and elected Franklin Roosevelt for a fourth term. He defeated Governor Thomas Dewey by a margin that was comfortable but smaller than in his three previous victories. Dewey did not concede until four in the morning. Harry Truman was elected vice president. He sent the reelected president a rather pedestrian congratulatory telegram: I AM VERY HAPPY OVER THE OVERWHELMING ENDORSEMENT WHICH YOU RECEIVED. ISOLATIONISM IS DEAD. HOPE TO SEE YOU SOON.

On December 16, as Harry Truman was preparing to become vice president, Dwight Eisenhower, in SHAEF headquarters in Versailles, received a report that the Germans had penetrated Allied lines in the Ardennes region—the first manifestation of Hitler's last gasp, the counteroffensive that would come to be called the Battle of the Bulge.

In August and September 1944, it had seemed that the war was almost over; the Allies had had their breakout from the battle of Normandy, and then a rapid progress across France to the border of Germany; around the map of Europe, nations had thrown off Nazi domination; German armies had been deeply depleted. In Allied capitals, the victory buzz was everywhere. But then on December 16, a wintry Saturday, the German armies launched an attack on the thin lines of the American First Army on the western front in the borderline Belgian-German region of forests, rivers, and hills called the Ardennes—which, when the Germans had punched deeply into the Allied lines, would become the Bulge. The size and significance of this counterattack was not at first recognized by the Allied commanders, and still less by the press and the public, which only gradually came to understand that at this late date the supposedly defeated Nazis had somehow launched a serious counterattack. This certainly was not supposed to have happened. The Germans had been defeated—as much, at least, as they had been in 1918 when they surrendered. So it had seemed that any day the war would be over.

But it was not over; it did not end. Instead, there was suddenly this attack. After the launching of the Ardennes offensive, as the Allies tried to understand what had happened, the thoughtful veterans' spokesman

Charles Bolte, writing in *The Nation*, said that we had been misled by the history of past wars, "in which nations quit when they have been defeated." But perhaps now it is otherwise: "Now we are engaged in a war in which nations do not quit when they are defeated, when there is no such thing as surrender, in which fascism is to either conquer the world or be utterly conquered."* Indeed, without Hitler's distinctive fanaticism, this battle would not have come about. But given that fanaticism, from December 16 until January 25 the not quite exhausted German armies took the initiative to fight an utterly self-destructive last counteroffensive, which proved to be one of the great battles of the war.

The inauguration on January 20, 1945, was a modest fifteen-minute ceremony in the South Portico of the White House, muted explicitly by the war and implicitly by Roosevelt's condition. Harry Truman stood in a blue overcoat to take the oath as vice president, which was administered by his predecessor, Henry Wallace. Then Roosevelt was helped to his feet, grasped the lectern, was inaugurated for the fourth time, and delivered his briefest inaugural address.

On January 26, Tom Pendergast died, and the new vice president immediately decided to attend the funeral, flying to Kansas City in an army bomber and joining those who filed by the casket—an action that provoked some sharply disapproving responses.

On March 1, President Roosevelt spoke in the House chamber about his meeting with Stalin and Churchill at Yalta. He spoke sitting down, which he had never done before, and he made explicit reference to the ten pounds of steel on his legs—the first public reference ever to his disability. After he finished, he spoke briefly to Vice President Truman, telling him he was leaving for Warm Springs for a rest.

In stark contrast to the immense collaborative accomplishment and inspiring unity of Operation Overlord, the last stages of the war in Europe would be a cauldron of controversy. Once the United States and Britain had joined together to bring that mighty host across the Channel and had deposited it on the hostile shore, the unity began to fray. As the armies broke out of their beachhead and fought across the Continent toward Germany and the war's climax approached, the differences in national

---

* In his excellent book on the Battle of the Bulge, *The Bitter Woods*, John S. D. Eisenhower usefully reprinted selections from the press response to the attack, of which this is one (see p. 32).

and personal understandings and purposes, present always but more or less submerged, now erupted into open dispute. The sharpest clash was between Supreme Commander Eisenhower and Gen. (later Field Marshal) Bernard Montgomery. The relationship between these two would be a central story of the whole war, and an epitome of the larger story, the troubled but ultimately successful coping of their two nations with each other.

General Montgomery, as commander of the British Eighth Army, had won a victory over the Germans at El Alamein in the West African desert in October–November 1942, when the British had desperately needed a victory. That iconic victory made him a major hero in Great Britain. He was a man whose brisk, peremptory style one can encounter directly by looking at his writings; one does get a sense that he would not have been easy to deal with. At one point in his 1958 memoirs, General Montgomery would write, "It was always clear to me that Ike and I were poles apart when it came to the conduct of war." But—alas, from Montgomery's point of view—Ike was the supreme commander and Monty was not. Montgomery made repeated efforts to have the command situation clarified, with one commander on the ground in Europe—himself.

On September 4, 1944, at a crucial moment of misleading euphoria, when the Allied armies had sped faster than anticipated across the Continent and it seemed (mistakenly) that the Germans were about to collapse, and when decisions about the war's last acts were being made, Montgomery sent to Eisenhower this blunt statement of his view, a sample of his presumptuous audacity, of which a great many further samples could be cited. He sent it in an effort, as he said with characteristic condescension, "to get a sound plan adopted." (Plans already made, indeed from the start of Operation Overlord, were, by implication, unsound.)

1. I consider we have now reached a stage where one really powerful and full-blooded thrust towards Berlin is likely to get there and thus end the German war.
2. We have not enough maintenance resources for two full-blooded thrusts.
3. The selected thrust must have all the maintenance resources it needs without any qualification and any other operation must do the best it can with what is left over.
4. There are only two possible thrusts: one via the Ruhr and the other via Metz and the Saar.
5. In my opinion the thrust likely to give the best and quickest result is the northern one via the Ruhr.
6. Time is vital . . .

7. If we attempt a compromise solution and split our maintenance resources so that neither thrust is full-blooded we will prolong the war.
8. I consider the problem viewed as above is very simple and clear cut.

It is no surprise to discover that the "full-blooded thrust" that Montgomery believed should be supported, leaving the other "thrust" to do the best
it could "with what is left over," was the one that he himself would command, in the north via the Ruhr. Although Eisenhower made accommodating compromises with Monty, he did not adopt Monty's plan. Where
Montgomery argued vigorously for this single "full-blooded thrust,"
Eisenhower supported a "broad front" advance, in which the armies under
Patton and Bradley, as well as under Montgomery, would advance toward
and into Germany.

Montgomery, although he was the worst, was not the only difficult
general. Eisenhower's friend Patton certainly was often troublesome, too,
as was even his calmer friend, Omar Bradley. These two American generals
claimed that General Eisenhower allowed himself to be too much influ-
enced by his British advisers and subordinates and had become pro-British.
Bradley told Eisenhower that he would not serve under Montgomery—in
fact, would resign before he would do that.

And then in December and January, there came the surprise German
attack, the Battle of the Bulge, and the war did go over into 1945, not
ending until May of that year. In the week after victory in Europe, Montgomery wrote in his diary, "The point to understand is that if we had run
the show properly the war could have been finished by Xmas 1944. The
blame for this must rest with the Americans." The chief American to be
blamed, in Monty's view, was Eisenhower, although he thought that Marshall and others should share in it. These Americans refused to run the war
"properly"—to give the whole support of Allied logistics to make a single
thrust in the north to capture Berlin.

One may see to what depths this argument may sink by noting passages in the biography of Montgomery by his fully sympathetic biographer, Nigel Hamilton. Hamilton observed that failure to follow the sound
Montgomery program that would have ended the war in 1944, and instead
allowing the war to go on until May 1945, meant the death of "millions
more Jews, political opponents, and ordinary citizens," for whom the
Allied rescue came "too late." Hamilton sharpened the point still
further—this is the particularly low blow—by opening the last section of
his second volume with a paragraph about Anne Frank in her apartment
in Amsterdam, thrilled to hear the Allies had landed and anticipating liberation, and then ending his whole book with the end of her diary and her

capture by the SS. The last words are "too late."* So the obscene argument is that Ike's decision about the endgame of the war—rejecting Montgomery's proposal and thereby, it is alleged, prolonging the war—led to the death of Anne Frank.

Those who support Eisenhower's side in this dispute do not believe Montgomery's plan, even if it had been politically possible, would have played out as he claimed. In speculation and imagination, one can picture any result; in reality, the result may be something else. It is extremely unlikely that the Allied armies could have reached Berlin before the Russians did, and it is also unlikely that the result of the effort would have been the surrender of Germany and the end of the war. Providing Monty "all the maintenance resources [his plan] needs without any qualification" while leaving "any other operation"—the armies under Patton and Bradley—to "do the best it can with what is left over" was a totally unrealistic program for an Allied commander. Ike did not do it, and Monty never forgave him.

In the midst of that Ardennes offensive (a more formal name for the Battle of the Bulge) on December 30, 1944, Eisenhower received yet another communication from Montgomery, one that struck again Monty's usual notes. After many prior provocations, Montgomery had sent Eisenhower a message about the endgame of the Allied battle in Germany that seemed to Eisenhower to be an ultimatum. Montgomery proposed, in effect, that he be given operational control of the army group commanded by Omar Bradley, and, indeed, that he—instead of Ike—be given the single overall command of the land armies of the Allies in Europe ("you cannot possibly do it yourself"). Eisenhower in exasperated response was on the point of sending a wire to the Combined Chiefs that would in effect have forced them to choose between him and General Montgomery—an event that would have been an earthquake in Allied unity. By great good luck, Sir Francis Wilfred de Guingand, better known as Freddie, who served Montgomery as chief of staff and protected his boss in many difficult moments, was just then in a conference with Eisenhower in the Allied headquarters in Versailles, and according to Eisenhower's son, "Freddie de Guingand earned a year's pay in the course of a few minutes."

The message from Montgomery was the latest aggravation in a series that had its echoes in the British press, which was giving the impression that Montgomery had had to come to the rescue of an American

* Nigel Hamilton, *Master of the Battlefield* (McGraw-Hill, 1984), p. 835; Larrabee, p. 472.

command—Omar Bradley's—that had failed. Eisenhower explained to de Guingand how damaging this was to Bradley and to the entire Allied effort, and told him that he had decided that the whole matter now should be submitted for decision to the Combined Chiefs of Staff. De Guingand then performed his golden minutes by insisting most earnestly that Montgomery had no idea of the seriousness of the situation, and that when it was explained to him, he would swallow his complaints and cooperate. De Guingand had one great advantage: that he was trusted by both principals, Ike and Monty, and finally did persuade Ike to postpone sending his bombshell of a wire.

But his service was not done; de Guingand then had to fly, through wretched winter weather, to Monty's headquarters, where he arrived in time to interrupt tea and to explain to an uncomprehending Montgomery how close he had come to being dismissed. Forced to choose, the Combined Chiefs, with the now overwhelming preponderance of American troops in the Allied armies, and the essential requirement of support by the American public, could not possibly have chosen Montgomery over Eisenhower. Finally grasping the point, Montgomery wrote irenic notes to Eisenhower and to Bradley, and they responded in a like spirit, and for the moment the crisis was over.

But it never seemed to be over with Montgomery. On January 7, he held a press conference, which, although loaded with favorable comments about the American soldiers and generals, nevertheless managed, given Montgomery's inimitable manner, to condescend to these Allies; he still seemed to insinuate that he had had to come to the Americans' rescue, to save them from disaster. The tilted simplifications of the headlines in the British press made the situation worse. The mild-mannered Bradley, not given to taking offense, nevertheless felt he had to do something he had not done before—hold his own press conference to defend the soldiers in his command. One of the unhappy aspects of the situation was that a transfer of the American First and Ninth armies to Montgomery's command had been intended from the start to be temporary, but Allied announcements had not made clear that they were temporary, so when after this flap the armies were taken from Montgomery's command and restored to Bradley's, the British tabloids treated it as yet another slur on Monty, who, having saved the day in the Battle of the Bulge, was now to be shoved back into semiobscurity.

It fell to Winston Churchill to straighten this out. In Parliament on January 17, he pointed out that in the battle beginning December 16, American troops had done almost all the fighting, and had suffered almost all the losses: "The Americans have engaged 30 or 40 men for every one of ours, and they have lost 60 to 80 men for every one of ours."

That spring would bring Dwight Eisenhower a day—April 12, 1945—that it would be impossible to forget, with events it would be impossible to ignore, including news from home.

By that time, the German armies, having made their last-gasp effort in the Battle of the Bulge in December and January, were plainly in their last throes, but under the spur of the SS and the Gestapo, and Hitler's fanaticism, they fought on. The Allied armies had advanced into Germany, and Eisenhower was faced with the decision about the endgame: whether or not to conduct the advance on the broad front, south as well as north, which Ike had insisted upon, against the strong desire of Montgomery and the British that there be a single thrust in the north under Montgomery to take Berlin. Eisenhower spent April 12 with George Patton and the Third Army, and saw sporadic fighting, although there was no concerted resistance.

The first of the events that would make that April day memorable would be the discovery by the advancing American army of a vast underground treasure, found (as Eisenhower tells the story in *Crusade in Europe*) only through the accident of a kindness done by two American soldiers to some German women, who then in passing pointed out the entrance to a salt mine: "That is the mine in which the gold is buried." Ike, Bradley, and Patton descended by an old creaky elevator the two thousand feet into the mine. Patton made a wisecrack as they descended about the swift improvement in the prospect for promotion in the American officer corps if the cable should break. Safely deposited on the bottom, they found a vast cavern, filled with gold, silver, paintings, and other works of art—loot stolen from all over Europe—as well as gold and silver fillings from the teeth of the dead and their eyeglasses, stolen from the corpses of those who had been systematically murdered, all stored in the depths of an old salt mine—the evidence of raw Nazi greed, thievery, and cruelty. There was also an immense hoard of paper currency; when their interpreter observed that the reichsmarks could have been used to meet the German Army's payrolls, Bradley remarked that he doubted that there would be many more German Army payrolls.

The second memorable experience of that day showed more profoundly still the evil of the enemy that the armies led by these generals had been fighting. The Third Army, deeper into Germany now, had overrun what Ike would call a "horror camp"—a subcamp of Buchenwald, near the town of Gotha. This was his first encounter with a Nazi concentration camp, which, although it was not a "death camp" with gas chambers, was still horrendous, a part of the incredible Nazi system of extermination. This camp had just been liberated by the American forces.* Before abandoning it, the SS guards had murdered all the inhabitants. The three generals saw, among other horrors, piles of bodies, some of which had been set aflame, and plentiful evidence of torture. Patton vomited and refused to enter one room of prisoners starved to death. Ike made a point of visiting "every nook and cranny" of this loathsome place, in order to be able to contradict, from personal experience, "claims that the stories of Nazi brutality were just propaganda." When the men returned to Patton's headquarters, staggered by what they had seen that day, despite their war experience, Ike sent messages to Washington and London, urging that editors and legislators be sent to see these horrors, in order to place before the public evidence that would "leave no room for cynical doubt."†

The quick variations in the emotional and rational requirements of Ike's job certainly revealed themselves on April 12; that same evening, after the stunning descent into the cavern of purloined Nazi gold at Merkers, and then the odious exposure to Nazi hell in Ohrdruf, Supreme Commander Eisenhower made a decision about the role of the armies he commanded, one that would shape the postwar world: He told Patton that he would order the Anglo-American armies to halt at the Elbe River and allow the Russians to take Berlin. Of that decision, much would be heard throughout the rest of the war, and for decades afterward.

As if that were not enough for one April day, the night brought something more—news from home. Patton turned on the radio to learn about the weather and heard the news that Roosevelt had died that day at Warm Springs. He then awakened Bradley and Eisenhower. And so we have the picture of the three American generals, in their bathrobes, sitting up until two in the morning, talking about what it meant that their commander in chief was dead—the commander under whom they all had risen through the ranks to their present eminence. "We pondered over the effect the president's death might have on the future peace," Ike would write. ". . . [W]e were doubtful that there was any individual in America as expe-

* One soldier in the liberating army was an uncle of a later American president, Barack Obama. When Obama first mentioned his "uncle's" role, he said "Auschwitz"; vigorous research corrected the mistakes—the camp was the subpart of Buchenwald at Ohrdruf, and it was the president' great-uncle.

† The next day, the horror would be compounded when he and Patton visited Buchenwald itself. Ike wrote both to Mamie and to Marshall that the bestiality he saw went beyond anything he could have believed.

rienced as he in the business of dealing with the other allied leaders." In his book, written in 1948, giving his account of this moment in time, Eisenhower did not mention the particular individual upon whose shoulders that "business" would now fall.

He did follow his account with a brief encomium for Roosevelt, preceded by a careful distancing: "With some of Roosevelt's political acts I could not possibly agree. But I knew him only in his capacity as a leader of a nation at war—and in that capacity he seemed to me to fulfill all that could possibly be expected of him."

Apparently, the three generals in bathrobes, in their midnight requiem, did eventually discuss the particular individual coming onto the scene. General Bradley's account, in his second telling of his story in his book *A General's Life,* does mention that person: "[F]rom our distance, Truman did not appear at all qualified to fill Roosevelt's large shoes."* Eisenhower wrote about the end of that enormous day: " [W]e went to bed depressed and sad."

The way the war was brought to an end provoked a sweeping criticism of Eisenhower and of the Americans, both at the time and later, which reflects again distinctive national attitudes. The specific criticism was this: The Americans did not make the moves that would have forestalled the Russians. They did not try to beat the Russians to Berlin. They—namely, Eisenhower—stopped their advance at the Elbe River and let the Russians take the German capital. And they did not plan the Allies' last actions in ways that would have forestalled the Russians elsewhere.

The broader criticism was that the Americans did not, while fighting a war, look beyond it to the world they were shaping by the way they fought it. The Americans responded, Of course not. One should not fight wars with one eye on some political arrangement in the future; the only object should be victory in the war. And the critics responded, Thus the Americans displayed their naïveté.

General Montgomery gave characteristically blunt expression to the criticism. He wrote in his *Memoirs:*

> The important point was therefore to ensure that when that day arrived [the day the Germans were defeated] we would have a political balance in Europe which would help us, the Western nations, to win the peace. That meant getting possession of certain political centres in

* Bradley produced not just one but two books about his life and service. His story of the war, *A Soldier's Story,* with a profile by A. J. Liebling as an introduction, appeared in 1951; his autobiography, *A General's Life: An Autobiography* (coauthored by Clay Blair), appeared in 1983.

Europe before the Russians—notably, Vienna, Prague, and Berlin. If the higher direction of the war had been handled properly by the political leaders of the West, and suitable instructions given to the Supreme Commanders, we could have grabbed all three before the Russians.

But none of the three political centers had been "grabbed." Eisenhower was not a capital-grabber; in fact, he tended definitely to resist capital-grabbing. He would say that when these great cities lost any strictly military value, they became "prestige" objects only (Churchill might have responded that "prestige" was half of what the war was about). Ike would say that these cities were then not worth the casualties the capture of them would have entailed. He would argue further that once "grabbed," these cities then would have become a huge drain on resources with which to tend to the population. As the Allied armies after the breakout had crossed France, he had been, at first, not eager even to take Paris. He certainly had not been going to race against our Russian ally to try to beat him into Berlin and these other capitals. And Roosevelt and Marshall—the thoroughly American decision makers—were not going to order him to do so.

Montgomery—and many others, as well—thought that this was quite wrongheaded.

> The Americans could not understand [Montgomery went on] that it was of little avail to win the war strategically if we lost it politically; because of this curious viewpoint we suffered accordingly from V-E Day onwards and are still so suffering. [Monty's book was published in 1958.] War is a political instrument; once it is clear that you are going to win, political considerations must influence its further course.

For Eisenhower, this was anathema. In his education at West Point and throughout his career, he had been taught a strict separation of the military from the political. To be sure, he understood that military action was undertaken ultimately for national purposes, which one may say are "political," but those national political purposes should be decided upon by the civilian political leaders, not insinuated by generals into the planning of military campaigns. Within the military action itself, the only consideration should be military effectiveness toward the defined military purpose—in this case, the defeat of Nazi Germany. He would write, "Military plans, I believed, should be devised with the single aim of speeding victory." And the other American leaders—Roosevelt and Marshall most importantly—would have similar views. And behind them would stand the great American public. That broad public, up to this point in its national history, had tended to see warfare as a distinct and separate domain, now and again breaking into and interrupting the normal run of peaceful history but otherwise isolated from affairs. For Great Britain, as for many nations, war was indeed the Clausewitzian continuation of politics by other means—its purposes were continuous with the policies of the nation all the time—in peace as in war. But for the United States, they were discontinuous; war for the Americans was an abruptly different realm.

One can see the different outlook in Montgomery's statement quoted above: He referred to the ensuring that there be a "political balance in Europe." He spoke for a nation that had had a centuries-old policy of alliance to shape a favorable balance of power on the Continent, and he insisted that even as the war went on against one enemy, a calculation of the future balance with another possible enemy should be a guide to military action. One cannot imagine Dwight Eisenhower, George Marshall, or any American commander making that calculation—including in his military purposes today a shaping of the balance of power tomorrow, including calculating a balance against a present ally. Chester Wilmot, in the potent defense of the point of view that Monty expressed, wrote that by their unsophisticated response to the war's end, the Americans led to "the destruction of the European balance of power which England went to war to maintain." Americans in general would be unmoved by that protest: They had not gone to war to maintain any European balance of power, but to defeat a uniquely evil world-threatening regime.

For all their commonalities, the two nations had key differences in historic experience, and in their current situation that pulled on policy and shaped the attitudes out of which policy grew. We saw how that difference affected the original planning—the Americans immediately gung ho for a direct massive approach, to attack the Nazis not with subtlety on the edges but with a huge invasion at the center, while the British were for postponing that main action, proposing always a new project in the Mediterranean, in the Balkans, on the fringe. "They have had to win their campaigns by maneuver, not by mass," wrote Chester Wilmot. And now this difference in experience and outlook affected the war's ending.

Great Britain, a centuries-old imperial power set on an island a short jump from the rambunctious powers of Europe, had for centuries learned from necessity to calculate and respond to the power situation in Continental Europe—preserving the balance of power often by alliance with the second most powerful Continental nation in order to balance the first—and these continuing calculations were built into the leaders' mind-set, in peace and in war, as Montgomery's statement demonstrates.

Americans, on the other hand, had been fighting to defeat an evil regime, not to reestablish a balance of power. Americans had not had the shaping experience that Great Britain had had, but a contrasting history. They had come into being as a rebelling colonial power, an ocean away from Europe, stuffed to the brim with universal ideals, proposing to make the world anew, or in any case to make a new nation deliberately repudiating "entangling alliances" and the power balances of Europe. For more than a century, the United States had grown essentially independent of the affairs of Europe, fighting a tremendous civil war to rescue its own moral meaning, tiptoeing close to European politics by the side door in the splendid little war with Spain at the turn of the century, then coming into the Great War not at the beginning but in their own time, toward the end, keeping their troops under their own command. In one of those slurs that reveal an attitude, some Americans in 1918 said that the initials of their American force—AEF—stood for "after England failed."

The wars that the United States had fought were not wars continuous with calculations of national interest but intrusions into an otherwise-peaceful history; after each war, the nation had figuratively brushed off its hands and dismantled its armed forces.

There is this further contrast, more immediate and perhaps the most important of all: Great Britain had always had to husband resources; she was not an economic giant. Her tradition of fighting shrewdly around the edges, trying to win by maneuver, grew from that condition. And now at the end of World War II, she was, in addition, an exhausted power, having fought for five years and drawn down the available resources of manpower and material to the vanishing point. And then came the big ally, with a huge economy not damaged at all by its wartime production, but revived by it. The United States, still in the Depression when war came, had been able to double her economic output with the demands of the war.

For England, there was continuity and connection; for the United States, discontinuity and isolation. The commanders, in a British view, should have been thinking in those last weeks about the balance of power after the war. For an American, that proposal would have seemed outrageous.

The argument entailed more than the question of entering Berlin and beating the Russians in other places in the last days of the war; it applied to earlier decisions, as well. Churchill and other Englishmen had opposed Operation Anvil/Dragoon because that big project in southern France took troops away from the war in Italy and from any further action in the Balkans—disallowed, in other words, those approaches to Nazi Europe through its "soft underbelly" that Churchill and others had been tempted to propose. The soft underbelly program, in addition to its other justifications, would have led the Allies into the areas the Soviets would soon occupy. Critics of the American enthusiasm for Anvil point out that Stalin was a strong supporter of that project, which took the Allied armies away from the region his troops would invade.

In the last days of the war, the American president died. But although Churchill and other British leaders might have been tempted to wonder whether the American position on the war's ending might therefore change, of course it was not to be. Truman, newly dropped into this immensely powerful position, succeeding this political giant, and altogether unprepared for it, was not going to reverse the policy of the great president he had just succeeded, particularly since the chiefs of staff still held to it. Truman upheld the Roosevelt-Marshall-Eisenhower principle that "strategy should be determined without regard to post-war political considerations." In the first communication involving the two subjects of this book at the pinnacle of power, the new president said in a cable that the disposition of troops was a military matter, adding, "It is my belief that General Eisenhower should be given a certain latitude and discretion."

Harry Truman was to write in his memoirs, "I felt I had lived five lifetimes in my first five days as President." He wrote to his mother and sister at the time, "Before I was sworn in, I had to make two decisions of world-wide import—to carry on the war and to let the Peace Conference [that is, the founding meeting of the United Nations] go ahead at San Francisco." After the funeral and burial of President Roosevelt, and Monday morning's address to Congress, Truman, as he put it in his April 18 letter to "Momma and Mary," "spent Monday afternoon seeing people and making all sorts of decisions, every one of which would touch millions of people." Later, on April 21, in his third letter home as president, he wrote, "Well, I've been president for nine days. And such nine days no one ever went through before, I really believe. The job started at 5:30 on the afternoon of the 12th. It was necessary for me to begin making decisions an hour and a half before I was sworn in, and I've been making them ever since."

In his memoirs, he would write, "In the position I occupied a day seemed like an eternity." And again, as of the last day of April, after eighteen days as president: "I feel as if I had lived through several lifetimes." The most often quoted of Truman's statements about the sudden weight of the presidency is his heartfelt cry when he visited his old vice presidential Senate office on his first full day as president, April 13. A long line of white-shirted pages gathered outside to greet him, and some reporters joined the pages, and Truman, shaking hands with every one of them, said, "Boys, if you ever pray, pray for me now. I don't know if you fellows ever had a load of hay fall on you, but when they told me yesterday what had happened, I felt like the moon, the stars, and all the planets had fallen on me. I've got the most terribly responsible job a man ever had."

Dwight Eisenhower had a terribly responsible job at the same time, with several additional planets falling on his already-burdened shoulders in the decisions about the endgame of the war in Europe. David Eisenhower has written about the ordeals encountered by "Granddad" and his granddad's predecessor in the years after Roosevelt's death. As he saw it, Ike's prominence increased substantially during the vacuum of the post-Roosevelt years. Advocates of Harry Truman, however, might not be so quick to agree and instead hold that it is a little hard on Truman to say that what followed Franklin Roosevelt's death was a "void."

On that day in April 1945 when the two subjects of this book came to have a direct connection for the first time, Harry Truman was now "Commander-in-Chief of the Army and Navy of the United States, and of the Militia of the several States," as the Constitution says, which had been "called into the actual Service of the United States." Although Dwight Eisenhower was the supreme commander of an Allied force—responsible to an Anglo-American joint command—he was also an officer in the American army, commander of American forces in Europe, and Harry Truman was now formally, in his role, Eisenhower's boss. But he was an extremely deferential boss. In his first days as president, Truman suddenly had to make a battery of heavy decisions, but until the war's end those decisions did not involve Dwight Eisenhower, who had his own decisions to make.

The Russian armies from the east and the Anglo-American forces under Eisenhower from the west closed on the armies and the leaders of the Thousand-Year Reich. On April 30, in Berlin, Adolf Hitler took his own life. German soldiers wanted to surrender to the American and English forces, not the Russians. German leaders stalled to try to bring this about, but Eisenhower would not allow that. He had a high-ranking Russian present at his headquarters as the surrender approached. All the German units had to surrender unconditionally to all the Allies.

At the surrender ceremony, Eisenhower maintained the same aloofness from the German generals that he had displayed first in Tunisia. Others on the staff tried their hand at more elaborate messages to send the world the good news, but finally Eisenhower sent the elegantly simple message: "The Mission of this Allied Force was fulfilled at 0241, local time, May 7, 1945. Eisenhower."

Eisenhower had a distinctive role in the Allied conduct of World War II, as we have already seen—a role that came to be particularly important as the Allies invaded the Continent, the ending of the war came into view, and issues arose about how it should end, who would be presented as the victor, and what the shape of postwar Europe would be. He was the primary agent, and also the symbol and embodiment, of a quite unusual joining together of the two English-speaking Allies, an alliance that became almost a unity. And it can be maintained that his fulfilling that role laid a foundation for the postwar foreign policy instituted by President Harry Truman.

Ike and the role he played have no clear analogue in other wars or other figures in this war. The Napoléons and Caesars and Bismarcks of other wars might have gathered allies around their powerful original national force, but these additional forces did not come all the way into the inner chamber of command. In World War I, John J. Pershing was the commander of the American Expeditionary Force, not of any Allied collaboration; in fact, it was part of his role just to keep the American forces independent of the Allies. Gen. Ferdinand Foch became, in the spring of 1918, after commanding French forces to that point in the war, nominally the supreme commander of Allied forces, but that was late in the war, the Americans were not included, and the commands were not integrated, but "co-ordinated." The chiefs of staff who took the largest view in World War II, George Marshall and Alan Brooke, were still primarily agents of their nation's distinctive angle of vision. Bernard Montgomery, George Patton, Omar Bradley, and the other generals whose names would be spread across the history of this war were all defined in major part by their national allegiance even as they fought for the Allied cause. Montgomery was certainly a British general. But Eisenhower was, throughout the three years and five months of the American participation in the war, something different: the "supreme commander" of an Allied force in which both nations participating had a nominal equality. He had the distinctive duty to win the war with the Allies still united—that is, to keep the Allies allied while they won the war.

Eric Larrabee, analyzing Eisenhower's accomplishment, which "not many really noticed," finding it to be the deft removal of the conduct of the war from British hands without giving them cause for complaint, making sure that the honor and glory of victory would be shared by Americans and British together in unity, wrote that "the design of Roosevelt had been supplanted by the design of Eisenhower. America was not going to withdraw from European concerns as the president had wished but would embrace them as Eisenhower had learned to do. In the figure of this man we were in Europe to stay and on this rock would be built the Truman Doctrine, the Marshall Plan, the North Atlantic Treaty Organization, and the world we have lived in since."

The premise of this assertion is that FDR would have followed a different course from the one Truman followed in the years after the war—a more independent course for the United States. Larrabee suggests that FDR "had even a trace of the isolationist in him," and a bit of the "World War One imperialist" who underlined America's military power; that he was "fully determined that the United States not become enmeshed in the restoration of colonial rule"; that he was "standoffish about Europe," teasing Churchill that after the war France and Italy would be Britain's responsibility; that he believed that the European countries would "revert to their historic squabbles from which the United States should remain aloof." If this picture of FDR's intentions for the postwar world is correct, then there was indeed a considerable contrast in what actually happened with his successor, Harry Truman, who would really prove to be a liberal internationalist who sought the revival of the West with the central role of a European-American, and especially an Anglo-American, connection. And then one may find the beginning of Truman's postwar policy in the wartime action of Dwight Eisenhower, at the center of which was his nurturing the British-American alliance and making it serve the great purpose of winning the war.*

When they were in Europe, President Truman and General Eisenhower each had an occasion to speak in a large way about the meaning of the just-completed war—Eisenhower when he was being honored in a solemn ceremony with wigs, a mace, the Lord Mayor, Winston Churchill, and the elite of England in the ancient Guildhall in London in June 1945; Truman much more informally in the American sector of Berlin on the occasion of the raising of an American flag at the time of the Potsdam Conference a month later.

* The quotations and themes of this paragraph are taken from the epilogue to Larrabee's book, especially pp. 631–34.

Ike wrote his important speech himself, perhaps the best speech of his career.* He worked hard on it, he said, for three weeks. There is a certain unexplained oddity about his use of the English language that is not altogether absent from this generally successful address. He had been something of a writer in his days in the peacetime army, writing speeches, we are told, even for Douglas MacArthur (it is hard to imagine that chore). He would go on in 1948 to compose, in clear and competent prose, his own book about the war, *Crusade in Europe.* But then in his press conferences as president, he would display an awkwardly verbose inexactitude that was distinctive enough to provoke one of the best-known parodies in modern American politics, the Eisenhower version of the Gettysburg Address, produced by an attentive journalist in the fifties and ubiquitous ever since. "I haven't checked these figures, but 87 years ago, I think it was, a number of individuals organized a governmental set-up here in this country. I believe it covered certain Eastern areas, with this idea they were following up based on a sort of national independence arrangement and the program that every individual is just as good as every other individual."

The explanation by some defenders that this awkward inexactitude in his press conferences was deliberate, a tactic as part of his hidden hand method, is very hard to credit. What possible purpose could it serve? And how could one possibly bring off such a trick? There seems to have been, rather, something that invaded and complicated his utterance when he dealt not with the concrete but with large realms of the abstract and general.

In any case, the Guildhall address, excellent as it was, would have a faint hint of the style to come. It has a couple of backward-running sentences, including one quoted earlier: "Humility must always be the portion of any man who receives acclaim earned in blood of his followers," and "Hardly would it seem possible for the London council to have gone farther afield to find a man to honor." The speech includes one word that cannot be found in dictionaries ("disregardful"), and it includes some slightly odd modifiers and expressions ("this devoted city"; "the remotest hamlet and heart of all peoples"; "our eyes rounded"). Anyone who had

---

* Other important Eisenhower speeches, less personal, would be his address defining the Cold War, on behalf of Radio Free Europe, on Labor Day 1950, when he was president of Columbia University, and his farewell speech, with its resonating reference to the "military-industrial complex."

been exposed to his answers in presidential press conferences and then looked back at this speech would find little adumbrations of what was to come. Nevertheless, it was a moving and successful speech. It may even be that part of its effectiveness was a slightly awkward echo of Abilene.

Because it was a splendid formal occasion, during which he was made an honorary citizen of London, General Eisenhower spent the first part of his address scrupulously spreading the honor out to include "all allied men and women that have served with me in this war." He was himself, he said with humility, just a symbol of "the great human forces that have labored arduously and successfully for a righteous cause." And he noted that no honors could hide his memories of the crosses marking the resting places of the dead.

The general then shifted to the great story of the link between England and the United States, using his home in Abilene as one symbol and London as the other. Although he admitted that London was bigger and older than Abilene, he held that they nevertheless shared something significant:

> those inner things—call them what you will—I mean those intangibles that are the real treasures free men possess.
>
> To preserve his freedom of worship, his equality before law, his liberty to speak and act as he sees fit, subject only to provisions that he trespass not upon similar rights of others—a Londoner will fight. So will a citizen of Abilene.

In an important part of the speech, he gave quite explicit recognition to the role of England, and specifically of London, in the war:

> And what man who has followed the history of this war could fail to experience an inspiration from the example of this city?
>
> When the British Empire stood—alone but unconquered, almost naked but unafraid—to deny the Hitler hordes, it was on this devoted city that the first terroristic blows were launched.

It was an effective touch, to be quite specific about the length of the war as London experienced it: "Five years and eight months of war, much of it on the actual battle-line." And it was effective also to specify something of London's experience of battle: "blitzes big and little, flying V-bombs—all of them you took in your stride. . . . The Battle of Britain will take its place as another of your deathless traditions."

As an American, it was important to specify the longer service of the British, noting that they had been in the war two years before the Americans began swarming into the country. And it was also good to acknowledge the naïveté of these swarmers:

With awe our men gazed upon the empty spaces where once had stood buildings erected by the toil and sweat of peaceful folk. Our eyes rounded as we saw your women, serving quietly and efficiently in almost every kind of war effort, even with flak batteries. We became accustomed to the warning sirens which seemed to compel from the native Londoner not even a single hurried step. Gradually we drew closer together until we became true partners in war.

Of course he hoped that it would not be necessary again to fight for those intangibles that the Allies fought for, but if it became so, London and Abilene would once more be right there together.

The comment by Alan Brooke, who, as we have seen, had persistent reservations about Eisenhower, has been widely quoted: "I had never realized that Ike was as big a man until his performance today."

Truman's remarks in Berlin were much less formal and extended. On July 20, 1945, he took a tour of the city with Eisenhower, General Bradley, and others. In his speech, Truman specifically addressed Ike: "General Eisenhower, officers, and men," he began. He made his remarks informally, without notes:

> This is an historic occasion. We have conclusively proven that a free people can successfully look after the affairs of the world.
>
> We are here today to raise the flag of victory over the capital of our greatest adversary. In doing that, we must remember that in raising that flag we are raising it in the name of the people of the United States, who are looking forward to a better world, a peaceful world, a world in which all the people will have an opportunity to enjoy the good things of life, and not just a few at the top.
>
> Let us not forget that we are fighting for peace, and for the welfare of mankind. We are not fighting for conquest. There is not one piece of territory, or one thing of a monetary nature that we want out of this war. We want peace and prosperity for the world as a whole. We want to see the time come when we can do the things in peace that we have been able to do in war.
>
> If we can put this tremendous machine of ours, which has made this victory possible, to work for peace we can look forward to the greatest age in the history of mankind. That is what we propose to do.

It was a homely and unpretentious effort, a long way short of Woodrow Wilson, and not what Roosevelt would have had his speechwriters produce, and yet those who were there—General Lucius Clay, for one, and a *New York Times* reporter, for another—found it moving.*

---

* Truman's remarks and the responses to them are given in McCullough, p. 429.

In neither of these speeches was there the self-congratulatory trium-
phalism that often mars the utterance of victors after a war. Although both
of these men fully recognized the depth of the evil that the Nazis
represented—an evil both of them saw to be as dark and as deep as any in
the whole history of mankind—they did not on these valedictory occasions make reference to it. While the accomplishment they celebrated was
huge, their claim was modest; their remarks included no undue celebration of the merit of the victors.

The occasion of President Truman's remarks in Berlin was also the time
he made a celebratory comment to General Eisenhower that would later
become a matter of controversy. Full of enthusiasm after he made his
remarks, riding in a car with General Eisenhower, Truman made a rather
sweeping offer: "General, there is nothing you may want that I won't help
you get. That definitely includes the presidency in 1948."

It is amusing to read the account by Truman himself of the meeting of
the "Big Three" in July 1945 at Potsdam. Truman was then a total novice at world-class statesmanship, only four months into this new job;
he presided over the meeting with these great world figures—Churchill
and Stalin—with a no-nonsense attempt to get things done, to move the
agenda, to nail down one issue and move on to the next. (Stalin had proposed and Churchill had seconded the motion that Truman, the only head
of state, preside.) In his own account in the first volume of his memoirs,
Truman tells about this exchange, at the end of the first session, at which
the agenda was discussed:

> I told Stalin and Churchill that we should discuss the next day some
> of those points on which we could come to a conclusion. Churchill
> replied that the (foreign) secretaries should give us three or four
> points—enough to keep us busy.
>   I said I did not want just to discuss, I wanted to decide.
>   Churchill asked if I wanted something in the bag each day.
>   He was as right as he could be. I was there to get something accom-
> plished, and if we could not do that, I meant to go back home. I
> proposed that we meet at four o'clock instead of five in order to get
> more done.

After the second session the next day, he wrote, "I felt that some progress
had been made, but I was beginning to grow impatient for more action
and fewer words."

On the next day, after somewhat inconclusive discussions about, among other topics, what to do with the German navy, and Franco's Spain, and Yugoslavia, Truman felt "I had heard enough of this."

> I told Churchill and Stalin that I had come to the conference as a representative of the United States to discuss world affairs. I did not come to hold a police court hearing on something that was already settled or which would be eventually settled by the United Nations. . . . I told them frankly that I did not wish to waste time listening to grievances but wanted to deal with the problems which the three heads of government had come to settle. I said that if they did not get to the main issues I was going to pack up and go home.

Truman did not pack up and go home, but stayed on to the end, trying to get "something in the bag each day."

It was on that trip to Potsdam in the summer of 1945 that the new president, Harry Truman, made the decision to drop atomic bombs on Japan. Is it possible that had Dwight Eisenhower been in Truman's position he would have decided otherwise?

The bombs killed tens of thousands of people on the days they were dropped and thousands more from their aftereffects—more than ninety thousand in Hiroshima, more than sixty thousand in Nagasaki. Although in the planning, Secretary of War Stimson and others—Truman himself— had spoken of bombing only military installations, in the event most of the dead in both cities were civilians.

It is easy enough to say, in the comfortable distance and irresponsibility of someone writing a book decades later, that the bombs never should have been dropped, but it would have been extremely difficult for any American president—any statesman in Truman's place—actually to have decided not to use them.

The overwhelmingly potent argument for using the atomic bomb was, of course, that it would end the war and save lives—save the lives, first of all, of the American soldiers who would have been killed in the ferocious fighting that would have accompanied an invasion of the Japanese homeland, and second, of the citizens of other countries, including Japan, that would have been lost in a continued war. An invasion of the Japanese islands had been in the planning stages since 1943 and would have taken place on a scale that would have dwarfed the Normandy invasion. Soldiers and equipment were being moved from the European theater to the Pacific, and the invasion was set for November 1. But the Americans had a horrendous example of what invading Japan itself would be like: the fanatical resistance the Allies had met in taking the islands of Iwo Jima and Okinawa. The stated figures for casualties expected in the invasion, large from the start, grew larger as the argument about the use of the bomb intensified, until somehow the stunning round figure of one million casualties came into play, and then it was raised another step to one million fatalities. Imagine an American president being told that the military action he was ordering would lead to a million dead American soldiers. Whatever the true numbers would have been—not that many, but staggering nonetheless—the prospect of an invasion of Japan, and a battle on every inch of its difficult territory, was a terrifying prospect. Understandably, Truman said he wanted to prevent an Okinawa from one end of Japan to the other. And the new weapon promised a way to avoid that appalling result.

It was thought that bombing a Japanese city with this new weapon would shock the already effectively defeated Japanese into surrendering, thus bringing the war to an end without the invasion of the Japanese islands and thereby saving many lives. In one aspect, the decision about the bomb had already been made: Both the United States and Great Britain had already engaged in strategic bombing—saturation bombing—of cities as, to be sure, Nazi Germany and Japan had done as well. In the early days of the war, there was still a certain restriction that only military targets would be bombed, and the Americans tried to maintain that they were engaged in "precision" bombing, directing the explosives dropped from the air on facilities below that served the enemy's war-making machine; but when the enemy dispersed his war-making facilities, that was no longer possible, and the Allies not only attacked urban populations but now justified these attacks by declaring their intent to break the will to fight. The RAF bombed German cities at night; the USAAF bombed in the daytime. There were notable raids on Hamburg, Berlin, Cologne, and other German cities. The most controversial, of course, was the bombing of Dresden, in February 1945. It is estimated that some 600,000 German civilians were killed in these raids and 800,000 injured. In some cases—Hamburg, for one—conditions were such that a raging fire was created; it is said that water in the canals in Hamburg boiled. (Ike's connection to the strategic bombing, as we have seen, was that he interrupted it. He fought fiercely, against strong opposition from the bombing commanders, to transfer their bombers for a time to a task that served Operation Overlord: the destruction of the roads, railroads, and bridges that the Germans would travel on to bring forces to Normandy. Churchill's opposition to this "transportation plan" included the claim that thousands of Frenchmen would be killed. Eisenhower went ahead with it; the casualties were not extreme.)

Among the ironies of the saturation bombing was the revealing un-willingness of the British after the war to honor "Bomber" Harris, the blunt promoter of area bombing, with the peerage that all other major commanders received; his crew was denied a distinctive campaign medal. Although the British public wanted the saturation bombing of German cities, apparently it did not want to admit to itself that it had done it.

And another irony: Almost immediately at the end of the war in Europe, with the Allies inheriting administration of Germany, precisely the same planes that had flown overhead carrying bombs to be dropped on German cities now flew to those same cities carrying essential supplies for rebuilding what they had helped to destroy.

In Japan, the destruction was even more stark. Fire was a deliberate feature of the bombing. The American general Curtis LeMay led the Twenty-first Bomber Command in attacks by great fleets of bombers flying low and dropping incendiaries, first on Tokyo and then on other major Japanese cities—eventually on fifty-eight cities. The number given for Japanese killed in these raids is 260,000—greater than the numbers killed in Hiroshima and Nagasaki combined—so the atomic bombings did not have the novelty of unmatched destructiveness.*

Some of the moral boundaries had already been crossed before Harry Truman (or Dwight Eisenhower) arrived in the highest corridors of power; but still, this new weapon did pose a new question, just because it was a harbinger of a new dimension of human destructiveness.

The speculation that Dwight Eisenhower, had he been in Truman's place, might have resisted ordering that the bomb be dropped on Japanese cities springs from his own report of his response when he learned about it.

Eisenhower's account features an exchange with Secretary of War Henry Stimson—a key player—in July of 1945, at the time of the Potsdam Conference, which was when President Truman was actually making the decision to bomb Japan. Eisenhower, who had stayed on as commander of the American zone of occupation after accepting the German surrender on May 7, wrote in 1948 in his book on the war:

---

* Sometimes in arguments against the dropping of the atomic bombs, the official U.S. Strategic Bombing Survey of 1946 is quoted: "[I]t is this Survey's opinion that certainly prior to December 31, 1945, Japan would have surrendered even if the atomic bombs had not been dropped, even if Russia had not entered the war, and even if no invasion had been planned." That statement is one of a continuing series by the bomber commands, indicating their belief that saturation bombing alone could win the war.

In [July] 1945 Secretary of War Stimson, visiting my headquarters in Germany, informed me that our government was preparing to drop an atomic bomb on Japan. I was one of those who felt that there were a number of cogent reasons to question the wisdom of such an act. . . . The Secretary, upon giving me the news of the successful bomb test in New Mexico, and of the plan for using it, asked for my reaction, apparently expecting a vigorous assent.

During his recitation of the relevant facts, I had been conscious of a feeling of depression and so I voiced to him my grave misgivings, first on the basis of my belief that Japan was already defeated and that dropping the bomb was completely unnecessary, and secondly because I thought that our country should avoid shocking world opinion by the use of a weapon whose employment was, I thought, no longer mandatory as a measure to save American lives. It was my belief that Japan was, at that very moment, seeking some way to surrender with a minimum loss of "face." The Secretary was deeply perturbed by my attitude.

Eisenhower apparently had an opportunity to express his opinion to Truman himself. Truman invited Generals Bradley and Eisenhower to a lunch during the Potsdam Conference, on July 20, at which Truman held forth about war-ending issues. According to Bradley, Eisenhower, although not directly asked for his opinion, did argue against using the bomb.

Indulging in a retrospective improvement of history, one can imagine how it might have been had a president acted on Ike's stated position. If one had had his eagerness to avoid using this "awful thing" (as Ike called the bomb in an interview with *Newsweek*) and his awareness that, as he had said, the Japanese were already defeated, then one might have made sure that the Potsdam Declaration—the statement of the terms to end the war with Japan issued by Truman, Churchill, and Chiang Kai-shek—included the reassurance to the effectively defeated Japanese that the emperor could be retained, which, knowledgeable American diplomats would insist, was an essential in persuading them to surrender. The pernicious doctrine of "unconditional surrender," tossed into the war's goals all too casually by Roosevelt at Casablanca, the carrier of an absolutist attitude harmful to wise policy, would thus have been mitigated, and the Japanese given a face-saving way to surrender. In the end, after the dreadful weapons had been used, the Allies did allow the emperor to remain; how much better to have agreed to do so before the United States crossed the line into the new world of nuclear catastrophe and thousands were incinerated in Hiroshima and Nagasaki.

A president with the convictions that Eisenhower expressed might also have included in the communication with the Japanese the information that the Soviets were about to enter the war against them. The Soviets had agreed at Yalta that they would come into the war, and now at Potsdam the date was set: August 15. When in fact they did enter the war, that may have had as much effect on the surrender as the bombs—or more of an effect.

The Japanese, already long since effectively defeated, were putting out peace feelers, and in the view of those who argue that the bomb was unnecessary, they could have been brought to surrender by wise policy. If these two efforts at persuasion were not enough, then still there might have been a warning that the Allies had this new weapon of immense power, and if the warning alone were not enough, there could have been a demonstration of the power of the nuclear bomb without dropping it on a city. This possibility had been discussed but discarded; a chief executive determined not to use the horrendous weapons on the general population might have overcome the arguments for doing so.

Harry Truman decided otherwise. He gave his order to drop as many bombs as were available to General Spaatz of the Army Air Force on July 25, 1945. Henry Stimson had managed to have the ancient capital and cultural center Kyoto stricken from the list of targets, but Hiroshima and Nagasaki had no such reprieve.

The bomb was dropped on Nagasaki just three days after the one on Hiroshima, with no specific order. But that second bombing especially should not have been carried out without a specific order. After the Nagasaki raid, Truman belatedly did order that there be no more nuclear attacks without his explicit approval. On August 10, he saw reports and photographs from Hiroshima and told the cabinet that he had given orders to stop atomic bombing. And there would be no more, not just during the rest of his presidency but no more during the forty-five years of Cold War, no more during the twentieth century, and no more into the second decade of the twenty-first century. Truman made a comment that Henry Wallace put in his diary that evening, and that remark is quoted in most accounts: He said that the thought of wiping out another 100,000 people was too horrible, that he did not like the idea of killing "all those kids"—wording that Truman would reiterate in later remorseful moments.*

It is true that it would have been very difficult for any president to resist the momentum for the use of the bomb. Although its significance reached

* See John Blum, ed., *The Price of Vision: The Diary of Henry A. Wallace, 1942–1946* (Boston: Houghton Mifflin, 1973), pp. 473–74.

a level quite beyond that of the usual calculus of national interest, it nevertheless came to the president as yet another in the flow of presidential decisions guided by the nation's interest in a ferocious war. Truman had been abruptly dropped into the presidency, and abruptly dropped also into the already-developed project to make—and presumably to use—nuclear weapons. There was a history of the development of the weapons, about which Truman had known nothing before he became president. Albert Einstein had sent his famous letter to FDR explaining the science in 1939; the Manhattan Project to build the bomb began in 1942 and cost two billion dollars. The impetus at the start was a fear that the Nazis might get the weapon. Before his ascension to the presidency, Harry Truman had not known of the *existence* of atomic experiments. On Truman's first full day in office, Franklin Roosevelt's "assistant president," James F. Byrnes, told him about an explosive that the U.S. government was developing. Twelve days later, Secretary of War Henry Stimson and Gen. Leslie Groves, the military director of the Manhattan Project, held a long meeting with the new president and told him the whole stunning story—not just about a new weapon but about the threat to civilization that its power represented. To be sure, Truman, at whose desk the buck famously stopped, always took the responsibility himself for having made the decision, but General Groves said, "As time went on, and as we poured more and more money and effort into the project, the government became increasingly committed to the ultimate use of the bomb." So Truman's "decision" seemed to Groves basically a decision not to upset the decision already made.

Truman's first public statements of justification for the nuclear bombardment reflected a low level of raw vengeance. "They [the Japanese] have been repaid many fold," he said on the day of the first bomb. On the day of the second, he said: "Having found the bomb we have used it. We have used it against those who attacked us without warning at Pearl Harbor, against those who have starved and beaten and executed American prisoners of war, against those who have abandoned all pretense of obeying international laws of warfare." Perhaps this was not the most propitious moment for an American president to refer to the "international laws of warfare."

The war with Japan was drawing to a close; the Allies had conducted six months of devastating firebombing raids on Japanese cities. Japan was effectively defeated, but it had sturdy cultural barriers against the supposed dishonor of surrender.

While Truman was in Potsdam in late July, attending the conference with Churchill and Stalin, the word came that a test had succeeded "beyond expectations" and that the atomic bomb would be ready for use in the first days of August.

If there ever was an occasion in which a statesman should have risen to the highest level of moral consideration, for mankind and for the vast future, this was it. The key point was that nuclear weapons represented, as scientists kept explaining to the political leaders, something radically new, and that the possible destruction resulting from their further development extended to civilization itself, and to all mankind. The first explosion in the New Mexico desert and the bombs exploded over the two Japanese cities were mere anticipations of developments to come, of virtually unlimited destructive power. But that would have been a very hard message for an engaged leader of a nation at war to assimilate. To have decided not to use the weapons, after they had been developed in the multiyear two-billion-dollar Manhattan Project, and with the Japanese even when defeated refusing to surrender and fighting fanatically to the last man—as the Allies had discovered in the fighting on Iwo Jima and Okinawa as they approached the home islands—would have been a decision of the utmost difficulty. A chief executive's formal and explicit obligation is to the nation he heads, and to its people; the decision presented itself to Truman as first of all a way to save American soldiers' lives by ending the war and making unnecessary that invasion of the islands.

The history of nuclear weapons since this unfortunate beginning has had this fortunate surprise: that the weapons, elaborated and spreading in the arsenals of nations, have often been used as a threat, but they have not been used again as a weapon.

When it is said that the atomic bomb has never been used since 1945, one response is to say, yes, they have been—as a threat, like a pointed gun, explicitly and implicitly. They were used in this sense in the Truman administration during the Soviet blockade of Berlin in 1948, and then in the Korean War. They were used in this sense in the Eisenhower administration in ending the Korean War; in support of the French at Dien Bien Phu in 1954; in Lebanon in 1958; and in response to the Chinese threats to the islands of Quemoy and Matsu. And they have been implicitly threatened in multiple crises in almost every American administration since.

But none has been exploded on an enemy since Nagasaki.

On August 15, six days after the detonation over Nagasaki, Japan announced its surrender to the Allied powers, signing the Instrument of Surrender on September 2, officially ending the Pacific war and therefore World War II.

CHAPTER SIX

Containment

HARRY TRUMAN of Independence, Missouri, was the president whose decisions shaped the American grand strategy, the strategy of "containment," in what came to be called the Cold War. Dwight Eisenhower of Abilene, Kansas, was the president whose decisions first tested that grand strategy, and built it into the nation's continuing policies.

On Saturday, April 14, 1945, the new president of the United States, Harry S Truman, asked two men—Jimmy Byrnes and Henry Wallace—to accompany him to Washington's Union Station to meet the train bringing the coffin of the previous president, Franklin Roosevelt, from Warm Springs, Georgia. These two men had been chosen, presumably, because they represented a continuity with FDR—with New Deal liberalism in Henry Wallace's case; with the management of the home front during the war in Byrnes's case. But they represented something else as well, which the three men could scarcely have avoided being aware of: Each of the other two might have been standing there in Truman's place. Before the Democratic National Convention the previous summer, Jimmy Byrnes had been the leading contender for the vice presidential nomination. He had experience in all branches and levels of government that no one could match. Byrnes had been a congressman, a governor of South Carolina, and a senator; he had been appointed by FDR to the Supreme Court; he had resigned from the Court to administer wartime agencies; he came to be called the "assistant president"; he had accompanied Roosevelt to Yalta. It certainly sounded from his résumé as if Byrnes should be the one to be nominated as vice president—so much so that many key figures endorsed him and he asked a friend to nominate him. The friend was Harry Truman. When the switch came and Truman himself was to be the nominee instead of Byrnes, Truman had the awkward duty of extracting himself from his promise.

Byrnes was already a senator from South Carolina, an experienced senator, when Harry Truman came as a newcomer to that body, and Byrnes still had a tendency to look at Truman as a lesser figure, a recent arrival. And in 1945, even though he had been vice president, Harry Truman did not know much about the important Yalta Conference with Stalin and Churchill that Roosevelt had attended the previous February—but Jimmy Byrnes *did* know. Roosevelt had asked Byrnes to accompany him to Yalta, and Byrnes had taken notes. He could now instruct Truman about Yalta. Even though he had been vice president, Harry Truman did not know what that big secret Manhattan Project was all about, but Byrnes *did* know, and, along with Secretary of War Henry Stimson, he could tell Truman about the atomic bomb. On the day before this trip to Union Station, his first full day as president, Truman had conferred with Byrnes and all but promised to appoint him secretary of state.* Probably he should not have done that. In any case, Byrnes, whom he did appoint in July, was not going to be a subordinate who deferred gracefully to this chief whose authority he had a hard time acknowledging.

Henry Wallace had come even closer to becoming president. He had been Roosevelt's vice president in his third term, from 1941 to 1945. If he had been renominated he would have become president when Roosevelt died, instead of Truman; but even without that renomination, if Roosevelt had died just three months earlier, before January 20, 1945, Wallace still would have become president. Wallace and his supporters would have a hard time looking at Truman as anything other than a usurper.

Roosevelt, on replacing Wallace, had named him, rather oddly, to be secretary of commerce, and Wallace had, equally oddly, accepted, so there he was, when Truman had all the planets fall on his shoulders, as a member of the cabinet. Now it was *Truman's* cabinet.

These two almost presidents would be key figures in the disputes over foreign policy during the first year and a half of Truman's presidency. The story of those months would be one of growing disillusionment with the Soviet Union. When the war in Europe ended, three weeks after Truman succeeded Roosevelt, the American leaders, like the American people generally, still had something of the favorable attitude toward the Soviet Union generated by her enormous sacrifice and essential contribution during the war. But Soviet failure to keep to the Yalta agreements, and her insistence on domination of the nations of Eastern Europe, her intransigence about Poland, and Germany, and Iran, and the UN, were already causing American leaders at differing rates of speed to view the Soviet Union more negatively.

One of the first decisions Truman made was to proceed with the found-

---

* Dean Acheson said that Truman made the offer to Byrnes later, on the way back from the Roosevelt funeral (see *Present at the Creation,* p. 137).

ing of the United Nations in San Francisco, and coping with the Soviets in that setting was not easy. Stalin was persuaded, by American ambassador Averell Harriman, to send not just his ambassador but the Soviet foreign minister Molotov for the signing ceremony, and on the way to San Francisco Molotov had an exchange with the new president in Washington that would become a legend. Truman spoke bluntly and immediately about the Soviet failure to fulfill the pledges made at Yalta for free elections in Eastern Europe, and Molotov said he had never been talked to like that in his life. Thereupon, Truman—so the story goes—said bluntly, "Carry out your agreements and you won't be talked to like that." The story then goes that Charles "Chip" Bohlen, the American expert on Russia, who was translating, said that he never translated anything so happily as he did that riposte of Truman to Molotov. American diplomats like Harriman and Bohlen, who had close knowledge of and dealings with the Soviets, were already convinced of their unmovable intransigence, but Truman and Byrnes in the first days after the war still had some hope that cooperation with the Soviet Union might be possible.

Truman appointed Byrnes secretary of state, as he had said he would, replacing the handsome but vacuous Edward Stettinius, who had stayed through the founding of the UN. Truman, the newly minted president, took his newly minted secretary of state with him to the Big Three conference in Potsdam in July and August. That was certainly a big moment for Harry Truman: A few months earlier, he had been altogether ignorant of key facts and main players on the world stage, and he was now abruptly elevated to the pinnacle of world politics, coming in all his newness and ignorance not only to confer as an equal with Winston Churchill and Joseph Stalin but, because he was the only head of state, to preside. As we noted in the previous chapter, he tried to be the can-do American, working briskly through the agenda, getting "something in the bag each day." He was impressed with Stalin; his illusion that "Uncle Joe" was not unlike Boss Pendergast and could be dealt with man-to-man would persist and confuse matters into the year to come, leading to the notion that if he could send somebody—Harry Hopkins, Fred Vinson—just to talk to Uncle Joe, relations could be better. But that was a total illusion.

Whom did Truman have to help him at Potsdam? He left much of the detailed negotiating—on reparations from Germany, on the government of Poland, on the Baltic and Eastern European states—to Secretary of State Jimmy Byrnes; but despite his long résumé, Byrnes was almost as much a novice in this world as Truman. They both had the working politician's disdain for the Foreign Service and the State Department—those cookie pushers, as the cliché had it, with their striped pants. Averell Harriman, the millionaire public servant who had spent a year and a half as American ambassador to the Soviet Union and knew whereof he spoke—already a hard-liner—and Bohlen, a trained expert in matters regarding the Soviet Union, were not seriously consulted, but left at the margins. Two American politicians, both ex-senators, Byrnes and Truman, thought they could deal with world politics by personal deals, swaps, and compromises.

Truman did get what he wanted most at Potsdam—a pledge by Stalin to enter the war in the Pacific three months after the war ended in Europe. While in Potsdam, he received the news of the successful test of the bomb, and dropped the news of the bomb casually to Stalin (who already knew). And during that trip, he made the huge decision to use the atomic bomb. Both Truman and Byrnes thought the possession of the bomb would give the United States new leverage in dealings with the Soviets, but to their surprise, it didn't—at least not obviously. Stalin and Molotov made little deprecatory jokes about the Americans having the bomb in their pocket.

It fell to Byrnes to deal with the details of the first foreign ministers' conferences, in London in September and Moscow in December, and he did so without much reference to the State Department, of which he was the nominal head, or to the president, who was his nominal superior. And he found that it was not so easy to outdo Molotov and arrange the condition of affairs in Japan, or Finland, or anywhere else. In later meetings, Truman began to feel that Byrnes compromised too much with the Soviets, and he certainly failed to keep the president informed. A climax of these events involved the other almost president, Henry Wallace.

The "I should be sitting where you are sitting" problem with Henry Wallace was even greater than with Byrnes: Wallace's had been an even nearer miss; he had a much larger constituency, one that saw him as a link back to the New Deal; and he had radically different ideas about policy, which a considerable public shared. It made a very large difference in the course of human events that Harry Truman, instead of Henry Wallace, was the American president in the years to come. Wallace, whom Arthur Schlesinger, Jr., described as "perplexing and indomitably naïve," continued to believe against all evidence in a comparatively benign picture of the Soviet Union—by the summer of 1946, almost uniquely among the president's cabinet and advisers. In July, Wallace sent a letter to Truman, setting forth a full program for improved Soviet-American relations. It was not his territory, of course, but Truman, temporizing, sent him a noncommittal reply, promising to pass his comments on to Secretary Byrnes.

Then, in September, Wallace accepted an invitation to deliver a speech on foreign affairs at Madison Square Garden. Two days before he was to speak, he went to the Oval Office and personally showed his speech to Truman for his approval, going through it as he would a report, page by page. (Actually, he should have taken it not to the president but to the State Department—or perhaps one should say that, as secretary of commerce, he should not have been giving a speech on the core of foreign policy at all—but Wallace was marching to a different drummer.) Truman, preoccupied, nodded in apparent approval and somehow gave Wallace permission to say he agreed with the speech—or agreed to something. The point would come to be disputed.

Two days later, on the day of the speech, Truman, who often got into trouble with answers he gave too quickly at press conferences, held a press conference and got into trouble. Reporters asked whether he agreed with just one paragraph of Wallace's speech or with all of it. Truman replied he agreed with the whole speech, and when they then asked whether Wallace's speech was a departure from the policy with Russia that Secretary Byrnes was following, Truman replied too quickly, saying, no, it was not.

That evening, Wallace gave his speech in the bright pink atmosphere of a heavily left-leaning audience at the Garden; when the crowd booed some modest criticism of the Soviet Union, he omitted any further ventures in that direction. He gave his endorsement to Soviet spheres of influence in Eastern Europe. Of course the speech was worldwide news.

And so Byrnes, carrying on difficult negotiations in Paris to try to squeeze a smidgen of democracy into the Eastern European governments, found himself confronted with a view contrary to his own, presented by a fellow cabinet member. He and key senators Arthur Vandenberg and Tom Connally strenuously objected, saying the United States could not have two secretaries of state. Truman, recognizing his mistake, scrambled to recover by claiming that he had not meant to endorse the content of Wallace's speech but only the fact that he had the right to give it. That effort met hoots of scorn. *Time* magazine called it "a clumsy lie," and Clark Clifford, a newly important staff member, would write in his memoirs, "Even though I helped to draft it, I have to agree."

Truman tried to negotiate an agreement with Wallace to the effect that he would make no more policy speeches during the Paris conference, but then that letter Wallace had written to Truman back in July, even more critical of the administration's policy, was leaked. In response to this, Byrnes, Vandenberg, and Connally increased their attack. Back in Washington, Wallace blandly announced that he would keep on speaking on foreign affairs. On September 18, Truman, with his press secretary, Charlie Ross, had a two-and-a-half-hour meeting with Wallace, during which they expected him to resign, but the indefatigable Wallace instead tried to present part of his next speech and to argue policy. The next day, Byrnes teletyped a furious threat to resign. That night, Truman wrote—and this time mailed—one of his sizzling letters; this letter demanded that Wallace resign and assailed him with the vigor that Truman was capable of (these letters were, in the view of his staff, like the press conferences: trouble). The next day, this letter was recovered from Wallace; fortunately, it was never released. There are slightly differing stories about just how it was recovered, but Wallace behaved well in this matter and Truman's letter was destroyed; no one except Wallace ever saw it. And then on the following day, Truman asked, now in the calm and measured presidential tones he should have used in the first place, for Wallace's resignation, and Wallace sent a slightly snippy resignation, saying in it that he would "continue to fight for peace." And so one of the almost presidents was gone from the cabinet—but not from Truman's life or from national politics. There would be another chapter.

Dean Acheson, Truman's great collaborator and defender, made a sympathetically critical summary of Truman's performance in this case of the presidentially approved Wallace speech.

> Throughout this episode President Truman was naïve. This is not a serious indictment. In the first place he was still learning the awesome responsibilities of the President of the United States. It did not occur to him that Henry Wallace, as a responsible and experienced high officer of government, should not make a speech he had carefully prepared. Pleased that his permission was asked, he readily gave it without . . . worrying about the content of the speech. Years later he would order General MacArthur to withdraw a message that he had released but not yet delivered. Even after Mr. Byrnes' first message, he did not understand the deep damage that Wallace had done to the foreign confidence in the United States. It seemed a personal quarrel that could be patched up. Secondly, he was not good at the fast back-and-forth of the press conference. President Truman's mind is not so quick as his tongue. . . . [H]e could not wait for the end of a question before answering it. Not seeing where he was being led, he fell into traps. . . . This tendency was a constant danger to him and a bugbear to his advisers.

The other almost president would soon be gone, as well. Byrnes's fault was not so much policy disagreement as failure to collaborate. The president learned what he had done at foreign ministers' conferences from the newspapers; Byrnes sent no reports. Truman tried to remonstrate with him, but to no avail. Byrnes had submitted a resignation back in April 1946, to be acted upon at the president's discretion. Truman chose his successor long before the change actually took place. In the summer of 1946, Dwight Eisenhower, now, by Truman's appointment, chief of staff of the army, took an inspection trip to the Far East; Marshall was then in China, dutifully attempting the thankless and futile task of bringing together the warring Chinese factions. Truman asked Ike to inquire of Marshall whether he would serve as secretary of state when Byrnes left; Marshall, who always accepted these duties, said yes but that he could not conclude his efforts in China right away. Dean Acheson, who seems to have been the active head of the department during this period, wrote about the last half of 1946, "When Secretary Byrnes returned to Washington from a series of United Nations and foreign ministers' meetings . . . he had been absent almost continuously for six months."*

So in January 1947, George Marshall succeeded Jimmy Byrnes as secretary of state, and the first phase of the Truman presidency was over and the great period begun. As secretary of state, Marshall took the department seriously and organized it; Dean Acheson was undersecretary and a key figure; George Kennan, by Marshall's initiative, was asked to shape the new Policy Planning Staff. The administration and to a considerable extent the nation had now clarified its realistic picture of the Soviet Union. Truman as president had found his sea legs.

The great personal story of the Truman administration with regard to foreign policy then became the relationship between Harry Truman and Dean Acheson. Despite all the disdain eggheads had for some of his associates, Truman actually had—or came to have—an unusually able group around him in this field. George Kennan became the most widely known foreign policy thinker in recent American history, and served as the first head of the new Policy Planning Staff in the State Department. His successor, Paul Nitze, somewhat less well known, was also notable and influential. Truman appointed two great secretaries of state, George Marshall and Dean Acheson. Marshall, who was the most admired contemporary of both Dwight Eisenhower and Harry Truman, undertook, at Truman's request, the hopeless attempt to bring together the Nationalists and Communists in China; he then served as secretary of state for Truman for two

---

* Acheson, p. 210.

years, 1947–1949, and finally served as secretary of defense from 1950 to 1951. A number of other able men who had joined government in the New Deal or in wartime were given high posts. Robert Lovett carried over from the wartime administration and flourished under Truman, serving as secretary of defense during the Korean War. Many would add James Forrestal to the list of unusually able appointees, although the troubles of the job, as the first secretary of defense, finally unbalanced him. But the most distinctive subordinate to Truman in world politics was Dean Acheson, who was said to have been "more responsible for the Truman Doctrine than President Truman, and more responsible for the Marshall Plan than General Marshall."*

The close and surprising relationship between Truman and Acheson spoke well for both men—Truman, with his origins in a small town and on a farm and then in the rough big-city politics of Missouri, certainly did not go to any Groton, Yale, and Harvard Law as Acheson had done. Despite his not having attended any college, his failure as a haberdasher, and the scramble of his political career, Truman was able to bond with the products of the world of Ivy League colleges, eastern seaboard elites, and prestigious law firms from which Acheson came. Acheson was the son of an Episcopal bishop of Connecticut and the heiress to a whiskey fortune. He served as clerk to Supreme Court Justice Brandeis and joined a blue-ribbon law firm. And yet the two men formed as close a working relationship as any top figures in recent American history. Acheson was assistant secretary and then undersecretary of state in 1945, when Truman assumed the presidency. Acheson wrote in an early note, "The months since April 1945 had brought me into continuous and close relations with President Truman. My regard and affection for him had grown steadily."[†]

In the book that Acheson was to write in his retirement, *Present at the Creation,* about his career in the State Department, Truman is regularly celebrated, not only with respect but also with a touching affection. Acheson dedicated the book to "Harry S Truman, the Captain with the Mighty Heart." The last chapter, after the full narrative of his career in the State Department, entitled "Summing Up," includes as thorough an overview of Truman's qualities as a president as of Acheson's career as a diplomat. Of Truman as president, Acheson wrote, "Among the thirty-five men who have held the presidential office, Mr. Truman will stand with the few who in the midst of great difficulties managed their offices with eminent ben-

---

* Isaacson and Thomas, p. 22.
† Acheson, p. 184.

efit to the public interest."* He applied to Truman both the phrase that Shakespeare applied to Henry V before Agincourt ("A touch of Harry in the night") and the phrase from an Arizona tombstone ("Here lies Bill Jones. He done his damnedest"). Analyzing Truman's qualities, Acheson listed his capacity for decision making without regrets or second thoughts, as well as his drawing on and nurturing of others. "He was not afraid of the competition of others' ideas; he welcomed it. Free of the greatest vice in a leader, his ego never came between him and his job. He saw his job and its needs without distortion from that astigmatism."[†]

If Acheson's staunch loyalty to Truman was commendable and rare, Truman's to Acheson was perhaps even more so. In domestic politics, Acheson was certainly no asset; on the contrary, Acheson was a total political liability. His appearance (his mustache and his style) and his pedigree were almost as though designed to be offensive to senators and congressmen from the deepest hinterland—to those he called, revealingly, "the primitives." In his manner, he did not suffer fools gladly, and some of the fools knew it. And he could be blamed not only for the loss of China but, more distinctly and personally, for his extremely vulnerable defense of Alger Hiss—admirable, perhaps, in that he would not turn his back on Hiss, but by no means a help to an administration under assault for its alleged softness on subversives. Nevertheless, Truman's response to Acheson's unqualified testimony about Hiss was firm support, compounding his own taking the heat of disapproval when he traveled to Pendergast's funeral.

Acheson admitted that Truman, especially in the first days, made mistakes; he tended to be hasty, as though fearing that taking time to deliberate would be mistaken for indecisiveness, and he wanted to be decisive. In the first fall after the end of the war, when he was still in his first months as president, he abruptly canceled the Lend-Lease program, for which there was still a great need—a bad mistake. In the midst of his whistle-stop campaign in 1948, he accepted a proposal from aides that he send his friend Chief Justice Fred Vinson to Moscow to confer with Stalin in an attempt to reduce tensions—a foolhardy project, for which Vinson was totally unqualified. The radio networks were asked for time so that Truman could explain the plan. But when Secretary of State Marshall, who was in Paris conducting delicate talks on ending the Berlin blockade, heard about it, the message he sent by Teletype was vigorous enough to cause the president to cancel the plan immediately. Truman, as we have

* Ibid., p 729.
† Ibid., pp. 732–33.

seen, handled the break with Henry Wallace badly, saying he had read and approved the speech Wallace gave, which he had neither read nor approved. He said things in press conferences that he should not have said—notably about the use of nuclear weapons, as we shall see, in the midst of the Korean War. Despite his mistakes, said Acheson, he learned: He came to ask how long he had for a decision, to take that time to think well and to decide, and not to suffer second thoughts afterward.

Acheson presented this summing up of the accomplishments of President Truman, which were, of course, his own, as well:

> When the Truman administration found its footing in foreign affairs, its policies showed a sweep, a breadth of conception and boldness of action both new in this country's history and obviously centrally planned and directed. We had seen it in the early domestic policies of the New Deal and in our vast military effort in the 1941–45 war, but not before in foreign policy. The 1947 assumption of responsibility in the Eastern Mediterranean, the 1948 grandeur of the Marshall Plan, the response to the blockage of Berlin, the NATO defense of Europe in 1949, and the intervention in Korea in 1950—all those constituted expanding action in truly heroic mold. All of them were dangerous. All of them required rare capacity to decide and to act. All of them were decided rightly, and vigorously followed through.

In a well-informed book about the wise men of Washington in those years, it is written: "There are fifty-two monuments or outdoor statues in Washington honoring a wide assortment of long-forgotten as well as famous figures, but in the public spaces of the capital there is not so much as a park bench named after Dean Acheson."[*]

The time of peace after the end of World War II had been distressingly short. Already during the war, the seeds of a conflict had been sown between the great ally in the East and the Western powers. In March 1946, less than a year after the end of the war, the greatest leader of that previous effort, Winston Churchill, delivered an address marking the beginning of the next one. After crossing half of the country in the president's railroad car, with Truman joining him in playing poker and drinking whiskey, he made his famous speech at a small college in a little town in Missouri, with Harry Truman introducing him and sitting on the stage. He put the term *Iron Curtain* into wide circulation. "From Stettin in the Baltic to Trieste in the Adriatic," Churchill said, "an iron curtain has descended across the Continent."

[*] Isaacson and Thomas, p. 408.

An American who was following public affairs in those years after the end of the war will remember the alarming picture one could not avoid of a world in mortal danger from twin evils: the world-destroying power of atomic weapons, on the one hand, and the threat of the great power that had brought down that Iron Curtain on the other. How could the world make it through the years ahead without catastrophe? In August 1945, one learned that there was a new weapon, one of unimaginable destructive power. In 1946 and 1947, with the Soviets reestablishing hegemony in Eastern Europe, and definitely with the Communist coup d'état in Czechoslovakia in February 1948, one was forced to understand the menace of the Communist movement and the Soviet Union. The great ally in World War II, whose enormous contribution—essential contribution—to victory over fascism one had learned to appreciate, now revealed itself once more to be a cruel and ruthless regime that had worldwide ambitions. Once again, the essence of the Soviet Union, and the character of its leader, Joseph Stalin, would be revealed by the murder of millions of kulaks, by the purges of the thirties, by the relentless killing of any possible rival. In the simplified slogans in which alternatives were stated, in those days of deep foreboding, it was debated whether it was better to be Red than dead. It did not seem to be altogether absurd to think that those were the alternatives, and that it would be very difficult to get through the years ahead without some immense calamity.

In 1949, Mao and the Chinese Communists triumphed in China, with tremendous reverberations in American politics. In 1949 also, much earlier than Americans had expected, it was learned that the Soviets had an atomic bomb: It was not announced by the Soviets, but discovered by American flights detecting radioactive fallout and then announced by President Truman and confirmed by the Kremlin. Now there were the two superpowers both equipped with the bomb, facing each other. In 1949, Truman made the decision to build the still more horrific weapon, the thermonuclear hydrogen bomb. His decision to drop the two atomic bombs in 1945 had been almost an automatic outcome of his situation, as the inexperienced leader of a nation at war with the imperative to end it, and with the total expectation of those who had been involved with building the bomb that he would of course use it. This time was different. He really did make a more considered decision. There was deliberation in which the other side was argued. There were those in the circle around him who urged him not to develop the H-bomb—notably, the leading scientist, J. Robert Oppenheimer; the New Dealer David Lilienthal; and the key analyst, George Kennan—but he decided that if the Russians could build one, the United States had to build one also. The Americans tested an H-bomb in August 1952; the Soviets, again much sooner than Americans expected, did so in November 1953. The statements about the H-bomb's power—how many times larger than the Hiroshima bomb it would be—ranged up into staggering numbers. So now there were two giant powers with radically opposed social systems and universalistic pretensions, hostile to each other, and both equipped with weapons that now one could say even more forcefully could destroy civilization. How could the world make it through the years ahead without calamity? The policy of containment was put in place in the administration of Harry Truman, and President Truman took the first major actions in accord with that policy. They were his primary historical accomplishment, and the reason he ranks high among presidents.

The intellectual shaping of the policy took place beginning in 1946 and 1947 in exchanges among foreign policy professionals within the Truman administration, the most important of whom, initially, was George Kennan. Kennan was a Foreign Service officer who specialized in the Soviet Union; he was serving in Moscow in 1946 when the Treasury Department asked the State Department to explain why the Soviet Union was not willing to support the International Monetary Fund and the World Bank. And Stalin made a speech in February 1946 that drew a dire picture of the capitalist encirclement of the Soviet Union and of the inevitability of conflict with the capitalist powers that also cried out for interpretation. The State Department sent the questions to Kennan in Moscow and got a whopper of an answer, made particularly memorable because the whole thing—all 8,000, or perhaps only 5,500 words—was sent as a telegram, an "outrageous encumberment of the telegraphic process," as he admitted. In those days, telegrams were terse because they charged by the word; Kennan's long telegram, for all its verbosity in general, does in telegram style omit the article *the* in some places, although not consistently. Sometimes it sounds like an effort at English by a native speaker of a tongue without articles—Chinese, say. Thus he ended a summary paragraph with this sweeping statement, omitting the article before "Problem" and the first "greatest" but not the second: "Problem of how to cope with this force is undoubtedly greatest task our diplomacy has ever faced and probably the greatest it will ever have to face."

Problem of coping with the Soviet Union will be greatest task ever for American diplomacy because that nation's conduct did not spring from a response to anything the West had done or not done, or from any empirical situation, but from its own internal necessities. The leaders of the

Soviet Union had ideological prepossessions, said Kennan, that blinded them to empirical reality—in other words, to the facts of the world before them. Kennan linked the Kremlin's "neurotic" view of world affairs not only to its Marxist-Leninist ideology but also to the "traditional and instinctive Russian sense of insecurity" and even "Oriental secretiveness and conspiracy."

The Soviets, Kennan attested, are "committed fanatically" to the belief that there cannot be in the long run any "permanent modus vivendi" with the United States; it is from their point of view "desirable and necessary that the internal harmony of our society be disrupted, our traditional way of life be destroyed." "This is admittedly not a pleasant picture" was Kennan's unsurprising comment.

But Kennan argued that the Soviet Union, although not amenable to reason or gestures of goodwill, would be sensitive to force; he said that the Soviets were weak compared to the united Western world and that if they were resisted in the long run, they would prove vulnerable to internal instability.

The long telegram was widely circulated in the administration, chiefly by the secretary of the navy, James Forrestal, but biographers differ as to whether President Truman himself, the captain up on the bridge, even read it; it was produced and circulated by the crew working down below. Kennan later said he met Truman only once or twice and doubted that the president read anything he wrote.* But if the long telegram was read by everybody except Truman, he certainly did read the report—produced by two of his closest aides, George Elsey and Clark Clifford—that drew upon it and related it to policy. They took the analysis of the long telegram and, with further contributions from officials in the Departments of State, War, and Justice, the Joint Chiefs of Staff, and the Central Intelligence Group, as well as more from Kennan himself, they translated it into concrete policy recommendations. When he read the stark appraisal of Soviet conduct in that report, Truman called Clifford and asked how many copies there were. Told there were twenty, he instructed Clifford to gather up the twenty copies and give them all to him, and then he locked them away, so that for more than twenty years the existence of this report would be a secret. Whereas the long telegram had been written by one person and read by many, the Clifford-Elsey report was written by many persons and read by one—Harry Truman. This report made the explicit assertion that American policy should be the "restraining and confining" of the Soviet Union.

* Ferrell, p. 248.

In January 1947, Kennan produced, at Secretary Forrestal's request, a report entitled "The Sources of Soviet Conduct," which, although it was intended to be only a private government report, was published with Forrestal's permission as an article in *Foreign Affairs*, attributed to "X," and would become as famous as the telegram. In it, Kennan wrote that the "United States policy toward the Soviet Union must be that of a long-term, patient but firm and vigilant containment of Russian expansive tendencies." This "containment," by not allowing the Soviet Union to expand, would in the long run—not during the reign of Joseph Stalin, but at some future date—cause the Soviet Union and the Communist world to collapse from its internal contradictions. Indeed, after decades, that is what it did.

The first in the series of important decisions reflecting the policy of containment was the statement of purpose that came to be called the Truman Doctrine, and the aid to Greece and Turkey that accompanied and reflected it.

The economic conditions in England after the war—battered by "[f]ive years and eight months of war, much of it on the actual battle-line," as Ike had put it, were horrendous. Greece and Turkey were reported to be in a precarious state as a result of guerrilla activity, economic distress, and a feeble government. In early 1946, the British notified the State Department that they could no longer carry the burden that they had carried of support for the Greek government. Acheson had the State Department prepare a response. It was essential to bring Congress along, and now perhaps more difficult because in the 1946 elections the Republicans had gained control of both houses. At a session with congressional leaders from both parties, Secretary Marshall, "most unusually and unhappily, flubbed his opening statement." Acheson, who told of this incident, to his own credit, but let us assume accurately, whispered a request to speak.

> This was my crisis. For a week I had nurtured it. These congressmen had no conception of what challenged them; it was my task to bring it home. Both my superiors, equally perturbed, gave me the floor. Never have I spoken under such a pressing sense that the issue was up to me alone. No time was left for measured appraisal. In the past eighteen months, I said, Soviet pressure on the Straits, on Iran, and on Northern Greece had brought the Balkans to the point where a highly possible Soviet breakthrough might open three continents to Soviet penetration. Like apples in a barrel infected by one rotten one, the corruption of Greece would infect Iran and all to the east. It would also carry infection to Africa through Asia Minor and Egypt, and to

Europe through Italy and France, already threatened by the strongest domestic Communist parties. . . . The Soviet Union was playing one of the greatest gambles in history. . . . We and we alone were in a position to break up the play.*

When Acheson stopped speaking, there was a silence, and then the key figure, Republican senator Arthur Vandenberg, the chairman of the Foreign Relations Committee, told Truman that if he talked like that to Congress, they would pass the aid bill. He did, and they did.

In the speech announcing that action, Truman included a broader commitment: "I believe that it must be the policy of the United States to support free peoples who are resisting attempted subjugation by armed minorities or by outside pressures." In the custom of discourse since President Monroe, this broad statement of national purpose was given the name the Truman Doctrine. (George Kennan was not in favor of this sweeping commitment, which he said exemplified an unfortunate American tendency to make overly general and abstract commitments of this sort; Kennan would say each case would require specific investigation.) Truman went on to say that free peoples should work out their destinies in their own way, and that "our help should be primarily . . . economic and financial." It was not easy, but with Senator Vandenberg playing a key role, the Greek-Turkish Aid Act was signed by the president on May 22, 1947.

Even as the "doctrine" was being first applied to Greece and Turkey, the key figures in the administration were developing a still more ambitious project, a great plan for the revival of the economies of the devastated nations of Europe.

The Marshall Plan was one of those great victories that have a hundred fathers (while defeat is an orphan) to which President Kennedy would refer after the Bay of Pigs, employing the allegedly ancient saying that no one had heard of until he cited it. In a knowledgeable book, two public affairs writers who knew whereof they spoke wrote, "The plan was not Kennan's alone, by any means. Forrestal, Acheson, Bohlen, McCloy, Stimson, Harriman, and a few others, including General Marshall himself, all share paternity."† Ike might almost have been one of those many fathers. As the program of aid to Greece and Turkey was being considered in the upper reaches of the Truman administration in early 1946,

* Acheson, p. 219.
† Isaacson and Thomas, pp. 405–6.

according to Dean Acheson, there came from Dwight Eisenhower at the Pentagon (Ike was then serving, by Truman's appointment, as the chief of staff of the army) the proposal that they should include in their request funds for "other countries in need of bolstering"—this at a time when the need for bolstering was widespread indeed, as Eisenhower knew, having served after victory for most of the rest of 1945 as commander of the United States occupation zone in Germany. But the suggestion at that point, wrote Acheson, "was rejected because we already had more to deal with than the time available permitted." By early 1947, however, there came time to deal with the crying need in Europe, with the people in place to make it happen. The spring of that year was to be one of the stirring moments of great public action by the American government. Marshall was now secretary of state; Acheson was undersecretary; Kennan was head of the newly formed Policy Planning Staff in the State Department. One of those who should know—Clark Clifford—wrote that "this farsighted program . . . was almost entirely a State Department project."* But if that was true, it was also the case that the State Department's work took place in an environment of discussion in government offices and Georgetown parties, across the American establishment, including the persons named above. These were folk who had ties to Europe and were aware of its plight, and who were close enough to America's exercise of power in the war to see that there could be practical action to deal with that plight.

George Kennan, the brains behind this moment in American history, was an enthusiastic supporter of the emerging ideas of the Marshall Plan, as he had not been of the Truman Doctrine. Although Kennan had supported giving aid to Greece, he did not believe that the inclusion of Turkey was necessary, and he felt the sweeping language of the Truman Doctrine had the curse of overpromising universalism to which Americans are prone. The ferment now about economic aid to rescue Europe was a chance to rectify (thought Kennan) the overly broad commitment, and the excessive emphasis on military action, of the Truman Doctrine. This idea was finite, even though huge; it entailed the quite practical action of supplying Europe with the economic aid that would allow it to recover. And—a shrewd and essential point—it was not to be explicitly or purely anti-Soviet or anti-Communist (although it was to be implicitly and effectively so). The nations to whom the offer of recovery funds was made were all those "West of the Urals"—in other words, not only all of Western Europe but also the Soviet Union and her European satellites. Kennan

---

* Clifford, p. 143.

and Chip Bohlen, the experts who knew the Kremlin, had to keep reassuring the others that in the end the Soviet Union would not participate, or allow any government it controlled to participate, because of the openness that would be required of participating nations—and so it would come to be. "Stalin fell into the trap the Marshall Plan laid for him," a Cold War summary observes, "which was to get *him* to build the wall that would divide Europe. Caught off guard by Marshall's proposal, Stalin sent a large delegation to Paris to discuss Soviet participation, then withdrew it, while allowing the Eastern Europeans to stay, then forbade them—most dramatically the Czechs, whose leaders were flown to Moscow to get the word."[*] The shrewdness of this second point lay in that it kept the program from being understood as an anti-Soviet, anti-Communist undertaking, and it put upon the Soviets the blame for splitting the Continent when that happened. Although they sent delegates to the first Paris conference of European nations considering the plan, they abruptly withdrew on Stalin's order. Molotov would be sent to the first meeting of the nations in Paris but then would be abruptly called home, and Marshall Plan aid would flow to the nations of Western Europe only. The Continent would be split, but the onus for the division would rest not on the United States, but on Stalin and the Soviets.

Another shrewd point was that the plan would not be specified in detail by the United States, but, rather, was to be a response to a proposal, a request, made by European nations gathered for the purpose and making their own plans and allocations, to which the United States would then respond with helpful cash. The planners made sure that key Europeans knew about the offer, and Ernest Bevin, the British foreign secretary, in particular jumped at the chance. Foreign ministers assembled in Paris and talked about their needs. In the end, the United States would have to play a bigger role in making decisions for the distribution than had at first been envisioned.

Acheson stood in for Truman in a speech he was to give in Mississippi, offering what Truman described as "the Prologue to the Marshall Plan."[†] Europe and Asia were in a state of utter economic disaster as a result of the destruction carried out by both sides during the war, and the particular devastation of the defeated enemies Germany and Japan, and then the unprecedented fierce winters of 1945–1946 and 1946–1947.

[*] Gaddis, p. 32.
[†] Acheson, p. 228.

Marshall had been invited to receive an honorary degree and to speak at Harvard in June; and so Marshall presented the outline—not the details—of the European Recovery Program, a plan that would bear his name.

There is another name to add to the list of the Marshall Plan's fathers: the president of the United States, Harry Truman. Truman's role was at once small and essential. Clifford described the moment during the drafting of the key speech in the State Department when he said to the president that he should give the speech and that the proposal should be named the Truman Concept or the Truman Plan. Truman "smiled wryly" (wrote Clifford) and said no. "We have a Republican majority in both houses. Anything going up there with my name will quiver a couple of times, turn belly up, and die." A day or two later, Truman said it was going to be named for General Marshall. "The worst Republican on the Hill can vote for it if we name it after the general."[*] Harry Truman thus passed up a chance for his name to be remembered in a most positive association. The earlier Truman Doctrine is not a well-known positive symbol, but the Marshall Plan is—a unique example of efficacious action by government for human betterment on a large scale, which is often referred to: a "Marshall Plan" for this, a "Marshall Plan" for that. Those could all have been called a "Truman Plan" if the president had gone along with Clifford's proposal. But, as Truman said, maybe then they could not have gotten it enacted in Congress.

Truman's role, according to one biographer, resembled that "hidden hand" that has been credited to Eisenhower in his presidency.[†] He brought Marshall into the State Department, had the plan named for him, and aroused public support. At first, the Republican-controlled Eightieth Congress resisted this WPA for Europe, this "global New Dealism," but Truman established a Committee for the Marshall Plan, chaired by Henry Stimson, which fostered widespread support. About the effort, similar to the prewar Committee to Defend America by Aiding the Allies, Acheson made this observation: "Many private organizations, in the United States and elsewhere, protest, sometimes, against Governmental action, sometimes against social or economic disadvantages. But few organize privately to support Government, and fewer still organize to support policies or measures not directly beneficial to their group."[‡]

[*] Clifford, p. 144.
[†] This paragraph draws on Ferrell, p. 255.
[‡] Acheson, p. 240.

Then, as the Marshall Plan was making its way through the difficult passage in the Eightieth Congress, the Soviets inadvertently gave it a big boost. In February 1948, they swept into Czechoslovakia and took over that sympathetic, much-tormented nation in a bloodless but brutal coup. The Marshall Plan passed by bipartisan majorities in both houses and was signed into law in April 1948.

After the act was passed, Truman called Dean Acheson—then in a very brief retirement between government jobs—and proposed that he be the administrator. But Acheson talked him out of that idea—for a reason similar to Truman's declining to name it after himself. They still needed appropriations from Congress and the support of Senator Vandenberg in particular, so Truman chose the Republican businessman Paul Hoffman, who proved to be a good administrator. When it ended in 1952, the Marshall Plan had spent thirteen billion dollars, which was a lot of money in those days, on a recovered Europe.

The Marshall Plan was, and is, regarded as a national and international act of unusual wisdom and generosity, despite the fact that it was designed and sold to Congress and the public with mixed appeals to mixed motives. The national interest is never absent in the actions of a nation, and so it was present in this case; the United States needed a revived Europe as a trading partner. And even though the plan was not explicitly designed to be an anti-Communist effort, it did diminish the appeal of Communist parties in Western Europe and confront Soviet power with a stronger Europe. But there was also in the mixture some element of altruism and humanitarianism. A phrase that Winston Churchill used in another connection—about the Lend-Lease program of American aid to the Allies before the war—has seemed so appropriate for this later act as to be constantly, if erroneously, attached to it: "the most unsordid act in history." Dozens of commentators have said that Churchill applied that phrase to the Marshall Plan; that is wrong as to the fact but nevertheless right as to the sentiment. The Marshall Plan was even more unsordid than Lend-Lease.

At 6:11 p.m. on May 14, 1948, President Truman recognized the new Jewish state, which just hours before had been given the name Israel. It had just been proclaimed at 6:00 p.m. The United States was the first power to recognize the new state—before the Soviet Union or anyone else.

Truman's act was, to a quite unusual degree, his own doing, not the outcome of a staff consideration; in fact, almost all the key members of his administration were opposed to his action. Dean Acheson, not then in government, was opposed, as well as George Kennan, Robert Lovett, Dean Rusk, and all top figures in the State Department. James Forrestal and, most important, Secretary of State George Marshall, the man Truman admired above all others, were also opposed. In fact, the kernel of the drama was the stark confrontation between the president and his secretary of state. It was the view of Marshall, and of almost everyone else in the State Department, as well as of the opponents generally, that Truman was making this decision on the basis of domestic politics, at the behest of political advisers like Clark Clifford. It was thought that he was taking this action to secure Jewish votes in the election coming up in November—to carry New York City and therefore the state of New York. And in the critics' view, taking this action would, in addition to many other bad effects, destroy the American position throughout the Arab world, opening it to Soviet penetration.

The dramatic, crucial meeting on May 12—two days before decision day—featured Clifford, by Truman's instruction, speaking first, making the case for recognition, and then Marshall, growing red in the face, objecting to Clifford's even being at the meeting (this was an international issue and Clifford was a domestic political adviser) and then concluding with the sharpest dagger of any top official's statement in all of the Truman presidency: George Marshall said that if the president did this, "and if in the elections I were to vote, I would vote against the President."

This was a bombshell. If Marshall had resigned, it would have been disastrous for the as-yet-unelected Truman in the November election. After this stark, shocking moment, there had to have been painstaking consultations behind the scenes. Truman, who stood by his decision, did agree that the recognition would be de facto only, not de jure. Marshall never spoke to Clifford again, nor did he withdraw his comment to Truman, but in the end he did not resign.

Truman insisted he had other, humanitarian reasons for what he did. His old friend and business partner Eddie Jacobson came to see him often during this period, and on one occasion he brought with him an ardent Zionist to describe the plight of Jews in the aftermath of the Holocaust. Jacobson had managed to arrange a secret meeting between Chaim Weizmann, the most distinguished Zionist leader and a gently persuasive advocate, and Truman. We may surmise that Truman's acting as he did came from a mingling of motives, high and low; it must have been partly political, but it was also to some extent moral—decided on the merits. When David Ben-Gurion, the first prime minister of Israel, met with Truman once years after he had been president and told Truman that his actions had given him an immortal place in Jewish history, tears sprang into Truman's eyes, to the extent that reporters afterward asked Ben-Gurion why the president had been crying when he left him.

Back to 1948. What did Stalin think he was doing by blocking Allied access to Berlin? Whatever it was, it did not work. And Harry Truman once again was the prime mover of his administration's remarkable and successful response. At a crucial early meeting, he said, "We will stay. Period." And we did stay.

A defeated Germany had been divided into four zones, for the victors in the war, with France generously included. Berlin was 110 miles into the Soviet Zone, but the city was to be governed by a four-power arrangement. Britain and the United States joined their zones—Bizonia—and then later the three free nations joined their zones to make one unit, West Germany, the implicit threat of which was no doubt a source of Stalin's unhappiness. In mid-June, the Soviets turned back freight trains bearing coal, then passenger trains, and then all vehicles on the Autobahn that were headed for Berlin. On June 24, 1948, for whatever reasons, Stalin shut down all access by land between West Germany and the German capital; the Soviets totally blockaded Berlin, denying access by land or rail. (June 24 happened to be the day, back in the United States, that the Republican National Convention nominated Governor Dewey as its candidate for the fall election.) The military governor of Germany, which for a time after the war had been Dwight Eisenhower, was now Gen. Lucius Clay, and Clay ordered that the city be supplied by plane on June 25, but he did not expect this to continue; it did not seem possible that a city of two and a half million people could be supplied for very long exclusively by air with all that it takes to live.

The story of the Berlin blockade is a case study in responsible decision making. There were those who felt there was nothing that could be done but to give up the difficult, fragile effort to sustain a Western presence, under Soviet pressure, deep in their zone. But giving up Allied rights in Berlin would leave two and a half million more persons consigned to Soviet control; all those throughout the world who were watching would lose faith in the United States as an ally, and the Western alliance, just coming into being, would be stillborn. Something had to be done.

But the obvious alternative—to take some kind of armed action in response to the Russian blockade—was fraught with the other big difficulty: that it would invite a war, which it was everyone's prime interest to avoid. Clay wanted to mount a convoy with troop protection to ram through the blockade, but Robert Lovett and Dean Acheson did not think Stalin was bluffing; Acheson told about an effort Clay made in April to send a train through, which the Soviets shunted onto a siding, where it remained for a few days before it "withdrew rather ignominiously." The Russians were not bluffing. At this point, the United States had an atomic bomb it should not and could not use, and otherwise a much-depleted armed services; avoiding a military exchange had to be a primary criterion.

Some advisers suggested retaliatory actions elsewhere in the world— closing the Panama Canal to Soviet ships, blockading Vladivostok— but it was clear that such measures would certainly increase tensions and risk war, while they almost as certainly would not achieve Russian acquiescence.

The Allies did have access to Berlin by air. Although no rules had been agreed to for access by land, there was an agreement, signed in November 1945, for three twenty-mile-wide air corridors to Berlin. To stop the flights, the Soviets would have had to commit a blatant act of war, with devastating consequences. They could not claim that cargo planes carrying "Vittles" were some kind of military threat, and they could not stop them without shooting them down. So the flights began, and they increased in number and capacity. Planes were brought in from the Far East and from around the world. The British contributed their planes and pilots. In June, when the airlift began, the phone log of key adviser Robert Lovett read "Can feed by air. Cannot furnish coal." But by the time winter came, the airlift had been so enlarged that it could furnish coal, and everything else the Berliners needed. One day in April 1949, after ten months of expanding the airlift, the planes for one day brought nothing but coal. By then, it had reached the point where Western Berliners were now better supplied than they had been before the airlift began. Runways at Tempelhof Airport were improved and Berliners built a new airport. The use of the best cargo plane for the purpose, the C-54, was increased. The RAF joined the USAF in a combined task force. At the height of the airlift, when Berlin was being fully supplied, a plane would appear above the city every three minutes and forty-three seconds.

The airlift continued, despite the daily dangers, right smack through the presidential campaign of 1948, and this operation was decided on and guided by the president personally more directly than other great acts of this time. From late summer until the election in November, the daily report on the airlift was mingled with the turmoil of campaigning at whistle-stops across the country.

David McCullough has written about President Truman's distinct role in the Berlin airlift:

> In making his decision, for all the political heat and turmoil of the moment, Truman had consulted none of the White House staff or any of his political advisers. Indeed, throughout the blockade, as George Elsey would recall, the White House staff "had no direct role whatever in any decisions or in the execution of any of the carrying out of the airlift." There was no talk of how the President's handling of the crisis would make him look, or what political advantage was to be gained. And neither did Truman try to bolster the spirits of those around him by claiming the airlift would work. He simply emphasized his intention to stay in Berlin and left no doubt he meant exactly what he said.*

Finally, in May 1949, in an exchange with a newsman, there was a signal that the Soviets were ready to give up. They tried to extract something in return, but the Allies had no reason to concede anything. And so the blockade ended, after ten dangerous and remarkable months.

A new foreign policy required a new military. Clark Clifford, the Truman assistant who played a big role in making it happen, gave a summary. "Consider this achievement: in less than three years President Truman established the Department of Defense, the United States Air Force, the Central Intelligence Agency, the National Security Council, the position of Chairman of the Joint Chiefs of Staff, and the first foreign aid agencies."†
Truman brought this about because he considered an orderly government to be of major value, and he thought the multiple competing services made for a wasteful arrangement. Dwight Eisenhower, who was serving, by Truman's appointment, as chief of staff of the army from November 19, 1945, to February 8, 1948, supported the reorganization because, as we have seen, his experience in the war reinforced his commitment to unity of command and integration of the services. He knew from the most pertinent experience that there should be one commander in a theater and that modern warfare demanded the coordination of air, sea, and land forces. Generals Marshall and Bradley broadly supported these principles also: a single, integrated military, with a single commander.

The reordering of the military was not, however, easy to achieve. The opposition to his original proposals by the navy, including James Forrestal, who was then the secretary of the navy, by powerful congressmen

* McCullough, p. 631.
† Clifford, p. 147.

attached to the navy, and by the marine corps and its supporters was ferocious. Forrestal, who had also served in this position during the Roosevelt administration, was the most difficult negotiator; he had an ally in Congressman Carl Vinson, the obdurate chairman of a key congressional committee and a passionate supporter of the navy's interest—a battleship would be named for Vinson while he was still alive. Eisenhower, although clear from the start about the more desirable outcome, was more willing to compromise than were the representatives of the navy and marines. Finally, the National Security Act of 1947 was passed and signed into law by Truman; while it fell far short of the integration Truman and Eisenhower wanted, it still was a major piece of legislation. It set up the new position of secretary of defense, who would head the National Military Establishment, or NME (which was renamed the Department of Defense in 1949), and created the air force, now independent of the army; the Joint Chiefs; the CIA; and the National Security Council.

Truman wanted Robert Patterson, the secretary of war, to be the first secretary of defense, but Patterson preferred to return to private life. So whom would he appoint? Ironically, he chose James Forrestal, who had been the strongest and most difficult opponent of the whole reordering of the military. That led to the irony and tragedy of Forrestal. After he took over in the Pentagon as the first secretary of defense, Forrestal discovered that his views were changing; he found that he agreed more with Eisenhower and the generals and less with his old companions in the navy. He supported a further reorganization, enacted in 1949, which now downgraded the separate service departments, so that they were no longer independent executive agencies, but subordinate sections of the Department of Defense, and demoted the secretary of the army (formerly the secretary of war), the secretary of the navy, and the new secretary of the air force, so that they no longer had cabinet status or direct access to the president.* This further reordering also created the chairman of the Joint Chiefs.

In February 1948, Dwight Eisenhower resigned from the service to spend three months writing his book about the war, *Crusade in Europe,* and then to take his one civilian job, president of Columbia University. In December 1948, Truman asked Eisenhower to come to Washington for

* Those who when young had learned the acronym STWAPINACL as a way to remember the cabinet members and departments in the order of their establishment now had this mnemonic device shattered by the removal of the *W* and the *N* and the addition of a *D*. Soon the *P* would be gone also, with the demotion of the Post Office Department. And later the elevation and demotion of others and the addition of a Department of Homeland Security would bring unrememberable chaos.

"two or three months" to serve as military consultant to the first secretary of defense, James Forrestal.

All this was the military side of the new "pattern of responsibility"—to use a phrase Acheson used—of the United States' role in the world. Put less positively, it was a major part of the creation of the "national security state" decried by some. The other elements would be the increase in the supply, power, and delivery system for nuclear weapons, and the huge increase in the defense budget, starting with the Korean War in 1950.

Forrestal's mental illness led to his resignation in 1949 and then to his death, when, leaving a passage from Sophocles' *Ajax* open on his desk (" 'Woe, woe!' will be the cry/No quiet murmur like the tremulous wail/Of the lone bird"), he leaped out of a hospital window. Truman appointed as his replacement Louis Johnson, a West Virginia politician and American Legion leader who had been a fund-raiser for his 1948 campaign—not a good appointment. But later he appointed George Marshall, who served Truman and the country yet again, and Robert Lovett—excellent appointments.

George Kennan was succeeded as head of the State Department's Policy Planning Staff by Paul Nitze, whose outlook differed enough that in a book about the two of them, he was called the "hawk," while Kennan was the "dove." Where Kennan was a ruminative, nuanced thinker, an excellent writer, who would soon be disagreeing with many actions taken in the name of his own theories, Nitze was a much less complicated person, a straightforward, clear, and energetic activist, and a hawk indeed. In April 1950, he and his staff produced the most famous of National Security Council documents, NSC-68, which presented a blunt picture of a Soviet threat that required a large military buildup. Kennan's productions were the work of one man, writing and thinking alone; Nitze's production was the work of a committee, and showed it. The circumstances in which the document was produced were changed from the immediate postwar era: Now the illusions about the Soviet Union were gone, its menace established by her domination of her neighbors, with the Czech coup of February 1948 as the most recent and blatant example. As of August 1949, this Soviet regime now had an atomic bomb—the American monopoly was over. And the much more destructive thermonuclear dimension was already in prospect. So now, in this new situation, Nitze and his cowriters really beat the drum for a strong military response. Although they assumed or called for continuing production of atomic bombs, they argued for a buildup of conventional military power that would make those bombs less central.

For years, NSC-68 was a secret, but now one can read it, and if one looks at this famous document today, years after it was composed, one is startled to discover how unqualified, how stark, and how absolute it is—one might almost say how simple-minded. In any case, it is not marked by nuance, subtlety, or discriminate judgment. When Acheson wrote about it, he had a slightly embarrassed, slightly apologetic tone. He admitted that the document was hyperbolic, but he said that its purpose was "to so bludgeon the mass mind of 'top government' that not only could the President make a decision but that the decision would be carried out."* So it is written in mind-bludgeoning prose. Describing his own speeches built on NSC-68, Acheson wrote, "The task of a public officer seeking to explain and gain support for a major policy is not that of a writer of a doctoral thesis. Qualification must give way to simplicity of statement, nicety and nuance to bluntness, almost brutality, in carrying home a point."† So the Soviet Union is bluntly described as seeking absolute domination and promoting "slavery." In NSC-68, whereas the United States has a "purpose," the Soviet Union has a "design"—somehow the document manages to load the word *design* with sinister overtones. "The fundamental design of those who control the Soviet Union and the international communist movement is to retain and solidify their absolute power." The document goes on to state, "The implacable purpose of the slave state to eliminate the challenge of freedom has placed the two great powers at opposite poles."

NSC-68 was thus more of a work of advocacy, even of propaganda, than of original and fundamental analysis. It was an effort to persuade the government to support the massive expansion of military power that Nitze and Acheson felt was necessary. Actually, as has been written, NSC-68 was aimed at one person: Harry Truman. Truman was inclined to be a fiscally conservative budget balancer, and Acheson and Nitze did believe a costly military buildup was necessary. Nitze, at Acheson's direction, did not include in NSC-68 any estimate of the cost of the recommended military buildup, but its supporters estimated the cost to be as much as fifty billion dollars annually. At that time, the budget was thirteen billion a year, so the unstated size of the increase in military spending to do what NSC-68 rec-

---

* Robert Dallek, *The Lost Peace: Leadership in a Time of Horror and Hope, 1945–1953* (HarperCollins, 2010), p. 299.
† Acheson, p. 375.

ommended was more than triple the previous budget. Truman appointed a committee to examine whether such a buildup was necessary, and before it reported its findings, the outbreak of the Korean War—interpreted as an aggressive move by the Communist powers—gave NSC-68 a boost. The expenditure on the military would be markedly increased in the early 1950s, not precisely as a result of NSC-68 but, rather, of the Korean War, and what it was thought to indicate about the Communist "design."

The most lasting expression of the Truman administration's "pattern of responsibility" and policy of containment was a multilateral mutual defense treaty among the nations of the North Atlantic. The North Atlantic Treaty represented a sharp break with the whole sweep of American history back to George Washington—the determination to avoid peacetime alliances with other nations, for which Jefferson provided the inevitable adjective, "entangling." The United States was not to be entangled in the constant power struggles of other nations, particularly in Europe. Even in World War I, as the United States made its first great entrance back onto the world stage, it insisted on keeping its armed forces separated from those of the other nations fighting the same enemies. In World War II, the United States did join in an alliance, but that was a wartime necessity, not yet thought to be a continuing break with the long American tradition. But now Truman and company, and America's friends in Europe, were proposing such a break.

The initiative, in this case, arose abroad. Worry about a revived Germany led England and France to join in the Treaty of Dunkirk, and then threats and actions by the Soviet Union and Communist parties in European nations led them to join with the Benelux nations in March 1948 in the larger Brussels Treaty. Meanwhile, talk had begun with the U.S. secretary of state, George Marshall, about the participation of the giant across the ocean in the emerging mutual defense treaty. The treaty, a huge departure in American policy, would finally be signed in April 1949.

There was to be sure much resistance in Congress to a treaty obligation that would seem to require American arms to defend a long list of nations. Congress, of course, jealously guards its constitutional obligation and right to declare war—it has not defended it very well perhaps against the executive branch of its own government, but in this instance at least it did not want to be swept into war by a treaty obligation to some other nation. Delicate conversations had to define just what the obligation was in this mutual defense treaty. Acheson described the cultivation of Senator Vandenberg, the Republican chairman of the Foreign Relations Committee in the Eightieth Congress in 1947–1948. The Constitution requires that treaties be adopted with the "advice and consent" of the Senate. "Senators are a prolific source of advice," Acheson would write, "but most of it is bad."* But with careful cultivation, Vandenberg was brought to giving good advice. On July 21, 1949, the Senate voted 82–13 for ratification—Senator Robert Taft and a small band of isolationists were the only opposition. To be sure, the actions of the Soviet Union prodded the senators to vote for it, due to the Berlin blockade, the continuing apparent worldwide menace posed by the Soviets, and particularly because of the shock caused by the coup in Czechoslovakia in February 1948.

The nations of the North Atlantic left it to the big partner to pick the military commander, and there was no doubt whatever whom Truman would pick. He called upon the man who had led their forces to victory in World War II, Dwight Eisenhower. Ike would now be the agent preserving the victory won in 1945 from the new threat, the ally in that war, the Red Army. In October 1950, Truman rescued Ike from his uncomfortable post at Columbia University by asking him to accept appointment as the commander of the NATO forces, with headquarters in Paris. Truman put it in the form of a request; Eisenhower, as he always did, had Truman recast it as a command and a duty.

Ike began his service with a whirlwind trip to eleven European capitals in January 1951, giving encouraging talks at every stop. A key problem was the participation of German troops. The idea of rearming the Germans, who just five years earlier had swarmed across the Continent, was very difficult to accept. But without German participation, the European force could not begin to match the Red Army. The idea of rearming *in general* was hard to accept. But the Soviet menace was fearful enough to supply the motive. Eisenhower was the voice. And American participation provided the key element—a guarantee of American force, including the bomb.

Before he went to Paris, Eisenhower had a famous talk with Taft, the Ohio senator, son of a president, leader of the conservatives, and—more to the point for this conversation—the almost certain candidate of conservative Republicans for president in 1952. Ike was being constantly pushed to become a candidate for the presidency. One of his considerations was what would happen if the Republicans won in 1952, as in general he hoped they would—but which Republicans? He wrote out a statement that he said he would announce publicly if Taft gave the right answers to his

* Ibid., p. 266.

question. The statement was that he would not run for president. The question was whether Taft would support full American participation in NATO. Taft did not give the right answer, so the written statement was torn up and thrown away, and Eisenhower did become a candidate, did defeat Taft for the Republican nomination, was elected, and did serve as president.

Truman's final and most complete presidential comment on containment and the Cold War came in his last State of the Union message, sent to Congress on January 7, 1953. This document, Truman's last gasp, deserves to be better known than it is. The reason it has been neglected is obvious: Truman was by then the lamest of lame-duck presidents; both his party and his candidate, Adlai Stevenson, had been defeated in the election in November, and Truman and his policies were thought to have been a major reason for the defeat. The attention of the political world was now focused on the incoming president, the war hero Dwight Eisenhower, who would take office in a fortnight. Truman's approval rating was as low as any president's ever has been; he was yesterday's news, on his way out. He did not go to the Capitol to give the message orally; he just sent it to be read by a clerk, the way presidents used to do before Woodrow Wilson began the modern practice of presenting the message in person. But no matter who presented it, the message was very much worth listening to.

After an account of his administration's domestic accomplishments, Truman gave his view of what lay on the horizon of world politics and American policy. There was, of course, an analysis of the Communist threat. He made clear that the threat was, as the response must be, more than military: it was "a challenge partly military and partly economic, partly moral and partly intellectual, confronting us at every level of human endeavor and all around the world."

In an interesting paragraph, he described the European unity that he and Dwight Eisenhower had had a hand in developing, and suggested that it had lasting significance:

> It sometimes happens, in the course of history, that steps taken to meet an immediate necessity serve an ultimate purpose greater than may be apparent at the time. This, I believe, is the meaning of what has been going on in Europe under the threat of aggression. The free nations there, with our help, have been drawing together in defense of their free institutions. In so doing, they have laid the foundations of a unity that will endure as a major creative force beyond the exigencies of this period of history. We may, at this close range, be but dimly aware of

the creative surge this movement represents, but I believe it to be of historic importance. I believe its benefits will survive long after communist tyranny is nothing but an unhappy memory.

His description of the way containment would play out would be prophetic:

As we continue to confound Soviet expectations, as our world grows stronger, more united, more attractive to men on both sides of the iron curtain, then inevitably there will come a time of change within the communist world. We do not know how that change will come about, whether by deliberate decision in the Kremlin, by coup d'etat, by revolution, by defection of satellites, or perhaps by some unforeseen combination of factors such as these.

But if the communist rulers understand they cannot win by war, and if we frustrate their attempts to win by subversion, it is not too much to expect their world to change its character, moderate its aims, become more realistic and less implacable, and recede from the cold war they began.

And so, eventually, it would be.

Dwight Eisenhower did not run for president primarily to contest Harry Truman's foreign policy; on the contrary, he agreed with most of it and had been one agent carrying it out—as army chief of staff from 1945 to 1948, as adviser to Secretary of Defense Forrestal from 1948 to 1949, and then as supreme commander of NATO. His strongest foreign policy reason for running was his disagreement with Taft and Hoover over a new isolationism, over Fortress America. With regard to domestic policy, he did have reservations about Truman and the New Deal, and he did believe it was not healthy for one party to be so long in power, so he allowed himself to be persuaded that it was his duty to run, but a large part of his objective was accomplished when he defeated Robert Taft for the Republican nomination. But then, having done so, he had to cross the street to Taft headquarters and promote common cause and defeat the Democrats. And Taft and the right wing had an already-established attack on the policy of containment.

The objection to containment was that it seemed passively to accept the Soviet domination of Eastern Europe and indeed the Communist world itself, in the Soviet Union and now, since late 1949, in China. An extreme example of this attack on containment could be found in a characteristic thrust from Richard Nixon, the rising California politician who was rather uncomfortably joined to Ike on the Republican ticket. Nixon charged that the Democratic nominee, Adlai Stevenson, had a "Ph.D. from Dean Acheson's Cowardly College of Communist Containment." The real stink bomb in this formulation, the adjective "cowardly," directly modifies only that imaginary "college," so Nixon was able to insinuate that Acheson and containment were cowardly without directly saying so. Presumably, containment was cowardly, in this view, because it seemed to these critics not to stand up bravely to the Communist empire and to strive to overturn it, but only to contain it. The anticontainment view, put forward noisily by *Time* and *Life* magazines, as well as by Republican politicians, was that the aim of policy should be not to contain but to "roll-back" the Communist tide and to "liberate" the nations of Europe under Soviet sway. The 1952 Republican platform put the point, as platforms do, with flagrant bluntness, condemning the "negative, futile, and immoral policy of 'containment' that abandons countless human beings to a despotism and godless terrorism."

It hardly needs to be said that these attacks on containment as being cowardly, bankrupt, static, and immorally neglectful of the peoples under the Soviet yoke reflected a radical misunderstanding of the policy of containment either as Kennan presented it or as Truman applied it, or, indeed, as it would in the end be carried forward, after the hoopla of campaigning was over, by the Eisenhower administration itself. Kennan had been one of the earliest and best-informed critics of the Soviet Union and the Communist movement after the war. But he was also fully aware that an all-out war between the two superpowers with their atomic weapons would be an utter catastrophe; so the problem of policy was how to oppose the Communist world without bringing on that war.

Kennan also had been aware, as not many American political leaders were, of the way U.S. policy would affect the inner workings of the Soviet Union. He would spell out objections to the liberationists' proposal: "even if it did not lead to war (as it probably would have done) [it] would almost certainly be exploited by the Soviet leaders as an excuse, internally, for not agreeing to any sort of liberalization or any modification of the intensity of the cold war. It was bad enough for the Soviet leaders to be committed . . . to the overthrow of *our* government. For us to be committed to the overthrow of *theirs* would be to justify all that had ever been said in Moscow about the evil designs of the capitalist powers against the peoples of the Soviet Union."*

But of course the obvious objection to the liberationists' rollback

* Kennan, vol. 2, pp. 101–2.

theme was that in a pinch the proponents would not act on it, and that their leading some in the "captive nations" to believe that they would so act would have damaging effects. When Secretary John Foster Dulles would hold forth about liberating "captive nations," Ike would remind him to say by peaceful means, but Dulles did not always remember to say that. When in October and November 1956 a student demonstration in Budapest led to a widening revolt throughout Hungary and its pro-Communist government fell and the Hungarians began to liberate themselves, Soviet tanks then rumbled into the city. The Hungarian revolt was a sad case study in why the United States should not trumpet an implied announcement that it would roll back the Communist boundaries and liberate "captive nations"—they would not do it. Eisenhower and Dulles expressed their sympathy for the Hungarian people, Dulles even saying the United States stood with them, but that was it. The only rollback in the fall of 1956 was that of Britain, France, and Israel in the Suez crisis.

Once Dwight Eisenhower was in office, however, that attack on containment began to fade away. As a book written by insiders puts it, Eisenhower was not keen to "overhaul policies that he had helped the Truman administration to design and implement. Within a few months of arriving in Washington, he was burying his campaign platform in a cemetery at the farthest edge of town. It was the start of a grand tradition in Cold War politics. Each time the White House switched hands . . . the new president reverted toward policies of his predecessor that he had denounced on the stump."* Eisenhower rolled back any rollback and liberated his policy from liberation.

Six weeks after Eisenhower was sworn in as president in January, there came a much-anticipated event: Joseph Stalin died. When terrified underlings finally ventured into his room on March 1, they found Stalin collapsed on the carpet, unconscious. Summoning doctors was a problem because he had had his doctors imprisoned, charging them with a plot; no doubt, given Stalin's record, they were on their way to being executed. An understandably nervous new set of doctors were summoned the next day, but Stalin's condition worsened, and he was declared dead on March 5. A clutch of Soviet officials—Khrushchev, Beria, Molotov, Bulganin, Mikoyan, Malenkov—acted jointly, and jockeyed for the succession, with Georgy Malenkov at first in the forefront. The others, aware of Beria's habits, got him eliminated in the old Soviet pattern. But there

* Thompson, p. 150.

were some signs of a new line of conduct. For example, they freed the old doctors—they knew there had not been any doctors' plot.

So both superpowers had new men at the top. Did that mean containment had a new shape? Eisenhower responded to positive hints from the new Soviet leadership with an address—arduously worked out in a back-and-forth with his advisers—entitled "The Chance for Peace." Delivered to the American Society of Newspaper Editors on April 16, this address was an overture to the Soviets, proposing that in the new circumstance the two sides agree to restrict the expenditures for nuclear weapons and devote themselves instead to improving the standard of living of their peoples.

"Let us seize the chance for peace," Ike said. The speech received wide and strong approval in the American press, in England and in Europe, and also among those to whom it had been chiefly addressed, the new leaders of the Soviet Union. The new Kremlin leaders published Ike's speech in full, including the passage that claimed that the Cold War was Stalin's doing, and then published a thoughtful rejoinder in *Pravda*. It did appear for a time that there might be a chance for a major change in the Cold War, with a diminution of the nuclear confrontation.

But it did not happen. Why not? A distinguished Cold War historian, Melvyn Leffler, tells the story in the chapter "A Chance for Peace" in his book *For the Soul of Mankind*. Both sides did have some genuine desire to seize the moment of new leadership to begin that relaxation of tensions. But both sides also were heavily constrained by an ideology that kept this from happening. Professor Leffler wrote, "After Stalin's death the ray of hope that the Cold War might assume a different trajectory sparkled briefly, but then went out. Ike declared that there was a chance for peace but did little to make it a reality. Why? Fear and Power provide the answers."*

Truman had said that Ike would find that governing was not like being in command in the army; he would say do this and do that and think that it would be done, but it wouldn't. Not if he didn't follow it and keep pushing, that is. That would be particularly true in international affairs, and especially with respect to the Soviet Union. The resistant currents in his own government would be strong, and the Soviets would have their own contending currents. So aligning the inclinations of the two nations to

---

* Melvyn P. Leffler, *For the Soul of Mankind: The United States, the Soviet Union, and the Cold War* (Hill and Wang, 2007), p. 147.

negotiate a lessening of tensions and a slowing of the arms race would not have been easy. And it did not happen.

Ike, despite his friendship just after the war with General Zhukov and his interaction with other Soviet leaders, sometimes seemed to hold an unusually absolutist anticommunism, going a notch or two further than Harry Truman. In his inaugural address, Ike had described the Communist enemy with an extra jolt of the negative:

> The enemies of this faith [in the "deathless dignity of man"] know no god but force, no devotion but its use. . . . Whatever defies them, they torture, especially the truth. Here, then, is joined no argument between slightly differing philosophies. . . . Freedom is pitted against slavery; lightness against the dark.

It sometimes seemed that Eisenhower saw this battle against slavery and darkness in such stark terms as to obscure our common humanity—to interfere with the human links that would have allowed for a shared attack on the new worldwide problem of civilization-destroying weaponry. The extreme to which his anticommunism could sometimes go is suggested by his version of the common assertion of the time—that one would rather be dead than Red. He told the English ambassador that he would "rather be atomized than communized." Such an overwhelmingly negative view of Communist domination—that it was worse than the vaporizing of civilization itself—did not leave much room for even a minimum shared purpose with that enemy.

On the Soviet side, the question was whether the death of Stalin and the awareness of the destructiveness of thermonuclear weapons would cut deep enough for old Bolsheviks to renounce the doctrine of the inevitable war with capitalism. Malenkov did briefly come to that fresh conception, but the other new leaders sat on him, and the old ideology prevented the undertaking of a common purpose with the capitalist enemy.

Two days after Eisenhower held forth in his "Chance for Peace" speech, John Foster Dulles gave a quite different speech to the same audience of newspaper editors, and he took a very different line, with typical Dulles references to the Kremlin as a "vast power" that was "possessed by men who know no guidance from the moral law."

Presumably, Secretary Dulles believed he and his government, by contrast, were guided by that moral law. But when it appeared that the democratically elected Prime Minister Mohammad Mosaddegh in Iran might come to rely on the Communist party, the Eisenhower administration, through the CIA, helped to overthrow him and restore the Shah. That happened in July 1953, not long after "The Chance for Peace" speech. Having found this way of conducting foreign policy, with a CIA now equipped to carry out such covert operations, the administration did it again in Guatemala, where a reform government, popularly elected, under Jacobo Árbenz Guzmán introduced social reforms and threatened the United Fruit Company; Eisenhower and Dulles allocated three million dollars for the removal of Árbenz, and in July 1954 he was overthrown. It was tempting to employ this means elsewhere, but the attempt was not successful in Indonesia in 1958 or in Cuba in 1960. It may be that the CIA was involved in plans to assassinate leaders—Castro, Lumumba, Chou En-lai, Trujillo—but it is neither known nor not known (in the event, we are not supposed to know) whether any such efforts might have been explicitly ordered by the president. The moral law apparently could be stretched not only to allow these interventions but also to allow lying to protect them. Eisenhower would learn in the incident with CIA flights in the U-2 plane over the Soviet Union in May 1960 that if one is caught in such lying, it could be awkward indeed. In that sorry episode, near the end of his presidency, the Soviets shot down the American U-2 plane, captured its pilot, and set a trap for the American president. When Eisenhower issued the false cover story about a weather plane, Khrushchev gleefully pounced and kept exploiting his advantage until he broke up the summit in Paris by walking out of the talks on May 16.

Although its leader pointed to the chance for peace, the Eisenhower administration did not adapt its policies to that possibility. Professor Leffler writes, "The United States would not negotiate a ban on nuclear weapons, would not agree to limit strategic armaments, would not recognize the People's Republic of China, would not accept a communist victory in all of Vietnam, and would not settle the German question except on its own terms."* And the Soviet leaders did not want to appear weak.

Eisenhower made two further efforts to qualify containment with an agreement with the Soviet adversary: In December 1953, he gave a speech, entitled "Atoms for Peace," to the UN, and in July 1955, at a four-power summit in Geneva, he proposed a mutual aerial-inspection program, which gained another catchy title, Open Skies.

In the "Atoms for Peace" speech he proposed a specific program in which the nuclear powers (now including the UK as well as the United

---

* Ibid., p. 148.

States and the Soviet Union) would donate and share the materials for peaceful nuclear development through an International Atomic Energy Agency. The idea received an enthusiastic response in the UN hall and a positive response around the world. The Soviets appeared to be interested; in New Year's greetings, Malenkov indicated their willingness to talk.

But again Fear and Power interfered: Dulles and Eisenhower not only were not ready to negotiate limits on nuclear weapons; they were in that very period increasing the American reliance on those weapons in their "New Look" policy.

The Open Skies proposal in 1955, a last-minute spectacular ginned up for a summit at Geneva, was also well received around the world, including by Bulganin from the Soviet leadership, but at the cocktail party after Eisenhower presented it in Geneva, he received a swift education in current Soviet realities: Khrushchev said to him with a mirthless smile, "I don't agree with Bulganin." Ike learned two things in that moment: that the Open Skies proposal was not going to fly, and that Khrushchev, not Bulganin or any of the others, was now the commanding figure in the Soviet hierarchy. Open Skies was not really a balanced proposal; it had been much easier to accept in the more open society of the United States than, given the difference between the two societies, in the closed society of the USSR, which would have been giving up much more.

Eisenhower's version of containment contrasted itself to Truman's by claiming to have a new approach, a New Look, at the core of which was a greater reliance on nuclear weapons and a diminished reliance on "conventional" weapons, and therefore a lower cost. Dwight Eisenhower, on coming into this new field of politics, turned out to be a wholehearted believer in annually balanced budgets and fiscal austerity. One of the significant patterns of his life starting after the war in 1946 was his acquiring a cluster of new friends among the nation's wealthiest businessmen—the head of Coca-Cola, Robert Woodruff; the president of CBS; the chairman of the board of U.S Steel; and the president of Standard Oil. He was comfortable with them, and they shared a common outlook. Now he discovered he also shared a common outlook with the man he appointed as secretary of the treasury, an executive of the Mark Hanna company, George Humphrey, who famously said that unless the budget was balanced the United States would have a depression that would "curl your hair." Eisenhower had not known Humphrey before bringing him into his cabinet, but he became as responsive to his views as to those of any other adviser, and he made Humphrey a member, as the treasury secretary had not been before, of the National Security Council. So the avoidance of hair-curling depressions was given voice in the highest councils of American foreign and military policy. And the budgetary restriction became a reason for the heavy reliance on nuclear weapons. Ike and his advisers believed that continuing the buildup of conventional forces that Truman had begun—after the Soviets had the bomb and the Korean War broke out—would be devastating. Eisenhower wanted a policy that could be carried out over a long period. He reduced the expenditures for defense. Every service was cut, except for the Strategic Air Command, which now moved to the center as the carrier of the atomic bombs on which policy now relied. Where Harry Truman's last budget had asked for $41.2 billion for the Department of Defense, Eisenhower shrunk that budget to $35.8 billion and asked for only $30.9 billion for the first fiscal year for which he was responsible, 1955.

The U.S. military policy was, in a Dulles phrase, to threaten "massive retaliation"—retaliation "at places and with means of our own choosing." Relying on the threat of nuclear weapons instead of on conventional arms meant, in another memorable phrase, "a bigger bang for a buck."

Dwight Eisenhower had a heart attack in September 1955, fortunately at a time of relative calm in world affairs. Although at first there had been doubt that he would run for reelection in November 1956, he did run and won handily. In his second term, President Eisenhower and his country faced the full-fledged nuclear threat. The Soviet Union now had atomic bombs, had tested thermonuclear bombs, had long-range bombers capable of reaching the United States, and would soon acquire missiles that could deliver nuclear strikes on the United States in half an hour. In August 1957, it launched the first successful intercontinental missile, and in October another missile helped put *Sputnik,* the artificial satellite, into orbit, causing a general uproar and a widespread clamor for an American response (Ike was not as impressed as most others were by this feat).

The primary American response to *Sputnik* was an attempt to improve American education, particularly in math and science, through a National Defense Education Act. At the same time, there were pressures for an increased military buildup. A study commissioned by the president, the Gaither committee, reporting in November 1957, found that the Soviet Union, with only one-third the GNP of the United States, was matching the United States in defense production, and was pulling ahead. All the services and related industries seized on the report and sought increased spending. The demands for more bombs, for more bombers, for fallout shelters, for aircraft carriers, for research on behalf of more missiles and satellites were very strong and came not only from Democrats and the services and related industries but also from within Eisenhower's own administration. The argument for military "diversity," for "flexible response," for the ability to fight "limited war" arose on all sides, including within the administration itself. It is to be doubted that any other president could have resisted to the extent that Ike did. Eisenhower was able to resist huge pressures for additional expenditures for three reasons: First, he was himself a general with a war experience no one could match; second, he recognized the uselessness of the redundant extras that the military-industrial complex wanted to build—about the piling up of still more bombs, he asked, "How many times could you kill the same man?"—and third, he knew from U-2 overflights (to which he did not want to refer publicly) that the claimed Soviet military expansion was much exaggerated. Khrushchev would say that the Soviets were turning out missiles like sausages, when in fact they had a grand total of six. So the last years of the Eisenhower administration, the late fifties, was a distinctive period in the Cold War: it was a time of unique danger, because the United States, by Ike's doing, had a military policy that relied centrally on nuclear weapons. It was also a period in which the United States abstained from the crash program of military expenditures that many were insisting was required; that abstention was also Ike's doing. Although he did not stop the piling up of redundant bombs that continued throughout the Cold War, he did stop the further expenditure on fallout shelters, soldiers, ships, more missiles, more bombers, and more bombs that many wanted.

Eisenhower's presidency would end with a disappointing anticlimax. He and Khrushchev almost achieved a major breakthrough for peace, but they failed to do so. Both men were at fault in causing the effort to collapse. Eisenhower made the mistake of granting permission for one last U-2 flight over the Soviet Union, and the Soviets shot the plane down; Eisenhower then gave out a cover story that was false, and Khrushchev had the pilot and the plane to show that it was false and gleefully exploited his advantage. In the last years of Eisenhower's presidency, Khrushchev made his bumptious visit to the United States, and where he pounded the table with his shoe on TV, and then after the U-2 affair, he broke up the Geneva summit.

Containment was, by its nature, a policy for the long haul. Its requirement was patient firmness over time; its premise was that if the Soviets were stymied and confined in their efforts to expand the Communist world, kept within their own boundaries, thrown back on their own resources, that in time the limitations of their society would lead to some moderating changes. Keeping the Soviet empire contained, resisting its expansive inclinations without war or appeasement, put in place in the presidencies of Truman and Eisenhower, would be the thread running through the varying policies of nine presidents, for forty-five years, until the collapse of communism in 1989–1991. In the end, it was not the capitalist United States that would collapse from its internal conditions, but the Soviet Union and its Communist world.

A citizen back at the beginning would have been astonished indeed to know that the world would make it through four and a half decades of Cold War without a maximum catastrophe, without any expansion of the Communist empire, and without a major war. It would have been hard to believe that the dilemmas would be resolved, as fully as such things can be, given the complexities of history, by the breach in the Berlin Wall and the falling away of the nations dominated by the Soviet Union in 1989, then by the collapse of the Soviet Union itself in 1991. In those forty-five years, there had been no nuclear war, no use of nuclear weapons, and no expansion of Soviet totalitarianism beyond the boundaries reached in the early postwar period. Of course, there were many wrinkles and complications, but in the very large picture one could say that the policy put in place by the Truman administration and built into bipartisan continuity by the Eisenhower administration—the "pattern of responsibility," to use Acheson's phrase—did what its proponents said it would do. Containment worked.

CHAPTER SEVEN
Choosing a President

HARRY TRUMAN'S ascent to the presidency in 1945 and 1948 was, twice, a surprise; Dwight Eisenhower's coming to be president, in 1952 and 1956, was, twice, utterly unsurprising.

They came into the presidency in four sharply different ways: a quick trip from Capitol Hill to the White House on an April afternoon; an astounding victory overturning all predictions; a hard-fought factional battle in a long-subordinated party; a blowout reelection.

In 1952, the convention battle with Senator Taft for the Republican nomination was the real contest for Ike; the victory over the Democratic nominee that followed was relatively easy. And in 1956, there was no contest. A speechwriter for Eisenhower's Democratic opponent in 1956 said to another speechwriter, "I see you write that we have a spiritual crisis." The initial speechwriter replied, "That was the only kind of crisis I could think of."

There were plenty of crises in Harry Truman's day.

He first came into office as the result of two phone calls: one in 1944, when he was sitting on a bed in a room in the Blackstone Hotel in Chicago, was handed the phone, and heard the president's booming, indignant, and insistent voice asking whether he wanted to break up the party in the midst of a war (by declining to run for vice president); the other, nine months later, in April 1945, when in Sam Rayburn's office, he returned a call from Steve Early, the president's press secretary, who told him "in a strained voice" to come immediately to the White House. As he was later to say, he went to the White House thinking he would see the president and then found out it was he, that he was it.

In a letter to his mother and sister, Truman captured the surprise of that trip succinctly: "I had hurried to the White House to see the President, and when I got there I found that I was President. No one in the history of our country ever had it happen to him in just that way."

· · ·

No one in history had it happen to him in just the way it did the next time, either. His second ascent, in 1948, was a surprise of a quite different kind.

As the election approached, it was widely assumed—indeed, taken for granted—that Truman could not win. Given that circumstance, a number of Democrats wanted to nominate, instead of Truman, the great hero of the recent war, Dwight Eisenhower. This is perhaps a point to keep in mind when we examine later the relationships between the two men.

Arthur Schlesinger, Jr., wrote about the plight of Democratic liberals like himself as the 1948 election approached:

> We were stuck with the Democratic party and with a president who had no chance at all to win the election. . . . But who was the alternative to Truman? . . . [T]oward the end of March Franklin D. Roosevelt, Jr., urged Democrats to draft General Eisenhower. Others followed. No one knew how Eisenhower stood on the issues or whether he was even a Democrat; but his war-hero stature, his popularity and genial bearing were thought sufficient to assure a Democratic victory in November. Hardened political bosses—Jake Arvey in Chicago, Frank Hague in Jersey City, Harry Byrd in Virginia—joined the cry for Ike.

Schlesinger went on to say:

> Though Jimmy and Elliot Roosevelt had joined Franklin in backing Ike, their mother kept a skeptical silence. I regret to say that Jimmy Wechsler and I rather dubiously joined the boom. Truman's record, we thought, was not bad, and his intentions were good, but he was, Jimmy said, like a baseball player: "good field, no hit." Ike would at least assure the election of a Democratic congress and help liberal Democratic candidates like Adlai Stevenson and Paul Douglas in Illinois, Hubert Humphrey in Minnesota, Chester Bowles in Connecticut, Estes Kefauver in Tennessee, Lyndon Johnson in Texas, G. Mennen Williams in Michigan. So we went along with Ike.

The proposal that the Democrats should nominate Ike instead of Truman in 1948 did not come only from ADA liberals like Schlesinger. It is a significant feature of this boomlet that it came from a strikingly diverse range of Democrats, including ultraliberal Senator Claude Pepper of Florida and archconservative Senator John Stennis of Mississippi; Adolph Berle, the New Dealer, and Frank Hague, the boss of Jersey City; James B. Carey of the CIO and Senator Richard Russell of Georgia; and Governor Strom Thurmond of South Carolina, who in the event would organize the Dixiecrat walkout from the Democratic convention and run on its ticket. Jack Kroll, the political director of the CIO, announced his support for

Eisenhower. Boss Jake Arvey of Illinois said that perhaps that state's new governor-to-be, Adlai Stevenson, could place Eisenhower's name in nomination, and (to round out this little historical irony) another supporter for Ike in 1948 was Senator John Sparkman of Alabama, who would be Stevenson's running mate four years later.

Republicans also were interested in Eisenhower, but they were not as desperate for a candidate. Alfred Landon, the Kansas governor who lost to FDR in 1936, for example, was an early supporter of Ike. But there were two solid candidates for the nomination—Governor Thomas Dewey of New York, who had run a strong campaign against FDR in 1944, and the perennial conservative favorite, Senator Robert Taft of Ohio—and for a brief time a momentarily interesting new possibility, Harold Stassen of Minnesota. The GOP had strong candidates and felt sure of victory and therefore took Ike's demurrals seriously and dropped any idea of pursuing him for this election.

It is a significant indication both of Ike's suprapartisan appeal and of his own naïveté that at a later period he would inquire more than once of partisans visiting him to urge him into politics about the possibility of his being nominated by *both* parties. There you have the ingredients of the Eisenhower phenomenon—political leaders of all stripes urging his nomination in spite of the fact that they did not know what party he favored or where he stood on the issues of the day, and Eisenhower himself imagining that he might float into power on the wings of nominations by both parties.

There was another notable political leader who had endorsed Ike for the presidency without knowing where he stood: Harry Truman. Back in 1945, just plunged into the office and full of admiration for Ike, as was noted in an earlier chapter, Truman had at Potsdam abruptly told Ike he would support him for president—an episode that under changed circumstances would become disputed between them. Then, in July 1947, fearful that MacArthur might make a triumphal Roman emperor–like reentry into the United States just before the next year's Republican National Convention and run for president on the Republican ticket, President Truman, according to his own diary, "told Ike that if [MacArthur] did that Eisenhower should announce for the nomination on the Democratic ticket and that I'd be glad to be in second place, or vice president."

But if Truman had entertained such a possibility in previous years, he had no such view in 1948. He had borne the moon and stars and all the planets on his shoulders for almost a full presidential term and had grown into the job; he was no longer inclined to hand it to Ike—or to anyone else.

But the universal view was that he would lose it nonetheless.

Truman was furious with all those who wrote him off and sought to support Ike, but especially with the Roosevelt sons. In Los Angeles, Truman met with Jimmy Roosevelt and gave him a sizzling rebuke, one that a Secret Service man remembered and that Alonzo Hamby recorded in his biography of Truman: "Your father asked me to take this job. I didn't want it. I was happy in the Senate. But your father asked me to take it, and I took it. And if your father knew what you are doing to me, he would turn over in his grave. But get this straight: whether you like it or not, I am going to be the next President of the United States."

This Eisenhower boomlet of 1948 in the Democratic party was composed of two parts: positive on Eisenhower, negative on Truman. The negative on Truman was, in turn, composed of two parts: he couldn't win, and he wasn't what people wanted. This second part took various forms, depending on the politics of the person holding it. For those who had been devoted to FDR and the New Deal, the contrast now with his successor was stark, both in style and in policy. Back in 1946, Schlesinger had written to his parents, "Truman has put on a performance of incompetence unsurpassed in my memory of U.S. presidents." A year later, he would write in *The Atlantic,* after Truman's first two years in the office, "Not only is he himself a man of limited and mediocre capacity, but after considerable hiring and firing he has managed to surround himself with his intellectual equals." Although those sneering dismissals had been considerably qualified by 1948—Schlesinger and company thought more of Truman after the enactment of the Marshall Plan in 1947 and a New Dealish State of the Union message in 1948—still the influence of Truman's pals, like right-wing Democrats John Snyder, his secretary of the treasury, and Ed Pauley, the oilman, plus the residue of that earlier appraisal, put them off. And there was no need to sort that all out because—according to the first part—he absolutely could not win.

And there, sitting somewhat uncomfortably in the president's chair at Columbia University, was Dwight Eisenhower, with his huge prestige from the century's most important war. This prestige came from the combination of his accomplishment in the war and "his popularity and genial bearing," as Schlesinger had put it in the passage quoted earlier. His leadership was established beyond all argument by his military career. He had been the successful executive in an enterprise that, unlike any factional struggle, all Americans shared, and that, unlike any effort in politics, business, the arts, or intellectual pursuits, had ends that were endorsed by every citizen. The leader of Allied forces in the final subduing of the Nazi armies, and above all the commander of Operation Overlord on D-Day, needed no further demonstration to fix in the public mind firmly and forever his skill, his decisiveness, and his leadership.

Despite all the earlier American resistance to standing armies and the democratic rejection of militarism, Americans had nevertheless often chosen to consider for their chief executive victorious generals in major wars and battles—sometimes even minor wars. Indeed, this had happened right from the start: The first president, the father of his country, was the victorious general in the Revolution. In later years, Americans elected Andrew Jackson, William Henry Harrison, Zachary Taylor, and—twice—Ulysses S. Grant. Major parties nominated Winfield Scott and George McClellan, and there was a movement in 1920 to nominate John J. Pershing. And Ike's war, World War II, dwarfed all those previous wars in worldwide significance. The other notorious American general from that war—Douglas MacArthur—would also be mentioned as a possible president, but whereas MacArthur's support was intense, it was also narrow. Ike's appeal was perhaps less fervent, but it was vastly wider. In his case, "his popularity and genial bearing" significantly increased his appeal. He was a general of whom it could be said, "I like Ike." Supporters pushing the candidacy of George McClellan in 1864 presumably did not make a slogan of "I like George" (or "I back Mac!"). Neither, for that matter, did supporters of George Washington. Nor did the supporters of any other general celebrate his grin. It was known—part of his appeal—that Ike's leadership of the Allied cause had included the tactful management of the differing personalities from the collaborating nations—a work of diplomatic skill. His personality, which one might see to be a standard American type, and which might otherwise have seemed rather colorless and ordinary, became in this great captain of the Allied armies enormously attractive. Given his superlative career, his ordinariness became a virtue; the victor in history's mightiest battles was a nice guy, too. For all his victories, he was not a man on horseback; he was personable and democratic. Richard Rovere wrote in *The New Yorker:* "Eisenhower, with nothing to give them but his smile, made a neat and unpretentious appearance before the high and mighty of Europe in the kind of jacket worn here at home by fastidious gas station attendants." Political scientists who summarized the polls concluded that, on the evidence, it was "highly probable that Eisenhower could have been elected President on either major party ticket in either 1948 or 1952." One might add that the same would have been true in 1956, had he for some reason postponed his entrance into politics—in other words, it would have been true in either party in virtually any political year. And all this was true, independent of any position on any issue. Those Democrats of all stripes in 1948 were seeking to nominate Ike even though they did not know whether he was a Democrat or not, or where he stood on any issue. One knew, by inference from his career, that he was an internationalist, not an isolationist, but on all other questions, Ike's positions were not known.

The Eisenhower boomlet of 1948 among Democrats continued right up until a fortnight before the convention, when he declared, "I will not at this time identify myself with any political party and could not accept nomination for any public office." Truman seized on the phrase "at this time" and said the statement was weasel-worded. But then three days later, Ike made a statement of the sort that is always associated with the Civil War general William Tecumseh Sherman (yet another general the public thought might be president), who truly did take himself out of consideration.*

Schlesinger wrote about the ADA liberals as they gathered for the Democratic convention in Philadelphia: "We were a particularly dispirited lot. The Eisenhower bubble had been (fortunately) pricked by the general's own Shermanoid statement four days earlier. There was no alternative to Harry Truman."

Truman's situation was hopeless. Let us count the ways. First, there were his defects and liabilities. The opinion reflected in the snobbish comments from Schlesinger quoted earlier was not confined to East Coast liberals, but widely held: Truman was seen to be a mediocre product of the Pendergast Kansas City machine who had accidentally succeeded to the presidency and who surrounded himself with cronies. Truman's voice, his appearance, and his associates stood in stark contrast to those of Franklin Roosevelt. His flat, staccato voice with its Missouri twang was a total contrast to the skilled aristocratic voice of the president people had become accustomed to for a dozen years. Truman was a very poor public speaker, racing through prepared texts, sawing the air with his hand, drastically inferior not only to the superb communicator he followed into the White House but also to the man with the smooth baritone voice who would run

---

* In 1884, when Sherman was talked about for the Republican nomination, he set a high standard for memorably unambiguous declination, which often is shortened: "If drafted, I will not run; if nominated, I will not accept; if elected, I will not serve."

against him in 1948. His appearance in newsreels and photographs, with his eyes magnified by strong glasses, was not distinguished.

He seemed to have responded with impatient ineptitude to a string of crises as the nation converted from war to peace. One might say that history was unfair to Truman on this count, since the Truman committee in the Senate had been warning about the need to prepare for reconversion from wartime to peacetime as early as 1943, but Roosevelt, the Congress, and the nation did not pay much heed, and the military was wary of even talking about reconversion while there was still a war to be won—so all the troubles the Truman committee had warned about came to pass while Truman himself was president. All the pent-up demand after years of wartime restriction with rationing, shortages, and price and wage controls spun out into one fracas after another in 1946. No president would have had an easy or graceful time disentangling the nation from its wartime controls and limitations, but Truman's style of aggressive simplification, of combat and condemnation, seemed particularly vulnerable. In January 1946, labor and management in the steel industry could not agree, and 800,000 steelworkers went on the biggest strike in history. In the months to follow, there were strikes in a long list of industries, coming to a climax in the spring with a nationwide strike in the coal mines, called by the egregious John L. Lewis, and, even worse, a nationwide railroad strike that brought commerce to a standstill. It was a siege of labor troubles longer and more costly than any other in American history. In response to the railroad strike, Truman issued an executive order seizing the railroads, and he threatened to draft the striking railroad workers into the army. In a moment of high drama, as he was addressing Congress to ask for the legislation to take this drastic step, he was handed a note that said the strike had been settled. He was cheered at the time, but when the legislation that would have allowed his proposal came to the Senate, having passed the House in the first wave of passion, Senator Taft persuaded the Senate and perhaps the nation that using the power of government to seize industries and draft strikers was not a good idea.

He was then faced with a hopeless complexity on the issue of whether to continue wartime price controls; by vetoing one bill and then signing another, he managed to offend all parties and concentrate the nation's anger at the sudden shortages and high prices on himself.

For those like Schlesinger, who strongly supported the New Deal, Truman's actions, particularly his appointments, looked like a severe falling off. One by one, the Roosevelt cabinet members departed. Harold Ickes, the irascible but excellent secretary of the interior, resigned in a huff in a dispute over his testimony to a congressional committee about Ed Pauley, the oilman Truman tried to appoint as secretary of the navy. The word *crony* came into wide use, fairly or not, in the discussion of Truman's appointments and associates. He did make good appointments in key spots—particularly in the State Department—but his dubious ones were bigger news. He appointed, for example, his poker-playing crony Fred Vinson to the Supreme Court and his apparently undistinguished friend John Snyder as secretary of the treasury. The departure of the last surviving pure-bred New Dealer, Henry Wallace, was accompanied by another Truman fiasco: Wallace gave a speech at Madison Square Garden that Truman said he had read but which, in fact, he had only glanced at, and which defended a foreign policy position at odds with Truman's. He had to ask for Wallace's resignation, and Wallace went on to lead a competing third party to his left.

The Democratic prospects were poor enough that the party had a hard time raising money, and sometimes radio broadcasts of speeches were cut off abruptly and an appeal had to be made on the spot to get the campaign train out of the station.

The result for 1948, many believed, was already foreshadowed in the meat-shortage election of 1946. The voters in that midterm election, unsettled by postwar troubles, had given the Republicans a big victory; for the first time since the days of Herbert Hoover before the Great Depression, the Republican party won a solid majority in both houses of Congress. Such a victory in the midterm elections was usually the harbinger of a victory in the presidential election to follow, and this midterm victory had been widely regarded as a defeat for the inept new president, Harry Truman. Democratic senator William Fulbright of Arkansas, a Rhodes scholar, even proposed that the presidency might be rescued if Truman would appoint the leading Republican internationalist, Senator Arthur Vandenberg of Michigan, as secretary of state and then resign. Since there was no vice president (because Truman had succeeded to the presidency, leaving his old office vacant), and since in those days the secretary of state was the next in the line of succession, Vandenberg would thus become president.* It is a sign of the desperately low regard for Truman that this proposal was not dismissed out of hand. It was not, however, well regarded

---

* Truman himself proposed the change, signed into law in 1947, that made the Speaker of the House—an elected official—next in line after the vice president, instead of the unelected secretary of state.

by Truman, who thereafter was given to referring in private to Fulbright as "Senator Halfbright."

And if Truman appeared to be extremely vulnerable, the Republicans had an outstanding candidate in Tom Dewey, the efficient and moderate governor of the nation's then largest state, New York, who had been reelected to that important post by the largest margin in history, and who in 1944 had come closest among Republicans to challenging FDR in his four elections. Dewey, a swift success all his life, was an internationalist, much harder for Democrats to beat than his conservative rival Robert Taft. He had supported the Marshall Plan, the Truman Doctrine, recognition of Israel, and the Berlin airlift. He was a moderate, with a better record on civil rights than many Democrats. He chose another attractive moderate, Governor Earl Warren of California, as his running mate, thereby comprising, for independents and Republicans who were not followers of Senator Taft, a dream ticket.

The Democrats, moreover, had not one but two splits in their ranks. On the Left, there was the new Progressive party, which would nominate Henry Wallace, who had been FDR's vice president up until the time Truman supplanted him on the ticket in 1944, and who had then become secretary of commerce. Wallace resigned from Truman's cabinet (actually, he was dismissed) in 1946 after a disagreement over foreign policy; the party he led would draw off left-leaning voters in disagreement with Truman over the developing Cold War. On the Right, meanwhile, the Truman civil rights program and then the dramatic liberalization of the Democrats' civil rights plank at the convention drove southern segregationists out of the party. All of Mississippi's delegation and half of Alabama's walked out, and the remaining southern delegates voted for the nomination of Richard Russell of Georgia, and even denied Truman the usual courtesy of a concluding unanimous nomination by acclamation. The southern Democrats then formed a rival party, informally known as the Dixiecrats, which nominated Governor Strom Thurmond of South Carolina, who would surely deny Truman the electoral votes of some hitherto solidly Democratic southern states.

And it was time. The Democrats had won four presidential elections in a row and had led the nation through the Depression and the war, but now that was over and it was time to change, time for the Republicans to win. Everybody thought they would.

Every pollster and expert said Truman would lose. But he upset everything and won after all.

Harry Truman would win a victory that is unique in American history. There had never been a totally unexpected victory like his, and (one may assert) there never will be another. Truman biographer Robert Ferrell would write, "It was the biggest political upset in American history. Among all the presidential candidates, from 1788 on, no one had come from behind and won in the extraordinary way that Truman did."*

It was not a case of not knowing who would win. On the contrary: Everyone was certain that they *did* know who would win—and they were all wrong. Not just most but *all* were wrong, and not just a little wrong but *totally* wrong. Every pollster failed to call the result; no one got it right. No political columnist, commentator, or editorialist said Truman would win—all were mistaken. *Newsweek* conducted a poll of the fifty most eminent political commentators, asking who would win; the score: Dewey 50, Truman 0. Nothing like that would apply in any other election—the supremely confident unanimity in error. Historians and biographers have enjoyed recounting the embarrassing mistakes pollsters, news organizations, and political commentators made in assuming that they knew the result of the election before it happened. The best known, of course, is the headline on the front page of the *Chicago Daily Tribune:* DEWEY DEFEATS TRUMAN. A smiling Truman held aloft a copy of the paper in a ubiquitous photograph. But there are many examples. *Life* ran a picture of Dewey on a ferry in San Francisco Bay, calling him "the next president." Columnists anticipated who the members of the Dewey administration would be and what policies the administration would follow; or they examined Truman as a study in failure, or they speculated about how the government would manage for the interim with a lame-duck Truman awaiting the inauguration of Dewey.

After the election, there was a uniquely widespread discussion of eating crow.

How had this miracle happened? What were the reasons for it?

First of all, it was a triumph of Truman's own grit. Second, there was Dewey's complacency, Republican overconfidence.

In a peculiar reverse-English sort of a way, the unanimous prediction of his defeat, the apparent utter hopelessness of his effort, worked to Tru-

* Ferrell, p. 268.

man's advantage. It furnished the dramatic setting for his gutsy back-to-the-wall battle, which, given the huge odds, was hard not to admire. And it lulled the Dewey team into a static, self-satisfied complacency that implicitly furnished Truman a convenient foil, and left his charges unanswered.

The transformation of Truman's public persona started with his middle-of-the-night acceptance speech at the Democratic National Convention. As in the election as a whole, so it was in that event at its start: Everything was against its success—and Truman triumphed anyway.

It was now July and terribly hot—after the Republicans had been in the same Philadelphia hall in a cooler time in June. There was no air conditioning. The hall was still decorated with the buntings from the Republican National Convention, which were now drooping. The delegates were dispirited, demoralized, depressed. They were wilted, and not just from the weather. The jokes ran to the funereal: We need not bourbon but embalming fluid. The convention was so poorly managed that wrangles on the convention floor kept the president of the United States waiting offstage for three hours. When he was finally introduced, it was prime time on the radio far out in the Pacific, such as on Guam, but not anywhere in the continental United States. On the East Coast of the United States it was at two o'clock in the morning.

But Truman, looking trim despite everything, came on with a bang: "Senator Barkley and I will win this election and make the Republicans like it—and don't you forget that." It was not elegant, but it was effective, rousing the delegates with his combative approach—and that would persist in the campaign to come. In the fighting speech that roused them from their torpor, he announced that he would call the Republican-dominated Eightieth Congress back into session on July 26—Turnip Day in Missouri—and give them a chance to enact the measures that their convention platform claimed they supported but that this Congress had never acted upon. (The Republican National Convention, with the Dewey forces in strength, had written a more liberal platform than the Congress, where Taft forces dominated, would enact.)

And he did bring the disgruntled congressmen back for a two-week session. As he expected, they served the Democrats' purpose by putting "failed to act" after a list of proposals the convention platform had claimed they supported. So Truman had recent obvious evidence of the theme with which he would go roaring across the country: the do-nothing, good-for-nothing Eightieth Congress.

· · ·

Then Truman undertook the most remarkable campaign by a sitting president in American history. He traveled almost entirely by train, in the special presidential car built for Roosevelt—the Ferdinand Magellan—at the end of a seventeen-car special train, crisscrossing the country, speaking again and again and again at multiple small places that Taft referred to disdainfully as "whistle-stops," with a few major speeches in bigger cities.

He found his style, putting aside the prepared texts, speaking extemporaneously or from notes only, formulating his thought in his own words on the spot, keeping eye contact with the audience, attacking the "do-nothing" Republican-dominated Eightieth Congress, reminding voters once again in pungent layman's language about the Depression and the New Deal. Truman absorbed information well, had a good memory, and had read a great deal, and so he could formulate brief extemporaneous speeches. His style certainly was not fancy, but it worked.

There were three major trips: fifteen days across the country to California; six days in the Middle West; ten days in the big centers in the East. Truman spoke five, six, seven, and even as many as thirteen times a day. He made six speeches in six separate locations before the train reached Dexter, Iowa—for the plowing contest, a major performance including the famous pitchfork he said the Republicans put in the backs of farmers—and then three more times that day. He spoke twenty-five times during four days in Texas, where no previous Democratic nominee had thought it necessary to campaign.

He spoke at each stop from the rear of the train to citizens gathered on the platform. He would begin with references to local characteristics and local persons, and then, after a pungent attack on the Republicans, would end by introducing Bess ("the Boss") and Margaret.

The epithetical bluntness that had seemed a fault in a president following the adept Roosevelt and coping with a nation reconverting from wartime to peacetime in his first two years now became, in a president fighting bravely with his back to the wall, a virtue. Whatever one might say about the simplifications, the Truman campaign had the merit of the candidate's wholehearted belief in what he was saying.

Truman finished his remarkable campaign in St. Louis. Biographer Robert Ferrell wrote of his last appearance with the particularity that makes a reader infer that he was there himself as a witness. "On some of the major speeches of the campaign the president also introduced the verve that came from offhand remarks, notably in the St. Louis speech that closed the campaign, in which he took over a huge audience and turned it into a raging Democratic mob."

If Truman's spunky campaign was the first reason he won, Dewey's complacent campaign was the next reason. Dewey's team made a huge strategic mistake. They were certain they were going to win, so they did not fight. That might be the summary of the campaign: Truman fought; Dewey didn't. Dewey's speeches were polished platitudinous appeals for national unity. He furnished a perfect implicit foil for Truman because he tried to float into office on the cloud of assumed victory. The assumption that he would win was so universal and so solid that Dewey campaigned like an incumbent, while Truman, in this reversal of roles, was campaigning like a challenger. Truman's administration certainly was vulnerable, but Dewey made almost no attacks on it, and gave virtually no answers to Truman's charges against the Eightieth Congress and the Republicans. Actually, the Eightieth Congress was not by any means all bad; it approved the Marshall Plan, for example. In a sense, Truman was campaigning not primarily against Dewey but against Taft—and Herbert Hoover. Dewey, meanwhile, seemed to think he would coast into the White House.

The whole drama of the 1948 election was still intact when it came time for Election Day, and then even after all the voting, when Americans gathered around radios that evening to hear the results.

Despite the attractive drama of the Truman campaign, it was still the solid conviction of even strong Truman supporters that Dewey would win. Schlesinger wrote that he and his band of liberals in Cambridge gathered about their radio "were surprised early on by the doughty fight Truman seemed to be putting on and by apparent Democratic successes in the Congress." All of those liberals he had listed as likely to be carried to victory by an Eisenhower nomination—above all Hubert Humphrey, as well as Stevenson, Paul Douglas, Lyndon Johnson, and the rest—would win. But even as Democrats absorbed that good news, it still did not mean that they thought Truman would win. Schlesinger wrote, "The thought never occurred to me that Truman might win."

When people retired that night, perhaps at an early-morning hour, the expectation was still that Dewey would be elected president, even though Truman had a lead and it appeared that Democrats might control the new Congress. Truman himself awoke in the middle of the night and heard the radio commentator H. V. Kaltenborn, in a voice Truman would thereafter often imitate, insisting that although Truman was leading, Dewey would surge ahead when the "late results" from the provinces came in. But that never happened.

When people arose on the next morning and turned on their radios, there came the astonishing news that the presidential race had not been settled—not only had Truman not conceded but he was still leading. The Democrats had won a strong victory in Congress, but it was hard to believe that the whole world had been wrong about the election for president and that Truman would win. Then, in midmorning, there came the excited announcement of a miracle: Ohio had gone for Truman, and Harry Truman was reelected president! Governor Dewey confirmed the unbelievable by conceding at 10:14.

Professors who taught an eleven o'clock class in the right time zones that morning had the privilege (or the sad duty—depending upon their politics) of informing their classes of what had happened. Schlesinger reported a class breaking into applause. At Yale, on the other hand, it was reported that a conservative economics professor, known for his support of the gold standard, came before his eleven o'clock class, bowed his head, and said with infinite sadness, "Gentlemen, Mr. Dewey has been defeated."

The election was not particularly close—24.1 million for Truman, 21.9 million for Dewey. Four years earlier, Dewey had received slightly more votes—22 million. Because the total turnout in 1948 was low, many assumed that many potential Dewey voters had stayed home and that if the turnout had been larger, Dewey would have won. But an investigation by the journalist Samuel Lubell found that these nonvoters were not predominately Dewey voters but included many apathetic Democrats, so that a larger turnout would not have meant a Dewey win but an even larger Truman win.

One major error that this campaign corrected was the notion that campaigns don't matter—that voters have their minds made up by the end of the conventions and that the campaigning that follows is just ritual. One pollster stopped polling almost before the campaign began, announcing that Dewey, for that reason, already had the election won. But it appears that in this election, at least as many as 15 percent of the voters were undecided with two weeks to go and made up their minds thereafter.

Although Truman had big and enthusiastic crowds from the start, and although they got even bigger and more enthusiastic as the campaign progressed, reporters covering the campaigns were still not disabused of their expectation that Dewey would win. They thought the crowds could be explained by historical curiosity more than by political conviction: Parents held their children on their shoulders so that they could see a president, and multitudes turned out when Truman's train came through for that same reason. But when election night came, it turned out that the crowds had been affected by the campaign after all—not only had they turned out to see Truman but they also had voted for him.

In percentage terms, Truman won 49.6 percent to Dewey's 45.1 percent. Truman's total percentage means that more Americans voted against him than for him, by a very thin sliver. On the other hand, if the Wallace and Thurmond votes are added not to Dewey's in the against-Truman box but, rather, to Truman's in the Democratic box, these Democrats of various stripes received 54 percent of the vote. But, of course, many of the split-party voters—particularly in the South—would not be even nominal Democrats much longer.

To look ahead: In the popularity of Ike department, one of the most impressive numbers in these election statistics would be the difference between this Dewey vote in 1948—21.9 million votes—and the votes for Eisenhower when he was running for the same office on the ticket of the same party just four years later: 33 million. In 1956, Ike would be reelected with 35.5 million votes, which would be more than his successor would receive from an enlarged electorate.

Back in 1948, in the one count that matters, Truman received 303 electoral votes to 189 for Dewey—a comfortable but not overwhelming victory. The electoral college is a bad way to choose presidents, but it usually does perform this service: It exaggerates the margin of the popular-vote winner so that there is a more decisive result. Not always.

Truman won Illinois, California, and—the last to come through on that stunning Wednesday morning—Ohio, all by less than 1 percent of the vote. If all three had gone for Dewey, there would have been one of those royal screwups made possible by our crazy electoral college system: Dewey would have been chosen as president, even while the majority of citizens had voted for Truman. But if only two of those close big states had gone for Dewey, we would have had that still more dreadful situation threatened by the electoral college system: The election would have been "thrown into the House," which had been Thurmond's objective all along. If Thurmond's Dixiecrats (officially the States Rights party) had carried just a few more of the once-Confederate states—say, Georgia, North Carolina, and Virginia—he would have accomplished that feat and the nation would have learned what an anachronism the "thrown into the House" provision of the Constitution really is. (Each state has one vote—Wyoming one, New York one—and they choose from the top three candidates. In this case, it would have been a choice among Truman, Dewey, and, by a nineteen-thousand-vote whisker, Thurmond rather than Wallace—not a scenario to contemplate with equanimity.)

Redistributing only 33,000 votes in those three big close states—California, Illinois, and Ohio—would have given the election to Dewey. But shifting not many more in other states—Michigan, Maryland, Indiana, Connecticut, all of which Dewey carried by less than 2 percent—would have given Truman an electoral college landslide of historic proportions. There were five states carried by the winner (the three key ones by Truman, two by Dewey) with less than 1 percent of the vote, and four more, all carried by Dewey with less than 2 percent. Still, it was not exactly a close election; look at the popular vote. It was skewed, as all presidential elections are, by the division of the voting by states and the counting by the electoral college. We would be in far better shape if our president were chosen by the national popular vote.

In contrast to the two Eisenhower victories to follow, Truman's win in 1948 was not only a Truman victory but also a party victory. The Republican-dominated meat-shortage, do-nothing Eightieth Congress, fiercely condemned by Harry Truman, was decisively overturned. The Democrats won back control of both houses of Congress by electing fifty-four senators, to forty-two by the Republicans, and 263 House members, to 171 by the Republicans. That congressional victory was not necessarily the result of riding on Truman's coattails; there were attractive candidates for other offices who may have had their own coattails. In Illinois, which Truman carried by only 31,000 votes, Paul Douglas, an economics professor from the University of Chicago, the candidate for the Senate, won by 400,000 votes, and Adlai Stevenson, the Democratic candidate for governor, who would be the presidential nominee in the two next elections, won by a huge 570,000 margin.

To look ahead, in the 1950s that public opinion giant, the popularity of Ike, would at last get its political expression, and in Eisenhower's two enormous victories the story would be very different from what it had been in 1948. In 1952, the Republican candidates for Congress would run over five million votes—and 15 percent—behind Eisenhower's total in the presidential race; in 1954, they would lose control of Congress. In 1956, Eisenhower would run ahead of his party's candidates for Congress by the astounding total of ten million votes. For the only time in modern political history and the first time since 1848, the victorious party candidate for president would fail to carry his party to control of Congress. In 1958, that party would lose Congress again, and overwhelmingly. In 1954, 1956, and 1958, for the first time in American history, a president would face three Congresses controlled by the opposite party. The Eisenhower years would not be Republican years.

Were the Truman years, if we may use that term, Democratic years? Only in part. In the two years of the Eightieth Congress, the other party did control Congress, and in the 1950 midterm elections—the elections that would be shadowed by the Korean War and by McCarthyism—the Democratic party would suffer losses, losing five Senate seats and twenty-eight House seats, but Congress would still be just barely under Democratic control. In this central event, the 1948 election, Harry Truman ran and won unmistakably as a partisan, a Democrat.

It is almost true to say that Eisenhower would win in spite of his party, while Truman would win because of his party. Has there ever been in American history any more partisan campaign than Harry Truman's in 1948? He reminded voters, with insistent repetition and much invective and exaggeration, about the sins of the Republican party—about the Dust Bowl and the Depression and Herbert Hoover and the alleged wretched neglect of the nation's needs by the Republican-dominated do-nothing Eightieth Congress.

And what he did was to bring back for one last hurrah the Democratic party as it had been defined by the New Deal. The reasons for Truman's victory in the groups that supported him can be summarized by saying that by his sheer grit he pulled together most of the old New Deal coalition.

After his victory, Truman impulsively said that "labor did it," which had a limited truth: He recovered the support of a considerable part of the labor movement, in spite of his earlier actions in the troubles over reconversion from a wartime economy to a peacetime one in 1946—his dealings with the striking railroad workers and coal miners. The Eightieth Congress did him the service of passing the Taft-Hartley Act, which constrained unions by outlawing the closed-shop and mass picketing and industry-wide strikes, by requiring cooling-off periods before strikes, by giving the president power to use injunctions when strikes threatened the public good; it was called by the unions, with characteristic exaggeration, a "slave labor" act. Whereas events involving labor early in Truman's tenure had worked against his popularity with unions, now they worked for him. He vetoed the Taft-Hartley Act; Congress then conveniently passed it over his veto. So in the campaign, it served Truman's purpose as one of the great sins of the Eightieth Congress.

Dewey and his circle blamed his loss on the farm vote, with some justice. There was, among the farmers, one of those quite particular grievances that elections sometimes turn on. Congress—the Republican-dominated Eightieth Congress, as Truman would not let voters forget—when rewriting the charter of the Commodity Credit Corporation (the agency that dealt with farm loans), had voted, as an economy measure, to prohibit the CCC from acquiring any additional grain-storage bins. Farmers had to store their grain in such bins to receive price supports. When that congressional action was taken in June, it had not been a problem, but by the time Harry Truman went to Dexter, Iowa, to point to the pitchfork that Republicans had thrust into the farmers' backs, it was known that there would be a bumper crop of corn and wheat in the fall, too large for the existing bins to handle. And the bumper crop would mean not gains but big losses. A Congress that would let that happen— a *party* that would do that—did not care for the farmer and might even endanger all price supports. Remember, said Truman, what happened to the farmer during the long Republican rule in the twenties. Truman's cause was helped by the bumper crop in the fall of 1948, which meant falling farm prices. Truman carried Ohio, Iowa, and Wisconsin—states that Dewey had carried when running against FDR in 1944—and six of the eight biggest corn-growing states.

Truman's planners had focused particularly on the West, and he made whistle-stops throughout the West, vigorously defending New Deal projects; in the end, he won every western state except Oregon—most important of which was California, a state he just barely carried.

Truman's support for the new state of Israel, controversial and difficult within his own official family, nevertheless helped him to hold the votes of Jews, who had historically supported the Democrats by a big margin.

The two splinter parties—which he almost never mentioned in his campaigning—not only hurt Truman but also helped him. They each drew 1.1 million votes, most of which, one may assume, given past patterns, would have gone to the Democrats. The Wallace vote, by subtracting half a million liberal New Yorkers, denied Truman the biggest prize, New York State, which went to Dewey by only 60,000 votes. The Wallace vote also may have cost Truman Dewey's home state of Michigan: Dewey won by 35,000 votes; Wallace had 46,500 votes. The Dixiecrats carried four states, subtracting them from the Democratic total, but only four:

Alabama, Mississippi, South Carolina, and Louisiana. The other seven states of the old Confederacy, as well as the three border states, all stayed with the Democrats, as they had solidly since the Civil War. The old South's big switch to the Republicans would come later, as LBJ would predict, after the civil rights bills of 1964 and the Voting Rights Act of 1965.

If the two splinter parties made those subtractions from Truman's total, how, then, did they help? By shaping a greater appeal to other groups in another political direction. Politics is a dynamic field of action and reaction. The Wallace party's attack on Truman helped to insulate him from the charges of being, in the terms of the time, "soft on communism." With Wallace and his cohorts vigorously denouncing Truman from the point of view of real Reds and real Pinks sympathetic with communism and unwilling to criticize the Soviet Union, it was much less convincing to charge the Truman administration with redness and pinkness and softness. That helped to retain for Truman the votes of strongly anti-Communist Roman Catholics and other conservative bodies of opinion.

And the Dixiecrats' blatant segregationism and racism helped to invigorate the support of Truman by African-American voters and northern liberals. Truman's civil rights program, his ordering the integration of the armed services, and the dramatic strengthening of the civil rights plank in the Democratic platform in the floor fight led by Hubert Humphrey (a fight that did take place during good listening hours on the radio, so that all the nation could hear) all helped, as well. Truman was the first political candidate to make a speech in Harlem. Even against the relatively liberal Governor Dewey, Truman got more than two-thirds of the black vote, a bigger proportion than FDR ever had. That helped him win Illinois, Ohio, California, and other states, and was a harbinger of elections to come.

From a longer historical perspective, one might think the important steps the Truman administration had taken in world politics, shaping the response of the United States and even of the free world to the emerging challenge of the Soviet Union, would have been much discussed in the presidential election of 1948; the so-called Truman Doctrine and the Marshall Plan were more important in the larger history of the times than many of the items that the candidates did talk about, but they did not figure in the contest of 1948. Truman did not feature a defense of those policies, and Dewey did not attack them; indeed, Dewey supported these actions, while Taft and isolationist Republicans did not. Dewey just hoped that Truman would not mess up the nation's foreign policy before he had a chance to take it over.

The extraordinary accomplishment of the Berlin airlift was happening exactly during the time that this election played out. It started on June 24, 1948, on the very day that the Republicans in Philadelphia nominated Governor Dewey, and its early and more difficult stages continued straight through the campaign and the election. It is an example of the complex interweaving of many duties of a modern president that Truman would receive regular reports on the airlift in the White House pouch that came every day to the Ferdinand Magellan as he whistle-stopped across the country—going out on the rear of the train to upbraid the do-nothing Congress, the good-for-nothing Republicans, and to introduce Bess and Margaret, and then coming back into his railroad-car office and reading the latest report about getting supplies by air to the beleaguered German capital. In Dallas, during his four-day, twenty-five-stop campaign in Texas, the American ambassador to Moscow, Eisenhower's old associate Walter Bedell Smith, came unobserved aboard the train and reported to Truman on his reading of Stalin's attitude and the possibility of war.

And then it was back to campaigning at the next stop.

The airlift would finally end in triumph in May of the following year, after Truman had started his second term, when the Russians at last gave up their blockade and provided access to Berlin. But the extraordinary accomplishment of the airlift had played no part in the political campaign that accompanied its beginning.

It is true that among the congratulatory messages Truman received after his astonishing victory was one from the president's office at Columbia University. It gave about as good a summary of Truman's achievement as one could ask; the telegram said that never did American political history "record a greater accomplishment than yours, that can be traced so clearly to the stark courage and fighting heart of a single man." It is also true that the telegram included the sentence "It seems almost needless for me to reaffirm my loyalty to you as President"—which, one would think, really ought to have been needless.

It is further true that in the parade for Truman's inauguration in 1949, the sender of that telegram, passing the reviewing stand in an open car, stood and saluted the president—a gesture McCullough says the crowd loved.

The apparent warmth of these gestures, perhaps going a little beyond what civility required, is cooled a bit, however, by the knowledge, made

public four years later by Henry Cabot Lodge, that Dwight Eisenhower
had, in fact, voted in 1948, the very first vote in his life, not for Truman with his stark courage and fighting heart, but, rather, for the candidate that courage and fighting heart had been directed *against:* Governor
Thomas Dewey.

CHAPTER EIGHT

The Once-Forgotten War

HARRY TRUMAN made the decisions that brought the United States into war in Korea; Dwight Eisenhower made the decisions that brought the nation out of that war.

But Eisenhower had supported the original Truman decision.

David Halberstam, in his last book, *The Coldest Winter,* described Truman's predicament: He had to decide what to do when the North Koreans invaded South Korea on June 25, 1950. "Harry Truman was quite reluctantly going to have to be the commander in chief dealing with a war he did not want, in a part of the world his national security people had not thought important, and relying from the start on a commander in the field whom he did not like, and who in turn did not respect him."

The ending of World War II in the Pacific had left the Korean peninsula, which the Japanese had controlled for decades, divided at the soon-to-be-famous thirty-eighth parallel. The Soviet Union's forces, coming into the war in the last days, fighting the Japanese, had advanced that far south at war's end; that hastily drawn line became the dividing point between two zones of occupation, Soviet and American. Then, as efforts at unification failed, the line divided two new quasi-nations, the Republic of Korea in the south, backed by the United States, from the People's Democratic Republic of Korea in the north, backed by the Soviet Union.

The North Korean Army had crossed the boundary with the south—the thirty-eighth parallel—with a force of about 135,000 troops. The Republic of Korea (that is, South Korea) was taken completely by surprise by the invasion, and its much smaller armed forces, with the handful of American troops that had been left there, were soon in full retreat back down the peninsula.

Harry Truman had to decide how to respond to this event—perhaps the biggest decision of his presidency, apart from the decisions about the bombs. As had happened with Pearl Harbor when he was a senator, so it was with the Korean invasion when he was president: Truman happened not to be in Washington, but in Missouri, when the event occurred. This time, Secretary of State Dean Acheson called him with the news.

In his last State of the Union message, in January 1953, Truman gave a retrospective on his presidency, and described the events that followed the invasion in this way:

> I told the Secretary to lay the matter at once before the United Nations, and I came on back to Washington.
>
> So calling on the United Nations had been immediate, a decision right from the start.

Truman the history buff put the event in sequence with the past:

> Flying back over the flatlands of the Middle West and over the Appalachians that summer afternoon, I had a lot of time to think. I turned the problem over in my mind in many ways, but my thoughts kept coming back to the 1930's—to Manchuria, to Ethiopia, the Rhineland, Austria, and finally to Munich.
>
> Here was history repeating itself. Here was another probing action, another testing action. If we let the Republic of Korea go under, some other country would be next, and then another. And all the time, the courage and confidence of the free world would be ebbing away, just as it did in the 1930's. And the United Nations would go the way of the League of Nations.
>
> When I reached Washington, I met immediately with the Secretary of State, the Secretary of Defense, and General Bradley, and the other civilian and military officials who had information and advice to help me decide on what to do. We talked about the problems long and hard. We considered those problems very carefully.
>
> It was not easy to make the decision to send American boys again into battle. I was a soldier in the First World War, and I know what a soldier goes through. I know well the anguish that mothers and fathers and families go through. So I knew what was ahead if we acted in Korea.
>
> But after all this was said, we realized that the issue was whether there would be fighting in a limited area now or on a much larger scale later on—whether there would be some casualties now or many more casualties later.
>
> So a decision was reached—the decision I believe was the most important in my time as President of the United States.

When back in Washington, Truman assembled his advisers, of whom Acheson was the most important. He found general agreement that the North Korean incursion should be forcibly resisted by American armed forces and by United Nations action. As the president said in his account, he had, in his very first response, asked Acheson to lay the matter before the United Nations.

Dwight Eisenhower was in his one civilian role, as president of Columbia University, at the time of the start of the Korean War. He phoned Truman to support his action; told *The New York Times* the country should take a firm stand, as President Truman had done; talked to his friends in the Pentagon about that support; wrote in his diary that "we'll have a dozen Koreas if we don't take a firm stand"; and said he had "urged action in a dozen directions and left a memo for Brad." That was a reference to his close friend Gen. Omar Bradley, then chairman of the Joint Chiefs and a key Truman adviser. Truman had promptly sent naval and air support to the South Koreans; now the day after Eisenhower's call, he took the more portentous step of sending combat troops. At a lunch on July 5, Ike assured Truman that he believed his decision to intervene was "wise and necessary."

Ike, like Truman and almost everyone else considering this action, referred to Munich. (The events surrounding World War II had left two solid shorthand symbols now deployed around later wars: Munich and Dunkirk.)

As Truman and his advisers gathered at the temporary presidential residence at Blair House, they brought to this event two powerful themes: in shorthand, Munich and anticommunism.

Their anti-Communist theme was, in fact, too simple; the Communist world was not nearly as monolithic as they assumed, and also not as consistently expansionist. Truman and his policy makers instantly regarded this event as a Soviet-inspired move, and they asked themselves what the Soviets were up to. Perhaps, they said, this was just a feint—misdirecting the response while Stalin planned a move in Europe or elsewhere in the world.

But we now know that this was not a Soviet action, or part of any world Communist scheme. The agent for the incursion was not Stalin, but the North Korean dictator Kim Il Sung. Kim did seek Stalin's approval, but Stalin had turned him down repeatedly before he finally agreed that Kim might take this action, and Kim was disappointed in the sparse support he would receive from the Soviet Union. Stalin's role was not to initiate the action, but, after demurring for a time, to acquiesce. The invasion was initially decided upon not in Moscow but in Pyongyang.

It is not clear, however, that the response of Truman and the Americans would have been any different had they known the true story of the invasion's beginning and sponsorship, because of the strength of the other theme: Munich. The symbol of Munich and the words *aggression, aggressor,* and *appeasement* ran through all the discussions. As the site of the most egregious appeasement of the Nazis, Munich had come to stand for all the similar early failures to oppose aggression that the president rehearsed in his reflections as he flew back to Washington across the flatlands: Mussolini in Ethiopia, Japan in Manchuria, and Hitler in Austria and Czechoslovakia. The invasion of South Korea by the North Koreans was a clear violation of the agreed-upon division, plain aggression of the sort that the president and others hoped the world had learned to resist.

The Truman administration did take the case to the United Nations Security Council, and by a stroke of luck it was able to get United Nations authorization for a military response. The UN of that time was not yet the polyglot conglomeration of nations it would become as former colonies became states in the years to come. It was then just five years from its postwar inception, and still had the marks of its beginning as an organization with the great powers at the center, and European nations and the United States as primary participants.

And—the crucial accident—although the UN had had to bow to greatpower realities in its formation, and give five great powers a veto over any UN military action, the Soviet Union in January 1950 had walked out of the Security Council and boycotted the UN because Nationalist China, although driven off the mainland to the island of Formosa, still occupied the China seat. So when the United States brought the Korean case to the Security Council in June 1950, the nations voted, with the Soviet seat vacant and only two abstentions (India and Egypt), to authorize the use of force. And that meant that the army battling the North Koreans, and eventually the Chinese, was a United Nations force. It drew upon fifteen nations, mostly from Europe and the British Commonwealth. But the United States provided throughout the overwhelming preponderance of the armed forces, and the primary commanders.

On June 29, just before he sent American combat troops to fight the North Koreans, Truman held a press conference, at which he made definitions of the event that would have thorny repercussions. Because there is a certain value in hearing Truman's voice, part of the text of the press conference is reprinted here:

Q: Mr. President, everybody is asking in this country, are we or are we not at war?

THE PRESIDENT: We are not at war.

Q: Mr. President, another question that is being asked is, are we going to use ground troops in Korea?

THE PRESIDENT: No comment on that.

Q: Mr. President, in that connection it has been asked whether there might be any possibility of having to use the atomic bomb?

THE PRESIDENT: No comment.

After other questions, they returned to the issue of definition:

Q: Mr. President, could you elaborate on this statement that—I believe the direct quote was, "We are not at war." And could we use that quote in quotes?

THE PRESIDENT: Yes, I will allow you to use that. We are not at war.

Q: Could you elaborate, sir, a little more on the reason for this move, and the peace angle on it?

THE PRESIDENT: The Republic of Korea was set up with the United Nations' help. It is a recognized government by the members of the United Nations. It was unlawfully attacked by a bunch of bandits which are neighbors of North Korea. The United Nations Security Council held a meeting and passed on the situation and asked the members to go to the relief of the Korean Republic. And the members of the United Nations are going to the relief of the Korean Republic to suppress a bandit raid on the Republic of Korea.

Q: Mr. President, would it be correct, against your explanation, to call this a police action under the United Nations?

THE PRESIDENT: Yes. That is exactly what it amounts to.

The term *police action* would be used often in the three years that the whatever it was took place. Calling it a "police action" was unfortunate, however, in seeming to depreciate the very real killing and suffering of those who were fighting it; calling the event a United Nations police action would be much resented by soldiers who would fight in what surely seemed to them to be a war.

But the phrase "police action under the United Nations" nevertheless reflected a key definition—that this action was, in however distorted and partial a way, something like the concerted action of nations joining together to put down "aggression" that idealists had dreamed of for years. In theory, it was not a war between nations, but a military action by all the nations joined to stop one errant nation. Harry Truman, in his youthful reading days in Independence, had copied a visionary passage from Tennyson's "Locksley Hall," and he carried it with him (the biographers say) for fifty years—presumably he had it in his wallet when he made the decisions about the Korean incursion and took the case to the UN. Tennyson wrote of a day when

> *. . . the war-drum throbb'd no longer, and the battle-flags were furl'd*
> *In the Parliament of man, the Federation of the world.*

Harry Truman had been a supporter of Woodrow Wilson and a believer in the League of Nations, but he said in the discussions of what to do now that when the tests came, the League had failed. It did not resist the aggressions of the thirties. And now the United Nations must not fail. "It was our idea, and in this first big test we just can't let them down."

The UN was a conglomerate of national interests, not a "Parliament of man," and it certainly did not represent any furling of battle flags. Still, the Korean action could be said to be, partially and by a collection of accidents, a faint approximation of the idealistic dream. As David McCullough put it when referring to the Korean action: "For the first time in history a world organization had voted to use armed force to stop armed force."

For the Soviets, the Chinese, and especially the North Koreans, this event also was not exactly a "war" between nations; the action North Korea took was, for them, not an invasion of one nation by another, an "aggression" that a world body should put down, but, rather, an effort to unify, by force, their one country.

In the first hours and days after the invasion, when public support was immediate and virtually unanimous, Truman made a decision that would cast a long shadow. He decided not to ask for a congressional declaration of war or a resolution of support. He did not ask for that congressional concurrence because, he said, he did not want to set a precedent that would inhibit future chief executives. Some might say that was an admirable solicitude for the powers of the great office he held; but if there was time to go to the UN, surely there was also time to go to the United States Congress, and the inclination of presidents to protect and expand the office they hold has not proven to be an unequivocal blessing. This action by Truman of exercising presidential power alone was a worrisome precedent for the repeated actions by presidents who would follow him, a dubious feature of the modern age. And at the lower level of daily politics, a congressional action at the outset might have mitigated the fierce intensity of the denunciation of "Truman's War" as it dragged on. Wars always last longer than participants anticipate in the initial bravado; this war lasted not three weeks, but three years (and still was not firmly ended).

In the first stage of the war, the North Koreans drove the feebly resisting force of the Republic of Korea steadily back down the peninsula, rapidly but not quite as rapidly as Kim had predicted (he thought he could defeat the South Koreans and unify the country in three weeks: if the Americans had their illusions, the Communists also had theirs). They captured Seoul, one of four times the capital would change hands in the back-and-forth of the war. At Taejon, ninety miles south of Seoul, a gallant rear-guard action by parts of the Twenty-fourth Division of the U.S. Army helped to slow the North Korean advance, buying time for the buildup of American and UN forces. They feared and fought to avoid a Dunkirk—being driven off the peninsula. They fashioned a thumbprint of protected territory at the southeastern end of the peninsula, with a river and the seas as boundaries, the Pusan Perimeter; the Eighth Army commander, Walton Walker, issued a defiant last-ditch appeal, and the UN forces dug in and held that perimeter while the buildup continued.

Now the UN commander, Douglas MacArthur, planned his supreme accomplishment in this war—a daring amphibious landing well up the peninsula on the western side, much farther north than any planner would propose, at Inchon, behind the North Korean armies and twenty miles from Seoul. The landing there was fraught with difficulty, with very high tides, dangerous currents, tall seawalls, a small anchorage, and only two narrowly restricted entrances, which could easily have been blocked by mines. Officers of the U.S. Marine Corps and Navy had to be won over by a prodigious work of persuasion by MacArthur. Truman and the authorities in Washington have a small share in the credit for the event because they did not say no. And in any case, the landing was a complete success. The marines and others in the landing party met very little resistance. Meanwhile, General Walker's Eighth Army left the Pusan Perimeter and started north. The North Korean forces were caught in a giant pincer between that army coming from the south and the forces landed at Inchon to the north. The episode was a huge success for the UN, changing the fortunes of the war.

The fact that MacArthur planned the landing, picked the day (it had to be September 15 for reasons of the tide and daylight), and gave the go-ahead might remind one of his former subordinate Dwight Eisenhower's making the calculations and giving the go-ahead on D-Day at Normandy;

MacArthur surely would not have minded the comparison. As it had been for Eisenhower on June 6, 1944, so it was for MacArthur on September 15, 1950: He was lucky. It all worked. But there was this huge difference: Eisenhower had sent his multination invasion force into the teeth of one of the most formidable fighting machines that ever existed, the Nazi armies, whereas MacArthur's initial invading force of thirteen thousand American marines and soldiers faced very little opposition. Kim and the North Koreans were completely surprised. They had not mined Inchon harbor; they had not anticipated any such action coming around behind them. The North Korean forces, disciplined when winning and driving their fellow Koreans and a few Americans down the peninsula, suddenly found a formidable American force at their rear and did not fight so well.

There is this further comparison to MacArthur's onetime subordinate that one could make: Whereas Eisenhower, after the landing and the battles on the Continent, decided not to distort what he saw as the militarily sound action by a particular effort to capture the capital of Berlin for propaganda purposes, MacArthur, after the Inchon landing, *did* distort the sound military proceeding in order to capture the capital of Seoul. It was a public-relations coup but not a military one.

On this point, Truman and others in Washington were sharply on a different side from MacArthur: They wanted the action that would bag most of the North Korean Army. But MacArthur wanted a parade in the capital. MacArthur not only wanted to capture Seoul; he wanted it by a particular symbolic date, September 25, three months after the North Koreans crossed the parallel and started the war. They did not quite make that date, but after hard fighting that devastated the city, the UN forces— American marines in particular—did capture the city, but the North Korean Army slipped through the trap that might have caught and destroyed them, and the war therefore went on for two and a half more years.

Nevertheless, the war was transformed by the successful Inchon landing. Both Eisenhower and Truman sent MacArthur high praise for the accomplishment. With the unassailable prestige of Inchon, the fully inflated MacArthur took two disastrous actions. First, he attempted another amphibious landing, farther north, this time on the east side of the peninsula, at Wonsan; this time, the harbor was mined and the attempt, poorly planned, was a complete flop. Second, he divided his force into two armies, two commands, which is strictly forbidden by the dictates of army wisdom.

Meanwhile, a larger issue of policy had been presented by the UN success at Inchon: Should the UN forces now cross the thirty-eighth parallel and proceed northward?

It could certainly have been argued that the original mandate of the UN action had been fulfilled: to repel armed invasion and restore peace and stability in the area. But it would have been very hard actually to have stopped and negotiated for peace at that point. It would have meant, as David Halberstam wrote, "accepting a concept of a limited victory in a limited war, and negotiating with people Americans otherwise refused to talk to." The whole story of the Korean War is that Americans are not very good at accepting a limited war, and would have an even harder time calling its cessation a limited *victory*. It would certainly not have been the sort of victory dramatized in MacArthur's speeches.

Should the UN forces cross the thirty-eighth parallel and defeat the North Koreans on their home ground—perhaps occupy and unite the country, doing the reverse of what Kim Il Sung had intended when he started the invasion? There was no doubt that Syngman Rhee, the American-educated president of the Republic of Korea, wanted that to be done, since it was presumed that he would be the president of the unified Korea. MacArthur was loudly in favor of continuing the war in the North. Dwight Eisenhower, still a temporary civilian but the most respected of all American generals, "called for the destruction of the North Korean military capability," which might have been accomplished without going too far into the north.

However, not only MacArthur but in this case the other American officers, who were not always in accord with MacArthur, did want to go on pursuing the army that they had just defeated; there was a logic in military action that argued against stopping on one's own initiative at the artificial line drawn on a map. And Truman, Acheson, and advisers in Washington had not thought much ahead of time about this situation: suddenly to have accomplished the purpose of the "police action." Perhaps it would have been wiser to have stopped there, told MacArthur he had done his part, and negotiated a peace. But it would have been extremely difficult to have sold that program to the American public and to the military leadership; in any case, it was not done. The UN forces crossed the boundary and not only pursued the North Korean Army but proceeded farther and farther north.

Truman had to look at the Korean scene in a much larger context than MacArthur did—in the setting of global politics, and of the response of the Soviet Union and, particularly, because of the geography, China. Mao and the Chinese Communists had finally conquered the nation in late 1949, driving Chiang Kai-shek and the Nationalists onto the island of Formosa (Taiwan), and China had a long border with North Korea at the Yalu River.

On September 27, Truman sent a top secret National Security Council memorandum to MacArthur, reminding him that operations north of the thirty-eighth parallel were authorized only if "at the time of such operation there was no entry into North Korea by major Soviet or Chinese Communist forces, no announcements of intended entry, nor a threat to counter our operations militarily." As the UN forces drove north, they came at each stage closer to the boundary with China at the Yalu River, and some in command and in Washington were apprehensive about Chinese involvement. There were warnings, but these went unheeded. MacArthur insisted that the Chinese would not come into the war, and he repeatedly promised that the soldiers could be home by Christmas. But in fact, the Chinese were preparing "the largest ambush in the history of modern warfare." Suddenly, on November 25, the Chinese struck. The estimates by Allied commanders of the numbers they were facing fell far short of the stunning reality.

MacArthur's intelligence chief, adapting his reports to the desires of his boss, got *everything* wrong; according to Halberstam, he "placed the minimum number at 40,000, the maximum at 75,000. At that time there were 300,000 Chinese troops waiting patiently for the UN forces to come a little deeper into their trap."

There were two Korean wars: one with the North Koreans, from their June incursion until late November, and then one with the Chinese, from that date until the end. The Chinese were said to be "volunteers," to protect against this being an all-out war between nations, which Mao and the Chinese did not want any more than did the Americans (Douglas MacArthur excepted).

The last months of 1950 were a horrendous time for President Truman.

On November 1, there had been an assassination attempt by two Puerto Rican nationalists at Blair House, the temporary presidential residence, across the street from the White House. On November 4, the word came from Korea of the first encounter with the Chinese, at Unsan, an ambush and defeat that should have been a warning but that MacArthur refused to heed. On November 7, the Democrats lost heavily—they had to relinquish five Senate seats and twenty-eight House seats—in the midterm elections, in which the loudest noisemaker had been Senator Joseph McCarthy. On November 25, the report came from Korea of the full Chinese attack.

On November 30, the president made the huge mistake of answering a reporter's question about using the atomic bomb in Korea.

> Q: Mr. President, will attacks in Manchuria depend on action in the United Nations?
> THE PRESIDENT: Yes, entirely.
> Q: In other words, if the United Nations resolution should authorize General MacArthur to go further than he has, he will—
> THE PRESIDENT: We will take whatever steps are necessary to meet the military situation, just as we always have.
> Q: Will that include the atomic bomb?
> THE PRESIDENT: That includes every weapon that we have.
> Q: Mr. President, you said "every weapon that we have." Does that mean that there is active consideration of the use of the atomic bomb?
> THE PRESIDENT: There has always been active consideration of its use. I don't want to see it used. It is a terrible weapon, and it should not be used on innocent men, women, and children who have nothing whatever to do with this military aggression. That happens when it is used.

After a question on another topic, the reporters, perhaps in order to give the president a chance to correct what he had said, returned to the topic of the bomb:

> Q: Mr. President, I wonder if we could retrace that reference to the atom bomb? Did we understand you clearly that the use of the atomic bomb is under active consideration?
> THE PRESIDENT: Always has been. It is one of our weapons.
> Q: Does that mean, Mr. President, use against military objectives, or civilian—
> THE PRESIDENT: It's a matter that the military people will have to decide. I'm not a military authority that passes on those things.
> Q: Mr. President, perhaps it would be better if we are allowed to quote your remarks on that directly?
> THE PRESIDENT: I don't think—I don't think that is necessary.
> Q: Mr. President, you said this depends on United Nations action.

Does that mean that we wouldn't use the atomic bomb except on a
United Nations authorization?

THE PRESIDENT: No, it doesn't mean that at all. The action against
Communist China depends on the action of the United Nations. The
military commander in the field will have charge of the use of the
weapons, as he always has.

The press conference was a total disaster, one of the worst a president
has ever had. The White House did issue a statement in an attempt to stop
the panic: "The replies to the questions at today's press conference do not
represent any change in the situation." But the press reports the next day
were devastating, announcing under banner headlines that Truman had
said the use of the atom bomb in Korea was under consideration, and that
its use was up to MacArthur.

To say that Europeans were appalled is not nearly strong enough; their
anxiety carried them some notches beyond being appalled. In England,
the prime minister, Clement Atlee, dropped everything to fly to Washington to "confer" with the president.

On December 5, in the midst of the Atlee visit, Charlie Ross, Truman's
old friend and press secretary, abruptly slumped over at his desk and died.

Early the next morning, Truman read in the *Washington Post* a review
of his daughter's concert the previous evening, and he wrote a fierce letter
of protest, which should never have been sent but which he got into the
morning mail before his staff could prevent it. The angrily proud father
thus provoked an avalanche of opinion. There probably are citizens of the
United States whose knowledge of the thirty-third president includes, but
does not extend much beyond, the fact that he wrote an angry letter
attacking the music critic who criticized his daughter.

But then in Korea in December, there came an important change of subordinate command, which led to yet another change—this time for the
better—in the war. Gen. Walton Walker, who commanded the Eighth
Army, was killed in an accident in his jeep. MacArthur requested as his
replacement—not realizing what he would thereby get into—Matthew
Ridgeway, who had followed the war as deputy chief of staff for operations
and administration in the Pentagon. As a commander in Korea, Ridgeway was an instant success; he transformed the morale of the key army,
the U.S. Eighth Army, as it retreated down the peninsula. He stopped
the retreat, stabilized the line, and then started to fight back up the peninsula. He retook the battered capital of Seoul, the fourth time it had

changed hands. Ridgeway found ways to use the Americans' technological advantage—artillery in particular—to counter the huge Chinese advantage in numbers. After the dismissal of MacArthur in April 1951, he would be given the top command.

There followed a two-year stalemate, with efforts to negotiate a peace that never succeeded. There was a big snag, in that many of the North Korean prisoners captured by the UN forces did not want to be repatriated to North Korea, and Truman and the Americans refused to force them.

At the heart of the story of the Korean War, there is the altogether fraught relationship of Harry Truman to a general well known perforce to Dwight Eisenhower—the egregious Douglas MacArthur. Their immense later world fame in separate endeavors would put the story of the earlier close relationship between these two generals into the shade, so that the public in general would not realize how extended and how turbulent their relationship had been. But service under MacArthur was a long and drama-filled chunk of Ike's years in the army. Whereas Truman had to cope with MacArthur as an obstreperous subordinate, Eisenhower had had to cope with him as an obstreperous superior.

Eisenhower's coping lasted throughout the decade of the thirties, first in Washington and then in the Philippines. We have seen in chapter 3 how in Washington, as assistant to MacArthur, who was the chief of staff of the army, Eisenhower took a streetcar or a taxi, recovering his pennies by turning in the expense, while MacArthur grandly rode about in a limousine, in which he never offered Ike a ride; how MacArthur would summon Ike from his little broom-closet office just by raising his voice; how Ike resisted MacArthur's self-dramatizing overreaction in the Bonus Army episode. Eisenhower did not believe it was necessary or appropriate for the chief of staff of the army to put on his full uniform with five rows of medals and ride grandly on his horse in order to disperse an unarmed band of ragged civilians. Then when MacArthur's five years as chief of staff of the army ended in 1935 and Manuel Quezon, the president of the new Philippine Commonwealth, asked to have MacArthur's help in reorganizing the Philippine Army, Roosevelt was more than happy to grant the request, which would take MacArthur eleven thousand miles away from Washington.

The word *insubordination* occurs in accounts of the Eisenhower-MacArthur relationship in the Philippines. In this case, however, it applied not to MacArthur but to his restive subordinate Dwight Eisenhower, who would protest and object to MacArthur's egotistical and grandiose undertakings. MacArthur made it a condition of his accepting the job that he be promoted to the rank of field marshal in the Philippine Army—in violation of a strict American military tradition, in an army that barely existed—and he received extra pay from the Philippine government, making him the highest-paid military officer in the world. He was also presented with a gold baton as a symbol of his lofty position. All of these things were thoroughly objectionable to his chief assistant, Dwight Eisenhower. MacArthur wanted to have a grand parade of the Philippine forces; Eisenhower had to incur his wrath by insisting there was no money to pay for it. Eisenhower was eager to leave MacArthur and the Philippines, as he did in 1939, just as World War II began.

As he then rose to world fame, Eisenhower furnished MacArthur, his former superior, with a particular object of envy. MacArthur would try to put Eisenhower in his proper relative place by referring to him as "the best clerk I ever had." When grateful Canadians named a mountain for Eisenhower, MacArthur was heard to say that he understood it to be just a small mountain. A woman once asked Eisenhower whether he knew MacArthur. "Not only have I met him," Eisenhower replied; "I studied dramatics under him for five years in Washington and four in the Philippines."

Now MacArthur was the commander carrying out a military action initiated by Harry Truman under the United Nations.

The UN Security Council had ceded the appointment of a commander to the Americans, and Truman could hardly have avoided picking MacArthur, who was there in Tokyo serving as commander in chief, Far East Command, with all his prestige from the Pacific campaign in World War II and from implementing far-reaching democratic reforms as proconsul in Japan.

Perhaps there had been a chance that Truman could have avoided that appointment. None other than John Foster Dulles, who was no liberal, but the chief Republican foreign policy authority—and in the future Dwight Eisenhower's secretary of state—had by chance been visiting Tokyo as an adviser to the State Department. He was accompanied by a hard-liner from the department at the time of the North Korean attack, and they felt that MacArthur's response was altogether inadequate. Dulles told Truman that MacArthur, then seventy, seemed to him a little old to undertake the command. But Truman felt that appointing MacArthur was too obvious a decision to be avoided. The time would come when he would surely regret that decision.

On October 14, 1950, after the Inchon landing and after the subsequent crossing of the thirty-eighth parallel by UN forces headed north, President Truman flew all the way to Wake Island, in the Pacific, to confer with General MacArthur. They had never met. Truman had twice invited the general to come to Washington—the sort of presidential invitation that ordinary mortals would regard as a command, and surely accept— but the general had declined.

What was the reason for this Wake Island meeting? Straightening out policy about Korea (and China), no doubt, and hearing the general's report firsthand. But there was also some White House inclination to trade on some of MacArthur's prestige, after the huge success of the Inchon landing, in anticipation of the congressional election in November. Of course one expects a commander in chief to meet and confer with generals under his command personally, face-to-face, if possible. But usually a commander in chief does not fly a 14,404-mile round-trip, requiring an all-day and all-night flight, in order to have a meeting that will last less than two hours. In this case, the meeting was so brief that Assistant Secretary Dean Rusk handed the president a note suggesting that they slow down in order to make it longer. What was remembered about the event and entered into history was, chiefly, that MacArthur had not saluted when he met the president. In his memoirs, MacArthur reported a political conversation. When Truman asked if he had political ambitions, MacArthur replied, "None whatever. If you have any general running against you, his name will be Eisenhower not MacArthur." If Eisenhower would have difficulty appreciating the particular worth and merit of this Missouri politician, MacArthur would have even greater difficulty.

MacArthur's already-towering prestige had been greatly increased by the success of the Inchon invasion, but then toward the end of 1950, two of his oft-stated predictions—repeated to Truman at Wake Island—came spectacularly undone. One was that the boys fighting in Korea would be home by Christmas—that is, Christmas 1950. They were not—not then and not for two Christmases thereafter. And he had offered repeated assurances that the Chinese would not enter the war in any significant numbers. That assurance was contradicted in the most convincing manner by their sudden overwhelming presence in November.

With that event, and the new war, and the arrival of General Ridgeway to command the Eighth Army in Korea on December 25, 1950, MacArthur began to lose altitude. As he was forced to float back down to earth, his exuding of insubordinate opinions about the conduct of the war increased, until the president was forced to fire him.

Although the presidential decision to remove MacArthur on April 11, 1951, provoked a tremendous public outburst—the most extreme overt public reaction against a presidential decision in modern American history—it nevertheless was not as difficult for Truman to make as other decisions. MacArthur did him the service of making his insubordination so blatant and so continual, and his insistent policy positions so wrong-headed and dangerous, as to make his removal virtually mandatory.

On December 6, 1950—now with the new enemy, China, in the war en masse and the UN forces in retreat—Truman issued an explicit order that all statements about Korea be cleared through the State Department and the Pentagon, a gag rule that MacArthur mocked in private and quickly and repeatedly violated in public. One historian counted six distinct violations.

The most important of MacArthur's insubordinate acts was his upstaging and undercutting of a Truman feeler about peace in March 1951. Ridgeway had brought the Eighth Army back up the peninsula, retaking Inchon, retaking Seoul, and coming yet again to the thirty-eighth parallel. MacArthur sneered at this, calling it an "accordion war." Ridgeway was incensed at this insult from the commander, who was, after all, supposed to be on his side. Advisers in the Pentagon and State Department thought the time had come to inquire whether the Chinese might engage in peace talks. Truman and his staff worked on a proposal. MacArthur was informed, but he made no response to Washington. Then, on March 24, without warning, MacArthur issued his own pronouncement to the Chinese Communists, disparaging their effort, taunting them, and then grandly offering to meet with them at any time to arrange a settlement. It was an insult to Beijing as well as to Washington, and a flagrant violation of the rules of soldiers' conduct in general and of the gag rule of December 6 in particular. When news of this stunning utterance reached Washington, it provoked widespread fury; Truman's effort to begin peace talks was now impossible.

As the debris from this earthquake was settling, a MacArthur aftershock followed. Joseph Martin, the House Republican leader, had sent MacArthur a copy of a speech he had given, asking MacArthur's views on opening a second front against China, which Martin strongly favored. Asked to give his opinion, MacArthur gave it, and he did not insist that his letter be kept private. So Martin read it on the House floor. The Chinese on Formosa, said MacArthur, should be used in the conflict; the war in Asia was the key to the whole battle with communism; and—MacArthur's signature themes—"in war there is no substitute for victory."

Truman knew when he relieved MacArthur that every one of the Joint Chiefs, as well as George Marshall and all the top advisers, supported his action. Over in Paris now, Eisenhower privately observed that Mac-Arthur appeared to have forgotten the restrictions on those who put on a uniform, and Truman was sure enough of Ike's support to send him, the day after he removed MacArthur, an insider's letter: "I am sorry to have to reach a parting of the ways with the big man in Asia, but he asked for it and I had to give it to him."

So although immense crowds poured out to greet the deposed warrior in Tokyo, Honolulu, San Francisco, and New York (more even than at the parade for Dwight Eisenhower after the war), and although Republican leaders responded by immediately inviting MacArthur to address Congress (without consulting the Democratic majority), and even though the response to his treacly address to Congress ("old soldiers never die; they just fade away") on the part of many Republicans, including congressmen, could only be described as ecstasy, still Truman could be sure that when all that stardust had settled—if not right away, then later—his action could only be approved.

MacArthur was in the wrong, and Truman in the right, unmistakably, on two counts: constitutional propriety and policy. The constitutional point would be hard to miss: MacArthur had openly violated explicit orders of the commander in chief; in the U.S. system, the civilian authority commands the military, and he had radically disobeyed. And the policy point would become plain enough, as well—that MacArthur insisted on a policy that was not only at odds with that of his commander but also extremely unwise, and at root not what the public really would want, despite all their cheering. He kept hinting—or insisting—that he ought to be allowed to use the Nationalist Chinese force to widen the war against China, to bomb beyond the Yalu. But the public, confronted with what that would really mean, would not want to send American soldiers into a war with the Chinese on the mainland.

MacArthur's balloon would be punctured at the hearings held jointly by two Senate committees, at which the general would have to speak not in lonely grand rehearsed monologues on a stage, as had been his practice, but in response to questioning senators, who though they would defer would also probe. After three days of questioning, MacArthur had been brought back down to earth. In response to questions about the whole of American world policy, he had insisted he was simply a theater commander, not an expert on the larger picture. And when the committee heard reports on the Nationalist Chinese on Taiwan from military experts who had spent more time on the island than MacArthur's one day, his appeal to be allowed to use them in battle collapsed utterly. The Nationalists' condition was so feeble that they could not be depended upon to defend the island, let alone to attack the mainland; there was a reason the Nationalist Chinese had been driven from the mainland. American intervention with the Seventh Fleet, instead of preventing the Nationalists from assailing the mainland and recovering their homeland, was protecting the Nationalists from being overrun.

After MacArthur testified, the Joint Chiefs followed one by one, all of them supporting the president's decision. Eisenhower's good friend Omar Bradley memorably said that to pursue MacArthur's course would lead the United States to the "wrong war at the wrong place at the wrong time with the wrong enemy."

All through the MacArthur uproar, there would be a contrast in generals: not only between MacArthur, the grandiosely mistaken, and Ridgeway, the vigorously effective, in Korea but also between MacArthur, the insubordinate Asia Firster, in Asia and Eisenhower, the responsible instrument of policy, in Europe. Eisenhower, in Paris with NATO, quietly agreed that Truman did what he had to, that MacArthur had forgotten the restrictions army command imposes. Although it seemed in the furor of April 1951 that MacArthur might go on to become president by receiving the Republican nomination in 1952—if not, as the shouting millions lined the streets to greet him, by some swifter, more direct means—when after the air had been let out of his balloon and he spoke to the Republican convention of 1952, MacArthur, to change the metaphor, laid an egg. The convention would nominate a general, but it would not be Douglas MacArthur.

As would prove true of the Korean War, so it would of Truman's firing MacArthur: It would be severely damaging in terms of immediate politics and the short run, sharply drawing down Truman's already-low public approval, but looked at in a longer historical perspective, it would be seen to be a necessary act—and, considering the furor it would evoke and the damage to his own standing, a brave one.

Ike would end Truman's war. As the 1952 election approached, visitors to Eisenhower in Paris persuaded him to seek the Republican nomination for president in 1952. His supporters did manage to defeat Taft, in a fierce struggle, for that nomination, and then in the general election campaign as the Republican candidate, Eisenhower gave voice to common Republican themes. He criticized the Truman administration's conduct of the Korean War, which made Harry Truman hopping mad. Ike criticized the statements, like that of Acheson, made before the war that outlined an American defense perimeter from which Korea was excluded—but, said Truman, General MacArthur had said the same and so had the Joint Chiefs—when Ike was chief of staff. Eisenhower, the newly minted Republican politician, blamed the Truman administration for American casualties in the war, in just the way right-wing Republicans were doing, and said "let Asians fight Asians." Truman was particularly exasperated by this kind of criticism coming from a leader who just the other day had been a party to the decisions he now attacked. He made the mistake of saying that if Ike had a way to end the war, he should come out with it. In response, Eisenhower, in a televised speech from Detroit, said that "bringing the Korean War to an honorable end requires a personal trip to Korea and I shall make that trip." He said, "I will go to Korea," a master-stroke politically. He was the hero of World War II, the decision maker of D-Day, the Supreme Commander of the Allied force that had accepted the Nazi surrender—and he would go to Korea.

President Truman could not resist saying, in his telegram of congratulation on the day after the election, that the presidential plane, the *Independence,* would be available to Eisenhower for his trip to Korea "if you still want to go." Eisenhower's response to this gratuitous dig was, understandably, somewhat tight-lipped; he said any military transport would be fine.

After he was elected, he did go, on November 29, 1952, on a three-day trip to Korea. He conferred with Mark Clark, who had succeeded to the old MacArthur position, and with other commanders, and with Syngman Rhee, and he reviewed troops at the front. He toured the cold, mountainous front in a small plane. Clark wanted the limitations removed so that he could attack, but Eisenhower said no—he wanted out.

The settlement that both sides wanted was finally made possible by two changes in leadership: In January 1953, Dwight Eisenhower was inaugurated as the American president, and he was able to settle for an armistice that the Truman administration could never have signed. And Stalin (who did not mind watching the United States and China, an enemy and a rival, fight with each other) died in March 1953, making it easier for Mao and the Chinese to settle. President Eisenhower pushed the Chinese into serious negotiations over Korea by rattling Sabres, bombing irrigation ditches, and even planting atomic bombs on Okinawa and hinting at their use. On July 27, six months into Eisenhower's presidency, the United Nations, supported by the United States, on the one side, and the Chinese People's Volunteers on the other, signed a truce, agreeing to a line approximately at the thirty-eighth parallel, and a Demilitarized Zone between the two Koreas that has lasted to this day. South Korean president Syngman Rhee tried unsuccessfully to disrupt the negotiations, and refused to sign the armistice, so technically the Republic of Korea was not a party to it.

The Eisenhower administration signed an armistice that—as Dean Acheson and Truman himself would say—the Truman administration might have been impeached for doing, or certainly would have been pilloried for doing. That ended the war, after 55,000 Americans had died, at just about the situation at which it had begun.

The war was very damaging to Harry Truman politically; the ending of it was helpful to Ike politically. In the seven and a half years of Eisenhower's administration that followed, not a single American soldier would be killed in combat. For all the sacrifice in the long, drawn-out, and, in the end, apparently inconclusive war, there was no moment of victory—no signing of a peace with defeated enemies in a railroad car or a tent in the field or on the USS *Missouri.* The initial spurt of popular and establishment support, which had greeted Truman's decision in June 1950, had long since evaporated as the armies drove up the peninsula, back down the peninsula, back to the original dividing line, and then stalemated and settled at just about the point it had begun—no gain, no victory.

Harry Truman had to defend what he asserted was the necessity of a *limited* war—a war limited geographically, and also in terms of the weapons that could be used and the objectives to be achieved. The American public found that hard to accept. The popular tendency is to make sharp absolutes about war and peace; the popular view is that when war breaks out, an altogether distinct situation arises. MacArthur reflected this deep popular inclination when he said that in war there is no substitute for victory. But the complex world scene in the developing Cold War, with a superpower adversary equipped with nuclear weapons and another emerging adversary with an enormous population, with weapons that could destroy civilization, with the politics of the entire globe now figuring in the nation's responsibility, there had to be an understanding of the use of force that was not simple or absolute. Korea was a harbinger of the future of American policy.

Campaigning for the presidency, Ike implied that he would bring the war in Korea to an end, and six months after becoming president he did so. He ended the Korean War with a negotiated settlement at the thirty-eighth parallel, despite strong opposition from South Korean president Syngman Rhee, the United States' ally in South Korea, who wanted the United States to expand the war into the north, and unify the country under himself, using U.S. nuclear weapons to achieve that result. But when Ike made his trip to Korea, knowing he wanted peace, he ended the war in spite of Rhee's desires and in spite of the proposal from the American general now in command in Korea, his old companion in arms, Mark Clark, who, like most generals, wanted permission to expand the war. Ike wanted to shut it down. He ended that war despite opposition from his own moralistically belligerent secretary of state, John Foster Dulles, and from conservative members of his own party who said Americans always want victory, and from other advisers and Republicans and Democrats who would have continued the stalemate rather than settle. He ended the war with an armistice back at the place the war had started. There was not any celebration of the result, but Ike was proud of it, and one may say it was a considerable accomplishment of statesmanship to bring it about.

There were few positive appraisals of the Korean War at the time, or in its immediate aftermath. There was no credit given to Harry Truman, as his public approval ratings went down as low as those of any president before him and as low as Nixon's after Watergate. But as the years have gone by, there has come into view the possibility that there were positive results after all.

One positive result may be that the response to the North Korean invasion served the purpose of Cold War containment. Korea was the example of overt military containment, alongside the containment achieved by economic, military, and political collaboration elsewhere. Truman had said early in the event that Korea was the Greece of Asia—as the so-called Truman Doctrine of aid to Greece and Turkey had contained Soviet expansion in Europe, so the Korean War made possible a comparable containment in Asia. After distinguishing carefully the possible exceptions, one might be able to say that there would not be, in the forty years of the Cold War to follow, any further examples of the deliberate expansionist crossing of a line with military force by a Communist power.

Another positive result of Truman's war is the flourishing democracy and prosperous economy in South Korea. Imagine that Kim Il Sung's invaders had swept down the peninsula, conquered the south, and unified the nation as he intended—the nine million Koreans in the north ruling the twenty million in the south in a larger, unified version of today's repressive North Korean regime, under Kim's equally objectionable son, equipped now with nuclear weapons, a repugnant totalitarian state and a geopolitical menace to Japan and Formosa and to the peace of the world. The war prevented that—no small accomplishment.

But there is not only this negative accomplishment, preventing the consolidation of the peninsula under the regime from the north; there is also this positive one: Although Syngman Rhee was no democrat, and the regime at first had its authoritarian elements, with the passage of time, and the forced resignation of Rhee and the continuing influence of the free world, there would come into being in the most recent decades a new democracy and thriving economic success in South Korea. That would not have happened without Truman's war.

CHAPTER NINE

Two Moralities

I

ONE REASON the 1952 presidential campaign was drenched in moral language was the catalog of "scandals" in the administration of Harry Truman. The other reason was the mind-set of the Republican nominee, Dwight Eisenhower.

The 1952 campaign also exhibited varied understandings of *loyalty*, a theme introduced primarily by the incumbent president, against whom candidate Eisenhower directed much of his fire, and who certainly fired back, Harry Truman.

These themes arose in large part because of the "mess in Washington"—a phrase Harry Truman definitely did not like. There was nevertheless, unfortunately, a reason that phrase came to be widely used . . . was even used once, indeed, with implied quotation marks, to the great distress of President Truman, by his own party's nominee for president, Adlai Stevenson.

Truman was, in a peculiar way, and even though he came from a small town, a product of a big-city political machine. He represented its somewhat ambiguous "virtues" while personally avoiding its unambiguous vices. He remembered his benefactors, kept his word, stood by the Pendergast organization, and helped his friends. The organization gave him plenty of opportunity to practice those virtues, along with a certain amount of temptation to succumb to its vices, which, generally speaking, he did not do.

It does appear to be true that Truman did not profit financially in any illegitimate way from that relationship. His own summary, written in July 1954, has not drawn much of a challenge from biographers and researchers: "In all this long career I had certain rules I followed win, lose, or draw," he wrote. "I refused to handle any political money in any way whatever. I engaged in no private interests whatever that could be helped by local, state or national governments. I refused presents, hotel accommodations or trips which were paid for by private parties. . . . I made no speeches for money or expenses while I was in the Senate. . . . I lived on the salary I was legally entitled to and considered that I was employed by the taxpayers, and the people of my country, state, and nation."

The one (unconfessed) exception to this clean bill of health that Truman gave to himself—that as a senator in 1941 he put his wife on his Senate payroll—did not have anything to do with his relationship to Pendergast. Faced with the responsibilities of two places of residence and with no other income, the comparatively poor man Truman did do what many other senators and congressmen did: He put his wife on his office staff. The arrangement, which lasted from 1941 to 1944, probably was one of the secret reasons Bess Truman did not want her husband to be subjected to the intensified level of publicity as a vice presidential nominee.

On the whole, it does appear that Truman deserves his self-commendation on this score—he half-boasted about and half-lamented his financial probity more than once—that he lived as a poor man when "there were opportunities for the wholesale making of immense amounts of money."

But that exhibition of rectitude, commendable as it is, does not cover all the questions that might be asked about Harry Truman's relationship to Tom Pendergast. Did Truman protect public moneys under his (partial) control from the fat graft that marbled the organization's activities elsewhere? Again, the answer appears to be yes, on the whole, but not "perfectly." The story of his letting a contract go to the lowest bidder—from *South Dakota*—and of the outraged complaints thereafter by local contractors, and of the meeting then in Pendergast's office, at which Truman was adamant and Pendergast angrily exclaimed that Truman was as stubborn as a Missouri mule, is told in all the biographies. And Truman did build roads and courthouses not only within the limits of the bond issues but with a surplus with which to pay for the famous statue of Andrew Jackson in front of the courthouse in Independence.

Still, apparently there were compromises around the edges. The rule that we may infer Truman followed in dealing on behalf of the county with the Pendergast organization—graft, no, but patronage, yes—could not provide airtight honesty, because the latter leaked into the former. In some remarkable notes he wrote in the Pickwick Hotel in Kansas City in the early 1930s, he exhibited a confessional and morally troubled attitude that contrasts sharply with his usual briskly self-confident moral certitude. The notes were private musings; he was worried about some compromises he had made. "I wonder if I did right to put a lot of no account sons of bitches on the payroll," he wrote, "and pay other sons of bitches more money for supplies than they were worth in order to satisfy the political powers and save some $3,500,000 [this figure was the half of a seven-million-dollar bond issue that he estimated the "crooks" would take if he had not fended them off with smaller compromises and kept control]. I believe I did do right. Anyway, I'm not a partner of any of them and I'll go out poorer in every way than when I came into office." So, his own modest means notwithstanding, Harry Truman's conduct in coping with the Kansas City machine did not have the purity that the simplest popular morality—in small-town Kansas sectarians, but also in Harry Truman himself most of the time—would require. The pure, the right, and the good in that setting, as in most, had a flavoring at least of the slightly impure, the not quite right, and the not so good.

An unabsolute and complex moral understanding would be particularly important to Harry Truman if one were to ask (knowing the answer) yet one more question about his relationship to the Pendergast machine: Did he himself benefit from their ghost votes and repeat votes and Election Day shenanigans? The fraudulent voting practices of the Pendergast machine in the 1936 election were shown, by investigations after Pendergast's fall, to have been gargantuan.

A great value Truman did share with the Pendergast people, and which was manifest throughout his life in his own distinctive way, was that of loyalty. He would be steadfast in his loyalty to the organization and, in spite of their sins, to people who had helped him—very much including T. J. Pendergast himself. It could be argued that Tom Pendergast's pleading guilty and being sent to prison provided the moment when Senator Harry Truman might (sorrowfully, of course) have cut his ties with Pendergast—like Shakespeare's Prince Hal, when he becomes king, with Falstaff, or like Woodrow Wilson, as he rose in national politics, with the North Jersey bosses who had supported him for governor.

One could argue that Truman should have then made a break with Pendergast not only on moral grounds but on grounds of self-protective political strategy, as well. He could have argued—to himself, if to no one else—that the Pendergast organization had needed him as much as he had needed it, and therefore his obligation was now fulfilled. At the outset, the organization needed a well-respected veteran, a farmer, and a Baptist to provide its reach out into the rural part of the county; later, it needed his accomplishments as an honest, efficient, road-building, courthouse-building county judge to provide something of a deodorant for its doings of other kinds. So he might have said, with respect to his obligation. He might have acknowledged the sins of Tom Pendergast—not small, and determined now in a court of law, which found him guilty. And in addition to such arguments on the higher plane, there were others, on the lower, "pragmatic" plane: His ties to Pendergast were hurting his reputation, and the Pendergast machine, now in a shambles after Boss Tom's conviction, could not help him much in the forthcoming campaign.

But Harry Truman never made any such arguments, higher or lower. He never did repudiate Pendergast, or take any of the lesser steps he might have taken to distance himself, thereby signaling to the public his disapproval, or at least dramatizing his independence. He would be loyal to the end.*

He would make a revealing reference to his loyalty to Pendergast, five years after having attended Pendergast's funeral, in January 1950, when he was president of the United States and the immensely controversial Alger Hiss case was before the public. Hiss, a highly placed American foreign service officer, was charged with being a secret agent of the Soviet Union. Dean Acheson, Truman's new secretary of state, had been asked in a press conference about Hiss, and he had responded by saying, "I do not intend to turn my back on Alger Hiss," for which he was strenuously attacked. But Acheson immediately received sympathetic support from his chief. As Acheson put it in a letter to his daughter, "He [Truman] has been, as usual, wonderful about it and said that one who had gone to the funeral of a friendless old man just out of the penitentiary had no trouble knowing what I meant and approving it."

Two years later, in January 1952—his last year in the White House, as the "Truman scandals" were in the news—President Truman wrote a private memorandum about his relationship to the aforesaid "friendless old man." It contained no criticism of T. J. Pendergast but did include some praise and defense of him. Writing about the boss, Truman said, "His word was better than the contracts of other men and he never forgot his verbal commitments." And in that same memorandum, he said of him-

---

* Truman's defenders, like his daughter, Margaret, say he was not one to hold grudges, but it is admitted that if he did do so, high on the list would be Lloyd Stark, whose sins were those of betrayal. Truman had defended Stark to Pendergast, and helped him become governor—after which, when the wind changed, Stark condemned Pendergast and ran against Truman. That was not the sort of conduct Truman approved of, for himself or for anyone else. Actually, one might disagree with Margaret Truman's claim that her father did not hold grudges. Both Truman and Eisenhower fell a considerable distance short of Lincoln's superhuman magnanimity.

self, "I never deserted him when he needed friends. Many for whom he'd done much more than he'd ever done for me ran out on him when the going was rough. I didn't do that—and I am President of the United States in my own right!"

This steadfastness in his loyalties, we may infer, was not only something acquired from the ethos of a politician in a party organization but also a feature in the makeup of Harry Truman himself. He exhibited it in other relationships: in his spectacular lifelong fidelity to Bess Wallace Truman (from age six to death at age eighty-eight); as a ferociously defensive father; as "Captain Harry," in a reciprocal bond that lasted all their lives with his companions in the 129th Field Artillery in the Great War.

Truman made some poor appointments to the judiciary and the Department of Justice, and was loyal to them; made mostly rather good appointments to the White House staff, and was loyal to them; and made excellent appointments (Louis Johnson excepted) to the State and Defense Departments (Acheson, Marshall twice, Lovett), and was loyal to them. McCullough has noted the loyalty of Truman's staff to him, as well as Truman's to them; one expression of it was the complete absence of insider tale-telling books about the Truman administration:

> The loyalty of those around Truman was total and would never falter. In the years to come not one member of the Truman White House would ever speak or write scathingly of him or belittle him in any fashion.*
>
> When Truman had completed his service as President and retired, and his long time White House assistant Matt Connelly was sent to prison for income tax evasion, Ex-President Truman (for just one example of his standing by his friends) helped raise money for Connelly's defense, and wrote the then Attorney General Robert Kennedy in Connelly's behalf. When nothing happened Truman did not give up; he wrote a furious letter in longhand to the Attorney General, insisting that Connelly had been mistreated. When finally in 1962 President Kennedy pardoned Connelly, Connelly wrote his letter of gratitude not to Kennedy but to Truman.

---

* Contrast this with Lou Cannon's remarks about Ronald Reagan's colleagues: "While Reagan was still in the White House dismissed or disenchanted former members of his cabinet and staff produced ten memoirs that reflect the frustrations of those who made the mistake of trying to breach the personal barrier. The authors were Martin Anderson, Terrell Bell, Anne Buford, Michael Deaver, Alexander Haig, Donald Regan, Larry Speakes, David Stockman, Helene Van Damm, and James Watt . . . whoever they blame or say they blame, the memoirists show little sense of loyalty to Reagan and find even less loyalty in him." (See Lou Cannon, *President Reagan: The Role of a Lifetime* [PublicAffairs, 2000], pp. 175–76.)

But if this standing steadfastly by one's friends, feeling gratitude toward one's benefactors, and supporting one's organizational associates are admirable qualities, obviously they cannot be absolute. There are conflicts between personal loyalties (particularly in politics) and larger principles—the common good, the integrity of the law, justice to large numbers of unseen human beings.

When Prince Hal in Shakespeare's *Henry V* becomes king and repudiates his old pal Falstaff—"I know thee not, old man"—most audiences are by no means altogether on Hal's side; on the contrary, often there is a gasp of shock and disapproval, at least at the abruptness and harshness of the repudiation and probably also at the repudiation itself. Audiences love Falstaff, perhaps proportionately more than Shakespeare intended, and do not care about the proper royal conduct of the rulers of the ancient English state enough to give weight to the other side of the argument. But some interpreters, as perhaps Shakespeare did, see the young man making the right decision, although a difficult one, for a man about to become a king.

There would certainly be moral critics who would say that Harry Truman did *not* make the right decision about his rather Falstaffian friend Harry Vaughan, and his personal physician, Wallace Graham, and his assorted friends and associates on the Democratic National Committee, in the Reconstruction Finance Corporation (RFC), the IRS, the Justice Department, and the White House itself. Late in Truman's first term, his personal physician, Wallace Graham, was shown to have speculated in grain futures, presumably with insider knowledge (and just after President Truman, in the first television address broadcast from the White House, had condemned "gambling in grain" as a cause of high food prices). Graham, the son of the Truman family's physician in Independence, denied wrongdoing, said he had sold his holdings, was defended at a press conference by the president, then under congressional questioning admitted that he had not sold his holdings after all at the time he said he had. Graham was not relieved of his duties, but served on through the Truman presidency.

Early in Truman's second term, Harry Vaughan, an old Missouri friend, and certainly a jester, if not a fool, was found by investigating newspapermen and a Senate committee to have associates who, equipped with match folders bearing the legend "Stolen from Harry Truman," made a business of selling access to the White House for 5 percent of the resulting business contracts—hence a newsman's invention of the term *five percenter.* These newspaper investigations further revealed that another friend of Vaughan, a free-spending perfume tycoon, who, after overhearing reports of Mrs.

Truman's need to refrigerate gifts of food she was given in Independence, grandly donated to her a $390 freezer (which, as it turned out, did not work), and provided freezers to a number of others high in the administration. President Truman also never did fire his old friend Vaughan.

The more serious second wave of Truman scandals, in a series of ascending importance, came in February 1951, and again President Truman's unwillingness to admit fault in, to discipline, or to fire old friends and supporters made it worse than it would have been. This one revolved around the alleged systematic influence of some officials—including William M. Boyle, chairman of the Democratic National Committee, and Donald Dawson, on the White House staff—on the low-interest government loans made by the Reconstruction Finance Committee. This set of scandals acquired its symbol when a Washington attorney named Joseph Rosenbaum, who specialized in RFC matters, bought an expensive coat for one E. Merl Young, who had been an RFC examiner and sometime political operator for the Democratic National Committee and was another of those charged with improper influence. And Mr. Young gave the coat to his wife, who worked as a stenographer in the White House. Thus, in addition to Mrs. Truman's Deepfreeze, another potent symbol—that mink coat—was brought into the executive mansion itself. Both Texas delegations to the Republican convention in 1952 (the Taft people and the Eisenhower people) could join in singing to the tune of "Deep in the Heart of Texas":

> *Deep freeze and minks*
> *And all those pinks*
> *You bet they're not from Texas*

President Truman did not advance his own cause very much when he called the two senators leading the investigation of the RFC—Paul Douglas of Illinois, a Ph.D. who had been professor of economics at the University of Chicago, and J. William Fulbright, the Rhodes scholar who had been president of the University of Arkansas—"overeducated sons of bitches." It was noted earlier that he had already taken to calling Fulbright, in private, as a result of a previous episode, Senator Halfbright. Although Boyle was forced to resign, Truman did not dismiss Dawson from the White House. He did, however, reorganize and provide new safeguards and new administration for the RFC—albeit a little late.

The third and most significant wave of Truman scandals came in late 1951 and lasted into the election year of 1952. It involved the IRS and the Department of Justice, and was another tale of shady dealings by dubious individuals, except that this time a central character in the drama was the nation's chief law-enforcement officer, the attorney general of the United States: the dapper, hard-drinking, and wonderfully named J. Howard McGrath. Under his leadership the Department of Justice did not do much to discover miscreants in office, and thus did not mitigate the criticism of the president and his administration.

The original occasion for this series of unsavory events was fraud and malpractice on the part of some district commissioners of the Internal Revenue Service; citizens otherwise sympathetic to Mr. Truman shuddered a little when they said they hoped the problem did not reach into the *tax* system. The immediate occasion for the climactic events was the reluctance of the Justice Department, at the top, to investigate or take action.

There was a seriocomic episode involving a rather innocent special prosecutor from New York named Newbold Morris, who was finally appointed, under pressure, by McGrath, to find and prosecute the evildoers. After trying, with spectacular ineptitude, to do his job, Morris was fired by McGrath, after which Attorney General McGrath was, very reluctantly, fired in turn by President Truman. Truman did do some housecleaning this time, and, indeed, he reformed the IRS. Early in 1952, he submitted to Congress a plan to abolish the politically appointed district collectors of internal revenue and institute a new professional service under a single fully responsible commissioner. This huge improvement was passed into law over the contrary votes of thirty-seven presumably patronage-minded senators (senators had under the old system, of course, had a big influence on the choice of their district's collector—as, indeed, once upon a time, had Senator Harry Truman himself). This was a big and a worthy reform; while he was at it, Truman also proposed civil service status for postmasters, customs officials, and U.S. marshals, but Congress, in its wisdom, did not want to overdo this *reform,* and it rejected those further proposals.

Truman himself, an honest man personally, was vulnerable in these matters because of his excessive loyalty to, and support of, friends, friends of friends, and acquaintances of friends, and his lifelong unsubtle partisanship, which inclined him to interpret all the charges of corruption as being motivated only by partisan and ideological purposes. He would regularly assert that the investigators who exposed these matters were really striking at him. But those who exposed these corruptions were not all political opponents. The press played a role; Democrats controlled the investigating committees. Senators William Fulbright and Paul Douglas, whose educations Truman thought to be excessive, were both Democrats. At one point, Senator Douglas, the Democrat from Illinois, made a remark to Truman that went to the heart of the matter: "Mr. President, you have been loyal to friends who have not been loyal to you."

II

NOW, INTO THIS SITUATION in the spring of 1952 there came a man from the plains of Kansas, not young anymore but something of an innocent in politics, bearing as his banner the highest moral standards. Dwight David Eisenhower flew across the Atlantic from Paris, intending to enter American politics from above. He certainly knew, from his activities of the previous ten years, the difficult moral conflicts of great public affairs; surely the commander of Operations Torch, Husky, and Overlord had dealt with moral conflicts that dwarfed anything in that line that Jackson County, Missouri, had to offer. Nevertheless, he was new to the issues of *this* kind of domestic, democratic, civilian politics.

He had never liked, or been a part of, this kind of politics. His lifelong career in the peacetime army had insulated him from politics and public affairs to a unique extent: He came from a family with a three-hundred-year sectarian tradition on both sides; here we may translate *sectarian* as "antipolitical." He had grown up in a small town in Kansas, on the wrong side of the tracks, outside even that small town's structure of power. When accident took him to West Point, he held the strongest conviction that military men should stay out of politics, and his entire career reinforced that. He had many times insisted that the military and politics should be sharply separated. "It's like church and state!" he told Kay Summersby. He admired the career of Gen. George Marshall, whom one could not imagine ever running for political office, and he did not admire the political activities of his longtime boss, Gen. Douglas MacArthur.

And in addition to the general antipolitical principle, there was the added feature in his own case that he had been the leader of the Allied victory in Europe in World War II, and, as he said in the sentence from his Guildhall speech in London just after the war—which has been quoted earlier—"Humility must always be the portion of any man who receives acclaim earned in blood of his followers and sacrifices of his friends." His brother Milton later wrote about his attitude at this time: "He earnestly believed that it would be wrong to take advantage of the wave of popularity and affection that resulted from military victory, won by the toil and blood of men under his command."

In his notes and memoranda in 1950–1951, when political people of all stripes sought him out, Dwight Eisenhower strongly avowed his principled resistance to politics. He wrote in his diary on New Year's Day 1950, "I do not want a political career" and "I do not want to be associated with any political party." In that same extended diary entry, he spelled out a particularly interesting alternative conception of his role in the world. He wrote that he and his family were examples of what this country, "with its system of individual rights and freedoms," can do. "[My] greatest possible opportunity for service is to be found in supporting, in renewing public respect for, and encouraging greater thinking about, these fundamentals." And he came (again) to the no-party-for-me conclusion: "In the field in which I should work [just described—bringing basic American tenets to conscious attention] there is no difference between the two great parties. Therefore I should belong to neither." He continued to assert, "I do not want a political career," "I do not want to be associated with any political party," and, later (on October 29, 1951), "I do not want to be president of the United States."

So when clamoring multitudes, and perhaps also his own secret ambition, began to urge him to run for president after all, they had formidable barriers to surmount. And out of the need to surmount those barriers (one may surmise not least in his own mind) came a distinctive conception of the Eisenhower campaign and presidency. The theme was this: that this campaign and presidency were altogether different, distinctive, and on a higher plane. To be sure, many campaigns claim that—perhaps most do. But not many believe it. In the case of Eisenhower, the principal *did* believe it, and he had a strong, although vague, conception of the nature of his campaign's aboveboardness and distinctiveness.

In order for him to allow his name to be entered in the presidential race, he had to have that act defined as his *duty*—not his ambition, not his self-interest, not his ideological conviction, not even his free choice, but his *duty*. In one note to himself, he even raised the moral ante again: his *transcendent* duty! It was not to be the reflection of that merely personal aspiration, or even the desire to serve some ideological purpose, that marks the choices of others—for example, of mere politicians. It was the stern daughter of the voice of God, his *Duty*.

This insistent casting of his role in that way had appeared before. When, in October 1950, President Truman asked him to accept the appointment as commander of NATO, Eisenhower responded that as an old soldier, rather than acquiesce to a "request," he would accept "orders" from "his superiors" to take the post. So Truman, to fit Ike's moral makeup, had to "order" him to do it. And so, a little over a year later, he had even more insistently to regard his career decisions as submission to duty. But who, in this strange new world of civilian politics, could issue an authoritative command? Who could give him the *orders* that defined his duty? The answer was, the people.

Ike's persuaders flying back and forth to Paris in the winter of 1951–1952 learned that this was the effective appeal—his duty, made plain by the call of the people. They therefore orchestrated a campaign intended to bring that call to Eisenhower. The climax was a mass meeting in Madison Square Garden, with fifteen thousand people cheering his name, a mass of citizens directing their cheers, really, at an audience of one—the supreme commander over in Paris. A film was made of this event and immediately flown to Eisenhower in Paris by Jacqueline Cochran, the aviatrix. When he saw that film, he capitulated; he had been called to duty by the cheering thousands.

At various times later, he would give, in private, more ordinary "political" reasons for his decision to run for president. As we have seen, when he discovered that Taft would not necessarily support stationing American troops in Europe under NATO, he tore up a note he had written absolutely removing himself from the political race (he told this story in a book written during his retirement). So one could say he ran for president to stop Taft. On other occasions, he told interlocutors that he did so to bring to an end the twenty-year New Deal–Fair Deal expansion of the bureaucracy. But these purposes, ideological and partisan, like those of politicians, did not provide the primary reason for his decision to reverse a lifetime's commitment and go into politics. His life up to that point, and his presidency afterward, would show that although he was, loosely, a rather standard American mild conservative, his partisan and ideological commitments were not deep or strong or well informed. They were joined to this other feature, distinctive to Eisenhower, which goes back to his ruminations on New Year's Day of 1950: his role in articulating and restoring the American fundamentals shared by both parties—morality, spiritual values, American fundamentals, all of which superseded politics.

For his own reasons, his political undertaking had to be distinct from and superior to the ordinary political movements. It is now more or less forgotten, but it was much noted at the time, that the new candidate and new president made a quite marked, although also quite vague, appeal to the nation's religious or "spiritual" foundations. Ann Whitman, who would be his secretary throughout his presidency and beyond, was just joining the Eisenhower campaign in that first summer of 1952; she wrote to her husband and others, and put down in her diary, her surprise at Ike's repeated emphasis on "spiritual" matters: "Again I am amazed at the stress he always puts on spiritual matters." This emphasis would subsequently appear as the rather distinctive "piety along the Potomac" of the Eisenhower presidency.

And this was linked to, indeed almost identical with, "morality." Eisenhower continually described the political movement that it was his transcendent duty to lead, on the orders of the people, by using one of his favorite words: It was a "crusade." He had used that word also in the days of his supreme commandership, and had given his book about the war the title *Crusade in Europe.* In the first sentence of his acceptance speech at the 1952 Republican National Convention—his first words as a Republican candidate—he said, "Ladies and gentlemen, you have summoned me to lead a great crusade." The word *crusade* appeared three more times in the next sentences. Franklin Roosevelt had also used that word at the start of his acceptance speech in 1933, in the depths of the Depression, but with a difference: FDR did intend to bring about a sharp change, in a new direction, with new purposes. Did Eisenhower's political movement fit that metaphor, as the unified single-minded undertaking of the war or the New Deal had done? It was important to Ike to pretend that it did. In the very earliest days, he suggested that this "crusade" would be like that of Oliver Cromwell, but more experienced Republican politicos around him, explaining that he had a real chance to make inroads on the Irish-American vote, quickly squelched that particular comparison.

It is significant that this moral crusading appeared even before, and independent of, the attack on the Truman scandals, and that it persisted after that attack had resulted in the putative rascals being thrown out. There had been a ferocious squabble, long since forgotten but of central importance at the time, over the Texas delegation to the Republican National Convention. The Taft forces had controlled the state convention at Mineral Wells, chosen their slate of delegates, and excluded (because they said they were Democrats just converted for the purpose of nominating Eisenhower) all Eisenhower delegates. The Eisenhower people had withdrawn to a rump convention and nominated their own slate of delegates for Texas's thirty-eight votes in the Republican National Convention. These two separate slates of delegates continued to contest the seats, and the issue was projected onto the national scene by a press that the Taft forces charged—not without reason—with favoritism to Eisenhower.

It has also largely been forgotten now how close and hard fought the battle for the Republican nomination in 1952 really was; it was the last real convention fight for a nomination, and either side could have won. The fight over Texas provided the Eisenhower forces with both the votes and the momentum that they badly needed in order to win. And, one suspects, partly for that reason they cast the issue in moral terms: They charged the Taft people with a "steal"; they insisted that this was a *moral* issue. They needed to have *all* the delegates, not some compromised split. Looking back at the 1952 nominating process, a sober Johns Hopkins Press study conducted by a clutch of political scientists in the aftermath said that "Eisenhower, with fewer committed delegates, needed an issue . . . the issue of the Texas 'steal' seemed heaven-sent. His managers made the most of it." They presented the matter to Eisenhower, the novice politician, as a moral outrage by the Taft people. Eisenhower's very sympathetic biographer Merlo Pusey wrote that "his fighting blood had been aroused. . . . He was ready to roar across the country for clean and decent operations. [He would] fight to keep our party clean and fit to lead our nation!" Pusey said that it was Eisenhower himself who decided to fight on the Texas matter because it was a matter of *principle.* This struggle within the party was a matter—and this Pusey placed in quotation marks as coming from Eisenhower—of "straight out right and wrong."

"Straight out right and wrong"? Which delegation of Texas Republicans would be seated in the convention—*that's* an issue of "straight out right and wrong?" The political scientists writing in the calm objectivity of the aftermath would say that "there was little reason to consider either state convention *wholly* representative of Texas Republicanism."

So then the moral crusade rolled on through the campaign against the Democratic ticket. Any Republican candidate for president in 1952 would have made use of the Truman scandals as a campaign theme, but the Eisenhower campaign used that topic a little more centrally, and perhaps in a slightly different way, than a Taft campaign might have done. One reason for this was that the Eisenhower differences with the Democrats were not as deep, especially on foreign policy, as were those of Taft, and although an Eisenhower campaign would indeed make some use of the McCarthy theme—the attack on alleged Communists in government—it would not do so in the even more blatant and unrestrained way that a presidential campaign rooted in the Republican right wing might have done. The attack on "corruption"—on the Truman scandals—correspondingly would rise in importance.

But in addition, that issue fit the nature of the candidate. It was a conveniently unarguable, one-sided matter. When former Democratic governor of Ohio Mike DiSalle was asked whether "corruption" would be an issue in the campaign, he responded that he supposed so, but he did not know who was going to take the affirmative. That altogether one-sided issue fit the widely popular conception of Eisenhower as political candidate, and perhaps even more Eisenhower's conception of himself as a nonpolitical candidate.

After Eisenhower's moral crusade had swamped Adlai Stevenson, the Democratic nominee, in the general election, and Eisenhower had been inaugurated as president—thereby having thrown out the scandalous Truman infidels, as it were, and having taken over Washington, the rather unlikely Holy City—Eisenhower's use of the metaphor of the "crusade," somewhat surprisingly, did not stop. Commentators would then ask: What sort of "crusade" is this? The characteristics of Eisenhower in office were not those of single-minded zeal and resolute rallying cries. His characteristic merits for his supporters were moderation, conciliation, middle-of-the-roadness; his characteristic faults for his detractors were those of the "green fairways of complacency"—in both cases, in other words, for good or ill, in some sharp contrast to a crusader's singleness of purpose, a crusader's zeal, or a crusader's fanaticism. Its true point was not to accomplish some clear, single, radical goal, but to justify, to the man at the center, this new role.

The "moral crusade" did have this leftover effect, familiar to moralists of all flavors: Its strictures were now applied with increased strictness against the crusaders themselves. One could not successfully adopt the implied attitude of Charles "Engine Charlie" Wilson during the exploration of his ties to General Motors and other defense contractors in the hearings on his confirmation as Eisenhower's new secretary of defense. Wilson seemed to assume that "corruption" and immorality had been thrown out of government *by definition* when Truman and the Democrats were defeated and Eisenhower and the moral crusaders were brought in, and that therefore he should be allowed to hold on to his stock and not be subject to any such examination.

The Eisenhower movement had already experienced something of this kickback effect when, during the campaign, it was discovered that the Republican vice presidential nominee, Richard Nixon, had a special fund provided for his expenses by his backers. Ike, the moral crusader, insisted that Nixon—and everybody else in his administration—must be "clean as a hound's tooth." Nixon's superlative hound's-tooth cleanliness was demonstrated not by any extraordinary proof of his probity but by an extraordinary display of televised bathos, as many of Eisenhower's advisers, along with many other citizens, held his "Checkers" speech to be.

Each of the scandals of the Eisenhower years set off embarrassing reminders and comparisons. They came to a climax in his second term in the case of Ike's own enormously important White House chief of staff, Sherman Adams (Ike: "I need him"), whose sins were not so much scarlet as pastel pink; they actually had some similarity to the smallness and obtuseness of early Truman scandals. In place of a mink coat, there was now the vicuña coat. In June 1958, a Boston businessman, wonderfully named Bernard Goldfine, who was having problems with the Securities and Exchange Commission, had paid hotel bills for Sherman Adams, and given Adams an expensive fur coat, an act that would introduce the political world to the word *vicuña*. Adams did intercede for Goldfine with the SEC. The odor was sufficient to make it necessary for Ike to ask for his resignation—or rather, avoiding this task himself, to have Adams's resignation asked for by Hugh Meade Alcorn, Jr., the Republican chairman.

Truman's claim that the scandals of his administration were not worse than those of others, in a huge and complicated modern government, may have become a little more persuasive as those of Eisenhower's unfolded. But Truman's most serious criticism of Eisenhower—which takes us back to the 1952 campaign—was an issue of a radically different kind, at quite another level. This was Eisenhower's support of Senator Joseph McCarthy and his companion in demagoguery, William Jenner of Indiana, and, specifically, his deletion from his campaign speech in Milwaukee, with McCarthy sitting on the platform, of a paragraph praising George Marshall.

Before this episode, Eisenhower had already appeared (and, worse, had his picture taken) on an Indiana platform, grinning and holding the senatorial hand of McCarthy's notorious ally Jenner (who, among his other distinctions, had called General Marshall a "living lie"). And then Eisenhower, the novice candidate, in the hurly-burly of a campaign train, under pressure from Wisconsin Republican politicians, allowed himself to be persuaded to delete the praise of General Marshall that had already been pointedly written into the text of the speech he was to deliver in Milwaukee—a decision some of his staff deplored, and about which Eisenhower himself was chagrined for the rest of his life. The paragraph had been written, at Eisenhower's own instruction, and had appeared in the draft, but under the importuning of Wisconsin governor Walter J. Kohler Jr. and others on the campaign train, it had been, by Ike's own decision, removed. It had been included in texts of his speech that members of the press got hold of—so when it was cut, the political world knew.

It was surely galling to the moral crusader Dwight Eisenhower that among the most pungent critics of this Milwaukee deletion was none other than Harry S ("Scandal-a-Day") Truman. And Eisenhower, partly, no doubt, because his own remorse was eating at him, was furious at the things Truman said, and continued to be furious.

Truman, in his unvarnished style, said that Eisenhower's endorsement of senators who had attacked his great benefactor General Marshall showed a "kind of moral blindness" that "brands the Republican candidate as unfit to be president of the United States."

To be accused of moral blindness, and to have it said that one was therefore unfit to be president, and to be accused of compromising every principle of personal loyalty, would be a bit strong for anyone to take, even someone accustomed to the personal attacks and gross exaggerations of political campaigning. For a supreme commander, who had never liked politics, and who for years now had been deferred to and celebrated around the world, it was almost more than he could put up with. In *Ordeal of Power,* Eisenhower speechwriter Emmet Hughes wrote that in discussions during the campaign "a mere mention of Harry Truman's name brought fast flashes of antipathy." Eisenhower's fury was such that he said—aides and biographers report different times that he said these things, but there is wide agreement that he said either or both—he did not know how he could stand beside that fellow on Inauguration Day, and/or that he would never ride down Pennsylvania Avenue with that fellow. It was a vow he almost kept.

Truman, in his inimitable fashion, accused Ike of doing something "shameful," of having "betrayed his principles." And he put the point specifically in terms of loyalty: Eisenhower "had compromised every principle of personal loyalty by abetting the scurrilous big-lie attack" on General Marshall. The two men each discerned in the other a lowness he had not seen before. A furious Eisenhower said after Truman's comments, "How low can you get!" In Utica, New York, in October, Truman, speaking about candidate Eisenhower's endorsement of McCarthy and Jenner, said, "I had never thought the man who is now the Republican candidate would stoop so low."

Eisenhower's angry vehemence must have been made still more fierce by the obstreperous little voice within himself that kept whispering that Truman was right. That "memory," or intuition, or awareness of what human life and conduct ought to be, which provides the standards by which we praise and blame the conduct of others, cannot help but sometimes rebound on our own. The etymology of the word *remorse* evokes the picture of a person biting or stinging himself. On some matters on which others accuse us, we can nevertheless justify ourselves, because we have an insider's details about our choices that no one else can know; on other matters, we secretly condemn ourselves—we bite and sting ourselves—for the same reason.

Eisenhower himself would come up with the excuses that others would make for him with regard to that deleted paragraph, and perhaps be persuaded. But then—we may conjecture—the irrepressible small voice would whisper its stinging rebuke once again.

This was a speech *draft,* for crying out loud. It is nobody's business what a candidate and his staff put in and leave out of speech *drafts* before they are delivered. Changing drafts is just part of the process. Nobody should even know what is in suppressed drafts. But he might not have been able to suppress the inner voice that said, Wasn't this more than an ordinary draft? Hadn't that paragraph been written for a specific worthy purpose? And was it not then taken out under specific political pressure?

Had he not already spoken his piece, by his standards forcefully, about General Marshall's worthiness and patriotism in response to a question at a press conference on August 22 in Denver? But then would come an unhushable whisper of conscience: Not in Wisconsin. Not after the campaign had really started and the nation had really listened. Not in a way that joined the issue with the calumnies of Jenner and McCarthy. The answer to the question in Denver floated calmly by on the currents of public discourse without leaving a ripple. Since that time, Eisenhower had appeared on the platform with Senator Jenner in Indiana. And pictures of Eisenhower and Jenner, hands upraised and clasped together, had been publicized across the land.

Had not all of his staff, in the chaos of the campaign train traveling across Illinois toward Wisconsin, recommended that he drop the paragraph about Marshall from his Milwaukee speech? But, even if that were true, what a picture of the supreme commander that created, meekly deferring on so close a personal and a moral issue to these scrambling political advisers on the train! And it was not true. Sherman Adams, after his own consultations, had recommended the deletion, but his staff was divided, with at least Gabriel Hauge and Robert Cutler on the train and Emmet Hughes back in New York, and probably others, strongly in favor of retaining the paragraph, and dismayed when it was stricken.

Was it not true, as Sherman Adams said to Ike on the train, that the paragraph about Marshall was "out of context" and "didn't fit" and was gratuitously added to the speech? But what an extraordinary time and place—in the bedlam of a train in the slapdash of a campaign—suddenly to be appealing to the aesthetic and intellectual unities, as if that counted for beans in a campaign speech. And that wasn't true, either. The reference to Marshall that Emmet Hughes had written into the speech draft, with Eisenhower's approval, served all too well to illustrate the "wrong methods" for attacking Communists in government that that passage of the speech was condemning.

Was it not true, as was argued by Wisconsin's governor Kohler and others, that he was their "guest" in their great state, and—by implication—that it would be impolite while thus invited to condemn one of their own? But what a bizarre occasion on which to invoke such standards of courtesy! The Wisconsin Republicans had been desperate to get Ike, the popular candidate, to visit their state, for their reasons and their purposes. Ike had not wanted to go to Wisconsin and Indiana, exactly because of McCarthy and Jenner, both running for reelection on the Republican ticket with him. But to Eisenhower's dismay, the Republican leaders in Wisconsin and at national headquarters had scheduled a visit to those states anyway. He certainly did not owe them abject capitulation; as this was not an appropriate occasion for the criteria of aesthetic unity, so it was also hardly the moment to defer, on grounds of courtesy, to one's "host."

Eisenhower could say to himself that he had generated the passage at issue, in the calm of New York before the trip—as Emmet Hughes told the story—proposing to defend Marshall in McCarthy's own backyard. But having proposed it, and having had it written into the draft of the speech, to *remove* the passage under local political pressure was surely an act of quite another kind.

If Eisenhower was, as Stephen Ambrose, Emmet Hughes, and Piers Brandon all said it was clear he was, ashamed of this Milwaukee deletion, it cannot have improved his temper to realize that Harry Truman wholeheartedly agreed that he ought to have been. Of course one would say that a failure to defend a superbly honorable man against unconscionable attacks, in a situation in which such a defense was called for and had been planned, would be reprehensible already, even if the scheduled defender had no personal connection to the man under unfair attack. But for Harry Truman, there was another objectionable side to Eisenhower's failure to defend Marshall: Without Marshall's specific intervention on his behalf, Eisenhower would have remained a more or less lowly officer among many others—unheard of in the world of military affairs and world politics.

Truman said of Eisenhower, as Merle Miller recorded it in 1961, that "he was going to pay a tribute to General Marshall, but he took it out rather than stand up to McCarthy. It was one of the most shameful things I can ever remember. Why, General Marshall was responsible for his whole career. When Roosevelt jumped him from lieutenant colonel to general it was Marshall's recommendation. Three different times Marshall got him pushed upstairs, and in return . . . Eisenhower sold him out. It was just a shameful thing." For Harry Truman, the personal relationship of Marshall to Eisenhower as benefactor or patron added markedly to the shame—the disloyalty—of Eisenhower's deed.

Emmet Hughes, who was the speechwriter to whom Eisenhower had given the task originally of drafting the paragraph, and who did draft it, visited President Eisenhower in 1958, in response to a letter the president had written him. At one point, the discussion touched on the episode that still (apropos of the remarks about "remorse" earlier) "stung in his memory," as Hughes put it in his book *Ordeal of Power*. Some mention of Harry Truman "triggered an explosive exclamation. 'God, this man goes around,' he cried, 'saying that I let George Marshall be called a traitor in my presence and I never said a word. Why, I was never on any political platform where any such thing took place in my presence. George Marshall is really one of the few men I've ever known whom I'd call great!' " Hughes's own comment on this outburst was, "Thus do footnotes to history get garbled even in the minds of men who made the event. . . . [T]he recollection of compromise in 1952 was still too bitter to taste truly."

One striking feature of candidate Eisenhower's reasoning, back when that compromise was made, on the McCarthy issue in general, and on the Milwaukee deletion in particular, is how "political" it was, in exactly the pejorative sense that the crusaders, and Eisenhower himself, would use the term—that is, they altogether subordinated principle to perceived partisan advantage. Very early in Eisenhower's presidential campaign, he wrote a long response to a letter from Edward Meade Earle, a scholar whom he knew and respected, who had urged him forthrightly to denounce McCarthy. In response, Eisenhower made the tortured argument that because McCarthy had just won a primary victory by 100,000 votes, to oppose him on the ground that "he is morally unfit for office" would be "indirectly accusing the electorate of stupidity at best, and of immorality, at the most." And so he not only removed the paragraph but allowed it to be perceived that he was supporting McCarthy.

Truman, the politician, would sternly reject the argument by Eisenhower, the nonpolitician, that politics required his course toward Jenner and McCarthy. "Don't let anybody tell you that every presidential candidate has to do that—that it is just politics," Truman said. "Franklin Roosevelt did not endorse every Democrat, and neither did Harry Truman. Governor Dewey in 1948 did not endorse Republicans who had disgraced the Republican label. But the Republican candidate this year did, with the same betrayal of principle that he has shown throughout the campaign."

Eisenhower's action, or inaction, was widely deplored, well beyond the circle of Harry Truman and the Democrats; it was deplored by many of Eisenhower's original supporters and staff. Emmet Hughes was not with the campaign in the Middle West, but back in New York at campaign headquarters, when the deed was done. In his book *Ordeal of Power,* Hughes made a most interesting quasi-defense of Eisenhower on this matter, on which he had claim to be among those most deeply offended. First, Hughes quoted, as the "most compassionate response," the comment of one of those who was most dismayed, Harold Stassen, to the effect that it was hard for those back in New York to judge how it was there amid the pressures and the hurly-burly of the campaign train. But then Hughes drew back and said that there was more to it than that; that Eisenhower, if sure in his own mind, could not have been overborne by the staff, however hectic the conditions on the train. He then presented his interpretation: There was in him, said Hughes, "a profound humility—a refusal to *use* the full force of his personal authority or political position against a critical consensus." He saw himself as "a stranger to political affairs," and the people around him on the train as political experts. "He must show himself . . . a modest enough member of the team," Hughes wrote, noting how tiresome and stale the use of the word *team* would become in the Eisenhower entourage. (And how about the word *crusade*? one may ask.) And so—this is Hughes's interpretation—in an attempt to be a humble "team" player on a terrain in which he was unfamiliar, he took out the paragraph.

One can imagine how unpersuasive that would be to Harry Truman. He was by no means inclined to regard General Eisenhower, as he had become a world figure, as "humble" or "modest." "He had a very high opinion of himself," Truman said in 1961 to Merle Miller. "Somewhere along the line he seemed to forget all about the fact that he was just a poor boy from Kansas." For one who began his big two-volume biography with the flat assertion that Dwight Eisenhower was "both a great and a good man," Stephen Ambrose's conclusion about the Marshall deletion is rather stark: "Perhaps the best thing that can be said about the incident is that Eisenhower, having decided to run for president, was so determined to win that he was willing to do whatever seemed necessary to do." (If that is the *best* thing that can be said, one wonders what the worst could be.) "That he was ashamed of himself," Ambrose went on, "there can be little doubt." Eisenhower tried never to mention the event again. "When he came to write his memoirs, ten years later, he wanted to ignore it altogether," Ambrose wrote. "When his aides insisted that he could not simply pass it over, he wrote, discarded, wrote again, discarded again, and finally printed a version in which he said that if he had realized what the reaction to the deletion would be, 'I would never have acceded to the staff's arguments, logical as they sounded at the time.' "*

But that still dealt only with the *reaction* to his deed, not with its substance. How did it stand by Ike's campaign criterion "straight out right and wrong"? Throughout the rest of his life, one may infer, on this incident, Dwight Eisenhower of Abilene, Kansas, not only had a sore spot inside himself but also felt the eyes of Harry S Truman of Independence, Missouri, staring at him owl-like from behind thick glasses, his expression one of stern disapproval.

* Stephen Ambrose, *Eisenhower: Soldier and President* (Simon & Schuster, 1990), p. 284.

CHAPTER TEN

Reciprocating Animosities

I

THE FIRST THING TO SAY about Eisenhower's attitude toward Truman is that Truman was not Roosevelt. Eisenhower had many reservations about Roosevelt's political positions, but he still respected Roosevelt as a world leader, and understood from the most direct personal involvement the former president's role in shaping the Allied participation in the great events surrounding World War II. And Roosevelt had been the commander in chief under whom Eisenhower had been chosen for each of the giant steps in his own vertiginous ascent to the highest Allied command and to world fame. Roosevelt personally chose him, and told him he was chosen, to be the commander of Operation Overlord, the great moment of his life. Eisenhower felt no such debt, to put it mildly, to Harry Truman.

It is not easy to convey to those who did not live through it the depth of the shock—like that of the three generals in their bathrobes in Germany on April 12—when Roosevelt died. And then there was the subordinate and secondary realization after that first shock: Who was it—Harry Truman of Missouri?—that was now president? All transitions from one president to another require a little adjustment as one learns to pronounce such unfamiliar and slightly jarring locutions as "President Richard Nixon" or "President Lyndon Johnson." But learning to say "President Truman," after a lifetime of saying "President Roosevelt," was unusually disorienting.

Roosevelt was, in some ontological way, *the* president. Truman himself told in his memoirs (and all biographers and commentators since, including me, have repeated) the story of his telephoning, on the Saturday after Roosevelt had died, an old Rooseveltian Washington hand, administrator of the Reconstruction Finance Corporation Jesse Jones, to tell him that "the President" had appointed John Snyder as federal loan administrator.

"Did he make that appointment before he died?"

"No. He made it just now."

Roosevelt had been president *forever*. Republican wags in 1944 sarcastically altered the words to Irving Berlin's popular love song "Always": "Not for just two terms. Not for just three terms. Not for just four terms. But—*Always.*"

He was an active and stylish and very visible president through two pivotal episodes of the twentieth century, and of world history, the Great Depression and the New Deal response to it, and World War II. The twelve-plus years that he was president were to be measured not in chronological time only but also in that loaded and selective historical and psychological time, in which one afternoon's battle, one episode or vote or decision, can be the future's pivot, and a week, or a day, or a moment can count for more than whole years of quietly flowing years of more ordinary time.

Between March 4, 1933, when Roosevelt rode with his unsmiling predecessor down Pennsylvania Avenue, and April 12, 1945, when Harry Truman made his trip to see the president and learned that it was he who was president, both the nation, among the powers of the world, and the presidential office, among the powers of the nation, had been transformed. They had been ratcheted up and up, again and again and again. The first man after Roosevelt to occupy the vastly higher new pinnacle seemed to many not to belong there. *Harry Truman* of Missouri was *president*?

Might there also have been, mingled in Eisenhower's attitude toward Harry Truman (despite Eisenhower's origins in a poor family from the wrong side of the tracks in a little town in Kansas), just a touch of something approaching social disdain? Such an attitude toward Truman, implicitly contrasting him to the Harvard–Hyde Park aristocrat Franklin Roosevelt, to whom one had become accustomed in the office of president, or to some idealized picture of the president, was certainly not unknown in those days.

It does seem clear that Eisenhower did not approve of Truman's personal style. William Ewald, who had been an Eisenhower White House speechwriter, and then a writer on Eisenhower's memoirs, tells in his own book *Eisenhower the President* about Ike's remembering repeated invitations from Truman, as president, to Eisenhower, as army chief of staff (November 1945–February 1948), to come round at the end of the day for a drink, invitations that Eisenhower regularly declined. Ewald says Eisenhower's report of these repeated invitations was "tinged with faint contempt." That would seem to tell more about Eisenhower than about Truman—more than Ewald intended. Eisenhower was not averse to a certain amount of end-of-the-day relaxation and social life, involving a certain amount of alcohol, some jokes, and some card playing, even in the midst of the most serious events—as at Telegraph Cottage in England during the war—but not, apparently, with Harry Truman. The president of the United States invites you to come over for a drink at the end of the day; those of us who have never been a supreme commander surely would accept the invitation.

Eisenhower had this further shading in relationship to Truman: He had arrived at world fame first. Although Eisenhower was Truman's successor as president, he was his predecessor as a major world figure. Eisenhower had already had dealings with that difficult figure Charles de Gaulle, had been a regular weekend visitor with Winston Churchill at Chequers, had entertained the king of England in Algiers, and had had a spontaneous picnic featuring chicken sandwiches with President Roosevelt in a grove of trees in Tunisia, while Harry Truman was just another senator. Harry Truman never had a picnic with Franklin Roosevelt, featuring chicken sandwiches or anything else. Harry Truman's trip to Potsdam three months after he became president was his first trip outside the United States since he had been sent to Europe with the 129th Field Artillery in the Great War. Dwight Eisenhower had served for extended stretches in Panama and in Manila, had lived in Paris while writing a guide to the monuments of Harry Truman's war, and had had the world strategic picture in mind in conversations with the military intellectual Fox Conner, and in studies in the Army Command and General Staff College, while Harry Truman was dealing with bond issues for roads and courthouses in one Missouri county. Although Eisenhower's name had been unknown and sometimes misspelled when he burst upon the world scene in the summer of 1942, with the tremendous acceleration of events in wartime, by April 1945, when Truman suddenly became president, Eisenhower's name and nickname, his grin and character and jacket, had come to be among the best known not only in the United States but in the whole world. Eisenhower had already made decisions of the most staggering history-making kind at a time when Truman was still investigating defense plants.

In October 1950, the president of the United States, Harry Truman, called Dwight Eisenhower, now a university president, back into service again, to be the first commander of the North Atlantic Treaty Organization. This was to be, in historical terms, the high point of the collaboration between the two men. Even at this high point, however, there may have been a negative personal undertow. My evidence is slight—only one word, in fact. Maybe I make too much of it.

In *At Ease,* the amiable book Ike produced during his retirement, he told about his arduous takeover of the post of supreme Allied commander for Europe: he made a whirlwind trip (in very bad weather) in January 1951 to the European capitals, urging support of NATO; he spent four days at West Point in intense preparation for his defense of NATO to Congress; he flew with Mamie through more bad weather on the last day of January to have lunch with President Truman. Now comes the suspect word: "[A]pparently," Ike wrote, "traffic conditions were so bad that the President, who had insisted on meeting us [*insisted* is another word to notice], was late in arriving at the field. The plane's crew had to keep flying, circling the area so as to land just as the President reached the field." One can hear Ike's teeth grinding, even after the passage of the years: *Apparently,* traffic conditions were so bad that Ike's plane had to circle and circle until Truman's car got there. Truman would fly all the way to Wake Island, across seven time zones, 14,425 miles, to meet with General Mac-Arthur, who would not even salute or put on a tie to meet the president of the United States, and he could not get his presidential limousine to the Washington airport on time to meet General Eisenhower?

A news article once spoke about the onetime "mutual admiration" between the two men (as a dramatic antecedent to their "feud"), but it is not clear that Eisenhower ever admired Harry Truman. He did send him that congratulatory telegram on his 1948 election, as was noted in chapter 7, but, as was also noted, he voted for his opponent.

John Eisenhower, in his 1974 book, *Strictly Personal,* had this to say about his father's relationship to Truman: "Dad, being a secure and confident individual, could never carry a strong dislike for anyone for any length of time. But he also had a considerable capacity for simply writing off anyone whose abilities he did not particularly admire—and unfortunately Truman fell into that category."

Is "simply writing off anyone whose abilities he did not particularly admire" all that different from "a strong dislike"? In any case, the "writing off" of Truman's abilities lasted into Ike's retirement. William Ewald told about going over a late draft of Eisenhower's *Waging Peace,* in which Eisenhower gave an expansive list of "towering governmental figures of the West," including not only Churchill, Roosevelt, and George Marshall, whom no one could challenge, but also Herbert Hoover, John Foster Dulles, Lewis Strauss, and Ernest Bevin. "Given the expansiveness of this list," Ewald wrote, "I found one name conspicuously missing—Harry Truman's." Ewald pointed out that the omission appeared to glare from the page. "The General bridled for the briefest instant. Then he touched pencil to paper. 'Oh, hell, go ahead and put Truman's name in there.' " The bridling, and the grudging acquiescence, certainly tell the story.

The expectation of his high school class in Abilene that Dwight Eisenhower would become a "professor of history" was not to be realized in his career; rather, it was to skip his generation and realize itself to some extent in both generations to follow: his son John and his grandson David would both be, if not professors of history, serious historical writers. His grandson, exploring the doings of "Granddad" in 1943–1945, contrasting Eisenhower's situation in April 1945 with that in November 1942, would write in passing (once more, let me concentrate on just one word) that "in the course of two and a half years, Eisenhower's stature had grown, and by then [1945] he was acting in the *void* [emphasis added] left by Roosevelt's illness and death."* There is room to argue, if one were inclined to see Harry Truman's way, that what followed Franklin Delano Roosevelt's death was not a "void."

President Truman, in Europe for the meetings at Potsdam in the summer of 1945, and in office just three months, had in his meeting with Eisenhower in Frankfurt offered to support the supreme commander, then in the afterglow of the tremendous victory just two months earlier, for anything he wanted, specifically for the presidency in 1948. Eisenhower told about this offer, matter-of-factly enough, in *Crusade in Europe*, published in 1948, but the time would come when Truman would criticize him, attack him, and even (in 1958, on Edward R. Murrow's TV program, *See It Now*) deny he'd ever made that offer. Eisenhower, hearing of such denials, would be, understandably, "hopping mad." There had been other praise and other offers, not only in routine or ceremonial exchanges of birthday greetings, congratulations, and the like, and the awarding of oak-leaf clusters (in the citation for one of which Truman, as president, praised among other things Eisenhower's modesty), but also in private and personal communication about politics. Late in 1947, when Truman's fortunes were low, Truman again raised the possibility of Eisenhower's running on the Democratic ticket in 1948. It is reported, in fact—according to Secretary of the Army Kenneth Royall—that Truman went so far as to offer to go on the ticket himself as *vice president* if Ike would run in the top spot, but Ike turned him down again. Eisenhower, in his later years, angry with Truman, could recall other examples of his earlier extravagant praise

* David Eisenhower, *Eisenhower at War, 1943–1945* (Random House, 2010), p. xxv.

and support. How could a man turn from such commendation in one year to such disparagement in another?

Truman, on the other hand, surely had admired Eisenhower, perhaps, at first, extravagantly. He had been a United States senator and a strong supporter of the war effort during Eisenhower's rapid ascent, and, by the evidence of his response when they met, had been loaded with admiration. Their first real conversations had come there in Germany, when Truman was the new president, pluckily trying to fill the huge shoes into which he had been abruptly dropped. Truman made the offer mentioned above to the war hero Ike. At that time, it would certainly seem, Truman shared in the widespread adulation of Eisenhower. And thereafter the tone of his letters to Ike would exhibit more friendliness, and imply the expectation of a greater intimacy, than would Eisenhower's to Truman. But then as 1952 approached, it would appear that Truman experienced a considerable reversal of feeling regarding Eisenhower, a certain disillusionment, almost a sense of betrayal.

The nub of the matter may have been this: Truman, the partisan, had thought that he and Ike were not only friends but at least implicitly, in some broad way, members of the same political team. He therefore thought that if Eisenhower should enter politics (which toward the end he advised him not to do), it should be as a Democrat.

We may infer that Truman really did feel that there was something a little illegitimate, a touch of betrayal, in Eisenhower's now lending his immense prestige as a war hero to the service of the opposing party. From Truman's point of view, Eisenhower had participated in making and executing key policies that a large segment of the party he now joined had opposed. And Eisenhower would still have been a colonel had it not been for appointments made by a commander in chief who was a Democrat. Democratic administrations had appointed him to high posts and had encouraged the sudden flowering of his worldwide fame. John Snyder would say, "At bottom the president resented Ike running as a Republican. He thought Ike should have run as a Democrat. They had built him up."

Meanwhile, surely Truman himself changed. Harry Truman had been perhaps excessively modest during those first days of his abrupt and unprepared entry into the presidency, and he had asked everyone to pray for him. Then in Frankfurt, as we have noted, he had told General Eisenhower, that he would support him for anything, including the presidency in 1948, and had deprecated his own abilities to the point that Alben Barkley told him to stop it. When that very modest and very nervous new president first addressed his old colleagues in Congress (and the nation over radio), he started ripping right into his text in his midwestern twang, and Speaker Rayburn stopped him to say (with the microphones still open, so all the world heard), "Just a minute, Harry. I have to introduce you."

But that was then and this was now. With the passage of time, Harry Truman had become accustomed to carrying great responsibility on his presidential shoulders. He had made huge decisions of world import, a dozen of them before he'd gotten his breath back in 1945, decisions as big and as fraught as those Roosevelt had made, as big as those Eisenhower had made—or even bigger. He had been nominated in 1948, had given a gutsy and rousing middle-of-the-night acceptance speech, had called the Turnip Day congressional session, had toured the nation's whistle-stops, giving 'em hell, and, against all odds and all predictions save his own, had been elected.

As a history reader, Truman knew, vice presidents who succeeded upon the death of presidents in the nineteenth century (Tyler, Fillmore, Johnson, and Arthur) not only were not elected in their own right; they were not even nominated by their parties—those of them who still had parties. In the twentieth century, though, the pattern would be reversed; succeeding vice presidents (Teddy Roosevelt, Coolidge, Truman, and then Lyndon Johnson) were both nominated and, except in the special case of Gerald Ford, elected in their own right.

Surely there must come, with that vindicating event, a certain psychological transformation—even, let us suppose, in the case of Calvin Coolidge, although in his case jesters might insist on asking, How could you tell? Presumably this was true in the case of Theodore Roosevelt, although perhaps again, for opposite reasons, the question might be, How could you tell? Theodore Roosevelt's biographer Henry Pringle quoted him as saying, on March 3, 1905, "Tomorrow I shall come into office in my own right. Then watch out for me!" In the case of Lyndon Johnson, in more recent times, one *could* tell. Being elected in 1964 by that huge margin began to free him from that galling shadow of the young martyr who had chosen him for the ticket and then left him such an emotionally turbulent succession.

And surely in Harry Truman's case, the difference, against the backdrop of earlier expectations and assessments, must have been immense. A part of it was to take one big step out from under the gigantic shadow of

FDR. But surely being elected in his own right rearranged psychological and emotional relationships all around, including those to former general and now mere university president Dwight Eisenhower.

What a victory! Not only over Dewey, not only over the *Chicago Daily Tribune* with its DEWEY DEFEATS TRUMAN headline, not only over H. V. Kaltenborn, but also over all those, including that list of prominent Democrats, who had not wanted Truman to be the 1948 nominee! And whom had those Democrats proposed in Truman's place? Dwight Eisenhower, of course. What a victory, then, not two years after those despairing and demeaning proposals, for Harry Truman to be nominated and to win, by his own efforts!

Perhaps in his second term, there was a new spring in Harry Truman's step, a new authority in his voice.

Had Eisenhower also changed? During the heightened intensity of wartime, and the first flush of world fame, Eisenhower's democratic, nice-guy demeanor had been a large part of his distinctive appeal; it set him apart not only from German generals and from a British prima donna like Montgomery but also from fellow American generals like his friend George Patton and his sometime boss Douglas MacArthur. His grin and the nickname "Ike" were ubiquitous accompaniments of the great Allied victory. When in 1945 (before the war in Europe was over) Sam Goldwyn proposed a movie about him, Ike had insisted that the movie not glorify General Eisenhower but, rather, democracy, freedom, and the soldiers who fought; he further insisted that each British and American general who served with him "be portrayed as a leader of courage, intelligence, and as fully devoted as myself to the promotion of unity and effectiveness. . . . [T]he picture will have to be honest again in giving the same amount of credit to subordinates all the way down the line, as I have." All very admirable, but Goldwyn dropped the idea of the picture.

Eisenhower, still under the spell of the high wartime purpose and collaboration, stated with grace and simplicity, as we have seen, in his Guildhall speech in London in June 1945, that the honor given to him there had been won by the deeds and the blood of anonymous millions of others. But again, that was then and this was now. It was he, not those subordinates all the way down the line, or those bloodstained followers and friends, who had been given the duke of Wellington's sword and the keys to the city of London. And as the years went on and the war became only a potent recent memory and not a present reality, it was Eisenhower who kept on receiving the honors. The others would fade, the complexity of the collaboration would fade, and Ike would remain. The collective memory of nations and peoples must, by nature, simplify. Eisenhower was celebrated throughout the Allied world as not only the agent but also the symbol of the immense victorious collaboration. And in the United States, given the meaning of the American presidency (leader of the free world, political leader and national symbol, model and representative), politicians of both parties and citizens of both parties and of no party would, of course, keep insisting Ike should be president.

Harry Truman might say of Eisenhower that, for all your origins in a little town in Kansas, if you have grown accustomed to being called supreme commander, and to being saluted and deferred to, and to having a Filipino or black valet help you on with your clothes every morning, you, although Kansas-born, are now in the situation that Dorothy famously described to her dog Toto in *The Wizard of Oz:* You are not in Kansas anymore.

II

ENTERING POLITICS from outside and above leaves one unprepared for the constant barrage of criticism that it entails. Eisenhower's actions and policies had not been systematically and continually assailed from within the institution in which he had lived his daily life as Harry Truman's had been, as any politician's are. Any politician may read each morning in the paper "unfair" attacks upon himself by members of an organized opposition. Those attacks are institutionalized in the contests of parties. A general isn't used to that—not the regular, institutionalized opposition. A general may encounter attacks and criticisms, to be sure, including severe and mistaken ones, but those attacks are not a systematic part of one's own institution. They are not deliberately articulated by the system itself, which is not the case with democratic politics. On the contrary: Within any one army, the purpose is to suppress and subordinate differences and conflicts, in the interests of a unity that is important to victory over an external opponent.

During his rise, Eisenhower was subject to occasional press and political and popular criticism, notably about the Admiral Darlan matter in North Africa, and perhaps a little in the Patton slapping incident. Of course there were arguments over grand strategy—over invasion of the soft underbelly as against invasion across the Channel, over continuing on to Berlin as against stopping and letting the Russians take it (in these he had been but one voice, mostly in accord with his own nation's leaders)—

and there were continuing personal differences that reflected some national differences. But none of this took place in the setting of an overt, systematic, and continuing contest for power, whereas such differences do in the political sphere. However many disagreements there may have been in Operations Torch, Husky, and Overlord, the organizing commitment was to a great common cause with a common leader. The building up of that leader was an important part of the effort to achieve the objectives; the machinery of propaganda of several governments, and the willing cooperation of the press, celebrated the supreme commander as an aspect of the building of war-winning morale. Eisenhower himself was more aware of this feature of warfare, perhaps particularly big-army, long-distance, mass-communication modern warfare, than other military men.

And so he may not have been altogether prepared for what he got into when he allowed himself to be persuaded that it was his transcendent duty to enter politics. When he landed at the Kansas City airport in almost his first venture out into that world, he did not expect to be clapped on the back and greeted with "Hiya, Ike" by the governor of Colorado, Dan Thornton—a greeting unlike those to which he had become accustomed as supreme commander. He did not expect to be asked by a nosy Taft Republican from Nebraska about Mamie's drinking habits. He also did not expect to be attacked from several sides in the press and in political speeches.

Margaret Truman reported a meeting that her father had with Ike in the early summer of 1952, when the general, home from Europe, requested permission from the president to resign from NATO and come home to be a candidate. "Ike," according to Margaret Truman, "expressed considerable resentment over some nasty comments which certain segments of the press had already begun making about his candidacy. The General had thought he was going to get the Republican nomination on a platter. But Senator Taft had other ideas, and Ike found himself in the middle of a dogfight for delegates. Senator Taft had plenty of newspaper support, and Ike suddenly had become the target of numerous uncomplimentary remarks. Dad grinned. 'Ike,' he said, 'I suggest you go right down to the Office of the Republican National Committee and ask them to equip you with an elephant hide an inch thick. You're going to need it.'"

Eisenhower would need an elephant hide of some thickness not only to withstand shots from Taft and the press but also, of course, from Democrats, very much including Truman himself.

In the campaign of 1952, Eisenhower was a total novice in practical

American politics, the logic of whose political situation required the pla-
cating of the right wing, the Taft wing, of the party that had—against its
own true heart's desire—nominated him. Truman was a sitting president,
low in popularity, whose record and historical place were, in his eyes at
least, to be tested by the election's outcome. The logic of the situation
meant that Eisenhower would be attacking (as any Republican nominee
would have done) the record of the Truman administration, and that Truman would be defending it, belligerently, as he would have against any
Republican nominee.

And so these onetime collaborators went at it. The two men even had
an exchange or two about great issues at the very beginning of the Cold
War, in which they had been, in fact, collaborators and in basic agreement, and, if in error, both in the same error. Truman, for his part (of
course it was his speechwriters), went clear back to 1945 for statements by
Eisenhower about the USSR and the Communists (for example, "There is
no one thing, I believe, that guides the policy of Russia more today than
friendship with the United States," Truman quoted Eisenhower as having
testified to the House Military Affairs Committee in 1945) to say (in Mon-
tana, at the end of September) that Eisenhower's hindsight was better than
his foresight, and that if he had given better advice back then, "we wouldn't
have had so much trouble waking up the country to the danger of communist imperialism." Eisenhower responded a week later in Eugene, Oregon, with a quotation from Truman that (in turn) his staff had dug out:
Such a charge comes with poor grace from a man who once said "I like old
Uncle Joe Stalin. Joe is a decent fellow." It wasn't a particularly edifying
exchange.

Once, Truman attacked Eisenhower over the arrangements for access
to Berlin worked out at the end of the war.

On the home front, Eisenhower, speaking to the AFL, implied (in the
very first attack, in early September, that either one of them made on the
other) that when he was chief of staff, President Truman had wanted him
to play the role of "strikebreaker"—to "assume command of the railroad
workers who were going to be drafted into the army." (Apparently, that
was some Republican speechwriter's idea of the kind of speech to give to a
labor union audience.) The lowest blow of all was struck by President Truman, in one of those wild swings one is inclined to attribute, without
excusing the principal, to an overeager staff. This was a message President
Truman sent (that is to say, it was sent in Truman's name) to a Washington
conference of the National Jewish Welfare Board in October, in which

Truman charged that by his endorsements of conservative Republicans and his choice of Richard Nixon as his running mate, Eisenhower was linking himself to those who had voted to override his (Truman's) veto of the McCarran-Walter Immigration bill. That bill—in the view of Truman and many others—implicitly, by its geographical limits on immigration, discriminated against Jews and Catholics, and Eisenhower was by that chain of reasoning guilty of a "moral blindness" toward the "master race" theory we had fought against in the war. Eisenhower of course would respond angrily, but the far-fetched charge had already exploded in Truman's hand, with the prompt rejection of his attack by Jewish and interfaith groups.

But these matters, distressing though they might be, were not the main themes of the campaign. Corruption was a main theme, one C of the Republican campaign's K1C2 formula, and Eisenhower was more than willing to give voice to it; it fit him. The "scandal-a-day" administration of Harry Truman was, of course, the target of the highly moralistic attack on corruption.

Any Republican candidate, including Taft, would have attacked what Harry Truman did not enjoy hearing called the "mess in Washington," but corruption was an issue that particularly fit Dwight Eisenhower.

Still worse, from Truman's point of view, were the other two items in the Republican campaign formula, Korea and communism. Truman (and his staff) were particularly annoyed by items that Eisenhower (and his staff) had allowed to go into Eisenhower's speeches, items that implied criticisms of Truman *foreign* policies, in the making of which Ike himself (as chief of staff of the army and then as commander of NATO) had participated. Throughout this service in the Truman administration Eisenhower supported the developing Truman foreign policy. This point, like everything else about their relationship, would become disputed territory once the political contest and personal antagonism between the two men developed in 1952. From Truman's perspective, the story would be this: Eisenhower as chief of staff supported the Truman Doctrine's concrete expression in Greece and Turkey in the spring of 1947. He supported the Marshall Plan in the spring of 1948, when he was out of government and president of Columbia University. Eisenhower, while president of Columbia, served as an adviser to the first secretary of the new Department of Defense and as chairman of the new Joint Chiefs, and he supported President Truman's response to the North Korean attack in June 1950. Then at the end of 1950, he accepted Truman's appointment as the first commander of NATO. At the end of 1950 and the beginning of 1951, he toured NATO capitals to assess European commitment, and then defended NATO to Congress at the end of January, in testimony that was very important to NATO's success with Congress and the American public.

And so Truman and his associates would be particularly vexed by criticisms Ike would make or imply, under prodding from, and in an effort to placate, the Republican right wing, against the main outlines of postwar foreign policy. You helped to *shape* it, they would say; you were involved in making the policies which you now attack. The most severe irritants had to do with Senator McCarthy, and with the Korean War, which furnished a backdrop to McCarthy's exploits. As to the war: By the fall of 1952, it had become a major item in the indictment of Truman's administration. Although the initial American public response to President Truman's action, in June 1950, had been favorable and mostly bipartisan, as the war continued, and the complaints against the restrictions of a "limited" war—a UN police action—multiplied, and the casualties increased, it became, in right-wing opinion, "Truman's War."

Eisenhower, however, had supported that war. How, then, as the Republican candidate for president, would Eisenhower handle the matter? He spoke about the war often, in phrases that could be interpreted as reflecting the right-wing attack upon it. Then his earlier, somewhat dubious remarks about, for example, Korean natives taking over, were altogether upstaged by the most brilliant stroke of the campaign—considered simply as strategy—Eisenhower's famous "I will make that trip" speech in Detroit on October 24. This promise of a trip to Korea had the advantage, for the Eisenhower forces, of using his immense prestige as a war leader—such a promise by another candidate would not have had any comparable effect—with an implied, but entirely unstated, suggestion that the war would thereupon be concluded. One may surmise that Truman's angry counterattack was motivated, in part, by the frustration on the part of an actual war leader, facing the actual complexities, at that unspoken implication, but also partly by the frustration of a politician dealing with an unbeatable opponent's tactic. It was an unanswerably effective campaign device, juxtaposing the unpopular war with the very popular war hero, without saying anything specific about policy. Truman said that was "a piece of demagoguery," which in turn, of course, made Eisenhower furious. As noted in chapter 8, President Truman could not resist saying, in his telegram of congratulation on the day after the election, that the presidential plane, the *Independence,* would be available to Eisenhower for his trip to Korea "if you still want to go."

The two men's reciprocating fury would center most of all on Eisenhower's treatment of the McCarthy problem. (The 1952 presidential election took place at the height of the influence of Senator Joseph McCarthy.) Traces of the charges of "softness" on communism featured by the right wing of Eisenhower's new party, and directed at Harry Truman's party, would appear in Eisenhower's speeches. And then came Milwaukee, and the deleted paragraph that was discussed in the previous chapter.

III

WHEN ELECTION DAY CAME in 1952, Eisenhower won the expected large victory by the expected large margin, and prepared to move into the White House, where Harry Truman prepared to yield it to him. But there would be further aggravations before Inauguration Day.

When in the middle of December the outrageous MacArthur grandly announced that he wanted to talk to President-elect Eisenhower because he had a solution to the Korean War (the "solution" proved to be to use atomic bombs on China), and when President-elect Eisenhower did confer with him, President Truman told reporters that if MacArthur had a solution to the Korean War, he ought to come to Washington and tell the Defense Department immediately. And then he again attacked Eisenhower's trip to Korea as "a piece of demagoguery."

Nevertheless, President Truman, an experienced professional politician, expected to swallow his unhappiness and to play his public role properly. He was determined, because he read history and because he cared deeply about the office and because he himself had been so ill-prepared by Roosevelt, that this change of presidents would be as helpful to the incoming administration as it could be. But from Eisenhower's point of view, that was not so easy. It was as if he were saying, You mean, after all the nasty things you said about me, we are supposed to turn around and act as though it had never happened?

The one meeting between these two before the inauguration came in the middle of November. It was Truman's idea, an attempt to smooth the transition. But the adjectives used by all parties to describe both the meeting and, particularly, Eisenhower's demeanor do not suggest that it was a happy or a fruitful occasion: "grim," "unsmiling," "chip on his shoulder" (Harry on Ike); "stiff, formal, embarrassing, and unrewarding" (Stephen Ambrose on the meeting); "added little to my knowledge, nor did it affect my planning" (Eisenhower on the meeting); "I think all this went into one ear and out the other" (Truman on attempts to inform the president-elect); "cold and uncharacteristically taciturn" (Brownell on Eisenhower); "taciturn to the point of surliness" (Acheson on Eisenhower); " . . . the photograph taken when Dad visited the White House for a briefing portrays anything but an atmosphere of cordiality" (John Eisenhower).

President-elect Eisenhower's informal remarks to the press after this frigid meeting made a pointed distinction between two aspects of his day in Washington. "This meeting today we expected to be completely business," he began. "It has turned into a dual purpose meeting. One, a very warm reception here from the citizens of Washington, for which I thank them sincerely. It was an inspiring experience to come up the streets from the airfield here up to the White House." But at the door of the White House, the president-elect's remarks plainly implied, the warmth and the inspiration abruptly stopped. Eisenhower described this sharply antithetical aspect of the day in a sentence that reminds those who were alive then of the peculiar quality of Eisenhower's presidential speech pattern, a kind of awkwardly pompous excess of inexact words: "The other part of the meeting was that kind that has been reported in the papers for making certain arrangements for the orderly transition of the functions of government from the outgoing administration to the incoming." President Truman was not named, let alone thanked. As the first sentence of Eisenhower's statement spoke of his expectation that the meeting would be "completely business," so the last sentence flatly affirmed that the purpose was to make the transfer in "orderly," businesslike fashion. Meanwhile, there had been that warm reception and that inspiring experience from the airfield up the streets and to the door of the White House—but no further.

President Truman, by his account, offered the president-elect some pictures that had been given him by several governments: of Hidalgo, the Mexican liberator, given to him expressly for the presidential office; of San Martín, given to him by the Argentine government; and of Bolívar, given to him by the Venezuelan government. Truman's own account of the response to this gesture, in his diary, is that "I was informed, very curtly, that I'd do well to take them with me—that the governments of those countries would, no doubt, give the new President the same pictures!" Truman, who recorded that he was trying to be "pleasant and co-operative," offered Eisenhower the global map that Eisenhower had used during the war and, in friendlier times in Frankfurt at the time of the Potsdam conference, had given to Truman. Now, in the frost of 1952, Eisenhower did accept this map, but, according to Truman, he "didn't even say thanks." The aftermath of the presidential election of 1952 might be said to be unusual in this respect: that it was the victors, more than the vanquished, who behaved in a bitter, sullen, and uncooperative fashion.

So that was the emotional backdrop when these two Middle Americans, who had now become giants of twentieth-century world politics, met again, this time for the passing of the mightiest governmental power that had ever been passed, in the history of the world, from one hand to another. This inauguration was unusually noteworthy because it entailed the shifting not only of presidents but also of parties, after a long, multiply transforming twenty years, and that change took place under the new conditions of the Cold War and unbelievably potent weapons. And, of course, it is that peaceful and orderly passing, from hand to hand, and party to party, of immense governmental power that is the large story of that day—a moving example of the continuing success of this continent-size constitutional republic.

But it does not diminish that larger story (perhaps it even enhances it) to note that within and alongside it there were some smaller stories—very much smaller. First, there was the episode of the hats. Second, there was the matter of lunch. Third, there was the great question of getting out of the car.

Eisenhower had insisted to his advisers, who were meeting in the Commodore Hotel in New York, and then, without consulting Truman, had announced that he would wear a homburg instead of the traditional top hat. Truman, although a traditionalist, said he did not wish to have a quarrel over hats, and he shifted to a homburg.

Truman also believed it was customary for the president-elect and his wife to call on the president and his wife, and so the Trumans invited the Eisenhowers to lunch. But the Eisenhowers declined the invitation.

Then came Inauguration Day itself. Truman was incensed when Eisenhower tried to make Truman, the sitting president, come and pick *him* up at the Statler Hilton. Truman, of course, could cite the precedents: The incoming president had *always* called on the sitting president, and gone into the president's residence to greet him, except for two occasions, when John Adams fled Washington before the inauguration in 1801 and when Franklin Roosevelt did not get out of the car because of his crippled legs in 1933. (Truman may have omitted the case of John Quincy Adams in 1829.) The Eisenhowers did finally go to the North Portico of the White House to pick up the Trumans, but then they sat—grimly, we may suppose—in the car, waiting. Eisenhower's own account of this moment in history, in *Mandate for Change,* includes a detail that a reader unaware that there was a great issue involved might find puzzling. Why this peculiar specificity about getting into and out of cars? Choosing a verb from Abilene's Wild West days, Eisenhower wrote, "When Mamie and I dismounted from our car, President Truman and Mrs. Truman came to the front steps; we exchanged greetings and the President and I re-entered the first car, while Mamie and Mrs. Truman rode in the second."

But Eisenhower's account, if one accepts the report of others, papers over the issue: He and Mamie did not "dismount." According to Margaret Truman, the Eisenhowers "refused to get out and greet us in the traditional manner." David McCullough wrote, "Only when the Trumans appeared did they step out of the car to greet them." McCullough went on to quote Eric Sevareid of CBS, who was on the porch close by: "It was a shocking moment. Truman was gracious and he had been snubbed. He showed his superiority by what he did."* What Truman did was to walk over to the car and shake Ike's hand as he got out of the car. Margaret, still boiling twenty years later, wrote that her father, "rather than hold up the inauguration[,] came out and got in the car."

The chilly ride down Pennsylvania Avenue, once they managed to get in the cars, cannot have been easy for any of the passengers. One well-recorded exchange took place either in the car or in the sergeant at arms' office as they waited to go onto the platform. Ike suddenly inquired as to who had ordered his son John home from Korea. "Who is trying to embarrass me?" he asked. Truman replied, "The President of the United States ordered your son to attend your inauguration. If you think somebody was trying to embarrass you by this order, then the President assumes full responsibility." Margaret Truman, writing while her father was still alive for consultation, recalled, "[M]y father had ordered John Eisenhower home from Korea as a gesture of thoughtfulness. He was not serving on the front lines, or in any particularly vital role in the Army, so there was no reason to accuse either his father or Dad of favoritism, or of endangering the public interest. It astonished Dad that Ike resented this gesture. It still astonishes me." John Eisenhower, for his part, wrote (in 1974), "I always appreciated Mr. Truman's kind gesture, and only the frosty atmosphere of the time prevented my expressing it."

Three days into his presidency, Eisenhower would write a thank-you note to Truman, singling out "your thoughtfulness in ordering my son home from Korea . . . and even more especially for not allowing either

---

* McCullough, p. 921.

him or me to know that you had done so." By then, he had comprehended
that it was a gracious gesture. But it had not been his first impulse to consider it so. The two men had reached that point of wary hostility in which
even benign gestures were misinterpreted.

The English member of Parliament and writer Roy Jenkins remarked
on "the unfortunate picture of two gentlemen in their sixties, both outstanding servants of the greatest democracy in the world, behaving in a
way which would have been discreditable to two small boys of eight."

At the inaugural ceremonies, the brand-new ex-president sat on the
platform, trying to listen but finding his mind wandering, while the
brand-new president gave his inaugural address, and then the two went
their separate ways, with a car carrying Harry Truman stopping for red
lights for the first time in seven and a half years.

In the Eisenhower papers in Abilene, there is a memo signed by the
president on January 28, in his second week in the White House, addressed
to the ex-president, Harry Truman, which says, "I have just noticed the
inscribed plate you had attached to the globe [sic] in this office, and I
remember that I failed to thank you for your courtesy in returning it to
me. It was a friendly gesture that I appreciate." If that note smacks of good
corrective staff work (more than two months later, he suddenly remembered that he had forgotten to thank the then president?), another item in
the Eisenhower files may reflect one other effort that failed. A staff memo
drafted the following April (1953) suggested that the president might want
to send Mr. Truman the poker table from the presidential yacht, the *Wil-
liamsburg,* that was built especially for Truman, indicating that it would be
"a nice return for the favor" that Truman had done by giving Eisenhower
the global map. The memo carries the terse notation: "THE PRESIDENT
SAID NO."

CHAPTER ELEVEN

Judging Presidents

HARRY TRUMAN, according to the polls in the last months he was president, was one of the least popular of presidents. Dwight Eisenhower, throughout his eight years, was one of the most popular. In his last year, Truman received the lowest approval rating any president ever managed—22 percent in February 1952—lower even than Richard Nixon's at the time of Watergate and his resignation. Dwight Eisenhower, on the other hand, had consistently high numbers—typically 64 percent—throughout his presidency; only twice, in ninety-six monthly polls, did his approval rating slip just barely below 50 percent.

It is not hard to explain why Truman came to be severely unpopular: The Korean War dragged on, and it was a limited war—not the sort of war the American public was thrilled to support. The firing of MacArthur was hugely controversial. The scandals could not be defended by anybody. The McCarthy attack—alas—took its toll. The demands of the Cold War meant that Truman could not get much of his domestic program passed. In his first years, Truman had to cope with an economy recovering from the war, and in his last years, he had to grapple with an economy strained by a new war and rapid military expansion. Truman, coming into the presidency as a major war ended, had to deal with more severe labor troubles than any president ever faced; he seized the coal mines and the railroads in his first term, and in his second term he made the mistake of seizing the steel mills in anticipation of a strike, and was stopped by the Supreme Court. And he was not Roosevelt, in voice or appearance.

It is easy also to explain Ike's approval ratings: personality, peace, and prosperity. He was an immense hero and a nice guy. A large part of his popularity was already established by his role as supreme commander—money in the bank before he even became president. (Harry Truman had nothing in that bank.) Six months into Ike's administration, he ended the Korean War, and there was no more war for the seven and a half remaining years of his presidency. With the end of the war in 1953, and then the effective end of McCarthy in 1954, and a postwar economy finally allowed to flourish, there came a golden moment when Ike was in his White House and all was right with the world. After *Sputnik* in 1957, and with the U-2 affair and the breakup of the summit in 1960, the glow around Ike may have dimmed a little—but not much. Had the new two-terms constitutional amendment not prevented it, he probably could have been elected a third time.

But the later judgment of historians and other professional observers evaluating these presidencies as a whole almost reversed this popular response. Truman was regularly placed up in the top numbers, among the "near great" or even sometimes the "great" in those surveys of the greatness of presidents, while Eisenhower languished for a time down below with Chester A. Arthur.

Historians now appraising Truman looked not at the scandals and difficulties that defined him for the public at the time, but at the decisions of huge consequence in the foreign field that set American policy for a generation—the Truman Doctrine, the North Atlantic Treaty, and, above all, the Marshall Plan. And Truman's personal characteristics were seen to include, prominently, courage and decisiveness. Everyone knew Truman's motto, The Buck Stops Here. The quality that phrase embodies came to be a part of his persona—the gutsy president, making hard decisions, such as creating the Berlin airlift and firing MacArthur. Intellectuals looking at Ike, meanwhile, for a decade and more after he left office found bumbling answers at press conferences and not much happening. They found the belligerent moralism of John Foster Dulles and the danger of brinkmanship and massive retaliation in foreign policy, and no leader in the White House on the key moral issues of the time.

But that appraisal of Eisenhower would change drastically. The appraisals of Truman, after they reached a fairly high level, have tended to stay there, but those of Eisenhower, beginning at his lower level, have undergone a marked change. In 1967, the brilliant, idiosyncratic columnist Murray Kempton published in *Esquire* an article whose title makes its point: "The Underestimation of Dwight Eisenhower." His article was a colorful canary way out in front of the coal mine of historical revision that was coming. Kempton was a unique political commentator—a man of the Left, but by no means predictable. His stylistic legerdemain and startling insight were more notable than any ideological position. His Eisenhower article would make key points that would later be echoed, though by no means as entertainingly, in multiple "revisionist" books and articles changing, and mostly boosting, Eisenhower's presidential reputation. Kempton made those points in imaginative ways, with telling anecdotes, surprising interpretations of passages from Ike's own memoirs, and even with an Edward Lear poem about the Quangle Wangle ("nobody ever could see his face").

The first common impression to be overturned in these multiple revisions was that President Eisenhower was easy to interpret, the uncomplicated, straightforward, genial man from Abilene, plain and simple. No, said the revisers, he was quite a complicated fellow. Kempton quoted at the head of his essay the wonderful comment by Richard Nixon, who surely should have known: "He [Ike] was a far more complex and devious man than most people realized, and in the best sense of those words." Nixon felt he had to add that little fig leaf of self-protective rationalizing at the end ("the best sense") to cover the naked truth of what he had said about Ike's complexity and deviousness. But he conveyed something significant: Eisenhower, far from being simple, clear, easy to interpret, was immensely complicated. His position on thermonuclear weapons after his heart attack in 1955, for one hugely important example, which will be discussed in chapter 14, is still an enigma wrapped in a puzzle adding up to a mystery. But this complexity appears not just in specific policy areas; it marks the man himself.

The common stereotype held that this president was rather passive, that Dulles was the leader when it came to foreign policy, and Brownell on civil rights and legal affairs, and George Humphrey on economics, and other subordinates in other areas, and that Ike himself spent his time on the "green fairways of complacency." Those who looked at the matter more carefully, especially when they had a fuller record, saw that that was quite wrong; Eisenhower was an energetic, activist executive, fully involved in the actions of his administration. One specific thread of Eisenhower revision has shown that the actions Dulles took were fully in accord with his president's purposes. Dulles had been widely unpopular, while Ike was widely popular—but now it appeared, when the record of the telephone calls and other messages between them became available, that Dulles's policies were Ike's. One might now venture the suggestion that Acheson may have been a good deal more the independent originator of policy in the Truman administration than Dulles was in the Eisenhower administration. After the scholarly revisers thoroughly rejected the notion that Dulles determined foreign policy, they may have overcorrected and had Ike alone doing so, and then some would correct again and say the two were a team. But in any case, Ike was active rather than passive.

A third impression of Ike that the revisers corrected was the notion that he was naïve, not especially bright, not particularly intelligent, a bumbler. Kempton quoted an exchange, in which an Eisenhower bumble caused him to say that Ike was dumb, to which an admirer responded, "If he is so dumb, why is he such a good bridge player?" Kempton, finding that Ike "revealed, if only occasionally, in the vast and dreary acreage of his memoirs of the White House years" a rare quality of mind, produced this remarkable paragraph, which, if I read it correctly, makes a stunning claim about Eisenhower:

> The Eisenhower who emerges here [in his memoirs] intermittently free from his habitual veils is the President most superbly equipped for truly consequential decision we may ever have had, a mind neither rash nor hesitant, free of the slightest concern for how things might look, indifferent to any sentiment, as calm when he was demonstrating the wisdom of leaving a bad situation alone as when he was moving to meet it on those occasions when he absolutely had to.

One may rub one's eyes reading this ("most superbly equipped . . . we may ever have had") and ask, More than Abraham Lincoln? This is an aspect of the revision that then cries out for another revision—articles proposing that Ike be labeled a "genius" and the like go too far. In any case, it would be a consistent major point, in the revised professional view of Eisenhower, that he was abler intellectually than the earlier stereotype had allowed. The papers of his administration, as they became available, showed him engaging in clear and intelligent analyses. Kempton got illustrations for his picture of the decision-making Ike from—of all places—the thick books of his memoirs. Kempton formed this opinion after noting Eisenhower's response to what he saw in Korea ("one look had decided Eisenhower to fold the war"), in Lebanon (he was careful to say of American troops he sent in a 1958 invasion just that they were "stationed in" Lebanon), and in Indochina (the French had committed the classic military blunder, and the United States would not on his watch be involved in trying to rescue Vietnam), and his response to the U-2 affair (he bluntly acknowledged the truth after the U.S. cover story exploded).

Kempton's paragraph brings out a key feature of Ike's rationality: that it was controlled, "neither rash nor hesitant." Those who knew him in private report that Ike did have a volcanic temper but that its effects passed swiftly. One would not see that volcano in public, and it would not affect the making of policy. On this count, there may be more of a problem with Truman than with Ike: Truman also had a temper, and exploded on occa-

sion, and he did not necessarily insulate his anger from his political decisions. Take, for example, his coping with the labor troubles and the labor
leaders of his time—John L. Lewis of the United Mine Workers was the
worst, but the leaders of the railway brotherhoods were big aggravations,
too, in the strike-ridden spring of 1946. Truman had to cope with Lewis,
but Eisenhower had managed to get through a victorious war with Bernard Montgomery. Truman's fault would appear to be twofold: He became
enraged, and he sometimes made up his mind too quickly. The labor troubles of 1946, as the nation came out of the shortages and restrictions of the
war, were severely challenging; perhaps something like Truman's drastic
response—to seize industries and threaten to draft workers—was needed,
but if so, such measures should have been decided upon with calm, cool
reason, not with fury.

Another of the revisers' corrections of the stereotypes of Ike is not
unequivocally to his credit, although it may be; it is part of the complexity.
Eisenhower was, and is widely seen to be, a good man. Stephen Ambrose
began his one-volume biography claiming that he was writing about a
"great and good man," and moral uprightness would surely be part of the
popular impression of the man. *New York Times* columnist Arthur Krock
once wrote, "He fairly radiates 'goodness,' simple faith and the honest,
industrious background of his heritage." But Kempton saw a man more
willing to do what needed to be done, skating the corners of rectitude,
than either the popular or the professional impression of him allowed.
Kempton quoted "one of Nelson Rockefeller's captains" as saying of Ike,
believe it or not, "He is the most immoral man I have ever known." After
quoting this, Kempton takes it back a bit: Ike was moderate in all things,
so that he was only moderately immoral. What can that Rockefeller man
have experienced? Remember the second word in the quotation from
Nixon: Ike could be "devious." Ike, "of all people," said Kempton, proved
to be the perfect statesman of Voltaire's irony, who "could learn nothing
from Machiavelli except to denounce Machiavelli."

The key book back at the beginning of the revised view of President
Eisenhower was *The Hidden-Hand Presidency: Eisenhower as Leader,* by
political scientist Fred Greenstein, published in 1982. In analyzing Ike's
"political style," Greenstein focuses on six "strategies," which, one may
say, show Ike to be "political" and show that he preferred to take many
actions out of public view. Some of the "strategies" are not much different
from the practices of other public persons (delegating what can be delegated; attending to the personal characteristics of those with whom one

deals; adapting language to occasion; building public support), but if these strategies are not distinctive to Eisenhower, they are part of a package that is distinctive, because he was not known as a calculating politician and took pains not to be seen as one. So the distinctiveness of Eisenhower's leadership as seen by the new scholarship was that it was in considerable part unseen by the public, and that in his hidden activity he was a conscious and effective politician. So we may draw another correction to the stereotype: Ike was thought to be nonpolitical, even "above politics," but in fact he was, out of the view of the public, very "political" indeed. That means he analyzed the power relationships in situations he dealt with, calculated effects, and took manipulative actions to accomplish objectives without being seen, including preserving and enhancing his own power.

The hiddenness is a key that runs all through this change in perception: If it is thought that all of Eisenhower is on the surface, in the open, transparent, then that, too, is now seen to be wrong. A large part of Eisenhower's presidential leadership was not on the surface. The metaphor of the iceberg is not neglected. And this half-hidden condition was deliberate. What is hidden especially is his political manipulation. Much was done in the Eisenhower years by the unseen hand of the president. This point was made stronger as the papers from the administration began to be opened in the 1970s and then as more became available in the 1980s. The Eisenhower administration had been well documented behind the scenes. While Ike made phone calls, held meetings in the oval office, conferred with his subordinates, doodled on a pad while Dulles talked, his able, intelligent personal secretary, Ann Whitman, recorded and saved it all, providing an unusually full record of the inner workings of a presidency. Eventually, the minutes from all the 336 Thursday meetings of the National Security Council became available.

Greenstein found it important for understanding the Eisenhower leadership to remember the unusual dual role of the American president, who is both head of state and governmental executive. Ike played to the full the role as head of state, the noncontroversial agent and symbol of national unity. He was at the same time seen by the public to be "above politics," a perception he was at pains to preserve. He was unusually well equipped by his history to be the unifying national symbol; he had been the supreme commander of the Allies in a major war, an activity of the highest importance and the widest appeal. Ike's presidency was seen—by him, on his first day, as well as by others—as an extension of his lifetime role as supreme commander. So he was already in place as a unifying national figure when he came into politics. Both parties wanted to nominate him at one time or another. And then as president, Eisenhower consciously avoided being identified with trouble or failure; in one of the anecdotes repeated in the texts, he says "better you than me" to a subordinate, referring to the expected negative response to an unpopular action.

Of the six Eisenhower "strategies" Fred Greenstein identified, the one that can be said to be distinctive is the principle he enunciated repeatedly: "I don't deal in personalities." That meant he would not criticize anyone by name. It came to be most significant in his dealing with McCarthyism—when a member of the press regularly would ask something about McCarthy, Ike would always start by saying, "You know I don't deal in personalities"—but it was a principle that ran through his whole career. Thinking back to his role as supreme commander, one realizes he did not deal in the personality of Bernard Montgomery, or of Alan Brooke, or of George Patton, either; he did not articulate in public the negative judgments he surely felt. What Brooke and Eisenhower said about each other in their books has been noted in an earlier chapter: Ike's interpretation of Brooke was much less critical than Brooke's of Ike—in public. It is particularly notable that Eisenhower never articulated in public what he surely must have felt about the endlessly difficult Montgomery.

But meanwhile, while serving most fully as the head of state, a figure "above politics," Eisenhower also played, more than the public knew, the role of government executive—the leader of a party contending with another party, a faction contending with other factions—for policies that were controversial. That is a theme of the revised Ike: that he was "a politician with apolitical coloration."

When one asks, reading all this about Eisenhower, whether any of it applies to Harry Truman in the same office, the answer is no, almost none of it does. Truman's politics were obvious, forthright, and public; although of course there were some actions taken that were not revealed to the public—as in any presidency, or any organizational leadership—there was no pattern of actions by a hidden hand and certainly no pretense that he was above politics. If there ever was a president who was not separated from politics, it was Harry Truman. He was not to any degree, in popular perception, akin to a constitutional monarch. Although in the ending of one war and the beginning of another he played an important role as head of state, that aspect of the presidency did not play a large place in the perception of Harry Truman by the American public.

As a result of the revolution in what we may call "Eisenhower studies," Ike now ranks much higher than he did in those polls of various kinds of experts on presidential greatness. To be sure, rankings are affected by whom you poll as experts, and there has been some diversifying to larger and different groupings than in the original poll, conducted in 1948 by Arthur Schlesinger, Sr., of Harvard, of academic historians. In that poll, Eisenhower ranked twenty-second. He now comes in at twelve, eleven, ten, even, in one case, as high as eight, which puts him in the "near great" category. Truman comes in most often as the seventh-greatest president; twice on C-Span polls he has ranked as high as five, and twice he has slipped to nine. There is no poll in which he is named less "great" than Dwight Eisenhower. To state the point again, in stark contrast to the public's opinion during their presidencies, Truman's ranking on every known poll is still higher than Eisenhower's, although Eisenhower's has risen markedly.

Eisenhower's foreign policy has looked better as that of later presidents has looked worse. His accomplishment consisted in considerable part in what he did *not* do. He resisted strong pressures to get American forces involved in Vietnam as Dien Ben Phu fell and the French were driven out; as later presidents did get involved with Vietnam, with unhappy results, Ike's resistance looked better and better. He started his presidency by getting the country out of Korea, and then he steered the nation through multiple subsequent crises without committing troops or dropping bombs.

Although it had become part of the conventional wisdom that Ike had not provided leadership on the great moral issues of his time— McCarthyism, and racism at the time of the great Court decisions—that, too, came under reexamination with the revision and upgrading of the appraisal of his presidency. The revolution in Eisenhower interpretation has furnished the grounds for a defense of his activity on controversial issues: He did more, it could now be said, than had appeared. In the next two chapters, I will examine his and Truman's response to those two issues. In preparation, I now want to raise some questions, accepting the thorough revision of the view of the Eisenhower presidency, about conducting affairs by a hidden hand.

The new defense of Ike's doings tends to assert that where others talked and gave speeches, he acted. He moved behind the scenes and actually changed the situation. To this, one may respond, Maybe so, but don't discount that speech making entirely. There is a reason Theodore Roosevelt's expression "the bully pulpit" has become such a cliché; the role of the president has come to include, in a central place, his acting as an educator, a preacher, an advocate, a shaper of values. Think of Harry Truman out there on the farm in Grandview reading the speeches of Woodrow Wilson. The life of the American democracy is an unending work of mutual deliberation in which the consenting people shape their changing policies in accord with established but also subtly changing ideals. The nation's chief executive has come to stand often—one might say usually—in a prominent place, often at the center, in this ongoing national conversation; he has that bully pulpit. His words are carried to the public by the means of communication of his time, and are reinforced by visible, widely reported actions. He (so far always a he; one day soon a she) proposes legislation, grants honors, signs into effect new laws, calls out the armed forces, does myriad activities that reflect some values. Under Franklin Roosevelt's tutelage, the American public underwent two huge transformations: the acceptance of a minimal welfare state in the thirties and the strangling of isolationism in the forties. Presidential opinion shaping, value shaping, consists of more than speech making, to be sure; a president carries on a whole raft of activities that have as part of their intention and effect the shaping of public values. The Founding Fathers did not intend that the president would be a legislative leader, but as the nation developed, presidents have come to play that role, sending legislative programs to Congress, which programs reflect values that presidential speeches and other utterances interpret.

Now the application of this point: A hidden-hand president fails to serve to the full this important facet of a president's role. Ike came out of a career in which he did not need to express his political understanding, or to debate or change and develop it as he would have if he had come up through a political career, as Truman had done; on the contrary, all that political arguing and thinking were quite explicitly set aside. Ike had a career that included nothing but serving as an officer in the United States Army, for whom politics in its ordinary meaning was strictly set aside, and then as the supreme commander in an Allied military force, for whom unity across all differences was imperative. When he floated down into American politics, he brought a strong internationalism, a conviction about the importance of collective security with Europe, solidly based on his experience; but he did not come with convictions gained by experience in all the other fields with which American politics would deal. He organized the presidency with a chief assistant—Sherman Adams—who was not called by the army term but who functioned as a chief of staff. And he had National Security meetings every Thursday, generating the NSC resolutions that guide foreign policy. As a result, his two-term presidency would not leave a legacy in American political history the way the other two-term Republican president in the last half of the twentieth century, Ronald Reagan, would do. As a consequence, there was not an Eisenhower Republicanism playing its role—preserving and advancing a moderate Republicanism—in the decades that would follow. You can only do so much with a hidden hand.

This book begins with a quotation from George Kennan, and he is quoted again in chapter 6 about the intellectual shaping of high policy in the postwar years. Now let us ask what this key thinker had to say about these two presidents. In the two volumes of his memoirs, Kennan made brief references to President Truman, in the course of his narration of events, but then gave a quite interesting full-dress appraisal of Dwight Eisenhower.

Distributing credit for the Marshall Plan, Kennan wrote:

> But President Truman deserves that credit, too, for his perception and political courage in selecting as Secretary of State one of the most experienced, most selfless, and most honorable of America's professional public servants [George Marshall] in giving to that man his confidence and a wide latitude of action, and then supporting him in an individual initiative which, had it misfired, would have brought embarrassment and misfortune to the administration.

Kennan had specific policy quarrels with the Truman administration. He thought the 1945 Potsdam communiqué, like the Potsdam Conference ("confused and unreal discussions") reflected radical ignorance of the Soviet Union, with whom the English-speaking allies were dealing. But he did say, "Mr. Truman cannot, in all fairness, be blamed for the general tenor of these arrangements." They had already been approved by FDR and Churchill. He was critical, as has been said, of the sweeping universal language in which the Truman Doctrine was cast. But his comments on Truman himself, in the course of his memories, feature two qualities, decisiveness and courage. At a dark moment in the Korean War, when congressmen wanted to pull out entirely, Kennan had lunch with Acheson just after he had seen Truman and gave this report on Truman: "The President's decision, as always in great crises, was clear, firm and unhesitating." On another page about Korea, Kennan wrote of the "stoutness of the President." He noted "President Truman's courage in relieving MacArthur of his command and thus bringing our policy in Korea for the first time under Washington's control."

Kennan had dealings with Eisenhower, perhaps more than he ever did personally with Truman. Writing in 1971, before the Ike revisionism that was coming, he anticipated some of its themes, evincing the authority of one who had experience with the figure discussed and adding a twist of his own. In the second volume of his *Memoirs,* he described Ike as "one of the most enigmatic figures in American public life. " He went on: "Few Americans have had more liberally bestowed upon them the responsibility of command; and few have ever evinced a greater aversion to commanding. His view of the presidency resembled more closely the traditional pattern of the European head of state than that of his own country." We can imagine that this observation was grounded in some personal experience: "No royal personage ever possessed to a higher degree the art of repulsing, with a charming baffling evasiveness, any attempt by a casual visitor to come to grips with him over a serious political subject."

Although Kennan says Ike "was our national Boy Scout," he rejected the impression that Eisenhower was "an intellectually and politically superficial person. . . . That impression is quite erroneous. He was actually a man of keen political intelligence and penetration, particularly when it came to foreign affairs. . . . When he spoke of such matters seriously and in a protected official circle, insights of a high order flashed out time after time through the curious military gobbledygook in which he was accustomed both to expressing and concealing his thoughts. . . . Dwight Eisenhower's difficulties lay not in the absence of intellectual powers but in the unwillingness to use them except on the rarest of occasions." Why this was, Kennan—who was surely writing out of direct experience—could not say. But it was his impression that "[Ike] was a man who, given the high office he occupied, could have done a great deal more than he did." That is what Eisenhower's early critics had thought, too.

CHAPTER TWELVE

The Miasma of McCarthy

GEORGE KENNAN'S APPRAISAL of Dwight Eisenhower, and to a lesser extent his appraisal of Harry Truman, figured in a comment he made about the presidents and McCarthyism. Kennan had a close encounter with the mephitic atmosphere that would come to be called by that word. (As Dean Acheson observed, one could say that the Wisconsin senator's name, like those of Judge Lynch and Captain Boycott, enlarged the vocabulary.) John Paton Davies, Jr., a foreign service officer who would be driven out of the foreign service because of his views on China, was a subordinate and close associate of Kennan, who valiantly tried to defend Davies in letters and testimony and an article in *The New York Times*—to no avail in the end. Two other old China hands who suffered a similar fate were also associates of Kennan, and he felt it was only by chance that he escaped an ordeal like theirs. The disillusioning experience of deep injustices done by this poisonous movement caused him to deplore the actions and inactions not only of the State Department, which would not defend its own but simply left it to the accused to defend themselves, but of everyone else as well. In his *Memoirs,* Kennan lamented "the dismal failure of the American government . . . to cope with this phenomenon." The executive branch was almost as bad as Congress. He wrote:

> It is sad to observe that neither of the two presidents under whom these disgraceful things occurred gave fully adequate leadership in opposing them: Harry Truman not, God knows, from any lack of courage, but rather because he tended to attribute them to the normal political partisanship of his Republican opponents, ignoring their deeper roots and consequences; Dwight Eisenhower because of some curious bewilderment in his own mind about the true responsibilities and possibilities of the presidency.

Kennan's criterion for the adequate coping with McCarthyism was perhaps more demanding than the real world would ever allow to be fulfilled; he felt the need not simply for the quashing of Senator McCarthy himself but also for the repudiation of the larger movement and its mindless assumptions, which, he said, did not happen.

To be sure, it was not easy to deal with this dark cloud of unreason aroused in American public life in the early phase of the Cold War. It had a history. After the 1917 Bolshevik Revolution in Russia and World War I, there was in 1919–1920 an outbreak—a "Red Scare"—featuring raids by Woodrow Wilson's attorney general, A. Mitchell Palmer, whereby he arrested and tried to deport "radicals" and "anarchists." In the 1930s, in the turmoil of the Depression, another term was added to the vocabulary with the coming into being of the House Committee on Un-American Activities. Could there be such committees in other countries? Un-British Activities? Un-French? Un-Belgian? The United States has a distinctively creedal national self-understanding that along with its positive aspect has its perversities as well. As to the positive aspect: It is quite possible to say, as Harry Truman did in 1950, that the House Committee on Un-American Activities was itself "the most un-American thing in the country today," with civil liberties understood to be of the essence of the normative "Americanism" the committee violated.

From June 21, 1941, until August 9, 1945, the Soviet Union was an ally in World War II—an essential ally, making sacrifices well beyond those the other Allies made. But then abruptly, that wartime ally turned into a peacetime menace. It was the world's other superpower; the capitalist United States was its chief enemy; it had as an instrument of its attempted expansion a worldwide movement of thought and opinion: communism. As we have seen, the Soviet Union acquired an atomic bomb in 1949 and an H-bomb in 1953. In October 1949, the Communists came to power in China; strong American supporters of the Nationalist Chinese were inclined to suspect that some subversion in the American government had allowed that to happen—some Americans somehow "lost" China. There had been actual instances of espionage in the American, Canadian, and British governments. A Soviet embassy clerk, Igor Gouzenko, revealed a spy ring in Canada. While on loan to the Manhattan Project, Klaus Fuchs, who was the son of a German pastor and who became a British citizen and an outstanding physicist, supplied the Soviet nuclear program with information that really did accelerate its achievement of bombs. Julius and Ethel Rosenberg were arrested, tried, found guilty, and—with Eisenhower declining despite a worldwide appeal to pardon them, or pardon her—were executed, the only Americans ever executed for espionage. The ex-Communist and now *Time* editor Whittaker Chambers made sensational charges against a most proper member of the foreign policy elite, Alger Hiss. But the altogether legitimate and essential searching out of actual spies was not the real interest of the noisiest hunters of Reds and Pinks and fellow travelers and "subversives." Theirs was not an effort at counter-intelligence, but of ideological combat; they were attacking opinions, not actions. Red scares and hunts for subversives and those deemed un-American were ways to attack progressives and advance right-wing positions. And attacking alleged Communists and subversives in government became a fruitful theme for right-wing politicians even before Senator McCarthy's appearance in the headlines in 1950.

There was another key figure already on the scene, difficult for presidents to deal with: J. Edgar Hoover, the head of the FBI. He had been appointed by A. Mitchell Palmer in 1919, when he was twenty-four, and had since built a fortress of prestige that even presidents could not breach. His agency had nurtured a powerful public reputation as the scourge of gangsters. One grew up hearing about the G-men bringing down colorful legendary characters of the thirties—John Dillinger and Pretty Boy Floyd and Machine Gun Kelley—and also of the FBI's triumph over enemies of the republic of various stripes. But Hoover's own political outlook went well beyond the professional work of finding criminals and spies; his opinions resembled those of right-wing politicians. Like them, he saw the nation threatened not only by actual espionage but also by political opinions to the left—by socialists, leftists, fellow travelers, and even by social reformers and liberals. And dealing with the broader issues of disloyal and subversive opinion would justify larger budgets and a larger role for the FBI.

Truman was not in a strong position to resist pressures from a mogul of the permanent government like Hoover. As we have seen, Truman had abruptly dropped into the presidential role in April 1945, and then, after a tough first year during the nation's reconversion from wartime to peacetime, he had seen his party lose badly in 1946, a loss for which he was given much of the blame. Truman really did appear to be an unelected, accidental president. J. Edgar Hoover and his allies, wrote Clark Clifford, "treated the Administration as a group of very lame ducks." Hoover sensed his opportunity and with his allies in the press and in Congress began a campaign to broaden the FBI's investigative authority, to open the door to a hunt throughout the entire government for those whose "loyalty" Hoover and his ilk might regard as suspect. Truman's attorney general, Tom Clark, shared some of Hoover's views about the problem of "loyalty." In late November 1946—after the early November electoral defeat of Democrats and after Truman's lonely return from campaigning to Washington's Union Station, where he was met only by Dean Acheson—Truman yielded to a recommendation that he establish a temporary commission, headed by a Hoover ally, to examine what should be done about employee "loyalty." Then when the commission recommended, as it was plain from the outset it would, a thorough vetting of the entire federal workforce, Truman, in March 1947, established by executive order a far-reaching Federal Employees Loyalty and Security Program.

Truman had reservations about Hoover and the FBI; he is quoted in the biographies as saying he did not want to see a Gestapo in this country. He attempted to have the program run primarily by the Civil Service Commission, but in the fight over funding in Congress, Hoover and his allies won, and in October 1947, it was the FBI, with an enlarged budget, that began fingerprinting and checking on the "loyalty" of every one of the two to three million federal employees, down to janitors in the Agriculture Department. The attorney general's list of subversive organizations was instituted as part of this program, was, inevitably, made public, and had its nefarious effect. The existence of this official governmental program gave encouragement to similar exercises, like the most notorious, the blacklisting scourge in Hollywood that disrupted the careers of screenwriters, actors, directors, and other entertainers for the politics of their youth.

Truman's order called for dismissal from government employment if there were "reasonable grounds . . . for belief that the person involved is disloyal to the Government of the United States," but loyalty and disloyalty were not examined or defined, so that the program was an invitation to personal and ideological manipulation, and the disparaged could not confront their accusers. There were no procedural safeguards or standards of evidence. How many of the allegedly disloyal did they find? Varying numbers are given, depending on the source, but of the more than two million civil servants investigated, several thousand resigned, and only a very small number—212, according to one source—were dismissed for inadequate "loyalty." Clark Clifford wrote that his "greatest regret is that I did not make more of an effort to try to kill the loyalty program at its inception in 1946–47." There were no spies and no one indicted for espionage, or for any other disloyal activity (as distinct from someone's opinion of someone else's opinion). It was a huge waste. But it was worse than a waste. In his book *Truman*, David McCullough told about an interview Clifford had with the journalist Carl Bernstein, in which Clifford said, "It was a political problem. . . . [W]e never had a serious discussion about a real loyalty problem. . . . The President didn't attach fundamental importance to the so-called Communist scare. He thought it was a lot of baloney." McCullough added, "To Bernstein, this was a particularly chilling revelation, since his own parents had been among the victims of the Loyalty Program."

Careers were damaged and a noxious atmosphere generated. In the State Department, the most informed and competent experts on China had their careers destroyed because they had spoken frankly about what was happening in China; these were the colleagues whose cases George Kennan knew about and deplored. It was not "a lot of baloney" to them, or to many others. Although there were those who justified Truman's Loyalty Program in political terms—that it shielded the administration on the domestic front while the administration accomplished great things on the foreign front (the loyalty order came nine days after the speech announcing the Truman Doctrine) and thus improved Truman's standing markedly in 1947—that still is not a justification on the merits. The sign that it would not stand up by that test was this: that, as Clifford makes clear, Truman himself did not really believe in it. He and his administration knew that communism (in the form particularly of the Soviet Union) was a great external danger *to* the United States, but they did not believe it was a great danger *in* the United States. Although some in government posts had been Communists or fellow travelers in the Depression-era thirties, and to a lesser extent after the Hitler-Stalin pact—August 1939 to June 1941—that phase was pretty much past by the late forties. Truman instituted the Loyalty Program because he was in a political bind and felt he had to, and no doubt it would have been difficult to have held off Hoover and his many allies (sometimes presidents are not as powerful as the public thinks they are), but it would have been better if he had resisted this capitulation to the worst spirit of the times.

In 1953, then, at the height of the eruption of McCarthy himself, the incoming Eisenhower administration put its own stamp on the Loyalty Program. As we have seen was true with regard to other topics, so doubly and triply was it true on this one: As an incoming administration taking over from an administration of the opposing party, whom it has attacked— and been attacked by—Ike and company were determined to do things differently from the Truman folks. Ike announced in his first cabinet meeting after taking office that he would revise the Loyalty Program as it had been under Truman. The aim of the Truman program had been to determine whether a public servant was *loyal,* and not many were found who warranted being discharged. Ike's program now broadened the question to be asked. The issue about public servants was now to be not only whether they were *loyal* to the United States but also, much more broadly, whether they had personal characteristics that made them a *security risk*—

another rebarbative term this topic contributed to the dark side of the lexicon of American politics. Studying Eisenhower's actions, Fred Greenstein wrote, "The new program did not turn up many alleged Communist sympathizers, but lumping them with homosexuals, alcoholics, and other 'unreliables' enabled the administration periodically to cite statistics on increasing numbers of 'security risks' who had been denied government employment. Eisenhower took care not to say that the people enumerated were disloyal, but on a number of occasions his associates quoted the new security risk statistics in ways suggesting that an Augean stable of subversives had been swept out of government." There was thus introduced into American politics a perverse criterion that administrations boasted about—the number of persons fired. By lumping in blabbermouths, drunks, and gays, the Eisenhower administration gave itself distinct bragging rights in that unseemly contest. Richard Rovere would observe: "McCarthyism rampant managed, for a time, to make politics in America seem almost entirely a matter of idiotic chatter about 'loyalty risks' and 'security risks.' . . . The parties seldom argued over the number of gifted people brought into government; the test was how many rotten apples each had been able to find."* Putting a premium on finding multiple rotten apples had destructive effects at several levels: Careers were damaged, persons stigmatized, lives uprooted; recruitment and morale were severely and adversely affected.

One might wish that these two presidents, honorable men and loaded to the brim themselves with loyalty to the nation, both of them lifelong public servants, had seen it to be their primary duty, in this season of unreason, to defend, rather than to facilitate the attack upon, the beleaguered federal public service, which they oversaw as the chief executive. President Eisenhower himself actually expressed the point very well in a "Personal and Confidential" memo sent to all department and agency heads on March 5, 1954, in the midst of the buildup to the Army-McCarthy extravaganza, when Secretary of the Army Stevens was being tormented by McCarthy. This memorandum was entitled "Treatment of Governmental Personnel" and read as follows:

> Each superior, including me, must remember the obligations he has to his own subordinates. These obligations comprise, among other things, the protection of those subordinates, through all legal and proper means available, against attacks of a character under which they might otherwise be helpless.

* Rovere, pp. 17, 18.

No hope of any kind of political advantage, no threat from any source, should lead anyone to forsake these principles of organizational leadership.

Exactly. But the defect of this memo is its date. This worthy admonition came after thirteen months of McCarthy's outrages during Ike's administration. Would that he had said this at the start—on March 5, 1953, say, instead of on March 5, 1954, and would that he had followed it himself. (It is interesting that he inserted that phrase "including me.") But I don't believe it can be held that these sound instructions were followed, in particular by Eisenhower himself throughout most of 1953, while McCarthy's unspeakable representatives Roy Cohn and G. David Schine devastated the Voice of America and the libraries in the embassies of Europe, and his minion Scott McLeod and McCarthy himself continued harassment of the State Department. General Eisenhower, commanding Allied forces in Europe, had conveyed to the lowliest private the fact that he cared for him, empathized with him; think of the scenes of Ike showing up at camps of soldiers in England who were waiting to embark on the perilous trip across the Channel during Operation Overlord. To be sure, his relationship to the federal employees in 1953 was considerably different from his relationship to American soldiers in England in 1944. It is probable that Ike himself, and certainly many of those around him, looked upon the federal bureaucracy that he inherited as loaded with Democrats. And to some extent, perhaps it was. But even if so, there was the relationship he stated in his memo: *the obligations he has to his own subordinates.*

It was against this background, then, that there arose one of the most bizarre episodes in the colorful history of the American republic: the sudden discovery by a thoroughly undistinguished senator from Wisconsin named Joseph McCarthy of the stunning possibilities of the Communists-in-government theme, if presented with a sufficiently audacious falsity, a big-enough untruth, a bold-enough lie. McCarthy seized with unbridled opportunism on that theme, starting his peculiar career as a demagogue with a makeshift speech in Wheeling, West Virginia, on February 9, 1950, in which he alleged that "I have here in my hand" the names of a certain number (for starters, he said 205) of known Communists in the State Department still making policy, and that he and the secretary of state knew their names. The charge, which he amplified with various other numbers in subsequent speeches, was totally false; if there were any Communists in the State Department, he did not know it, and he certainly did not know their names, as investigations by Senate committees soon established. But having nothing actually to reveal did not stop McCarthy from making revelations; he kept making charges with an audacious mendacity and the tinder of public anxiety burst into flame. For the last two years and eleven months of Truman's presidency, as he made the decisions about the Korean War, the menace of McCarthy always lurked in the background. Truman thought McCarthy's influence would evaporate when it became evident that he was making it all up, but it did not. Of course McCarthy never answered anything; he just moved on to new charges. And somehow it all worked and he became a world-class menace. Richard Rovere wrote, "Sir Winston Churchill became sufficiently exercised to write an eloquent anti-McCarthy passage into Elizabeth II's Coronation speech." McCarthy, Rovere wrote, was "the first American ever to be actively hated and feared by foreigners in large numbers."*

An essential ingredient in McCarthy's power was the support by conservative Republican senators for what he was doing. Senator Taft, the leader of those Republicans, was at first put off—as most senators were—by the efforts of the undistinguished senator. But then he discovered that McCarthy had struck some kind of nerve and was getting a public response after all. Taft is reported to have encouraged McCarthy by saying, "If one case doesn't work, try another."

It is to be noted, however, that a small group of Republican senators took a more honorable stand, and said what not only other senators but also presidents should have been saying. In June 1950, less than four months after McCarthy's Wheeling speech, Senator Margaret Chase Smith of Maine wrote a "Declaration of Conscience," which, although it did not mention McCarthy by name, was clearly directed against his activities: "I think that it is high time for the United States Senate and its members to do some soul-searching—for us to weigh our consciences—on the manner in which we are performing our duty to the people of America—on the manner in which we are using or abusing our individual powers and privileges."

As Truman had done, so Senator Smith would do, setting a genuine morally substantive "Americanism" over against the loudly touted "Americanism" of the McCarthy stripe:

> Those of us who shout the loudest about Americanism in making character assassinations are all too frequently those who, by our own words and acts, ignore some of the basic principles of Americanism:

* Ibid., p. 10.

The right to criticize;
The right to hold unpopular beliefs;
The right to protest;
The right of independent thought.

The exercise of these rights should not cost one single American citizen his reputation or his right to a livelihood nor should he be in danger of losing his reputation or livelihood merely because he happens to know someone who holds unpopular beliefs. Who of us doesn't?

But Senator Smith's was not the voice of most Republicans in the Senate; her protest was signed by only six other moderate Republicans, and it was McCarthy, not Senator Smith, who addressed the cheering convention that nominated Ike in 1952. McCarthy's staff took to referring to Senator Smith as "Moscow Maggie," and to her and the group that signed her declaration as "Snow White and the six dwarfs." McCarthy supported an opponent of hers in the Republican primary in 1954, but by that time McCarthy's trumpet was broken and she won easily.

The two presidents dealt with McCarthy in quite different ways. Truman responded with a small number of blunt and spontaneous hostile comments, without a general plan; Eisenhower felt that the brusque, dismissive comments by Truman and by Acheson built up McCarthy by making him the victim/martyr, and he resolved to deal with him otherwise. Eisenhower refrained from quick denunciations or rejections of McCarthy, but—eventually—he dealt with him in a carefully planned way (Fred Greenstein used this as his most complete example of Eisenhower's "hidden-hand" technique). Both presidents would insist that as chief executive they should not dignify McCarthy by directly engaging him, and in making that point both would refer to the gutter. Truman's pungent way of putting it was, "You must not ask the President of the United States to get down in the gutter with a guttersnipe." Eisenhower firmly refused to respond; he said, "I will not—I refuse—to get into the gutter [with McCarthy]."

Truman and his administration were, to be sure, the immediate objects of McCarthy's attack; it was in his State Department that McCarthy claimed to have found those 205 or 87 or 53 or however many card-carrying Communists, and Truman's presidential years were entirely included in what McCarthy would call "twenty years of treason." Truman and his advisers made a deliberate decision, not unlike the decision that Eisenhower would make, not to overreact to McCarthy, not to build him up with presidential attention, not to devote a whole speech to the phenomenon he represented. But in spite of his announced resolve not to get down in gutter with McCarthy, Truman did make comments about the senator of a sort that Eisenhower did not make. When asked about McCarthy's charges at a press conference on February 16, 1950—after McCarthy's first explosion in Wheeling on February 9—Truman said that the State Department had answered them "by saying there was not a word of truth in what the Senator said."

On March 30, much of the press conference was devoted to McCarthy and to the damage Truman said he was doing to the nation's bipartisan foreign policy.

> Q: Mr. President, do you think Senator McCarthy is getting anywhere in his attempt to win the case against the State Department?
> THE PRESIDENT: What's that?
> Q: Do you think that Senator McCarthy can show any disloyalty exists in the State Department?
> THE PRESIDENT: I think the greatest asset that the Kremlin has is Senator McCarthy.
> Q: Would you care to elaborate on that?
> THE PRESIDENT: I don't think it needs any elaboration—I don't think it needs any elaboration.
> Q: Brother, will that hit page one tomorrow!

This last observation proved to be an accurate prediction.

At that press conference, Truman went on to give a summary of the nation's bipartisan foreign policy since World War II, and he then alleged that McCarthy and some other Republican senators were trying to "sabotage" that policy.

The president: "To try to sabotage the foreign policy of the United States is just as bad in this cold war as it would be to shoot our soldiers in the back in a hot war."

On April 13, Truman was asked about a remark Senator Taft had made in a column he wrote for Ohio newspapers.

> Q: Mr. President, Senator Taft said this week that you had libeled Senator McCarthy. Would you care to make any comment?
> THE PRESIDENT: Do you think that is possible? [*Laughter*]
> Q: May we quote that?
> THE PRESIDENT: . . . Yes.

But that was about as far as presidential comment on the senator went.

The Senate investigation of McCarthy's charges by a committee chaired by Senator Millard Tydings of Maryland found that none of those charges held up—that they were a "fraud and a hoax." This diminished McCarthy's effect briefly in the late spring of 1950. Then the start of the Korean War, in June of that year, pushed him out of the center of events, but only for a time. The Tydings committee report had been supported only by the Democrats on the committee, so its impact was limited. As the war continued, the frustrations were a reinforcement of, rather than a distraction from, further McCarthy outrages. When Truman relieved General MacArthur in April 1951, McCarthy said of Truman, "The son of a bitch ought to be impeached."

And then as McCarthy saw the spotlight move from him to the hearings of joint congressional committees that followed that spectacularly controversial presidential action—the MacArthur hearings, the most widely watched before the even more sensational Army-McCarthy hearings of 1954—he brought attention back to himself by going to the Senate one day with a bulging briefcase and a load of utterly ungrounded accusations and delivered his most brazen assault: his famous speech assailing George Marshall. Richard Rovere, who actually read the printed version of this mammoth production, explains that nobody ever heard it, and almost nobody, perhaps including McCarthy himself, ever read it. It was far too long for McCarthy to have presented the whole thing on the floor, and he gave only a token presentation. Printed in book form, it is a long revisionist attack on American foreign policy since the rise of the Soviet Union, in language and concepts clearly beyond the reach of McCarthy or his staff. Rovere wrote: "None of the campus queens or former detectives on McCarthy's staff would have been capable of such an aside as this: 'I am reminded of a wise and axiomatic utterance in this connection by the great Swedish chancellor Oxenstiern, to his son on departing on the tour of Europe: he said, "go forth my son and see with what folly the affairs of mankind are governed." ' "*

One cannot imagine the rampaging senator uttering or writing those words. Rovere gives other samples of material from this composition that clearly did not come from his pen or brain or from his staff. Rovere knew from whom they did come, a representative of "a school of revisionist historians" centered at Georgetown University critical of American diplomacy "because it failed to focus single-mindedly on Soviet power."

But the news from McCarthy's speech was not this bizarre academic enlargement—most of which was not presented by him on the Senate floor, or covered by the press in their reports—but the core accusation

* Ibid., p. 176.

against the most respected of Americans, George Marshall. McCarthy called him a "man steeped in falsehood"; he said Marshall had been party to "a conspiracy so immense and an infamy so black as to dwarf any previous such venture in the history of man"—language that had more of the authentic McCarthy touch. Truman, when asked about the attack on General Marshall in a press conference on May 4, 1950, said only, "I have no comment to make on anything McCarthy may say. It isn't worth commenting."

It was widely assumed—and asserted sometimes as an argument—that with the election of Dwight Eisenhower and the Republicans in 1952, McCarthy's depredations would come to an end. The new administration came from McCarthy's own party, and he had tepidly endorsed Ike, who had tepidly endorsed him—the two men had run together on the same ticket in Wisconsin; Ike had made that fateful venture into Wisconsin during the campaign in which he and McCarthy rode together on the train, had their picture taken, and Ike made the scandalous deletion from his Milwaukee speech. McCarthy's attacks had been directed at Democrats, the Democratic party, at a Democratic president and secretary of state, and had been supported by a considerable segment of top Republicans, both in the Senate and elsewhere. And the new administration was headed by a great war hero. So surely now the attack on the alleged coddling of Communists would stop.

But that is not what happened. There was a brief period of restraint, soon concluded. McCarthy's whole mode of being required him to attack and condemn. Richard Rovere wrote, "Before the Eisenhower administration and the new Congress were a month old, before John Foster Dulles had had time to hang the pictures on the wall in his Foggy Bottom office, McCarthy was raising his usual kind of hell in the State Department."* There were two surprises about McCarthy when Eisenhower succeeded Truman: that McCarthy's depredations did not stop and that for more than a full year Eisenhower did not do anything to counter them.

The damage that was done to American government, and to the nation's reputation around the world, was at least as bad during the twenty-three and a half months that McCarthy tormented the Eisenhower administration as during the thirty-three months he had done the same to the Truman administration.

And McCarthy now had new powers. Because Ike had brought with him (for the first two years of his first term only) Republican control in

---

* Ibid., p. 189.

the Senate, McCarthy was now a committee chairman, with subpoena powers and a staff—chairman of the Committee on Governmental Operations and of its subcommittee, which became the actual committee, the Committee on Investigations. Investigating was what McCarthy wanted to do, and not investigating the dull world of government contracts, but the spellbinding world of traitors, subversives, Pinks, and security risks. Having a staff meant he could hire the young Roy Cohn, of whose essence ruthlessness was a crucial part. Cohn, in turn, brought in young G. David Schine. The qualifications of the twenty-eight-year-old Schine to be an investigator of government subversives rested entirely on a six-page pamphlet he had composed, entitled *Definition of Communism*. Richard Rovere memorably described its content: "In a couple of thousand deplorably chosen words, Schine managed to put the Russian Revolution, the founding of the Communist Party, and the start of the first Five-Year Plan in years when these events did not occur; he gave Lenin the wrong first name, hopelessly confused Stalin with Trotsky, Marx with Lenin, Alexander Kerensky with Prince Lvov, and fifteenth-century utopianism with twentieth-century Communism. Copies of this bedside treasury of wrong dates and mistaken identities and misunderstood principles were to be found in Schine Hotels . . . from Miami to Hollywood."*

McCarthy, with Cohn and Schine as his agents, then introduced one of the wildest sequences of bizarre events in the rich panoply of American history. They started investigating the State Department's overseas information program—the International Information Agency (IIA), which included the Voice of America and the government's overseas libraries; it was a program that was intended to help the United States in the worldwide struggle of ideas. Cohn and Schine first set up shop in Schine's suite at the Waldorf-Astoria in New York and tormented the VOA about the siting of transmitters, alleging that subversive influence caused them to be located in less than optimum places for converting Communists. In the VOA, as in other agencies, McCarthy was able to establish what he called his "loyal underground"—disgruntled employees who brought him material of the sort he fed on. After causing chaos and perhaps one suicide in the VOA, the team moved on to the more promising territory of books—all those books in the libraries had to be a rich vein for investigation.

A distinguished businessman named Martin Merson persuaded his even more distinguished friend Robert Johnson, the president of Temple University, that as a fellow idealistic supporter of the Eisenhower crusade

* Ibid., p. 194.

he should not turn down the State Department invitation to head the International Information Agency. Merson, in turn, was told by Johnson that he would take the post if Merson would join him. So these two idealistic supporters of the Eisenhower "crusade," believing in what Ike would do while leading the country, went to Washington, at some personal sacrifice—only to be brutally disillusioned. Merson told the story in a long account after it was over—"My Education in Government," published in *The Reporter* magazine on October 7, 1954. The two honorable and distinguished Eisenhower supporters found on starting out in the IIA in March 1953 that the McCarthy juggernaut had already battered the agency before they arrived. The previous leaders of the agency, cowering apparently before the McCarthy onslaught, had issued a new directive about books in the agency's worldwide system of libraries—a directive that was to replace the carefully drawn policy of selection of materials that had been written by a serious panel of intellectual leaders. The new order, issued on February 19, 1953, made this command: "No material by any Communists, fellow travelers, et cetera, will be used under any circumstances by any IIA media." The order further directed that all material in these categories in any IIA outpost should be removed forthwith. This directive went out to all of America's 201 information-center libraries abroad; they had more than two million volumes. "Overnight the U.S. government," Merson wrote, "became the butt of worldwide ridicule and contempt."

Merson's abrupt education in government in the age of McCarthy continued when he learned the history of the "et cetera" order: Incredibly, it had been reviewed by top officials at the State Department, recent Dulles appointees, who, he wrote, "were evidently unwilling to consider the implications of that et cetera." One man who was willing to face what was happening was the Voice of America's chief, a former NBC radio and television executive named Alfred Morton. He fired back a response to the "et cetera" order that said the VOA would continue its established policy of using the words of Communists (e.g., Stalin) in exposing their lies and failures. The State Department's policy desk, in turn, fired back— unbelievably—the insistence that under the new order they could not use *any* words by a Communist for *any* purpose.

Merson continued his tale of his brush with government in the McCarthy days by relating what happened next: the word about Morton's defiance was carried by a member of the McCarthy underground to the State Department, and the atmosphere of capitulation to McCarthy was so strong that Ike's old comrade Walter Bedell Smith, now undersecretary of state, promptly and publicly suspended Morton. Cooler heads prevailed and he was reinstated the next day, but, wrote Merson, "when I saw him soon after at the Voice, he seemed a broken man, his control over his staff shattered."

Merson and Johnson had written to Secretary Dulles, indicating the absurdity of the directive—particularly with its grand "et cetera"—expecting that the secretary, who had, after all, requested that they interrupt their successful careers to help carry out national policy, would support them; to their astonishment, the word came back that the directive had to stand.

They tried to accommodate. Were there indeed cadres of coddled Communists crowding the halls of the agency? They discovered that there were not, but rather a serious and able and loyal workforce whom they had to respect. When McCarthy and Cohn on the one side and the budget cutters on the other forced them to fire people, and they did, Cohn and Schine then attacked them for firing members of the "loyal underground"—as they had unwittingly done.

They tried to get in to speak to the president, asking for help from C. D. Jackson, the writer for *Fortune* who was a leading opponent of McCarthy on the White House staff. "But Jackson blandly answered that he wouldn't dream of approaching the President on the subject," Merson wrote. "It was Eisenhower's passion . . . not to offend anybody in congress." This feature of Ike's outlook as a novice in the political world has not received the notice it deserves: At least at the outset, he had a civics-book fundamentalism about the separation of powers. Asked about McCarthy's attacks by the press on March 5, he said, after the usual declination to deal in personalities, that there was a constitutional "right of congress to conduct such investigations as it sees fit," and further that "I don't believe it is really a proper thing for me to be discussing publicly a coordinate branch of government." In the little prayer he had composed and read at his inauguration, Ike had been careful to explain to God that he was praying only on behalf of the executive branch. He began: "Almighty God, as we stand here at this moment my future associates in the executive branch of Government join me in beseeching that Thou will make full and complete our dedication to the service of the people in this throng, and their fellow citizens everywhere."

So neither Dulles nor Ike himself was any support, and the two honorable Eisenhower crusaders, Merson and Johnson, deeply disillusioned, were left to the mercies of Cohn, Schine, and McCarthy. The dark tragicomedy of the McCarthy attack on the information services included their having to issue lists of banned authors, and finding that scared officials abroad got ahead of them and removed books that were not on any list, and that some had even the bad taste to burn banned books. A conservative consultant tried to get Aaron Copland taken off the blacklist of musicians because the consultant liked his music. Ike himself objected at a press conference to the blacklisting of Dashiell Hammett, whose mysteries he liked, but he did not extend that particular objection to a rejection of the blacklist itself.

Suddenly, there was another display of McCarthy's magic with numbers: He publicly made the astounding claim that the IIA was holding on its shelves overseas thirty thousand copies of books by Communist authors. How in the world had he come up with that huge number? It developed that over time the McCarthy staff had asked about 418 authors of books, plus some playwrights and artists, about whom they sought information. When the list was examined, it was found to include many of the most distinguished writers and thinkers in the contemporary world, most of whom had no connection whatever with communism: John Dewey, W. H. Auden, Robert Hutchins, Arthur Schlesinger, Theodore Dreiser, and many, many more. They were on the list because some McCarthy staff person had asked about them. When all the books by these 418 were counted, the number turned out to be just over thirty thousand.

There were other chapters in the sad story of the McCarthy attack on the information services, none more loaded with comedy than the infamous trip of Cohn and Schine through major cities in Europe, causing havoc, indignant resignations, bitter mirth, and widespread contempt. The pair spent forty hours in Paris, sixteen in Bonn, nineteen in Frankfurt, sixty in Munich, forty-one in Vienna, twenty-three in Belgrade, twenty-four in Athens, twenty in Rome, and six in London.

Merson and Johnson, finding that they were not given any support at all from their superiors—including from the man at the top, who was the reason they had gone to Washington—were disillusioned, and they resigned after five months with the IIA.

Meanwhile, ironically, on June 14, 1953, in the midst of all of his IIA subordinates' troubles with the McCarthy book burners, President Eisenhower gave a talk in which he said, "Don't join the book burners." The occasion for this speech was that the president was being awarded an honorary degree by Dartmouth College. Dartmouth's president had told him that his address should be informal, so Eisenhower did not read a prepared text put together by his speechwriting staff, but spoke more personally. He had just two points for the graduates: first, about fun, happiness, and joy, and second, about courage. In the course of his brief remarks on the second point, he said, "It is not enough merely to say I love America, and to salute the flag and take off your hat as it goes by, and to help sing the Star Spangled Banner. Wonderful! We love to do them, and our hearts swell with pride, because those who went before you worked to give to us today, standing here, this pride."

Wearing his academic robe, the president told the graduates and the assembled crowd that they must do their part to add to that heritage; rather suddenly, he uttered the words that would resound and be widely quoted: "Don't join the book burners. Don't think you are going to conceal faults by concealing evidence that they ever existed. Don't be afraid to go in your library and read every book, as long as that document does not offend our own ideas of decency. That should be the only censorship."

The next paragraphs made plain what was already implicit—that he said this not only in the context of the worldwide ideological battle of the Cold War but also in the domestic contest over what was coming to be called McCarthyism:

> How will we defeat communism unless we know what it is, and what it teaches, and why does it have such an appeal for men, why are so many people swearing allegiance to it? It is almost a religion, albeit one of the nether regions.
>
> And we have got to fight it with something better, not try to conceal the thinking of our own people. They are part of America. And even if they think ideas that are contrary to ours, their right to say them, their right to record them, and their right to have them at places where they are accessible to others is unquestioned, or it isn't America.

The president's remarks won much favorable coverage in the Monday papers. This statement was the sort of thing a significant part of the American citizenry thought he should have done earlier, and should do persistently. The problem with it was not in anything he said on Sunday at Dartmouth but what he then said on Wednesday at a press conference back in Washington. He seemed to take back most of what he had said.

The Wednesday press conference started off with a question about the Dartmouth remarks against book burning, and there were several later questions on that topic. They were mingled with questions on other matters—the Korean War, the H-bomb, a new security order, which was about classifying documents top secret, and, the next-to-last question, from May Craig of Maine, about the Agriculture Department selling surplus butter for ten cents a pound: Was that free enterprise? (Presidents do have to spread themselves, speaking of butter, over a wide stretch of subjects.)

The first question at that Wednesday press conference from Merriman Smith of the United Press was, not surprisingly, this: "Mr. President, your speech this last Sunday at Dartmouth was interpreted or accepted by a great many people as being critical of a school of thought represented by Senator McCarthy; is that right or wrong?" To which the president, also not surprisingly, responded, "Now, Merriman, you have been around me long enough to know I never talk personalities." But then as Eisenhower took up the substance, he started off with the sharp qualification of his Dartmouth remarks: "[B]y no means am I talking, when I talk about books or the right of dissemination of knowledge, am I talking about any document or any other kind of thing that attempts to persuade or propagandize America into communism."

Later, he added:

I would say this: if the State Department is burning a book which is an open appeal to everybody in those foreign countries to be a Communist, then I would say that falls outside of the limits in which I was speaking; and they can do as they please to get rid of them, because I see no reason for the Federal Government of the United States to be supporting something that advocates its own destruction. That seems to me to be about the acme of silliness.

In other words, a certain amount of book burning is okay. Having started off on the wrong foot, he never got back in step. Fred Greenstein wrote, "The effect of Monday's headlines [on the Dartmouth speech] was virtually obliterated in the haze of Wednesday's press conference."[*] Although he made some remarks that reinforced his Dartmouth comments, in other responses he volunteered an anti-Communist exception that ruined the effect. The confusion reflected two defects in his approach to McCarthyism in general: He was not fully clear on the principle involved, and he had not measured the power of the phenomenon he was to some extent resisting. His remarks at the press conference were fuzzy enough, or bad enough, for McCarthy himself to make the patronizing comment that it was a "commendable clarification."

In July 1953, David Schine was selected by his draft board, and Roy Cohn commenced a campaign to make sure that his great Communist-hunting

[*] Greenstein, p. 176.

talents were not wasted in service as a mere private. He tried to get Schine a commission, and when that did not work, he tried to have him assigned to special Communist-detecting work, and when that did not work, he tried at least to make his basic training less basic than that of an ordinary soldier. The secretary of the army would testify, in the encounters that came later, that Cohn and other McCarthy staff members had made sixty-five phone calls on David Schine's behalf and arranged about nineteen meetings between army and McCarthy representatives to deal with the great subject of Schine's role—all the way from whether he could get a commission to whether he would do KP.

Meanwhile, McCarthy himself had also taken on the army. In September 1953, he said he would go after subversion in the military, and he started hearings on alleged wartime espionage at the Army Signal Corps Engineering Laboratories, at Fort Monmouth, New Jersey, leading to the suspension of thirty-three Fort Monmouth employees and a severe crisis in morale (most of the thirty-three were later restored to their jobs). So McCarthy was investigating the army while simultaneously Cohn was harassing the army on behalf of special treatment for Schine. When McCarthy found that Irving Peress, a drafted dentist at Camp Kilmer in New Jersey, had refused to sign a loyalty oath but had been promoted to major nevertheless (the promotion actually was automatic, part of the program of drafting medical personnel), the cry went up from McCarthy and his acolytes: "Who promoted Peress?" McCarthy called Gen. Ralph Zwicker, the commander of Camp Kilmer, to a one-man hearing and savagely attacked, saying he did not have the brains of a five-year-old and was not fit to wear the uniform. (Zwicker was a decorated hero from D-Day.) McCarthy went after Secretary of the Army Robert Stevens, a gentlemanly textile manufacturer not accustomed to this sort of thing, and extracted from him the admission that there might have been spying at Monmouth during the war.

The army charged that McCarthy's staff had relentlessly sought privileges for Schine; McCarthy countercharged that the army was retaliating for his investigation. The conflicting charges then led to the Army-McCarthy hearings, which were supposed to take just a few days and instead lasted from April 22 to June 17, 1954. The charges were investigated in hearings held by the committee of which McCarthy was chairman, with another senator, Karl Mundt of South Dakota, substituting as chairman and McCarthy vocally participating and making the repeated cry "Point of order! Point of order!"—which became notorious. The hearings, in which McCarthy exposed himself as an intemperate bully, were the cause of his collapse as a public menace.

The moment McCarthy's perverse career was brought to an end can be identified precisely, and it is one of those moments that those who saw it will never forget. To be sure, it did not end abruptly with this event; McCarthy went on for some months. But his spooky public power was broken. Those who saw it on the new medium of television—much of the nation, indeed—can recall the voice of Joseph Welch, the attorney for the army, speaking the climactic lines. In the midst of the insane Army-McCarthy hearings, McCarthy abruptly brought before the national television audience the name of a young member of Welch's law firm, Fred Fisher, who, when younger, joined the National Lawyers Guild, a left-wing organization that J. Edgar Hoover wanted put on the attorney general's list of subversive organizations. Welch's devastating response had three memorable passages. First, he exclaimed, "Until this moment, Senator, I think I have never really gauged your cruelty or your recklessness." He then explained that Fisher was a young man starting out on what looked to be a brilliant career but who would always bear a scar needlessly inflicted by McCarthy, and Welch used the words *reckless* two more times and the words *cruel* and *cruelty* each once.

When the obtuse McCarthy attempted to pursue the topic of Fisher, Welch's next comment included the most memorable lines: "Have you no decency, sir? At long last, have you no decency?"

When McCarthy yet again tried to pursue the subject (Roy Cohn, who was on the witness stand, clearly tried to signal him to stop), Welch cut him off: "Senator, may we not drop this? . . . Let us not assassinate this lad further. . . . You have sat within six feet of me and could have asked me about Fred Fisher. I will not discuss it further. I will not ask Mr. Cohn any more questions. You, Mr. Chairman, may, if you will call the next witness." At this, those in the gallery, who were, of course, supposed to refrain from such expressions, burst into applause.

At the moment Welch made those remarks, followed by that applause, McCarthy was effectively finished. There had been passages earlier in which Welch's questions made clear McCarthy's view of himself as above the law; there had been, before the Army-McCarthy hearings, two famous programs by the noted CBS newsman Ed Murrow that exposed McCarthy's arrogance and cruelty by showing him in action; and now twenty million people saw McCarthy behaving like the bully and villain that he was. The air went out of his balloon very rapidly. The Army-McCarthy hearings wound down and gave a predictably inconclusive result, but in the fall the Senate Select Committee to Study Censure Charges held that McCarthy's conduct should be condemned and the Senate voted 67–22 to condemn him. The grounds of this condemnation were predictably narrow—he was condemned only for his treatment of fellow senators—but that did not matter. He was abruptly demoted from senatorial and press attention and suddenly became a nonperson. Democrats won control of the Senate in 1954, and he lost his committee, and in two years he drank himself to death.

Was George Kennan right when he said that neither president during those memorable days "gave fully adequate leadership" against "these disgraceful things"? As to Truman's response, we may grant that Eisenhower was probably right in saying that Truman's unvarnished and dismissive comments on McCarthy—that he was the Kremlin's greatest asset, that he was so appalling, it was not possible to libel him—for all their satisfying appeal to those who already agreed that McCarthy was an abomination, were not effective with the larger public, which had not reached that conclusion. These blunt dismissals may, as Eisenhower claimed, have helped rather than hurt McCarthy by adding to his visibility and making him seem the victim of a presidential slur. Such a response seemed to set up a name-calling contest on the senator's own turf. But Ike's "I don't deal in personalities" disinclination to mix it up explicitly with McCarthy was also not all by itself the effective strategy that he seemed for a time to think it would be. Eisenhower said, "The President of the United States has a position that gives his name a terrific headline value. Therefore if he points his finger at any particular individual—meaning to name anyone specifically—he automatically gives that individual an increased publicity value." And he held that denying an individual that publicity would diminish his power, his public presence. But that is not what happened. All through 1953, McCarthy did not need presidential mentionings in order to be a major figure in the headlines; he had already developed the means of making himself inescapable. He had a following, and he had knowledge of the function of the press; he knew how to make his name appear in the public discourse without any help from a presidential mention. Eisenhower's theory was that "nothing will be so effective in combating this particular kind of trouble-making as to ignore him. This he cannot stand." But although it was quite true that publicity was the lifeblood of McCarthyism, it was not true that the virus required condemnations from presidents in order to obtain publicity. He was a senator, he had found the ways to use the press (the "media," as it was coming to be called), he had accomplices in the upper reaches of government and the press, and he had developed his own perverse talent at the demagogic capture of the headlines.

But Eisenhower did more, behind the scenes and out of sight, than simply to deny McCarthy his public attention. It used to be said, critically of Ike, that during all these events he played almost no role; in his benign one-volume biography, Stephen Ambrose said that "[Eisenhower's] sole significant action against McCarthy" was "his denial of access to executive personnel and records." But Greenstein's book on "the hidden-hand presidency," a harbinger of the revised view of Eisenhower, corrected these earlier claims and impressions. The book makes clear that that was far from being Eisenhower's only significant action against McCarthy. Using Eisenhower's diary and other sources that had not been available to earlier writers, Greenstein followed Ike's response, from his early attempts at accommodation of the rapacious senator, through the silence of 1953, and to a more active behind-the-scenes opposition in 1954. At the beginning of his administration, the new president was able to defeat McCarthy on one nomination, that of "Chip" Bohlen, whom Ike knew personally, but both Dulles and Eisenhower were silent when McCarthy and his crew made the attack on the VOA and the libraries that drove Merson and Johnson out of the administration. In November 1953, Attorney General Brownell tried to sharpen the contrast with the Truman administration by a little competitive McCarthyism: In a speech to Chicago executives, Brownell claimed that President Truman had allowed a man named Harry Dexter White to be appointed to the International Monetary Fund even after having been informed by the FBI that White had been part of a spy ring that passed information to the Soviet Union. But Brownell's effort, from which Ike was more or less insulated, exploded in his hand; Truman insisted that on learning about White's past, he had fired him, and it turned out that three days after the House Committee on Un-American Activities had charged him with a Communist connection, White had died of a heart attack. So Brownell had tried to get McCarthyist mileage out of "a five-year-old story about a dead person." Truman was given time on the networks to respond, and his use of the term *McCarthyism* meant that the senator, in his turn, was given time. He not only attacked Truman but also took a swipe at Eisenhower. And then Eisenhower and Dulles in their turn responded in statements to newspapers; that is the way things went in those days. Ike's "Atoms for Peace" speech in early December lifted the tone of American politics.

But if the Eisenhower administration was not an effective opponent of

McCarthy in 1953, it would do better in 1954. On January 21, it took what would be called its "first move," a planning meeting in Brownell's office between John Adams, the counsel to the Department of the Army, which was under attack, and three of Ike's top political advisers, Brownell, Henry Cabot Lodge, and Sherman Adams. When John Adams described the relentless efforts of Cohn and the McCarthy staff to get privileges for Schine, the group knew it had a weapon. Sherman Adams proposed that John Adams compose a complete listing of all the efforts to obtain favors for Schine—those sixty-five phone calls and nineteen meetings. That devastating document would then be the basis of the charge that, joined with a countercharge by McCarthy, brought on the Army-McCarthy hearings. In the run-up to that event, Ike did much behind-the-scenes managing; during the critical month of March 1954, Eisenhower conducted what Greenstein described as a "covert anti-McCarthy campaign." He met with the Republican leaders in the Senate to try to get the Republicans on the committee to curb McCarthy-style "investigating" and browbeating of witnesses before the television cameras. When it was being debated whether McCarthy could serve on the committee that was judging him, Ike observed at a press conference that the American tradition was that a man did not sit in judgment on his own case. Secretary Dulles, with at least Ike's agreement, if not his instigation, eliminated the personnel role of McCarthy henchman Scott McLeod in the State Department. At a March 3 press conference, Ike explicitly defended Secretary of the Army Robert Stevens, whom McCarthy had been excoriating. While granting that the army had slipped in the Peress case (the kind of protective concession that had to be made in this McCarthy atmosphere), he said that subordinates should not "submit to personal humiliation when testifying before congressional committees," the application of which, when McCarthy had just savaged General Zwicker and Secretary Stevens, was plain enough. He praised the military, and then specifically named "General Zwicker, who was decorated for gallantry in the field." Ike went out of his way to appear in public with Secretary Stevens, who ruled that Zwicker should not testify further; he intervened with Republican members of the committee to assure fair treatment henceforth; he commented on the removal of McLeod from his State Department post in a way that was understood by the press, without his saying so, as a move against McCarthy. On March 5, Ike issued the worthy instruction to each superior, "including me," to remember his obligation to his subordinates, a statement that was quoted earlier.

When in a TV speech Democratic leader Adlai Stevenson described the Republican party as half McCarthy and half Eisenhower, and McCarthy demanded television time to respond, Ike insisted that since the Republican party had been the object of the attack, the Republican National Committee should name who would respond, and the chairman, Leonard Hall, named the vice president. Hall and his staff coached and encouraged Stevens after he was browbeaten by McCarthy. Although Greenstein acknowledged along the way the limitations of Ike's performance and the difficulties it created, he nevertheless ended with the claim that "it is difficult to see how, at least for the purposes of defusing McCarthy, another technique would have worked faster or more decisively in the context of the time"—another technique, that is, beyond "refusing to exchange invective."* Greenstein ended with a quotation from Eisenhower strategist Henry Cabot Lodge, listing what had happened after Ike's "first move," a meeting on January 21, 1954, which, he said, had led to the televised hearings, McCarthy's collapse, and the Senate motion of censure. "These wholesome things would not have happened if Eisenhower had magnified McCarthy by confronting him face to face."[†]

So Ike played a role—that is all Greenstein contended—in stopping McCarthy, more of a role than had been understood. There were several actors in the drama of the puncturing of the demagogue; Ike was one of them. By two higher standards, he did not do so well. By the standard of his own March 5, 1954, "including me" statement on the "Treatment of Government Personnel," he did not protect and support beleaguered government employees during the first year of his presidency. He himself wrote in his memoirs about the toll on individuals and the cost to the nation of McCarthyism—innocent people accused, unable to clear their names fully—but his own refusal to confront McCarthy throughout 1953 and into 1954 allowed that result, and his own loyalty-security program, shaped in the McCarthy atmosphere, added to it. Greenstein, though an Ike defender in the main, nevertheless wrote, "Most government insiders . . . remember [the program] as having driven able people from government and fostered bureaucratic cautiousness. . . . The morale of civil servants also undoubtedly suffered adverse effects because Eisenhower, even though he was more popular than McCarthy, failed to confront him."[‡]

* Ibid., p. 227.
† Ibid.
‡ Ibid., p. 224.

And by the still higher criterion of George Kennan's requirement, which may be described as the clarification of the public's moral understanding, one may find "the hidden-hand" activity to have been severely limited. The issue was not only how to stop McCarthy himself; it was also how to lift the public understanding. Eisenhower had both the great bully pulpit that all presidents have and the immense prestige as the supreme commander in a great world war; no president since Grant, perhaps no president since the Founding Fathers, had come into the office with the already-established prestige that Eisenhower possessed. He could have used all that prestige for yet another service to his country. One aspect of those "hidden-hand" techniques, of that emphasis on the constitutional monarch aspects of the presidency, would appear to have been self-protection. One has subordinates do the dirty work and take the blame, thereby protecting oneself. A columnist back in those years, Marquis Childs, wrote that Ike's "chalice of fame had been filled to the brim in 1945 and he was reluctant to spill a drop." Would that he had risked a drop or two in worthy battle.

CHAPTER THIRTEEN

Ike and Harry on Race

I

BOTH DWIGHT EISENHOWER of once-bleeding Kansas and Harry S Truman of once–slave state Missouri would make, as president, a considerable contribution to the overcoming of the racial patterns that a later president would call the nation's "one huge wrong." Harry Truman's contribution would be more than might have been expected from his geographical background; it has been widely accepted that Dwight Eisenhower's was less. But as with other topics, the revised appraisal of Eisenhower's presidency has led some to argue for a more positive view of Ike's activity than had previously prevailed.

In Truman's case, the surprise, often noted, would be that he personally made such a contribution despite his origins in a onetime slave state, despite his own Confederate ancestors, despite the quite particular family memories of depredations by Yankees and Unionists, despite his many links to segregationist politicians in Missouri and in the Senate and the South, despite the racial prejudices of his friends, his brother, his sister, and his Lincoln-hating mother, and, for that matter, despite his own racial prejudice as reflected in a lifelong political incorrectness of speech.

One component in the complicated politics of replacing Henry Wallace with Harry Truman as the Democratic party's nominee for vice president at the convention in Chicago in 1944 had been Truman's greater acceptability to the white South. In the caucuses of delegates from state after state at the 1944 Democratic National Convention, it is reported, the strongest supporters of Henry Wallace, instead of Harry Truman, were the black delegates. When the radio carried the news that Harry Truman of Missouri had replaced the racial liberal Henry Wallace as the nominee, there was much angry rattling of dishes by the waiters—all black, to be sure—in a Pullman dining car. And yet, Harry Truman did more to advance racial equality than Franklin Roosevelt, more than any president since Lincoln.

Dwight Eisenhower's case would be quite different: Enormously important advances would come on his watch, and some by his administration, and to some extent by his own action. But there was at the time, and has continued to be, a perception that the advances of the Eisenhower years would fall short of what they might have been, exactly because of the limitations of the man at the top. In the revised appraisal of the Eisenhower presidency that view has been qualified.

It is possible to assemble, from almost all biographies and relevant histories, a long list of negative comments about Dwight Eisenhower's failures to lead in civil rights. David Nichols, in the early pages of his 2007 book, *A Matter of Justice*, did just that; he had scholars and writers saying of Ike on civil rights that he was "no leader at all"; that his "refusal to lead was almost criminal"; that his sympathies lay with southern whites, not southern blacks; that he "evaded" the great moral issue of civil rights; that he was guilty of a moral failing and a lack of vision. Those quotations Nichols put in his text. Having gathered still more of these, he put the overflow in his footnotes: Ike on civil rights provided little direction; comforted those who raged against the Court; appeared insensitive and ignorant about the plight of the black man; and—perhaps the worst—was a "closet racist." Nichols's reason for assembling this devastating collection was to reject it, to refute its claims, and to argue that all those scholars and writers had been wrong, and to assert that Eisenhower played a positive role in the civil rights revolution. And in the course of making his case, he deprecated Truman's contribution, compared to Eisenhower's. He evidently shares Eisenhower's own view that previous presidents—Truman in particular—"made promises they could not keep and submitted legislation they knew would fail." They made speeches. But Ike acted. Partisans of Truman, needless to say, disagree.

Both men would lead their adult lives in a racially segregated society. Eisenhower's would be more diversified geographically, although very often in army camps in the South, sometimes in the North, and for extended stretches in places outside the United States (Panama, Paris, the Philippines). But the American armed services took Jim Crow everywhere they went.

Southern attitudes permeated the army; officers believed blacks to be incapable of leadership but good at menial tasks. Blacks, called upon when fighting got tough, had proved themselves in combat in every American war, but the proof, after these wars had ended, always came unstuck. It is not true, as many white Americans have complacently assumed, that progress on race is continually unfolding and that gains once made will stay made; a deep undercurrent keeps pulling the nation backward and downward after each advance. One such powerful undertow, after the end of Reconstruction, brought the nation Jim Crow (*not* continuous with slavery) and pulled the nation back down to a nadir of race relations exactly during the turn-of-the-century youth of Harry Truman and Dwight Eisenhower. The deep undercurrents of stereotype and prejudice would wash away the memory of black success in battle. Black bravery in World War I was forgotten and denied; black inadequacy and failure was remembered, exaggerated, generalized. African-American units were segregated. African-American officers were few, lowly, not allowed to command white troops, often barred from officers' clubs. It was believed that *southern* whites made the best officers for African-American troops. In the navy, blacks were the stewards, serving in the mess. There were no African-American marines. There were (before World War II) no African-American fighter pilots; little black boys (not to mention girls) who saw airplanes and wanted to do aerial combat like heroes in the movies were like the little black girl in Langston Hughes's poem asking, "Where is the Jim Crow section / On this merry-go-round?"—except that there was no Jim Crow section of the U.S. Army Air Forces.

When he rose to be supreme commander, General Eisenhower had a black soldier, Sgt. John Moaney, as his personal valet throughout the war. In the small, tightly knit "family" in Telegraph Cottage, Moaney was present, although not a member of Ike's group: He did not join in the bridge games or the dinners, but he prepared the dinners and brought the drinks, peanuts, and cards for the games. He stayed with Ike not just through the war years but through his presidency and retirement, as well, serving as valet for twenty-seven years—until Eisenhower's death. The two men were said to be devoted to each other, but it was not a relationship of equals. John Moaney's oral history is closed.

Harry Truman would lead his life in all-white Grandview; in segregated Independence; in an all-white road crew, bank, theater, and night law school; in an all-white unit of the National Guard and an all-white battery in the Field Artillery; in an all-white store with (one may guess) an all-white customers; in a white-dominated political machine and in an all-white county board; and in an all-white and southern-dominated Senate in a segregated capital city.

One may glimpse a pattern of life from a tiny episode regarding a 1921 reunion of Truman's much-romanticized Battery D of the 129th Field Artillery (romanticized for, among other things, the democracy of its makeup, which included Irish plebeians). The secretary of the Benevolent and Protective Order of Elks Lodge Number 26 in Kansas City found it necessary to write to Harry Truman as the responsible official to request reimbursement for a Battery D party held at the Elks Club Lodge: "[S]ome members of your party . . . seemed to have taken it for granted that they could stage an 'up-roarious' time. Three members of your company went into our kitchen and threw dishes and glass-ware at the colored help working therein." The secretary of the Elks Lodge asked no apology or recompense for the "colored help," who furnished the target in this event, but he did ask Truman to pay for two-thirds of $2.24 for coffee cups; $2.03 for saucers; $1.13 for ten tumblers, $2.40 for a dozen punch cups (these are 1921 prices)—and some money for extra help to clean up the "muss" the veterans made during their "up-roarious" time throwing these coffee cups, saucers, tumblers, and punch cups at the African-Americans in the kitchen.

With the 1940s, there came war, and, for Truman and Eisenhower, great and sudden fame and power. All-out war unsettles the society that fights it, and makes deep change possible. America's "civil rights revolution," although center stage from 1954 to 1965, did not begin with the great Court decision or the Montgomery bus boycott; its roots were in the war. The war changed blacks as well as whites and sharpened ideals. Black Americans sought war work and went north, or joined the army and were sent south. Northern African-Americans, who were drafted and sent to army camps in the South, were forced to the back of the bus, to the last seats in the theater, to the separated tables in the mess hall (southern African-Americans were, too, but the northerners were not accustomed to it). White Americans as well as black Americans were sent to England, to the Continent, to the Pacific. Civilians changed jobs and geography. Millions of blacks and whites moved to the North. Detroit exploded. There were "incidents," protests, riots. Black activists, including A. Philip Randolph, threatened to march on Washington to protest discrimination, and as a result, Roosevelt signed the Fair Employment Act. The blatant racism of the enemy heightened awareness of national ideals; it also heightened frustration and moral outrage.

When Americans, white and black, landed in large numbers in England in 1942 ("over-paid, over-fed, over-sexed—and over here"), they came in segregated units, bringing their back-home prejudices into a country that did not share them.

A. J. Liebling, the great *New Yorker* reporter, talked to Ike in London in August 1942, according to Harry Butcher's diary, about "possible ways of dealing with colored problem [!] in this theater; rightly feels it will cast long shadows into future race relationships. . . . Ike said colored troops were being given equality of treatment with such segregation as the situation permits." Notice Butcher's phrasing of Eisenhower's report to Liebling. Would it be overinterpreting to hear in it ("with such segregation as the situation permits") the implication that segregation of the races was the *desirable* arrangement, with occasional mixing less desirable, allowable only by necessity? Apparently, it would not be. Butcher followed with "the directive policy with respect to Negro troops" sent by the adjutant general to the American Red Cross. In this directive the word *obviously* and the phrase "needlessly intermingled" carry a considerable message:

> Negro troops are to be allowed the same pass and furlough privileges as white troops—consequently Negro soldiers will come to London and other cities.
>
> They will expect to use the facilities of Red Cross Clubs. While obviously desirable that wherever possible, separate sleeping accommodations be provided for Negro soldiers; whenever that is not possible, Negro soldiers properly on pass or furlough should be given accommodations in the Red Cross Clubs on the same basis as other soldiers.
>
> It is believed that to avoid friction between white and Negro soldiers, care should be taken so that men of the two races are not needlessly intermingled in the same dormitory or at the same table in dining halls.

White English girls, not understanding how "obviously desirable" it was to avoid "needless" intermingling, would date black American soldiers. Southern white American soldiers would beat up the black American soldiers. Should such incidents be reported back home? Ike, to his credit, said yes—even when some reporters urged him to say no. There was to be no censorship. Further, he issued an order, distributed to every officer in England, which eased things somewhat. He said that the British had a different attitude toward race than did Americans (thereby taking for granted an "American" attitude of racial discrimination). Any effort to curtail association by official order or restriction, he said, "is unjustified and must not be attempted."

But the American part of the war that followed, fought in Europe under Eisenhower's command against a virulent racist enemy, was fought almost entirely by a white air force, a segregated navy, and a segregated army.

However, in 1941, pressure from FDR's White House finally brought, against great resistance, training of African-American pilots, which took place at a segregated African-American flying school located at Tuskegee (complete with a white commander who forbade social contact between white officers and the few black officers, and who had signs posted over segregated—"white" and "colored"—toilets). Many protests and the indignant resignation of the black aide to Secretary of War William Hastie finally did bring some broadening and change and the development of the first African-American military pilots, and of the all-African-American Ninety-ninth Pursuit Squadron, which went on to have, contradicting stereotypes, a fine combat record and lasting fame, at least in the African-American community.

On Saturday, July 3, 1943, Supreme Commander Dwight Eisenhower, in Algiers during the fighting in North Africa, paid a visit to the Ninety-ninth Pursuit Squadron—"the all Negro unit," as Harry Butcher put it in his diary. "One of its members," Butcher went on to say, "Lieutenant Hall of Brazil, Indiana, had just shot down the first enemy plane for the group. It is probably the first time in history that a Negro in a pursuit plane has shot down an enemy plane in aerial combat." Probably, indeed.

The navy began the war as the service most outspoken in its racism and most bitterly resented by African-Americans. Although all the services were segregated and discriminatory, if they admitted any African-Americans at all, the navy's insistence that blacks could serve only in the menial capacity of messmen was particularly insulting. A committee calmly reported to the secretary of the navy just after Pearl Harbor that the policy was perfectly fine; the enlistment of African-Americans other than as messmen would lead to "disruptive and undermining conditions." And the report (one can understand the fury of a black person reading this claim by an official committee reporting to the navy secretary) stated that there was no discrimination in the navy because the African-American's "characteristics" made him fit only to be a messman.

But the navy was to move, during the war, from being the most intransigent branch of the armed services to being more nearly integrated than any other branch. Under pressure from the Roosevelt White House in 1942, some blacks were allowed navy roles other than messmen; by 1944, two ships of the fleet had all-African-American crews; in 1944, the new secretary of the navy, James Forrestal (a key figure in changing the racial pattern of the navy), approved a plan to integrate the crews of twenty-five auxiliary ships; in 1945, Lester Granger of the Urban League had been asked to advise the navy, and by the end of the war, the navy had, on paper, the most progressive racial policy of the services; it had moved, so to speak, from worst to least bad.

But the great bastion of segregation was the army. It was argued that integration would lead to turmoil and violence. The army was not the place for social experiment. Segregation was efficient.

Eventually, there would come, through necessity, an opportunity to change. Supreme Commander Eisenhower was desperately looking for additional infantry in the Battle of the Bulge. An offer of pardon was made to men under court-martial sentences, and to white soldiers in "Com Z," the supply services. Maj. Gen. John C. H. Lee, the head of Com Z, pointed out that black troops, who were driving trucks and unloading ships but who were not allowed to carry rifles in the infantry, might be a considerable source of infantry manpower, if asked to volunteer, particularly if the invitation included service in racially integrated units. Eisenhower thereupon did put out a circular offering black soldiers a chance to volunteer for infantry units, promising that they would be assigned "without regard to color or race to the units where assistance is most needed." Those black soldiers who volunteered would have the opportunity of fighting "shoulder to shoulder [with white soldiers] to bring about victory." At that moment, there loomed upon the horizon the immense possibility of this war: genuine *racial integration* on a large scale, black and white together in the core institution of the armed forces, indeed the core of the core, the rifle-bearing foot soldiers, in the climactic battles of the great struggle against a racist enemy. That would have been another hinge of history. But it did not happen.

Eisenhower's chief of staff, "Beetle" Smith, exploded. He said the proposed racial integration of the infantry was directly contrary to War Department policy and was "dangerous"; "every negro organization, pressure group and newspaper" would say that the army segregated colored troops but then mixed them with whites in the front lines when an emergency arose. Henry Stimson, secretary of war in Washington, expressed the received view of the department and the army that came to be called, sardonically, by its critics the "Negroes are too dumb to fight" policy.

Eisenhower abandoned the key point: full racial integration. The circular was rewritten. Black volunteers did fight in the infantry in the last months of the war, but not "shoulder to shoulder" with white comrades; instead, they fought in segregated all-black platoons with white officers. It was, even so, an advance, but not the advance it might have been.

Eisenhower had sentimentally positive memories of these black soldiers. Seven years later, on the train back to New York City from West

Point, Eisenhower, as presidential candidate, would tell the young black staff man on the campaign team, E. Frederic Morrow, about the black soldiers. In his oral history, Morrow quoted Eisenhower as saying, "The thing I will never forget as long as I live is the sacrifice that black soldiers made at the Battle of the Bulge when I had to call for every able-bodied man, no matter what his situation or position in the army, to help to stem the tide. . . . The inferior training these men received [!] . . . Some of them would die with a rifle in their hands they'd never fired before. They came off the trucks and out of the kitchens and out of the labor battalions and they fought nobly for their country. And I will never forget."

The aroused passions of the war spilled out into the postwar years. Blacks, and many whites as well, insisted with a new intensity that Jim Crow must go. One focus of change was, of course, the armed services, and particularly the army. The greatest of the heroes of the army, and for almost two and a half postwar years (November 1945–February 1948) its chief of staff, was Dwight D. Eisenhower. In the aftermath of the war, which had been fought by a segregated army against a racist enemy, many sought full integration of the army—but not General Eisenhower.

When the pressure came to integrate the National Guard, Eisenhower allowed separate African-American companies within white battalions, but he joined with the army general staff in the decision not only to refuse to allow integration of National Guard units but even to withdraw federal recognition from units that did integrate African-Americans into "white" units.

The postwar deed of General Eisenhower that would stun black soldiers most was his testimony before a Senate committee against integration of the army of the future. E. Frederic Morrow, as a black man in the Eisenhower White House who was campaigning for candidate Eisenhower, felt he had to ask him about this (because it was a constant topic whenever the candidate spoke to black audiences). Morrow guessed that the date of the testimony was 1945, but it was later than that—April 1948. At these hearings before the Senate Committee on Armed Services regarding the Universal Military Training program, a proposal both President Truman and General Eisenhower supported, Eisenhower testified that the future army drawn from that training should still be racially segregated. The quotation that was to be remembered particularly, and to plague him when he became a politician, was this: "I do believe that if we attempt merely by passing a lot of laws to force someone to like someone else, we are just going to get into trouble."

Here is the way E. Frederic Morrow put it in his 1977 oral history:

One of the great crosses I had to bear as the black pioneer in the White House was trying to answer for blacks—and, particularly, for black servicemen—why General Eisenhower vetoed an integrated army when he came back from Europe to testify . . . was it 1945? [No, it was 1948.] A bill had been introduced in the Congress to integrate the armed forces. The feeling had been that here we are, strung around the world, fighting for something—for somebody else—that a great many of our own citizens do not share, and the bill had been introduced and the General had been called back to testify. And he testified that no, absolutely no, the time had not come when we should or could integrate the forces with any marked success. And this was a tremendous blow because we still had blacks overseas in segregated units, and—their morale just went to the bottom.

So then Morrow, as he would remember it in 1977, put the question to his candidate on the train ride in 1952: "General, you expect me to go out and stand on platforms all over this country and make speeches in your behalf but I have to be armed with information about questions that are going to be asked . . . One of them is, why, in your testimony . . . did you testify against integrating the armed forces?"

According to Morrow, Eisenhower "got very red." He hesitated for a minute. The dialogue that followed, as recorded by Morrow fifteen years later, went like this:

> "Son, your father's a minister, isn't he?"
> "That's right."
> "Did your father ever teach you anything about forgiveness?"
> "Yes, he did."
> "Well, that's where I am now. When I was called back to the United States to testify on that problem, I sent for all my field commanders to let me have their viewpoints. Their viewpoints were negative. I never, never questioned them. I just thought that here, a man commanding these men, and they had a responsibility, they ought to know. So the bulk of my testimony came from reports from these field commanders. I want to confess to you that it has only been in the last few months that it dawned on me that most of these men had a southern exposure and this, in itself, would color their decision."

This naïve acceptance of the point of view of racially prejudiced white southerners—regularly in those days Eisenhower's primary impulse on matters of race—was not lost on Morrow, much as the latter wanted to think well of his war hero/president/boss: "I could sit in the office . . . and we could talk about . . . a lot of the problems that afflicted the Negroes in this country, and this man's reaction was just a wonderful thing to see, because he was fair and decent and honest. But perhaps that night he might have a bridge game with his cronies from the South, and the next day his attitude was just altogether different. Because I guess, every man wants to be well thought of by his cronies and his close friends. . . . The problem was that most of his close friends were from the deep south."

Although Eisenhower's anti-integrationist testimony would be forgotten or unknown in the community at large, two groups would remember it: black soldiers and white racists. The latter, in the congressional battles, would quote General Eisenhower against racial integration of the army and insist that the "Eisenhower policy" of segregation should be continued. His successor as army chief of staff, Omar Bradley, was praised on the House floor by a South Carolina representative "for his courage in continuing the policy of General Eisenhower on segregation."

When some years passed and Dwight Eisenhower found himself running for president, he would be held to account for his testimony against the integration of the armed services; among those doing so would be Harry Truman. Campaigning for the Democratic ticket in 1952, Truman would say in Harlem that "while the Republican candidate was in uniform he told the Armed Services Committee of the Senate that a certain amount of segregation is necessary in the Army. You and I know that this is morally wrong. And what's more, it's even militarily wrong." Eisenhower and his defenders would try to counter with the claim that because he had favored placing all-African-American platoons in white companies, he had actually *started* integration. Making such a claim would split his audience: The broad white public might accept that claim; blacks and the whites who cared most deeply about the matter would not. For the latter group, putting all-African-American units into otherwise-white battalions was not yet "integration."

Eisenhower, the war hero, won a huge victory in the presidential election of 1952, drawing nearly 34 million votes, to 27 million for his opponent, winning surprising pluralities even in many traditional Democratic groups. But there was one constituency he did not win. Even though his Democratic opponent, Adlai Stevenson, was a little tepid on civil rights, had courted the South, and had chosen an Alabama senator (John Sparkman) as his running mate, still, the Democratic ticket received, in the teeth of the Eisenhower landslide, 73 percent of the African-American vote. Ironically, that was 4 percent more than Harry Truman received in 1948. Nevertheless, we may infer that the 1952 vote was not so much a vote for the somewhat unknown Stevenson-Sparkman ticket as an ironically belated tribute to Harry Truman, and a reproof to General Eisenhower.

II

TRUMAN'S PRESIDENTIAL RECORD on civil rights was a considerable surprise not only to the bigots in his past but also to the angry rattlers of dishes in a Pullman dining car.

The wartime turbulence on race had spilled out into the postwar years, augmented by the return of black and white soldiers. In Batesburg, South Carolina, in February 1946, a black veteran named Isaac Woodard, still wearing his uniform, had been taken off a bus, beaten, and blinded in one eye by policemen who jammed their night sticks into his eyes. (In a letter, Truman would tell Ernie Roberts about that incident.) In July 1946, two black veterans and their wives had been taken from a car near Monroe, Louisiana, by a mob of white men, lined up, and pumped full of as many as sixty bullets.

Not long after these brutalities happened, a former commander of the American Legion named Alvin Owsley, having seen pictures of black American soldiers dancing with German girls, had written to General Eisenhower, in September 1946, a letter reflecting the attitude out of which such incidents arose. "My dear General," Owsley wrote, speaking of the pictures of black American soldiers dancing with white, albeit German, girls, "I do not know . . . where these negroes come from, but it is certain that if they expect to be returned to the south, they very likely are on the way to being hanged or burned alive at public lynchings by the white men of the south." When he wrote this letter, not long after the two episodes reported above, former commander Owsley was chairman of the Legion's Americanism Endowment Fund.

Truman learned of these two particularly shocking incidents and was specifically stimulated to take action by a visit paid to him in the White House on September 19, 1946, by a group of black and white laymen and churchmen for whom Walter White of the NAACP served as spokesman. When Walter White told about the acts of violence, including the blinding of Isaac Woodard, Truman was not only shocked—as anybody would have been—but did something about it.

The first thing that Truman did that fall of 1946 was to establish his extraordinary Committee on Civil Rights—the first such body in American history—whose report would recommend most of the actions that would eventually come in the next twenty years. The second action, when the committee reported, was to make a major presidential address—the first address on the rights of African-Americans ever made by an American president. And the third and most consequential act was, in July 1948, to order the racial integration of the federal workforce and, most notably, of the armed services.

He gave his address to the NAACP at the Lincoln Memorial on June 28, 1947—the first time that a president had addressed that organization. The report and the speech included a long list of specific proposals to combat racial discrimination, legislation for the appropriate parts of which the Truman administration would introduce in Congress.

In his book defending Eisenhower's role, David A. Nichols cites an Eisenhower claim that Truman's role was "all talk and no action"; that he introduced measures in Congress that he knew could not be passed, and did not fight for them. But in their time, Truman's proposals were the center of the battle over civil rights. That they were taken seriously might be indicated by the shrill reaction of opponents: Senator Eastland of Mississippi—to quote just one phrase from a rich supply—said that the "organized mongrel minorities" that controlled the Truman administration were seeking to "Harlemize the country." Even making a presidential speech explicitly endorsing change toward racial equality, by means of the federal government, was a major step—not to mention that the speech was given at the Lincoln Memorial and addressed to the NAACP. Franklin Roosevelt had not done such a thing. Certainly no president before him had done such a thing. And appointing a serious commission was a major step. Moreover, much of Truman's program—although blocked by a southern-dominated Congress, especially the filibuster, during Truman's own administration—*was* to be enacted later.

The providing of legal machinery to advance civil rights, recommended by the Truman committee, would be slightly less controversial than other recommendations, and could be accomplished fairly soon; the Civil Rights Division of the Department of Justice could be enlarged and upgraded, and an independent Civil Rights Commission within the executive branch would be established by the modest Civil Rights Act of 1957, during the Eisenhower administration.

The Truman committee recommended federal statutory protection of every qualified person's right to vote, preventing interference not only by private persons but by public officials, as well. The poll tax would be outlawed in federal elections, as the Truman committee proposed, by the Twenty-fourth Amendment to the Constitution, ratified in January 1964. The Civil Rights Act of 1964 would include provisions outlawing a string of devices that had been used to keep blacks from voting in the South, including those that had hitherto maintained the white party primary; the

Voting Rights Act of 1965 would clinch the matter by providing *federal* registrars of voters in districts with long histories of voting discrimination.

The long-sought compulsory federal Fair Employment Practices Commission (FEPC)—against discrimination in employment—the center of argument about race in the politics of the 1940s, and recommended by the Truman committee, was in effect enacted by provisions for fair employment practices in the Civil Rights Act of 1964, and so were provisions against segregation or discrimination in entities receiving federal grants and assistance, in public health facilities, and in college admissions, also all recommended by the Truman Committee.

The Truman committee recommended a constitutional amendment granting residents of the already then predominantly black District of Columbia the right to vote in presidential elections; the Twenty-third Amendment, establishing that right, would be ratified in 1961. The committee recommended home rule for the District, which would be won in 1974.

So the proposals of the Truman committee would eventually be enacted, albeit some years after Harry Truman's presidency. But there would be two other routes, not blocked by the filibuster and white supremacist committee chairmen, through which Truman could pursue some of the recommendations more immediately. One of these was the Supreme Court. The long battle by the NAACP and its heroes—among them Thurgood Marshall and Charles Houston—had focused on the making real of the Constitution in the actual lives of African-Americans by appeal to the Court. It would be a key moment, of large significance, when the United States government, through the Department of Justice, would *intervene,* as a friend of the Court, on the side of the plaintiffs in cases attacking racial segregation. The first case was *Shelly v. Kramer,* decided in 1948, which said that racially restrictive covenants violated the Fourteenth Amendment. Then three cases in 1950 also held that particular forms of racial segregation violated the Interstate Commerce Act. *Henderson v. United States* struck down segregation in railroad dining cars; *McLaurin v. Oklahoma State Regents* did not permit the separating of a black student from others in a state university; and *Sweatt v. Painter* rejected a Texas effort to set up a separate black law school. There were no dissenting votes in any of these cases, although some justices did disqualify themselves. These cases found unconstitutional particular applications of the doctrine of separate but equal that furnished justification for racial segregation by law. They were victories for the forces of civil rights, but they fell short of the big victory because they did not quite challenge the constitutionality of segregation as such. They did, however, prepare the way for the Court's momentous, unanimous decision in the great school segregation case in 1954, *Brown v. Board of Education,* which would explicitly repudiate the separate-but-equal doctrine of *Plessy v. Ferguson* and say that segregated facilities are inherently unequal. The way had been prepared by decisions of the Court in Truman's day, aided by amicus curiae briefs prepared by Harry Truman's Department of Justice. So the deprecation of Truman's role as mere talk, perhaps by Ike and certainly by his defender Nichols, needs correction.

And there was one other route by which the aims of the Truman committee could be carried out: by executive order. This brings us back to the very large subject of the armed forces, about which there is clear-cut dispute. The Truman committee's report in December 1947, and then Truman's civil rights address in February 1948, called for an end to racial segregation in the armed forces. On July 9, 1948, the president issued Executive Order 9981, which declared it to be the policy that "there shall be equality of treatment and opportunity for all persons in the armed services regardless of race." But Nichols (and Eisenhower) would say that the declaration by itself did not accomplish its aim, which of course is true. Nichols objects to all the history books that say that Truman integrated the armed services; I believe he would sooner say Eisenhower integrated the armed services. So what is the truth of the matter?

The truth, as you might have guessed, is that both played a role, but a great deal did happen during Truman's administration. Truman did do more than simply issue the order; he established a President's Committee on the Equality of Treatment and Opportunity in the Armed Services to oversee its realization. That committee—called informally the Fahy committee, after its chairman, a soft-spoken liberal Georgian, former solicitor general Charles Fahy—had seven members, two of them black, and an energetic executive secretary, a strong integrationist who would later be a distinguished *New York Times* reporter, E. W. Kenworthy. They did prod and push the services, over the months that followed, into varying degrees of compliance. And some Truman appointees heading the services helped to push integration. We have noted that James Forrestal, as secretary of the navy, pushed the racial integration of that branch, which had begun even before Truman's order; as the first secretary of defense, Forrestal pushed all the services. Stuart Symington, the secretary of the air force, newly established as a separate service in 1947, pushed integration; the all-black Ninety-ninth Pursuit Squadron, which had in its time been an advance, now had to be broken up. These were no longer the more recalcitrant services; the greatest resistance came now from the army. Ike's friend "Brad"—Omar Bradley—had taken over as army chief of staff from Eisenhower in February 1948, and Secretary of the Army Kenneth Royall reflected the resistant opinion within the traditional army. They argued that attempts to integrate the army would undercut its efficiency as a fighting force, damaging morale, and they stood by the standard army position, repeating its dictum on race—that the army was no place for social experiments and that the army would change only when the rest of the nation changed.

When the Korean War broke out in the summer of 1950, the United States fought with the Eighth Army, which was still segregated. Blacks occupied service units in the rear. But when the United Nations forces were driven stumbling back down the peninsula in defeat, the generals, dealing with huge losses, put black soldiers into hitherto all-white units, and it worked. In July 1951, in the midst of the Korean War, the United States Army formally announced its plan to do what its commander in chief had ordered it to do three years earlier—desegregate. The Korean War was an important engine of the integration of the armed services, with the Truman order as the background.

It is nevertheless true that when Eisenhower became president in January 1953, there were still major sections of the armed services that were segregated, especially the facilities and services that surrounded bases in the South. And he could, with the prestige of his rank and military accomplishment, command obedience. The last segregated units were integrated, and in October 1954, the secretary of defense announced that the last racially segregated unit in the armed services had been abolished. When you think what a huge undertaking it was to take the armed services of a major power, deeply traditional, as all armies are, and loaded with prejudice, and turn it clear around in a mere six years—from Truman's order in 1948 to the announced completion in October 1954—you perceive what a huge social accomplishment this was. I believe the accurate statement on the racial integration of the American armed services is that Eisenhower completed what Truman had begun. What they accomplished (jointly, in a sense) was quite extraordinary. In a mere six years, they transformed the huge tradition-bound, prejudice-loaded, southern-tilted institutions of the American armed services from being, among national institutions, perhaps the most potent repositories and nurturers of racial discrimination and prejudice to being, perhaps, the opposite.

Truman issued another executive order on the same day as the one integrating the armed services, July 26, 1948, with a parallel purpose and number. This was Executive Order 9980, mandating the elimination of racial discrimination throughout the federal government. The embarrassing fact for a Democrat was that segregation had been instituted clear back in the Wilson administration, when the Democrats (which means southern politicians, of whom, on this topic, Wilson himself was one) returned to power after an enormous stretch of post–Civil War Republican rule. That newly instituted segregation had continued thereafter not only through the Republican administrations of the 1920s but also during the Democratic administration of Franklin Roosevelt, except for the Department of the Interior, where FDR's colorful secretary of the interior, Harold Ickes, insisted on an island of racial integration. But now Truman was ordering an end to racially separate cafeterias. As with the armed services, so with the federal government: Truman appointed another seven-man committee, with two black members, to prod and oversee the results, and his order established two ways a black person denied equal treatment could appeal.

Who ended racial discrimination in the federal bureaucracy? A Truman book (Michael Gardner, *Harry Truman and Civil Rights*) says that Truman did. An Eisenhower book (Nichols, *A Matter of Justice*) says that Eisenhower did. As with the armed services, I believe we can conclude that a process begun under Truman was completed under Eisenhower. But the tendency of Nichols, and perhaps Eisenhower as well, to claim that Truman was all talk and no action, all promise and no performance, is not accurate. There was effective action as well, as many black persons living then could attest.

An anecdote is told—originally by an early Truman biographer and journalist covering the Truman White House, Alfred Steinberg, who may have seen it happen—about an exchange at a White House luncheon for the executive committee of the Democratic National Committee shortly after Truman's executive orders on civil rights. The national committeewoman from Alabama, Mrs. Leonard Thomas, said to the President, "I want to take a message back to the South. Can I tell them you're not ramming miscegenation down our throats? That you're for all the people, not just the North?" In response, Truman first read to her from—so Mr. Steinberg reported—a copy of the Bill of Rights, which he carried in his pocket, and then said, "I'm everybody's President. I take back nothing of what I said." A "Negro White House waiter," according to Steinberg—here's the reason for citing this anecdote—"got so excited listening to the argument that he accidentally knocked a cup of coffee out of Truman's hands."

So there was a sharply contrasting rattling of dishes: unlike the rattling of cups and saucers around the heads of the African-Americans in the kitchen of the Kansas City Elks Club in 1921, when some veterans of Battery D had an "up-roarious" time, and unlike the angry rattling of dishes on the dining car when the radio said that Harry Truman of Missouri, instead of Henry Wallace, had received the nomination for vice president by the Democrats in 1944, now the dishes rattled in excitement when a black waiter heard his president, under challenge from an Alabama committeewoman, stick by his integrationist proposals.

How did it come about that Harry Truman of segregated Missouri and Confederate antecedents, whose attitudes one biographer, Richard Miller, bluntly calls "bigoted," did more for the rights of African-Americans than any president since Lincoln? The answer some scholars would give is: African-American votes. The answer another, and now larger, group of scholars would give is: He had a "conversion."

The first answer was given wide currency by a widely read book called *The Future of American Politics*, published in 1956 by a political writer, mostly for *The Saturday Evening Post*, named Samuel Lubell. Harry Truman figured prominently in the early part of this book, and the centerpiece of Lubell's analysis was a quotation he had extracted from a southern senator (not named) who reported what Senator Truman had said to him way back in 1938 about an antilynching bill: "[Y]ou know I am against this bill, but if it comes to a vote, I'll have to vote for it. All my sympathies are with you but the Negro vote in Kansas City and St. Louis is too important." A scholarly book entitled *The Policies of Civil Rights in the Truman Administration*, by William C. Berman, published in 1970, followed, although waveringly, that line of interpretation: Truman did what he did for Negro votes, and for that reason alone—almost. Some of Berman's material argues against his own conclusion. Berman himself oscillated. "Truman," Berman wrote in his concluding chapter, "moved only because he had no choice: Negro votes and the demands of the Cold War, not simple humanitarianism—though there may have been some of that— produced whatever token gains African-Americans were to make." Other and later interpreters, after the opening of more papers, especially from Truman aides, have been less reluctant than Berman to grant that "there may have been some of that," indeed quite a bit of that, of "simple humanitarianism." Michael Gardner's 2002 book presents Harry Truman as, at his core, a conscientious and idealistic young believer in American democracy at the same time that he held "racist" attitudes. He read books—not a small point—and he carried in his wallet a copy of Tennyson's poem

"Locksley Hall," idealistic in the extreme. Although his Missouri life was segregated and although it taught him racial slurs and jokes and prejudiced attitudes—probably more than Kansas or even the peacetime army and his Georgia golfing buddies taught Dwight Eisenhower—his political life had had a positive effect. By running for nationwide office, he paid some attention to the plight of the African-Americans of Kansas City in a way he might otherwise not have done. The Pendergast machine courted, and received a large share of, the African-American vote in Kansas City, and Harry Truman, as a loyal operative of that organization, came to do so, too. This enlarged his view, beyond what his sister, Mary Jane, or his brother, John Vivian, held, insulated in Grandview or Independence. Then when he ran for the Senate, with the entire state as the arena, he had the African-American population of St. Louis as well as that of Kansas City as a constituency. Although Missouri was a segregated ex–slave state, it was not Mississippi. Blacks did vote. Missouri was a border state with two big urban concentrations, which included blacks in significant numbers. Do not convictions come into play when deciding to *which* of the available groups of voters one should appeal? Other Missouri politicians—Bennet Champ Clark, the other senator from Missouri, and Lloyd Stark, the former governor who opposed Truman for the nomination for the Senate in 1940, both of them Democrats, with the same constituency as Truman—certainly did not make as definite statements on civil rights as Truman did.

Truman inaugurated his difficult second campaign for the Senate in 1940 with a speech on civil rights. It was a strong one for that time, that place, and, one might say, for that speaker, for these reasons: He delivered it not to a black audience but to a largely white audience (in Sedalia, a moderate-size town set in rural Missouri); he included not only the safely broad affirmations that almost any American politician might make ("I believe in the brotherhood of man") but also the explicit point, slightly less safe, that not every Missouri politician in that day would have ("not merely the brotherhood of white men"). He also then was more specific than politicians endorsing, in general, the brotherhood of man usually were back then: "If any class or race can be permanently set apart from, or pushed down below, the rest in political and civil rights, so may any other class or race. . . . Negroes have been preyed upon by all types of exploiters, from the installment salesmen of clothing, pianos, and furniture to the vendors of vice. The majority of our Negro people find but cold comfort in shanties and tenements. Surely, as freemen, they are entitled to something better than this."

The reader will notice the taking for granted, or perhaps acceptance, of a separated life for those patronizingly described as "our Negro people." That taking for granted would be even more explicit, and the condescension even more blatant, in a speech that Senator Truman would give a month later to a black audience at the Democratic National Convention in Chicago: "I am not appealing for social equality for the Negro. The Negro himself knows better than that, and the highest types of Negro leaders say quite frankly that they prefer the society of their own people." Those extremely patronizing references—"the highest types of Negro leaders" and "their own people"—and, particularly, the explicit rejection of something called "social equality" would recur in Truman's speeches and statements. But, offsetting that fault, was Truman's plain and clear-eyed comprehension of the central point: "Negroes want justice, not social relations," he said, immediately after delivering the sentences quoted above. To be sure, in the longer run one cannot accomplish "justice" without breaking down the barriers to "social relations," but for the time and place that sentence was an advance, especially as Truman went on, again, to name specific deprivations: "Every community owes the Negro a fair deal [notice this phrase, in 1940] in regard to public utilities, lights, sewers, street improvement, and water mains. [This was an experienced, down-to-earth local politician speaking; these specifics do imply a separated Negro district.] We owe the Negro legal equality . . . because he is a human being and a natural born American."

In 1949, when he was in the White House, Truman said in an interview with Jonathan Daniels, "I got to thinking about the Negro problem [while I was] in the Senate. We had no real problem at home." Richard Miller, a Missouri biographer who wrote about Truman's life before he entered the White House, and who sometimes showed a certain eagerness to find fault with Mr. Truman, pointedly juxtaposed this second sentence—"We had no real problem at home"—with an account of a particularly gruesome lynching of a black man at Marysville, in northwestern Missouri, while Truman was chief judge in Jackson County, not far away. "No problem in Missouri?" But if one reads that comment in context, one discovers it means that Harry Truman didn't have a problem. He didn't focus his mind on the problem, which Missouri, along with other states, surely had, until he was a senator. When he told Daniels, "I got to thinking about the Negro problem in the Senate," one must, given his track record for conscientiously doing his homework, believe him. And he went right on after the aside about "no problem" to describe a problem he did think about, as a result of his service on the Wheeler committee, investigating the railroads, during his first term in the Senate. This was his perception of the unjust treatment of the Negro fireman on an old southern railroad. He described it briefly in the "got to thinking . . . in the Senate" interview with Jonathan Daniels, and mentioned it on other occasions—apparently, it made a real impression on him. One of the fullest and most pungent of his references to this injustice came in a letter (now in the Truman Library) in which he tried to set straight a thoroughly bigoted racist old friend named Ernie Roberts, who had written him a sharp complaint about his egalitarianism. Truman told of a specific measure in his letter of response:

> On the Louisiana and Arkansas Railway when coal burning locomo-
> tives were used, the Negro firemen were the thing because it was a
> back-breaking job and a dirty one. As soon as they turned to oil as a
> fuel it became customary for people to take shots at the Negro firemen
> and a number were murdered because it was thought that this was not
> a white-collar job and should go to a white man. I can't approve of
> such goings on and I shall never approve it, as long as I am here.

The point about this railroad case is that it entailed the discerning and rejecting of a social *pattern*. The actual *shooting* of African-American fire-men would, presumably, be deplored by almost anyone, but in terms of Truman's enlarging awareness, the point was not only that the African-American firemen, after the job was a tidy one, were shot at and some-times killed but that the underlying patterns of employment and social attitudes were also deplorable: that African-Americans should do back-breaking, dirty jobs, but clean, white-collar jobs should be reserved for whites. About both the acts of brutal violence (of course) and, more sig-nificantly, the underlying social patterns and attitudes to which they were linked, Truman reached a moral judgment: They were wrong. "I can't approve of such goings on and I shall never approve it, as long as I am here," he wrote to Ernie Roberts. But then he went another step, which not everybody who morally disapproved of those acts and patterns did: "I am going to try to remedy it." Moreover, Truman responded grandly to friend Ernie's implicit threat of huge southern defections: "[A]nd if that [his trying to remedy such racial injustices] ends up in my failure to be reelected, that failure will be in a good cause."

III

THE DEFENSE OF IKE on race would be this: that he made two outstand-ing appointments, Earl Warren as chief justice and Herbert Brownell as

attorney general; that he shored up those appointments with able integrationist judges in the federal courts and a strongly pro–civil rights Justice Department; and that he undertook, with his executive power, to
make sure that whatever the federal tax dollar supported should surely be
racially integrated. In his first State of the Union address, Dwight Eisenhower committed himself to serve "the equality of all citizens of every race
and color and creed." The most concrete promise he made in fulfillment
of the pledge was "to use whatever authority exists in the office of the
President to end segregation in the District of Columbia, including the
Federal Government, and any segregation in the armed services." And
his administration would take steps to end the racial segregation that still
prevailed, in spite of a Reconstruction-era ordinance, in the hotels, restaurants, parks, swimming pools, and theaters of the nation's capital. The
Eisenhower administration did remove the last vestiges of the formal racial
segregation in the federal civil service—in the post office, for an important
example. (The Eisenhower administration had the great advantage, in its
first two years, that Republicans controlled Congress, which meant that
southern Democrats with seniority didn't.) As noted earlier, Ike not only
would complete the integration of the armed services begun by Harry
Truman; he would go beyond that to end the segregation in the schools
for the children of the military operated, in the South, by the military
itself, with federal tax dollars. ("All are taxed to provide these funds," he
would typically say.) These were accomplishments the executive branch
could put in place, within its own domain. His textbook sense of the
separation of powers—of the division between the state and federal governments—and of the gulf between the government and the private world
led him to a narrow but clear area of responsibility for the federal executive: "[W]herever Federal funds are expended . . . I do not see how any
American can justify a discrimination."

End discrimination in the nation's capital. End it wherever federal tax
dollars are used, and in the armed services. Defend everybody's right to
vote. And enforce the law—"faithfully execute" the laws, as the Constitution says. That's the role of the *federal executive*—so Eisenhower would
believe, and he would act on that belief.

In the most visible showdown over school desegregation with defiant
southern power, after much turbulence and when he had been backed
into a corner, President Eisenhower did send paratroops to Little Rock to
enforce a court order that Arkansas governor Orval Faubus and many
Little Rock citizens were intent on defying. A criticism at the time said
that he went "from platitudes to paratroops," arguing that if he had done

more *before,* he might have avoided having to do so much in the end. But when push came to shove, he did give the order and enforce the law.

E. Frederic Morrow was said to be the first African-American ever to serve on the White House staff, and he sat quite visibly at a baseball game with the president just before the 1956 elections. J. Ernest Wilkins, Sr. (an assistant secretary of labor filling in for the secretary), was said—in a memo from Maxwell Rabb to the president—to be "the first Negro in American history" to sit in a cabinet meeting. (When Wilkins resigned, in the second term, a white successor was appointed.)

So Eisenhower had a list of accomplishments that, in the view of his defenders, should cause him to be well regarded. They—and perhaps Ike himself—would be inclined to contrast the action of his administration with the mere talk, the speech making and empty promises, of previous administrations (meaning mainly Truman's). But important as Ike's accomplishments would have been in an earlier time, they were swamped in these years by a gigantic wave of history. In May 1954, the Supreme Court handed down its decision regarding school desegregation: Segregation is inherently unequal. In that great event and its tumultuous aftermath, the Eisenhower *administration* did play a curious sort of a positive part—but not Mr. Eisenhower *himself.* His critics argue that his failure to speak out was a negative. It is his failure on this point—on the explicit defense of the moral rightness of the Brown decision—that is the chief reason for all those negative views mentioned earlier.

The case (or the five consolidated cases) of *Brown v. Board of Education* had already worked its (their) way through the courts before Eisenhower became president. But President Eisenhower did then make one contribution "of the Highest Consequence" (as Roger Williams used to say, back in the seventeenth century) to the result of the case—an enormously important contribution that was inadvertent. In September 1953, just nine months after he became president, he appointed a new chief justice of the United States—Earl Warren.

The cases had already been argued before the Supreme Court in December 1952, and judgment postponed, before Eisenhower became president, and well before Earl Warren became chief. His chiefship was essential to the clear, unanimous, and ringing decision the Court rendered. And, as president, Dwight Eisenhower was essential to the appointing of Earl Warren.

Would the previous chief justice, Harry Truman's poker-playing friend and appointee Fred Vinson, have achieved a unanimous Court decision had he not died in September 1953? Almost certainly not, say those who are in a position to speculate with knowledge. More than that: The Court, conceivably, might even have left in place the *Plessy* doctrine of constitutionally legitimate racial segregation by law.

Would the Democratic presidential nominee in 1952, Adlai Stevenson, had he been elected instead of Eisenhower, have appointed on Vinson's death a new chief justice comparable to Earl Warren? With respect to this case? It is to be doubted. To have been elected, Stevenson would have had to carry the solidly Democratic South—the only states he *did* carry in 1952, nine of them, were in the solidly *Deep* South. He had chosen as his running mate Senator John Sparkman of Alabama, who, although a liberal by Alabama standards, did conform—would feel he had to conform—to the strong white southern support for segregation; for example, later, in signing the "Southern Manifesto" opposing the Supreme Court's decision. Although Stevenson's own record and attitudes were those of a liberal northern urban Democrat, they did not feature opposition to segregation as a major point. He had friendships and temperamental affinities with southern gentlemen. On the key racial issue of the time, the FEPC, he endorsed, in the 1952 campaign, only a "voluntary" version—which, to its true supporters, meant nothing at all. Had he been elected, he would almost certainly have brought the one seat necessary for the Democrats to retain control of the Senate (the Eisenhower victory resulted in Republican control by the narrowest possible margin, 48–47) and certainly a southern vice president—John Sparkman—to break ties; such a Democratic Senate would have increased President Stevenson's dependence on, and presumably deference to, segregationist southern Democratic committee chairmen. So a President Stevenson probably would not have appointed an Earl Warren equivalent to the chief justiceship in September 1953.

And therefore an Eisenhower administration was essential to that appointment, which, in turn, was essential to the unanimous antisegregation result in *Brown*. Yet that great result, for which President Eisenhower deserves a huge but indirect credit, was at best inadvertent. The view had been that Ike did not want, and perhaps actually opposed, the consequences of appointing Warren.

President Truman, as we have seen, encouraged his attorney general and the Justice Department to enter, as a friend of the Court, the segregation cases then coming before the Supreme Court: *Shelly v. Kraemer* and the others. That was a big step. These cases prepared the ground for the historic *Brown v. Board of Education*. And as the cases challenging school segregation wound their way from their several locations toward the great consummation at the Supreme Court, the Truman administration again entered the consolidated case as a friend of the Court—another big step—and took an explicit position against the constitutionality of segregation.

But these steps toward a Supreme Court decision unequivocally declaring that segregation is unconstitutional may not have been advanced by President Harry Truman's own appointments to the Supreme Court. The problem was not that the Truman appointees would have been *against* desegregation, although there was an undercurrent in some of the justices in that direction; the problem was, rather, that they did not provide the forceful intellectual leadership such a breakthrough decision would require.

It fell to Truman, in his seven and three-quarter years in the White House, to appoint four men to the Supreme Court, and none of these was outstanding. Two were old friends from the Senate—the straitlaced Harold Burton from Ohio, whom Truman had come to know on the Truman committee, the one Republican, and the Democrat Sherman Minton of Indiana, who had been a first-term senator with Truman from 1933 to 1939. Neither was a giant. The other two men were former members of his cabinet, poker-playing friends, both from states with racially segregated schools: former attorney general Tom Clark of Texas and—by far the most important, potentially—the former secretary of the treasury, a close Truman friend, Fred Vinson of Kentucky, as chief justice. Taken together, they were not as intellectually gifted as the five remaining Roosevelt appointees, four of whom (Black, Douglas, Jackson, and Frankfurter) were outstanding not only in intellectual ability and force but also in diverse and spectacular forms of prima-donnaism. This Roosevelt group was also notable for its feuds and conflicts, ideological and personal. And the fifth Roosevelt appointee, Stanley Reed of Kentucky, although not as "difficult" as the other Roosevelt appointees, also was not as able, and had strong inclinations to support the pattern of segregation he had known. These would be the nine justices—five appointed by FDR, four by Truman—who heard arguments on the long-anticipated school segregation cases, now combined into one, in December 1952, not long after Dwight Eisenhower's election but before Harry Truman turned the White House over to him in January.

It was by no means clear that the Court would take the fateful step and overturn *Plessy,* thereby rejecting segregation on constitutional grounds. And it was more than likely that it would *not* do so unanimously—that there would be dissent, and a scattering of opinions concurring with, and dissenting from, whatever decision was made. Various countings were, and have been, made (not by the Court—they prudently avoided a vote in their early conference), and these shifted and changed, because the issue was not only the bald question of whether to overturn *Plessy* and outlaw segregation but also what kind of an order for enforcement there would be, and what the justification would be. Justice Reed was disinclined, throughout, to overturn segregation. Black, Burton, and Douglas were rather clearly throughout going to vote to strike down *Plessy* and segregation. But the other five were not altogether predictable, for a variety of reasons. It was not at all absurd for John W. Davis, the distinguished South Carolina lawyer and 1924 Democratic nominee for president, who was the leading advocate for the segregationist side, to be fairly sure, after argument, that his side would win 5–4, maybe even 6–3. Convinced of the strength of his case, given seventy years of constitutionally justified segregation, and the acceptance even by the Congress that proposed the Fourteenth Amendment and its "Equal Protection of the Laws" of racially segregated schools in the nation's capital, and convinced as well of the weakness of the opposing case, relying, as it seemed, on "sociology," Davis might have believed he could win the votes of all, or almost all, of the five doubtful justices, plus Reed, to make a solid 6–3 vote to leave segregation in place.

The justices themselves did not, looking back, go that far—to believe that a vote by the Vinson Court in the spring of 1953 would have left segregation as it was—but they did believe that any vote to overturn it would have been divided, and perhaps even close, with many dissenters. There are two later estimates by justices then on the Court of the result that might have been in 1953. Justice Frankfurter, in a letter to his colleague Stanley Reed shortly after the unanimous decision in May 1954, wrote that "if the *Segregation* cases had reached decision last term there would have been four dissenters—Vinson, Reed, Jackson, and Clark—and certainly several opinions for the majority view." At about the same time, Justice Harold Burton guessed in his diary that a 1953 vote would have been 6–3, "with the Chief Justice one of the dissenters." All who commented on the matter, on whatever side they might have voted in 1953, and observers of the Court and interpreters since, agree that a *divided* decision on this subject, with strong dissents, would have been, in Frankfurter's word, "catastrophic."

And it is to be noted that both of these guesses from informed participants about a 1953 result indicated that one of the dissenters would have been Harry Truman's poker-playing friend and regular telephone pal, the chief justice, Fred Vinson.

The first key, in 1953, to achieving the great result of a unanimous over-turning of segregation was postponement. The brilliant and complicated Harvard professor and proponent of judicial restraint, Justice Felix Frank-furter, was a chief agent of that postponement. The Court did not hand down a decision in the spring of 1953, after having heard the argument the previous December, but, instead, asked of the parties a series of questions and ordered a reargument for the next Court term, beginning in October. In September, though, Harry Truman's appointee Fred Vinson died. Felix Frankfurter's cruel joke is, understandably, repeated in all the books: "It is the first indication I have ever had," he is reported to have said to a former clerk about Vinson's death, "that there is a God."

And so it came to pass that the chief justice who brought to its conclusion the historic case against segregation was appointed not by Harry Truman but by Dwight Eisenhower.

President Eisenhower appointed Earl Warren, governor of California. He had a political debt to Warren for leading California to the victory-determining switch (against Warren's own interest, as a long-shot candidate for the nomination, as well as that of Eisenhower's chief rival for the nomination, Robert Taft) on the so-called fair play amendment in the fight over contested Texas delegations to the Republican National Convention in 1952—a victory essential to, and decisive for, Eisenhower's winning the nomination. In addition, Eisenhower liked what he perceived to be Warren's practicality and middle-of-the-road philosophy, and, of course, Warren was one of the most eminent Republicans in the nation, in his third term as governor of a huge state. When picking his cabinet, Eisenhower told Warren that he would not offer him a cabinet post but would promise him—personally *promise* him—the first opening on the Supreme Court. When Vinson died, Warren held Eisenhower to that promise, insisting that it included the chief justiceship.

It was another important decision of the Eisenhower White House to appoint Warren in September—a recess appointment, because Congress was not in session. His confirmation would encounter a further delay when his name was formally submitted in January—he finally was con-firmed in March—but meanwhile he had been serving through the months of the winter of 1953–1954 in one of the most remarkable examples of potent small-group politics in American history.

Warren brought all the justices around not only to vote to overturn segregation but to do so unanimously and even without concurring opinions. The achievement of unanimity was of enormous importance, and, indeed, the justices' perceptions of its importance was one of the arguments Warren could use to bring it about. It was of immense importance in vindicating to a reluctant white public not only the *constitutional* authority but also the *moral* authority of the Court's decision. Suppose it had been 5–4, as in so many cases in the modern era, or even 7–2, as in the Dred Scott case. Or suppose there had been a ringing dissent reaffirming the *Plessy* doctrine that segregation is not inequality, and attacking the (widely admitted) defects of the vulnerable majority opinion. Or just suppose there had been a scattering of dissenting and concurring opinions. The effect on the subsequent politics of the matter would have been devastating. The resistance would be ferocious enough as it was, with not only white citizens' councils and acts of intimidation and violence spreading across the South but also with a defiant "Southern Manifesto" from virtually the entire representation of the South in Congress, and with governors and state legislatures and school boards outdoing one another in making defiant arrangements. All of this would have been incalculably worse had the Court's decision itself given the opposition an opening.

But the Court, under Dwight Eisenhower's appointee Earl Warren, provided no such opening. Its decision, written by Warren, was not only unanimous but also clear, short, to the point, noninflammatory, almost matter-of-fact, and—a key strategic point—did not say, as is often done, that compliance must come "forthwith." It provided, instead, for a reargument about compliance, inviting the segregating states to participate. (It is probable that the Court could not have achieved unanimity, perhaps not gotten a decision, if it had tried to say "forthwith.") And in the decision about compliance a year later—*Brown II,* as it is sometimes called—the Court did not set a "date certain" (as the NAACP and others wanted), but used the now-famous phrase "with all deliberate speed," and placed the judgment of compliance in the hands of the federal *district* courts, with their close links to the affected communities.

Those close links included being appointed by presidents on recommendation of the *senators* from the relevant states. Therefore, many of these judges in the South were themselves in their private heart gentlemanly segregationists—albeit some not so gentlemanly. Largely because of the link to Democratic senators, the appointments by Harry Truman, before Eisenhower, and even by John Kennedy, after Eisenhower, would include judges who would not be stalwart opponents of segregation. But on this point President Eisenhower made another important contribution to racial justice in America. His appointments to the federal bench were better than Truman's for these reasons: He was less deferential to segregationist southern Democratic senators than the presidents before and after him; Dwight Eisenhower had a kind of civics-book high standard (Truman appointed cronies; Eisenhower did not appoint cronies); and—by far the most important—Eisenhower's attorney general, Herbert Brownell, was more able, more influential with the president, and more devoted to civil rights than any of Truman's attorneys general. Truman had high standards for appointments in the fields of foreign policy and defense, but it proved to be otherwise with judges.

Eisenhower appointed four more justices to the Supreme Court after appointing Warren: John Harlan, a distinguished New York lawyer, who was not necessarily the racial liberal that his name implied—he was the namesake and grandson of the famous lone dissenter on *Plessy,* who said the Constitution is color-blind—but he did furnish intelligent conservative support to the Warren Court's further decisions on race; William Brennan, a Democrat, who went on to be an important longtime progressive on race as on other matters, and a strong supporter of the chief justice; Potter "I Know It When I See It" Stewart, an Ohio judge and lawyerly lawyer of good background, who became a swing vote on many issues but who joined all the others on race; and—the one truly mediocre appointment—a man named Charles Whittaker, who served only five years. Taken as a group, Eisenhower's five appointees would be judged by most observers to be superior in general to Truman's four appointees and, because of the importance of Chief Justice Warren, and also William Brennan, particularly superior on racial issues. The Warren Court, now with a steadily increasing number of Eisenhower appointees, would go on to make a long string of decisions applying the doctrine of *Brown* against state-sanctioned segregation in public parks, in libraries, in courtrooms, on buses (not only between states but *within* one state), on municipal golf courses, on public bathing beaches, in public housing, and even in hotels and restaurants and other enterprises accommodating the public. It was declared unlawful to list the race of candidates on the ballot and, with surprisingly little public outcry, in 1967, the Supreme Court struck down state laws forbidding the marriage of a white to an African-American. Jim Crow, as far as the *law* was concerned, was gone. The Court's decisions on all these cases dealing with race continued to be unanimous. The number of judges appointed by President Eisenhower kept increasing, until, with the appointment of Potter Stewart in 1959, it became an Eisenhower *majority*—still deciding unanimously that Jim Crow must go. Whatever the appointing president and his Georgia friends might think, Jim Crow must go.

But the big fight continued to be about the schools. And to that struggle, once again, Eisenhower would make a considerable contribution by his appointment of federal judges. These included not only the justices of the Supreme Court already listed, who continued to join in unanimous decisions against school segregation and the subterfuges that were invented to sustain it, but also—usually on the recommendation of his attorney general, Herbert Brownell—judges in the lower courts.

The superiority of Eisenhower's judicial appointees to Truman's would be, on the subject of race in particular, especially important in the districts that covered the South. As the story of desegregating the schools unfolded, while the man who appointed them remained silent and hinted disapproval, Eisenhower appointees Frank Johnson of Alabama, Elbert Tuttle of Georgia, John Minor Wisdom of Louisiana, and John Brown of Texas made brave decisions on the firing line of local prejudice. Eisenhower's judicial appointments were better than Truman's, and those who know say they were also better than Kennedy's.

For the same reason that a unanimous vote of the Court was important, it was of the highest importance that the president of the United States give the decision of the Court his clear moral support. But, in the view of Earl Warren and most civil rights leaders, President Eisenhower did not do that—never did that. And that failure is the primary reason for the repeated negative statements about his role on racial issues.

By hints and evasions and "neutrality" and references to "extremists on both sides" and, repeatedly, to the alleged inefficacy of "law" to "change hearts," he declined to put the full authority of his office behind the moral principle of the Court's decision. It was concluded by some that in his private heart, he did not accept the Court's position. But the problem does not really appear to be that he was anything like a "closet racist"; it lies, rather, in his concept of his role as president, as we have seen on other matters. He did not fully recognize the immense importance of the president as a leader of opinion, a shaper of the moral interpretation of events.

One of the reports most damaging to Eisenhower on race came from Earl Warren himself very early, even before the Court's decision in *Brown*, in the curious episode of the presidential stag dinner. While the case was pending, the president invited Earl Warren—now the chief justice of the United States—to an exclusive dinner at the White House, along with some other lawyers, including, significantly, John W. Davis, who, as noted, was now the leading counsel for the segregationists before the Court. Surely there was something more than a little dubious about the fact that the president had invited to an unannounced—should we say secret?—dinner the new chief justice (his appointee) and the leading counsel for one side in a most controversial case then before the Court.

More than that: Eisenhower "went to considerable lengths" (according to Warren in his memoirs) "to tell me what a great man Davis was," and arranged to have Davis seated near Warren, who, in turn, was seated next to the president. Furthermore, after dinner, Eisenhower took Warren by the arm as they moved to another room to be served coffee and said to him, referring to southerners like Davis, "These are not bad people. All they are concerned about is to see that their sweet little girls are not required to sit in school along-side big black bucks." Bernard Schwartz unearthed this unvarnished version of Eisenhower's remark in his research. Earl Warren gave a slightly cleaned-up version—"big overgrown Negroes" instead of "big black bucks"—in his memoirs. Herbert Brownell, who was present, also reconstructed, and perhaps cleaned up still further, the controversial substance (although Brownell was referring to the general conversation at dinner and not a remark Ike made to Warren personally). "As best I can reconstruct the scene at dinner," Brownell wrote, "Ike had expressed his personal sympathy for the mothers of young white children in the South who had been reared in a segregated society and feared the unknown—the arrival of a time when the public schools would be desegregated."

But even of this most softened version of the episode, one still may ask, Why was the president of the United States expressing such sympathy, altogether for one side, in a current case, with the chief justice and a counsel for one side present, by presidential invitation? Can anyone imagine that Ike would have invited Thurgood Marshall, the leading counsel for the other side, to a stag dinner to talk about the case? Didn't the young black children have mothers, too, and their fears, not only about the unknown but about the *known*? *Well-justified* fears about the known? It surely did seem that Ike's sympathies, throughout the years of turbulence, strife, and decision that would follow the *Brown* decision, were invariably for those white mothers, and never for the black ones.

One constant and striking theme in Eisenhower's comments on racial matters was ignorance—not only plain, everyday ignorance but that further conspicuously distant ignorance that implies that the subject is of less importance than the questioner seems to believe. He would often say at press conferences, not only those on race but on other issues as well, that he had not heard of the matter a reporter asked about (saying he hadn't been told about that, or that nobody had brought that to him). Of course, reporters do sometimes ask specialized or parochial questions a president should not be expected to answer, and other presidents have pleaded justifiable ignorance in such situations. But Ike on race was a special case. June 16, 1956: "The Attorney General hasn't given me any opinion on those bills [banning segregation in interstate travel]; I haven't seen them; I know nothing about them. . . . I don't know what my opinion is, really, at this minute on that particular law." December 8, 1954: "I never heard of this particular point" [about following a mandate from him to abolish discrimination in public places in the District]. "Whatever it is, I think the courts should decide whether there is any injustice done here or not. I never heard of this point." January 14, 1955: "You will have to go and ask the Secretary of Defense or the Secretary of the Navy, one of the two [about U.S. Navy crews segregated by race in foreign ports]." Sometimes his answers displayed the peculiar Eisenhower syntax. August 4, 1954: "You have asked me a question that if I would say what was going to be done [about housing discrimination], I would have to say I haven't any plan here I can expose to you."

December 16, 1953
Q: ALICE A. DUNNIGAN, ASSOCIATED NEGRO PRESS: Mr. President, I was wondering whether you could tell us whether the legislative conference will this week discuss any civil rights legislation?
THE PRESIDENT: Civil rights legislation?
Q: MISS DUNNIGAN: In the legislative conferences.
THE PRESIDENT: As I remarked, I am not going to talk about the details of this program. But civil rights legislation, identified as such, I doubt will come up.
There will be many things, I hope, that will be affecting the people of the United States as a whole, but I am sure that there is nothing that could be identified just as civil rights legislation.

It was hard to continue the pattern of avoidance and denial after the *Brown* decision and its ensuing uproar. But in his way, President Eisenhower did, still, deny and avoid it as far as he could, and, at least, keep *himself* at a lofty distance from it.

He was, of course, asked his response at the next press conference, on May 19, after the school segregation decision was handed down on May 17, 1954:

Q: HARRY C. DENT, COLUMBIA (S.C.) *STATE AND RECORD:* Mr. President, do you have any advice to give the South as to just how to react to this recent Supreme Court decision banning segregation, sir?

THE PRESIDENT: Not in the slightest. . . .

The Supreme Court has spoken and I am sworn to uphold the constitutional processes in this country; and I will obey.

Not "the slightest" advice? The President of the United States with his bully pulpit? Just "I will obey"?

He would be asked again and again to endorse the Court's decision; again and again he would avoid doing so.

August 8, 1956

Q: CHALMERS M. ROBERTS, *WASHINGTON POST AND TIMES HERALD:* Mr. President, do you believe, sir, that the Republican Party plank on civil rights should contain a specific endorsement of the Supreme Court decision voiding segregation in the public schools?

THE PRESIDENT: I don't know, Mr. Roberts, how the Republican plank on this particular point is going to be stated, and I haven't given any thought of my own as to whether it should just state it in that way.

September 5, 1956

Q: ARTHUR SYLVESTER, *NEWARK (N.J.) NEWS:* . . . Do you endorse the finding of the Supreme Court on segregation or merely accept it as the Republican platform does?

THE PRESIDENT: I think it makes no difference whether or not I endorse it. The Constitution is as the Supreme Court interprets it; and I must conform to that and do my very best to see that it is carried out in this country.

October 11, 1956

Q: CHARLES W. ROBERTS, *NEWSWEEK:* On September 5 you stated that it was not important whether you endorsed the Supreme Court's decision on integration so long as it was enforced. Since then a number of people, mostly Democrats, have said that it is important whether you endorse the decision. Could you amplify your position on that?

THE PRESIDENT: Look, I put that in this way: We start out with article I of the Constitution, and we go on right down to the end, including its amendments, and the Constitution as it is interpreted by the Supreme Court, I am sworn to uphold it.

I don't ask myself whether every single phrase of that Constitution, with all its amendments, are exactly what I agree with or not.

So he would not endorse the Court's historic decision. Would he, nevertheless, use the prestige of his office and his heroic reputation to give counsel or guidance to those caught in the struggle? No, he wouldn't do that, either.

September 5, 1956

Q: ROBERT E. CLARK, INTERNATIONAL NEWS SERVICE: Mr. President, there have been several instances of violence and near violence on the segregation issue as the fall school term begins. In some cases Negro children are risking physical injury to attend school. Do you think there is anything that can be said or done on the national level to help local communities meet this problem without violence?

THE PRESIDENT: Well, in each case I think the local governments have moved promptly to stop the violence. And let us remember this: under the law the Federal Government cannot, on the ordinary normal case of keeping order and preventing rioting, cannot move into a State until the State is not able to handle the matter.

. . .

Q: JOHN L. STEELE, *TIME* MAGAZINE: Mr. President, referring back to Mr. Clark's question of a moment ago, regardless of politics, you seem to have a tremendous reservoir of good will on the part of young people all over the country. With the schools opening up this week and next in places of serious tension, I wonder if there is anything you would like to say through us to the younger people who are going to school regarding this problem?

THE PRESIDENT: Well, I can say what I have said so often: it is difficult through law and through force to change a man's heart.

As the segregationist opposition spread wider and grew more intense, the nation's chief executive, sworn to take care that the laws be faithfully executed, was asked about it.

February 29, 1956

Q: WILLIAM V. SHANNON, *NEW YORK POST:* As you may know, four of the southern State legislatures have passed interposition resolutions stating that the Supreme Court decision outlawing segregation has no force and effect in their States; and I was wondering what you thought about this concept of interposition, and what you thought was the role of the Federal Government in enforcing the Supreme Court decision?

THE PRESIDENT: Well, of course, you have asked a very vast question that is filled with argument on both sides. You have raised the question of States rights versus Federal power; [the president is suggesting that the states' rights opposition is one legitimate position?] . . . you have particularly brought up the question whether the Supreme Court is the last word we have in the interpretation of our Constitution. [Is that a question? Is the president of the United States suggesting this can be debated?]

Now, this is what I say: there are adequate legal means of determining all of these factors.

[The president was asked where he stood.] The Supreme Court has issued its own operational directives ["Its own"? Not the law for the executive branch?] and delegated power to the district courts.

I expect that we are going to make progress, and the Supreme Court itself said it does not expect revolutionary action suddenly executed.

Suppose you were Earl Warren or any other member of the Court, all of whom had been so careful to present an unbroken, unanimous position to a reluctant white public, and then you heard the most visible and prestigious officer of the government—by far—give this kind of answer, treating a decision of the Supreme Court as though it were a proposal from one side, which one might argue with from another.

As the 1956 election approached, other Republicans would see the political possibilities in a historic Supreme Court decision made during years of a Republican administration by a Court headed by a Republican chief justice appointed by a Republican president, and would endeavor to exploit those possibilities—for example, in the party platform. But the platform writers received a protest from the White House: Ike was careful to insist that the Court decision was *not* to be associated with the administration, with the executive branch; it was the decision of a separate and independent branch of government. In his first press conference response after the *Brown* decision, he rejected the implication that southern segregationists who supported him in 1952 had cause for disappointment because this decision "was brought out under a Republican administration." "The Supreme Court, as I understand it," he said curtly, "is not under any administration."

The events in the lower schools were not the only developments in those years. Eisenhower had insisted that institutions of higher learning would be the proper place to start—very slowly—integration, and in 1956 Autherine Lucy, braving a racist mob, enrolled in the University of Alabama. Her right to do so was confirmed by a federal court. The president of the United States was asked about the result at a press conference on February 8:

Q: ALICE A. DUNNIGAN, ASSOCIATED NEGRO PRESS: Mr. President, do you feel, sir, that the recent outbreak at the University of Alabama is a violation of Federal law and order? If so, do you plan to recommend that the Justice Department investigate the situation?
THE PRESIDENT: Well, the Justice Department is already looking into it. I don't have to plan to order them. . . .

While there has been an outbreak that all of us deplore, when there is a defiance of law, still the chancellor and the trustees, the local authorities, the student body and all the rest of them have not yet had an opportunity, I should think, to settle this thing as it ought to be settled. I would certainly hope that we could avoid any interference with anybody else as long as that State, from its governor on down, will do its best to straighten it out.

When the state and its governor (George Wallace) did "straighten it out" by expelling Miss Lucy, there was no word from the White House.

But then, in 1957, events in Arkansas escalated to the point that he did indeed have to send federal troops to enforce a Court order that nine black students should be admitted to Little Rock's Central High School. His obey-the-law theme might have been a contribution had it been accompanied by surrounding moral affirmations, but it never was, and so it came to convey the message that one should obey *only* because one must, because it was the law—even if it be against one's own conviction. (From his radio and TV address on the situation in Little Rock: "Our personal opinions about the decision have no bearing on the matter of enforcement.")

And he constantly accompanied that theme with the two leading platitudes of white avoidance and undercover resistance on race: that "you can't change hearts by law" and that racial change could come about only by "a long slow process of education."

The civil rights community had long since worked out its answers to the cliché about not changing hearts by law: Law—the formal change of social structures—can be one of the best ways to "change hearts." Dwight Eisenhower had himself had his heart misdirected, exactly by a social structure, imposed by law—the U.S. Army's rigid segregation by race throughout his whole career. And in the next generation, because of Harry Truman's order and the Eisenhower administration's follow-up, and the changes effected by the needs of war in Korea, thousands of men would be educated, have their hearts changed, in the opposite way—by the experience of racial integration in the armed services, instituted by law.

President Eisenhower continually emphasized—to read through his press conferences and speeches is to be struck by how constantly he emphasized—the "emotionalism," the strong feelings, on this matter. He meant, of course, the feelings of white resisters to racial integration; that there were strong feelings on the other side, he knew only abstractly, and did not emphasize. His acquaintance with the black community was zero.

So with feelings and hearts on both sides, should not law, the Court, justice decide? And the law be enforced? The president was asked about this.

September 11, 1956

Q: LOUIS R. LAUTIER, NATIONAL NEGRO PRESS: Mr. President . . . If, as you say, changing of traditions and the hearts of men will unfortunately take a long time, is not the solution of the present disorders in many parts of the South over segregation this, namely, that citizens must be restrained from expressing their prejudices in public actions when such public acts are in violation of the law?

THE PRESIDENT: Well, I say again, the local court must determine whether there is someone in contempt of that court. And I know of no way from this distance that those things can be determined. But when the courts do call properly upon the Attorney General, I am sure he will assist in every possible way.

The president's continual equating of the "two sides," each with its "extremists," was particularly exasperating; on one such occasion, in the midst of the Little Rock crisis, Thurgood Marshall asked whether Ike meant to equate lawless mobs with the federal courts as "extremist."

There is truth, of course, in the point that law alone cannot function against total community opposition, and that education and attitudes must support law. But those who made this point in racial matters often did none of the educating and persuading they insisted on in place of law. President Eisenhower did appeal, privately, to Billy Graham to do his bit, but his own remarks tended to undercut what Graham may have attempted. The president recommended education but did no educating. He declined, on this issue, to use the bulliest of bully pulpits.

Both what he did and did not say was startling and very displeasing to Earl Warren and to others on the Court—to all of them, as far as is known. David Nichols, defending Eisenhower on race, tends to deprecate not only Truman but also Earl Warren. He sees Warren as an ambitious politician who would like to have run for president in Eisenhower's place, and implies that that ambition colored his attitude toward Ike on race. But it certainly was not Warren alone who objected to the presidential silence. Justice Minton wrote that "the fact that the Court has not received support from sources it had a right to expect support [from] has given the South a propaganda victory." Justice Tom Clark said in retirement, "If Mr. Eisenhower had come through it would have changed things a lot." Justice William Douglas wrote in his autobiography that "Ike's ominous silence on our 1954 decision gave courage to racists who decided to resist the decision ward by ward, precinct by precinct, town by town, and county by county." As President Eisenhower, by appointing Earl Warren, helped to produce a result he did not intend, so he received a credit he did not deserve. Indeed, he received credit he had sought actively to avoid.

Nevertheless, on Election Day of 1956, Eisenhower himself did reap a considerable benefit, however undeserved and unwanted. So one may infer, at any rate, from the election returns. For the first time since the switch to Roosevelt and the New Deal, and the last time down to the present writing, the Republican nominee received a majority—60 percent—of African-American votes. To be sure, there were reasons, other than racial ones and other than the *Brown* decision, that might help to explain that historic (momentary) shift. Ike was broadly popular in a time, as the Republicans said, of peace and prosperity, and the themes that affected other Americans of course affected blacks, too. And Adlai Stevenson, on the other side, made the least appeal on issues of racial equality, and the least appeal on other issues and personally, to the broad mass of African-American voters, of any Democratic candidate for the presidency since the Rooseveltian string began.

And then there was the great lift of the *Brown* decision. As is continually observed, presidents get credit (and blame) for much that happens in the years they are in office, whether they deserve it or not. But usually they deserve it a little more than Dwight Eisenhower deserved the black vote in 1956.

Eisenhower's failure, when *Brown* was first handed down, to lead the civil rights crusade that was handed to him on a platter by the Court had ramifications on into the future. Again, the speechless presidency left a vacuum in public discourse. Clearly, Ike thought his duty, as chief executive, was to insist on obeying the law, whatever you think of it. But there is more to the American presidency than can be learned just by reading the words of the Constitution.

There would be another, different chapter in the story of Ike and race. Attorney General Herbert Brownell persuaded the president to include in his 1956 election-year State of the Union message proposals that had been made in 1947 by Truman's Committee on Civil Rights: an independent Civil Rights Commission; a civil rights division in the Department of Justice; broader authority to enforce voters' rights. Reelected in 1956, Ike would in his second term successfully bring forward, and see through to congressional enactment, civil rights legislation built from these proposals—the first successful enactments since Reconstruction. For all those years, civil rights legislation had banged up against the power of the southern senators and the filibuster in the Senate. The bill Ike proposed would be considerably weakened in its passage, under the management of Lyndon Johnson, the majority leader in a Democratic Senate. Johnson, who was not unaware that candidates would be nominated for president in a short time, tried to arrange the passage of the act so that he would receive simultaneous credit from liberals for passing it and segregationists for weakening it. In 1960, the Eisenhower administration proposed, and again Johnson saw through to passage, a further Civil Rights Act, providing more protection for black citizens voting; again Johnson was the key to passage, against the threat of a filibuster, and got most of the credit. Eisenhower partisans believe Ike should receive credit as well for these civil rights initiatives.

But the big event in Eisenhower's second term, on civil rights to be sure but also in domestic affairs generally, was his sending the 101st Airborne Division to Little Rock to resist a mob and protect nine black students attending—or trying to attend—Central High School.

There was a long history to this controversy, which was an epitome of battles going on across the South: The Court orders school integration; officials and a segment of the public use every method to resist. The governor of the state, Orval Faubus, was the chief opponent of the integration ordered by the Court. Faubus, citing the threat of violence, had called the National Guard but given them orders not to protect the nine black students but, rather, to *prevent* them from attending. Faubus and the president had a long and complicated interaction, which included the governor's making a visit to the president during the latter's vacation in Newport, Rhode Island; Ike and his aides had thought the governor had agreed to change the orders for the National Guard, but he had not. The mob of some fifteen hundred that swarmed the school thereafter was called out and guided by an associate of the governor. The president, after much deliberation, found it necessary to call out military force; it was suggested that he federalize the Arkansas Guard, but he worried that that might set "brother against brother." He called upon his famous unit, to which he had a historic relationship: the 101st Airborne. This unit, with which he had had a memorable time on the evening of D-Day in England, was now given this different task. The president made clear throughout that the operative point of the action was not racial integration, but, rather, the integrity of the Constitution and the law: They must be obeyed, whatever one's opinion on some underlying issue.

David Nichols, an Eisenhower defender, says that this president had come to have different views on race in 1959–1960 from what he had held in 1953–1954.

As an ex-president, Ike had a mild disagreement with his party leaders on civil rights, as he moved somewhat to the left and party leaders moved markedly to the right, particularly after the passage of the strong 1964 Civil Rights Act and the nomination of Barry Goldwater, who had voted against it, as presidential candidate. The ex-president did exert some pull on the party and its leaders—getting Goldwater to come to Gettysburg and issue a joint statement—but he had never been a party leader or a factional leader, so there was no body of Eisenhower Republicans to contend with the new wave of Republicans conservative on race. On this topic, his party moved a long way from the point at which he had arrived after his instructive adventures in the White House.

Harry Truman's views on race were at their most enlightened while he was president, when they were reinforced by the liberal ideology of many in his administration; two episodes suggest that Truman's views deteriorated when he was on his own, after he left office. Dwight Eisenhower, on the other hand, having started from a less enlightened beginning, appears to have gained knowledge on this topic while in office.

One incident involving ex-president Truman was reported on an inside page of *The New York Times* on September 12, 1963; this little story bore the headline TRUMAN OPPOSES BIRACIAL MARRIAGE. Truman had made a comment in an exchange with a reporter on his usual early-morning walk, while he was visiting his daughter and son-in-law in New York City. He was asked whether he thought racial intermarriage would become widespread in the United States. "I hope not," Truman is reported as replying. "I don't believe in it. What's that word about four feet long? Miscegenation?" (*Miscegenation* is not an ancient European word, but a coinage that was given wide currency by Mr. Truman's own party in its disgraceful racist campaign against Abraham Lincoln in 1864.) Truman turned to the reporter—according to the *Times* story—and asked, "Would you want your daughter to marry a Negro?"

What is disappointing about this is not only that it reveals an essential racial prejudice but also that it is such a whopping cliché. It is a totally shopworn question out of the long and ugly history of race in America, utterly predictable in certain contexts repeated and repeated a million times, being uttered now by the distinguished ex-president on his morning walk.

When the reporter responded that he would want his daughter to marry the man she loved, Mr. Truman said, "Well, she won't love someone who isn't her color. You'll edit the man she goes out with. I did, and mine married the right man."

The *Times* then helpfully added that Mr. Truman's daughter, Margaret, was married to Clifton Daniel, assistant managing editor of *The New York Times,* who was not an African-American.

That is one distressing event from Truman's postpresidential years. Another came in 1960 when four students from North Carolina A&T State University sat at the lunch counter in Woolworth's, waiting to be served. This was the beginning, the new movement of direct social action for racial justice—the sit-ins, Freedom Rides, and marches that confronted racial discrimination with nonviolent direct action. Truman disapproved, and said so in public. He referred to "mob rule" (four young black men sitting at a counter hoping to be served looked like a "mob"?). He said if they did that in a store he owned he would throw them out—and he even seemed to accept J. Edgar Hoover's claim that these efforts were Communist-inspired. Dean Acheson wrote a remarkable letter to his old chief, suggesting gently, firmly, and clearly in numbered points that the two of them make a "treaty" about what they would say and not say in the current campaign (this was in 1960, when one issue was whether the Democrats would nominate young John Kennedy, and whether they could beat Nixon). Acheson included several points beyond the civil rights issues—that they would never say any of the Democratic contenders was not qualified to be president, or couldn't win, and that for the duration of the campaign they wouldn't say that in foreign policy they must support the president (because in Acheson's view, the president, then Eisenhower, did not have a "policy"). But the core of the letter dealt with the sit-ins: They would not say they disapproved and would not say the sit-ins were Communist-inspired, nor make any reference to J. Edgar Hoover, who, Acheson believed, should never be trusted. Acheson was telling Truman not to do what he had already done. At least Truman stopped. His response to this extraordinary letter of implicit admonishment from a former subordinate was altogether positive: "You'll never know how much I appreciate your call and your good letter. . . . I tried to do my best to profit by both. . . . Thanks for being a real friend." But of course his original statements, to which Acheson was objecting, were out there in the public record. The world still knew that Truman disapproved of the sit-ins.

Surprisingly, Eisenhower apparently did not. Asked at a press conference on March 16, 1960, whether he approved of the "Gandhi-like demonstrations," he gave, amidst a certain amount of hemming and hawing, an objective and positive approval. Whereas Truman, looking at the sit-ins, identified with the shop owner whose counter was filled with young activists, and then looked only at the tactic and intemperately condemned it, Eisenhower looked at the group's purpose and, so long as its method was nonviolent, approved it. "I am deeply sympathetic with the efforts of any group to enjoy the rights of equality that are guaranteed by the Constitution," he said. Assuming nonviolence, "if a person is expressing such an aspiration as this in a perfectly legal way, then I don't see any reason why he should not do it."

In clarifying his position, he stated, "I was talking about demonstrations, of marching in the streets, or any other kind of peaceful assembly that is trying to show what the aspirations and the desires of a people are. Those, to my mind, as long as they are in orderly fashion, are not only constitutional, they have been recognized in our country as proper since we have been founded."

Eisenhower specifically endorsed the position of the activists, that if you are open to the public, you have to be open to the *entire* public—a view Harry Truman, and many of Ike's southern friends, definitely did not hold. President Eisenhower said at a press conference, "My own understanding is that when an establishment belongs to the public, opened under public charter and so on, equal rights are involved."

In their retirement, Ike and Harry might thus have disagreed in terms that reversed their earlier positions.

CHAPTER FOURTEEN

Bombs

HARRY TRUMAN, the first human being to hold in his hands the catastrophic power of thermonuclear weapons, was also the first to discover the paradox that they were so destructive that they couldn't be used. More than that: He discovered they were such potent instruments, supposedly of warfare, that those who possessed them couldn't fight wars anymore—not "total" wars, major wars.

Dwight Eisenhower, the second American (the third human being, after Joseph Stalin) to hold that power, apparently came to those realizations also, but his position on nuclear weapons would be extremely complex. He would give voice to contradictions that would puzzle not only historians later but also observers, and even his own colleagues, at the time. Maybe he did the world another great service.

Both of these men made a variety of contrasting statements, changing over time and in varying venues, about those weapons. The views of both evolved, and they said different things in different contexts. One has to imagine how it was for them: encountering this terrible new power not just as an interested citizen or one among many governmental officials, but as the one human being at the center of the whole thing, holding the decision in his own hands.

Both presidents would at some stage give voice to the ridiculous position that these weapons were no different from other weapons—just like bows and arrows, swords and sabers, and muskets and rifles, and like the 75mm artillery that Capt. Harry Truman fired in World War I. In 1955, Harry Truman would write in his memoirs about the attitude he had back in 1945, that "I regarded the bomb as a military weapon, and never had any doubt that it should be used." Ike would say, as late as 1955, that in any contest in which they could be used on strictly military targets, "I can see no reason why they should not be used just exactly as you would bullets or anything else." He did not quite comprehend yet, apparently, that it was intrinsically impossible to confine the bomb to "military targets." Truman had said in conversation with Henry Stimson—the venerable secretary of war, a key figure in the early ruminations, before the bombs were actually dropped—that they should be used just on military targets. But in the event, they were used on two cities that, whatever military installations they might have had, had in them thousands of men, women, and children who had nothing to do with the military; given its massive destructiveness, the bomb could not avoid killing people. Apparently, after he received the report on Hiroshima, that did register with Truman.

Nevertheless, when he was questioned or criticized for having ordered the dropping of the bombs, Truman responded with defensive bravado. When J. Robert Oppenheimer met with him and said he felt he had blood on his hands (or, in another version, that the atomic scientists in general felt that they had blood on their hands), Truman responded with dismissive disdain; reports on this famous meeting have him responding that he had far more blood on his hands, and one report, which is hard to believe, even has him offering Oppenheimer a handkerchief to wipe his hands. Most reports have him saying something quite disdainful about Oppenheimer afterward, the most pungent being that he did not want to see that son of a bitch again.

But for all the instant defensiveness about his own past decision, Truman came to treat the bombs with a seriousness that indicated that they were something more than just another weapon. In the early days, he made an effort to bring the weapons under international control; in 1945–1946, he assigned the development of a proposal to a good committee of two—Acheson and David Lilienthal, the excellent TVA administrator—but then, when their proposal was ready, he made the mistake of giving it to Bernard Baruch, appointing Baruch to the United Nations Atomic Energy Commission to present it. Baruch revised it and attached his own name to the result, and the Soviet Union rejected it and it went nowhere. (Baruch, a financier turned presidential adviser, made contributions to Democratic politicians and somehow acquired a bigger reputation, in the view of many, than he had done anything to deserve.) Public attitudes probably made any international control impossible, even if the Soviets had been open to some arrangement, which they surely were not and could not be, because international control would have required openness to international inspection, something that Stalin's Soviet Union could not allow.

The Soviets, helped by spies, detonated their atomic bomb much sooner than the world expected—on August 29, 1949. Stalin did not announce it, but when American sampling flights detected fallout, Truman announced that it had happened, and the Kremlin confirmed it. So the United States had had a nuclear monopoly for almost exactly four years—August 1945 to August 1949—and that was now ended.

Having the world's only nuclear weapon had not had any overt benefit to American foreign policy. Stalin and Molotov, however nervous they may have been in private, made a point in public of dismissing the Americans' bomb with jokes and deprecatory comments. When in the middle of those four years, in 1948, the Soviets cut off Berlin, blocking all access by land, and the Truman administration discussed what to do about the Berlin blockade, Secretary of the Army Kenneth Royall urged a nuclear strike against the Soviets. Truman flatly rejected that proposal, and with it the notion that the bomb could actually be used: "You have got to understand that this isn't a military weapon. It is used to wipe out women and children and unarmed people, and not for military uses. You have got to understand that I have got to think about the effect of such a thing on international relations. This is no time to be juggling an atom bomb around."

Truman did not juggle an atomic bomb in that tense situation, but he did approve a subtler hint that the bomb might have a bearing on the matter: Some B-29s, the only plane that could deliver the bomb, were sent to bases in Great Britain, closer to Berlin and Moscow than American bases. But those who knew could see just by looking at them that these planes had not been modified in the way they needed to be to deliver the bomb, so the hint was very mild indeed.

Then, after the Soviets acquired their first atomic device, the North Koreans attacked South Korea in June 1950, and by Truman's decision the United States was involved in what most people regarded as a war, even though Truman once described it as a United Nations "police action." Despite the Soviet acquisition, the United States still had a huge advantage in numbers of bombs. John Lewis Gaddis, in his good short summary *The Cold War,* gave the numbers: "The United States at the end of 1950 had 369 operational atomic bombs, all of them easily deliverable on Korean battlefields or Chinese supply lines from bases in Japan or Okinawa. The Soviet Union had probably no more than five such weapons at the time, and they could hardly have been as reliable as their American counterparts."*

Yet Truman did not use an atomic bomb in the Korean War, even though American forces and their South Korean allies were twice driven down the peninsula—first by the North Koreans and then by the Chinese after their

* Gaddis, p. 58.

intervention—in as thorough defeats as any the American military has ever experienced. Nevertheless, there was no use of the most powerful weapon. As we have seen, Truman made the mistake of saying in answer to a question at a press conference that all weapons were being considered, and (perhaps worse) that commanders in the field could de-cide whether to use them (taken to mean that MacArthur could decide), thereby causing instant heartburn in Europe and a quick scuttling across the Atlantic by the British prime minister to forestall any such idiocy. Truman sharply corrected his mistake and insisted on presidential control—æthat is, civilian control—of these particular weapons. The use of these weapons was not left to the military to decide, which was not the case with all other weapons. About the use of these weapons, only the president would decide.

One can say that it was a constraint that the armed forces in the Korean War were fighting under the United Nations mandate, by Truman's initiative, so that opinions of other countries counted more heavily than they might have done. But, given the larger record, one may doubt that Truman would have used atomic weapons in Korea even if that constraint by other nations had not been a factor.

As a result not only of the Korean action but of the Soviet bomb test that had tipped the balances nine months earlier—in August 1949—Truman ordered, as we have seen, a buildup of what were now called "conventional" forces, the nonnuclear armed force that had been much reduced after World War II by demobilization and by budgetary restrictions. A fundamental planning document that he ordered—NSC-68—called for drastic rearmament. He also ordered the increased production of atomic weapons, so the United States was piling up these things even as it learned that they could not be used. And he made the big decision to build the much more powerful thermonuclear bomb, which would also never be used.

Scientists came to Truman after the report of the successful Soviet test with a new possibility: whether to build the still more destructive weapon, the thermonuclear bomb, or the H-bomb. His deciding to do it or not really was, this time, a considered determination. His decision to drop the two atomic bombs, a determination that he made in Potsdam in the summer of 1945, had been almost automatic, an outcome of his situation, as the inexperienced leader of a nation at war with the imperative to end it, and with the total expectation of those around him and those in the apparatus that built the bomb that he would of course use it. It would have been very hard, as has been noted, to have decided then to disallow using the bomb. But now with the new bomb, the situation was different. He was the president and it was he who could decide which way to go. There was deliberation, in which the argument against making the bomb was well represented. There were those in the circle around Truman who urged him not to develop the H-bomb—notably, the distinguished New Dealer David Lilienthal; the key analyst George Kennan; and the leading scientist J. Robert Oppenheimer. Oppenheimer was, for his pains, attacked by pro-bomb scientists and found to be a security risk. Truman made his decision on the dubious grounds that all these bomb-building decisions were made: If the Russians could build one, the United States had to build one also. (Critics would say that if the United States had enough bombs to create a catastrophe in the Soviet Union—as indeed it did—then it had enough bombs, without building any new ones.) But Truman decided to make the big bomb, and the Americans exploded the world's first hydrogen bomb at Eniwetok, an atoll in the South Pacific, on November 1, 1952, just two and a half months before the end of Truman's presidency. This explosion, set off from a control ship thirty miles away, was in an altogether different realm from the atomic bomb; even those who had witnessed atomic blasts were stunned by this explosion. The fireball reached 57,000 feet; the cloud, when it had reached its farthest extent, was about one hundred miles wide. The eruption wiped the island of Elugelab off the face of the planet, leaving only a crater behind, and it destroyed life on the surrounding islands. Human beings who saw it were particularly struck by what happened to birds for miles around: They were incinerated, singed, sick, grounded, struggling to fly. The blast yielded 10.4 megatons of explosive energy, 750 times greater than the explosion that leveled Hiroshima. Truman absorbed the profounder implication of this most destructive instrument so that he could take its sober measure in his final message.

In the discussion of foreign policy in chapter 8, mention was made of Truman's last State of the Union message, sent to Congress on January 7, 1953. The passage quoted there concerned the lasting effect of the unity of European nations that had been achieved and the long-term effect of containment. In that valedictory address, President Truman also dealt, of course, with the overwhelming issue of nuclear weapons.

> [W]e have entered the atomic age, and war has undergone a technological change which makes it a very different thing from what it used to be. War today between the Soviet empire and the free nations might dig the grave not only of our Stalinist opponents, but of our own society, our world as well as theirs.

This transformation has been brought to pass in the seven years from Alamogordo to Eniwetok. It is only seven years, but the new force of atomic energy has turned the world into a very different kind of place.

. . . From now on, man moves into a new era of destructive power, capable of creating explosions of a new order of magnitude, dwarfing the mushroom clouds of Hiroshima and Nagasaki.

. . . And we must realize that no advance we make is unattainable by others, that no advantage in this race can be more than temporary.

The war of the future would be one in which man could extinguish millions of lives at one blow, demolish the great cities of the world, wipe out the cultural achievements of the past—and destroy the very structure of a civilization that has been slowly and painfully built up through hundreds of generations.

Such a war is not a possible policy for rational men.

President Truman then addressed himself directly to Joseph Stalin:

You claim belief in Lenin's prophecy that one stage in the development of communist society would be war between your world and ours. But Lenin was a pre-atomic man, who viewed society and history with pre-atomic eyes. Something profound has happened since he wrote. War has changed its shape and its dimension. It cannot now be a "stage" in the development of anything save ruin for your regime and your homeland.

A week after his sending this last State of the Union to Congress, just before his final departure and the inauguration of the new president, President Truman did deliver in person, on the new medium of television from the White House, a much shorter message. This was a graceful statement of farewell, which included a shorter version of some of the themes in the State of the Union message. Once again, he spoke about weapons:

Now we have entered the atomic age, and war has undergone a technological change which makes it a very different thing from what it used to be. War today between the Soviet Empire and the free nations might dig the grave not only of our Stalinist opponents but of our own society, our world as well as theirs.

War's new meaning may not yet be grasped by all the peoples who would be its victims; nor, perhaps by all the rulers of the Kremlin. . . . The war of the future would be one in which man could extinguish millions of lives at one blow, demolish the great cities of the world, wipe out the cultural achievements of the past—and destroy the very structure of a civilization that has been slowly and painfully built up through hundreds of generations.

Such a war is not a possible policy for rational man.

John Lewis Gaddis drew this conclusion about the point at which Harry Truman had arrived:

> [A]fter August 1945 [Harry Truman] had the ability, by issuing a single order, to bring about more death and destruction than any other individual in history had ever been able to accomplish. That stark fact caused this ordinary man to do an extraordinary thing. He reversed a pattern in human behavior so ancient that its origins lay shrouded in the mists of time: that when weapons are developed, they will be used.*

Did the next individual to hold that unique power continue that reversal? Did Dwight Eisenhower also perceive that war with the new weapons was not a possible policy for rational men? No—but on the other hand, maybe yes, after a time, maybe an emphatic *yes*. Campbell Craig's book on Eisenhower and thermonuclear war observes: "A word to describe recent scholarship on Dwight Eisenhower and nuclear weapons might be *puzzled*."†

I. MAN OF PEACE: IKE THE DOVE

THERE IS A CERTAIN POPULAR INCLINATION to see Eisenhower, the genial general, not only as a man of peace in the White House but also as an opponent of the use of nuclear weapons. It is true, as we have seen, that in his first encounter with nuclear weapons, in his exchange with Secretary Stimson at the time of the Potsdam Conference in the summer of 1945, he did express a clear negative response to the proposal to drop the bomb on the already-defeated Japanese, and he gave cogent reasons. (And it is significant that he is the source for that incident, in the book he wrote and published in 1948, well after the bomb had been used and incorporated into the national arsenal. He might have engaged in politically convenient forgetting and just let that Stimson incident drop out of sight—but he didn't. He referred to it again in his memoir of his presidency, *Mandate for Change*.)

It is true that, coming into the presidency with a war in progress, in just six months he would bring that war to a kind of an end—an armistice. He would resist the pressures of the South Korean leader, Syngman Rhee, and of the American commander on the scene, his old friend Mark Clark, to enlarge the Korean War he had inherited by using nuclear weapons. The war in Korea was ended, brought to an armistice so that

---

* Ibid., p. 55.
† Craig, p. 67.

the shooting stopped, very much by Ike's initiative, and then for the rest of his two-term presidency, there was no further war—no Americans killing and being killed anywhere, a rare accomplishment among modern presidents.

It is true that the "Chance for Peace" speech that he gave in April of his first year as president, after the death of Stalin, would include a riff on the waste that advanced military expenditures represent:

> Every gun that is made, every warship launched, every rocket fired signifies, in the final sense, a theft from those who hunger and are not fed, those who are cold and are not clothed. . . .
>
> The cost of one modern heavy bomber is this: a modern brick school in more than 30 cities.
>
> It is two electric power plants, each serving a town of 60,000 population. It is two fine, fully equipped hospitals.
>
> It is some fifty miles of concrete pavement. [Eisenhower, the interstate highway builder, was impressed by miles of concrete.]
>
> We pay for a single fighter plane with a half million bushels of wheat.
>
> We pay for a single destroyer with new homes that could have housed more than 8,000 people. . . .
>
> This is not a way of life at all, in any true sense. Under the cloud of threatening war, it is humanity hanging from a cross of iron.

It is further true, as we saw in chapter 8, that the following December he would give an address to the UN that would submit a specific "atoms for peace" program, proposing that the nuclear powers donate and share the materials for peaceful nuclear development. And that speech would include striking statements deploring the level of destruction that the stockpile of nuclear weapons could now achieve:

> Today, the United States stockpile of atomic weapons, which, of course, increases daily, exceeds by many times the explosive equivalent of the total of all bombs and all shells that came from every plane and every gun in every theatre of war in all the years of World War II.
>
> A single air group, whether afloat or land-based, can now deliver to any reachable target a destructive cargo exceeding in power all the bombs that fell on Britain in all of World War II.

It is true that the administration would make its way through a gauntlet of crises in Indochina, twice with the Chinese islands of Quemoy and Matsu, in Hungary, at the Suez Canal, and again in Berlin without armed conflict or the use of the terrible weapon in its command.

And it is true that Eisenhower often expressed the horror of an all-out thermonuclear war—expressed it even redundantly. He condemned the use of that "awful thing," when he first heard of the bomb, and said not to shock world opinion that way; he was particularly sensitive to the use of the bomb on Asian peoples. In his last message, he contributed to the language an idea and a phrase of warning—about the "military-industrial complex"—that has had lasting effect.

So that is one story: Ike as a dovish opponent of nuclear weapons.

Why does the story not stop there? Because there are radically contrasting stories interwoven with it.

II. Massive Retaliation and a Bigger Bang for a Buck

FOR ALL HIS PEACEFUL INCLINATIONS and deploring of the destructiveness of nuclear weapons, President Eisenhower's administration increased reliance upon the threatened use of those weapons. The reasons that it did so were, first, that it was animated by the desire to spend less, to balance the budget, which purpose could be served by putting nuclear weapons at the center of military policy and making cuts in all the expensive conventional military forces—army, navy, unstrategic air force units; second, that it was like all change-of-party administrations, eager to distinguish itself from the administration it was succeeding; third, that the incoming Republicans had been out of executive power through all the world's changes since March 1933, and had accumulated the nation's most insistent strands of belligerent hard-line nationalism. The Eisenhower administration, as we have seen in chapter 8, proposed a New Look policy, which featured diminished support for the navy and the army—for "conventional" arms—with increased emphasis on the Strategic Air Command, which would deliver the bombs. It featured increased reliance on allies— a point sometimes overlooked—and it featured in particular a central threat to use nuclear weapons: massive retaliation. "The way to deter aggression," wrote Secretary of State Dulles, "is for the free community to be willing and able to respond vigorously at places and with means of its own choosing." That was taken to mean, of course, that this American administration might respond to any threat with nuclear weapons. The incoming Eisenhower administration moved nuclear weapons to the center of its military posture and built its policy around them. If the Eisenhower administration helped to maintain a peaceful world for eight years, it did so while constantly perched in the most precarious position on the brink—to use its own metaphor—of horrendous warfare.

The source of the concept of brinkmanship was the man Eisenhower picked—almost had to pick, given his eminence as a Republican foreign policy expert—as his secretary of state, John Foster Dulles. In an article written for *Life* magazine, Dulles defined his policy of brinkmanship: "The ability to get to the verge without getting into the war is the necessary art." Dulles called for "a policy of boldness." He explicitly rejected the understandings that Harry Truman had come to, that nuclear weapons were to be radically distinguished from other weapons and that nuclear war was not a possible policy for rational human beings. To the contrary: As they came into power, the new president and his secretary of state attacked the "false distinction" between nuclear and other weapons; Dulles even went so far as to charge that the making of that distinction was a Soviet ploy. Eisenhower himself said that "somehow or other the tabu [*sic*] that surrounds the use of nuclear weapons would have to be destroyed." Although on the surface the Korean War was ended—brought to an armistice—without using or explicitly threatening to use nuclear weapons, both Dulles and Eisenhower came to believe that the implicit threat of these weapons helped to bring and keep the armistice in Korea.

III. THE BIGGEST BOMBS

BUT TIME AND CHANGE, some psalmist surely tells us, come to us all. The Eisenhower years saw huge new events in the world of weaponry. The first American thermonuclear explosion came, as has been noted, in November 1952, just at the end of the Truman administration, not much more than two months before Ike became president. The world was just beginning to assimilate that event when Ike took over. And, as we have seen, in March the Soviets would have new leaders when Stalin died. These new men in the Kremlin would then have their first thermonuclear explosion, in a remote area of Kazakhstan, on August 12, 1953. And the effect on those who saw it would be the same as that of the American explosion nine months earlier: awe and wonder. Those Russians who actually saw the tests found themselves staggered, overwhelmed, awestruck, just as the Americans at Eniwetok had been. Ideologies differ, but the impact of raw physics is universal. The effect of the earlier atomic bombs had not necessarily been so great on those who saw the explosions, but it was on those who actually witnessed the explosions of the vastly more powerful H-bomb. These explosions were so profound as to have a psychological effect; the Soviet scientist Andrei Sakharov said "something within you changes." Another key Soviet scientist, after seeing the actual effect of a thermonuclear explosion he had worked to produce, vowed to work on it no more.

The American test code-named Bravo, on Bikini, an atoll in the Pacific, on March 1, 1954, carried the impact to another level; it was the largest blast with which human beings had ever assaulted their earthly habitat to that point, and showed the damage the tests themselves would do. Bravo had been planned to yield five megatons but yielded fifteen. It led to the first human illness and death produced by nuclear weapons since Nagasaki; the radioactive fallout spread hundreds of miles from the huge blast site, and affected some Americans, some Marshall Islanders, and the crew of a Japanese fishing boat, one of whom died. Among those deeply affected by the huge destructive explosion was Georgy Malenkov, for a moment the Soviet leader, himself. The impact was powerful enough to move him to reject, for a time, the received Marxist line that there had to be a war with the capitalist world. Another staggered by the new bomb, reversing previous positions, was the aging Winston Churchill, who noted that it would not take many such explosions to obliterate Great Britain (eight bombs, Harold Macmillan would say repeatedly at a later stage).

The threat to public health resulting from the fallout caused by the tests was a new dimension, and it now wound through the domestic and international politics of the next years. In 1956, the Democratic campaign of Adlai Stevenson, opposing Dwight Eisenhower's second term, tried, without success, to make the dangers of the continuing tests a political issue. A speechwriter would remark that this campaign turned on two words that a few months ago no one had heard: *ileitis* and *strontium 90*. Ileitis was an intestinal inflammation that Ike suffered in June 1956, which, on top of his heart attack the previous November, gave the opponents hope that voters might be persuaded that his health was a reason not to vote for him. Eager volunteers would phone in proposals for an Operation Crocodile Tears, which would, for his own good, force him to retire. Strontium 90 is a radioactive isotope cast up by nuclear fission. In the event, it was evident that Ike's reelection could have withstood any number of unfamiliar words.

Efforts to reach agreements about banning H-bomb tests would continue through the rest of Ike's presidency; a Limited Test Ban Treaty would finally be achieved in the next administration.

IV. CHANGES OF HEART

IN THE SUMMER OF 1955, in response to reports that the Soviets were producing missiles, President Eisenhower ordered the Pentagon to accelerate the production of missiles that could cross the oceans, ICBMs; he said to give that production the highest priority. Both superpowers now had tested and equipped themselves with thermonuclear weapons, and both now had long-range bombers, capable of reaching any target in the United States or the Soviet Union with thermonuclear weapons, but the advent of long-range missiles gave the world's plight a prospect more ominous still. The bombers would take hours to reach their destinations, but the missiles could make it in minutes. And while bombers have pilots and crews that may be called back and have a human reaction to what they are doing, there is no moral agent on a missile.

A short time after this decision, in September 1955, Ike, while fishing on vacation in Colorado, had a heart attack. What did he think about during the next four months while he was recuperating and staying out of the furnace room of decision making? Did his convalescence provide a fortuitous chance to think in a larger and more detached way about the horrendous world-shaking peril at the center of which he stood? When he returned to an active role at the start of 1956, attending his first National Security Council meeting, he made sweeping statements about war in the thermonuclear age. He said that war in the future would now be completely different from wars fought in the past; he spoke of the need to pause and think about the use of nuclear weapons; and he was particularly insistent that no one would be a winner in a nuclear war.

This last was a note that Dulles, the Joint Chiefs, and most of his other advisers did not want to hear from the president. If they were to play any role in planning the nation's military posture, they needed to believe—they needed the United States to believe—in a winnable war . . . a winnable *nuclear* war. At the next National Security Council meeting, a week later, the president again insisted "nobody can win a thermonuclear war." It does appear that a remarkable configuration then emerged: the president on one side, with essentially all his top advisers, including Secretary Dulles and Gen. Maxwell Taylor, and the remaining Joint Chiefs on the other side. They did not want to give up the notion that there could be a nuclear war that the United States could win. Otherwise, the country was stuck. The Soviets were more powerful in terms of conventional arms than the United States and its allies; only the superior American nuclear capability began to provide a balance, protecting free Europe and the free world. The military chieftains needed to have an operating plan for the contingencies that might arise, needed to count on using nuclear weapons, and needed to believe that when using those weapons, they could win a war. Secretary Dulles, whose attitude had shifted a good deal from the "massive retaliation" first days of the administration, now argued for "diversity of capability" and "flexibility." Maxwell Taylor's phrase "flexible response" came to be the phrase for the military posture the chiefs and the secretaries endorsed, and it carried over into the Kennedy administration.

In the broader foreign policy community, the discussion of high policy in the Eisenhower years often centered around the concept of limited war, a phrase that was the title of a widely read book. The reason is obvious: There were these two superpowers with thermonuclear weapons and, in the latest years, missiles for their delivery, ready to explode into the holocaust; warfare at that level would be an utter catastrophe, and yet conflicts of interest and power among nations did not go away. The United States, as the leading power of the free world, needed to be able to oppose the Communist powers militarily. Therefore—said most of the foreign policy community—create a capacity for warfare short of total war, a capacity for conventional warfare of various sizes and shapes, fought conventionally, while the missiles and the thermonuclear warheads pointed at each other deterred each other.

Henry Kissinger's book *Nuclear Weapons and Foreign Policy* argued for the possibility of limited *nuclear* war. The American policy makers wanted to plan on using nuclear weapons because the Soviets were so far ahead in terms of old-fashioned military power. Army chief of staff Maxwell Taylor and his navy counterpart, Arthur Radford, argued with Ike that the missiles with thermonuclear warheads would deter both sides from a big war and compel smaller wars (and thus, incidentally, keep the army and navy relevant; in the talk about the instant thermonuclear horrors, these military chieftains could see their institutions, and their careers, vanishing). But President Eisenhower did not accept this analysis. He insisted that war with the Soviet Union could not be kept limited; that commanders in a pinch could not leave a powerful weapon unused; and, to repeat, he insisted that in an all-out thermonuclear exchange there could be no winner. Given his quite strong statements of these points—to the dismay of the listening staff—it is then astonishing to see how he applied these to policy. Although he sounded almost like a nuclear abolitionist, his policy proposals were something else. He said plans should concentrate on "the first week of the war" because it would all be over in that time. He is quoted as having said, "We might as well put all our resources into SAC and into hydrogen bombs." But such statements did not become official policy immediately; in the official statements, limited war and limited nuclear war were still options, until May 1957, when Eisenhower's view prevailed (presidents do not simply pull national policy out of their own hip pocket; they have to go through a process).

Basic American military policy now assumed that war with the Soviet Union would escalate, automatically, into general thermonuclear war. An illuminating close study of these matters states, "By getting rid of NSC plans for conventional or limited nuclear warfare in the event of a conflict with the Soviet Union, Eisenhower put the Cold War on a hair trigger. In any confrontation between the two sides the United States would soon face a choice between capitulation and initiating thermonuclear war. Eisenhower regularly assured his colleagues that when the moment came he would be ready to launch the missiles."* This is the aspect of Ike's view on thermonuclear war that is most baffling. He was as appalled as any at the devastation that could be anticipated to result from a war with super-bombs; in fact, he repeatedly described the overwhelming devastation of a thermonuclear exchange, stressing this in the National Security Council meetings, with sophisticated professionals in foreign and military affairs who probably did not need reminders of that point. But Ike's repeated invocation of that terrible prospect did not lead, as it did with his advisers, to proposed limited, "flexible" plans for smaller wars. Instead, it led him in exactly the opposite direction: to oppose all plans for smaller wars, the reason being his conviction that any war between the superpowers would inevitably lead to the ultimate level, total war with thermonuclear weapons and utter destruction. When General Taylor wrote about the "umbrella" of the threat of massive retaliation, under which then smaller wars might proceed, Ike wrote that it would be instead a "lightning rod," drawing an escalation to a thermonuclear exchange. He did not propose stopping the production of atomic and thermonuclear bombs, and of the long-range bombers and then missiles to deliver them that continued to be produced by the military-industrial complex; what he proposed instead, to the dismay of his staff, was the omission of the instruments of a more limited war, of "flexible response," which his advisers campaigned for.

* Ibid.

V. SAYING NO TO THE
MILITARY-INDUSTRIAL COMPLEX

THE RUSSIANS SUCCESSFULLY LAUNCHED the first man-made earth-orbiting satellite, *Sputnik,* in October 1957, and that dramatic event was taken to indicate that the Soviets had missiles that made every part of the United States vulnerable to nuclear attack. A short time later, a presidential commission, the Gaither committee, recommended radically increased military spending by the United States (the Gaither committee report was secret, not known to the public until 1973). But President Eisenhower resisted all the pressures generated to spend more on missiles, on bombs, and on fallout shelters. He insisted that he understood what the nation needed and that it had a "sufficiency"—enough military preparation to serve the purpose. The resistance to his view was fierce not only from outside but from within his own administration, and the alleged neglect of the nation's military needs—the alleged "missile gap"—became a major political issue.

Of course, the military services fiercely contended with one another for increases, and sought enlarged national defense expenditure. But Ike stuck to his—shall we put it this way?—guns; that is, he stuck to his belief that we had a sufficiency of guns. His insistence that we did not need any B-70 bombers, any federally sponsored fallout shelters, any more missiles and satellites was strongly resisted. His resistance was reinforced by the results of flights over the Soviet Union by the CIA's new U-2 planes, which did not show the missile sites Khrushchev bragged about. The navy, with the Polaris missile on nuclear submarines, argued that with its maneuverability it could supplant and take over the lumbering old method of the Strategic Air Command; SAC responded that if Polaris became the strategic weapon, then it should be taken over by SAC, despite the fact that SAC had no navy men. The leaders of the navy said, Over our dead bodies. Ike observed that he had been right back in 1947 when he had thought the services ought to have been united into one service.

VI. IKE'S ALL-OR-NOTHING EVASION OF WAR

WHY DID EISENHOWER take his position opposing preparation for smaller wars and putting all the emphasis on the big bombs? An imaginative answer by historian Campbell Craig, to some extent accepted by the leading Cold War historian John Lewis Gaddis, is that he did so to keep his own advisers from pushing the country—from pushing *him*—into a thermonuclear war. This is rather an astounding conception: that a president made an arrangement to protect himself against the pressure of his own staff. He had to do it that way, the theory goes, because he could not simply announce to the world that he would not wage any such war with the Soviet Union; such an announcement, undercutting deterrence, would have had drastic consequences for the world's psychological power balance. He therefore set it up so that that choice of total war would be so extreme as to be impossible. He bequeathed to his successor, John Kennedy, an operational plan, in the event of an imminent Soviet attack, in which we would have launched an enormous number of nuclear weapons—3,267—simultaneously! They would have been pointed against not just the Soviet Union but also all Marxist-Leninist states—China, Eastern Europe, North Korea, North Vietnam . . . a truly ridiculous overkill. The point of it was, if I understand the interpretation Craig came to, to make the choice so ridiculous, such overkill, as to be indeed impossible.

Craig gave this summary:

> Eisenhower determined in 1956 to make the primary objective of his presidency the avoidance of a thermonuclear war with the Soviet Union. His strategy to evade nuclear war was to make American military policy so dangerous that his advisers would find it impossible to push Eisenhower toward war and away from compromise. NSC-5707/8 [the official security statement Ike finally had written] in other words was not so much a military policy stating basic American approaches to warfare as a strategy to allow Eisenhower to avoid war altogether.*

The policy was tested in two crises in the last years of the Eisenhower administration. In the first and lesser of these, in August 1958, the Chinese Communists resumed their artillery bombardment of the Chinese Nationalists on the small islands of Quemoy and Matsu—which are very close to Taiwan—to which the Chinese Nationalists had fled. The Americans, as a result of a crisis in 1955, had pledged to defend the islands, and the Joint Chiefs' war plans stipulated a defense of Quemoy and Matsu by nuclear strikes deep in China—atomic bombs to be dropped on great cities on the Chinese mainland. Eisenhower said no. We would help the Chinese Nationalists hold those islands, but without any bombardment of Chinese bases. Chiang Kai-shek wanted more, and the American general commanding forces in Taiwan wanted to knock out Chinese batteries with nuclear weapons. Ike said no. He kept making public declarations of support for the Nationalists, but at the same time he kept ruling out the

* Ibid., p. 69.

war-causing actions urged by others. Eventually, a compromise was reached: The Americans pressed Chiang Kai-shek to demilitarize the islands, the Chinese Communists agreed not to invade, and after a time they cut back their shelling to symbolic alternate dates and the crisis faded away.

And then, on November 10, 1958, the bumptious Khrushchev initiated a more serious crisis at the heart of Western resolve, once again in Berlin: He said, in effect, it was time for the Western occupation of Berlin to come to an end. He had reason to say that. The occupation of the German capital, 110 miles into East Germany, by the onetime Allies in the war increasingly demonstrated to the world, and to Germans, the contrast between a capitalist and a Communist society, and not to the advantage of the latter. Thousands of East Germans, including many of the ablest, made their way to the West by way of West Berlin, which did not argue for the superiority of the Communist regime. Khrushchev announced that the Soviet Union would be signing a peace treaty with East Germany and that the Western powers would then have to quit the zones in Berlin they had occupied since the war. He gave his claim the form of an ultimatum and set a specific deadline, six months into the future, May 27, 1959. Of course this brought belligerent proposed responses by members of the Joint Chiefs and the National Security Council and State Department, bristling with anticipations of war, and worried responses by the European allies. The official American strategy, rooted in Harry Truman's decision back in 1948 to make Berlin a basic American stake, was to treat a Soviet attempt to deny access to West Berlin as an attack upon the United States and a prelude to war. The chairman of the Joint Chiefs, General Twining, said we must be prepared for nuclear war over Berlin; Gen. Maxwell Taylor said the United States should make a military probe in East Germany to test the Soviets' will to escalate the war. But Ike supported none of this.

For the half year leading up to the Khrushchev deadline, Eisenhower's subordinates pressed him to commit to an explicit plan for the day Khrushchev had named. But Ike kept responding to anything they proposed in ways that historians describe with unusual verbs for presidential action: *sidestepping, evading, stonewalling*. He did not yield to their demand for a contingency military plan. He resisted the widespread demand for more troops, missiles, and weapons. He spoke of firmness in Berlin but at the same time instituted a *cut* of fifty thousand troops from American forces. When congressmen and reporters challenged him, Eisenhower asked, "What would I do with 50,000 troops in Europe; we are not going to fight a ground war in Europe." He thought Khrushchev was bluffing, and he did not match Khrushchev's belligerency with a belligerency of his own. Ike's handling of this Berlin crisis was one of his most distinctive episodes. Khrushchev wanted a summit to deal with Berlin, but Ike demurred; he said there had to be progress at a foreign ministers' conference before there could be a summit. The British prime minister, Harold Macmillan, fearful of what might happen, came to the United States to try to talk the Americans out of confrontation; in the case of the American president, that was easy, because he already agreed. The British wanted conciliation, and a summit; the Americans said they would not "negotiate under ultimatum," but in the end, they did.

The coming of Khrushchev's day of reckoning had an ironic twist. Dulles, who had cancer, died on May 24 and was buried on May 27, the very day Khrushchev had set for the ultimatum. One is tempted to imagine some variant of the famous comment attributed usually to Metternich about Talleyrand's death: What can he have meant by doing that? So there were all the foreign ministers, including Gromyko from the Soviet Union, coming to Washington not for a showdown about war but for a funeral.

Khrushchev was thrilled to be invited to visit the United States, which he did in a memorable excursion in November 1959. This pulled the plug on any ultimatums.

One has the picture of the president of the United States resisting all of his own Joint Chiefs and cabinet members to come through this Berlin crisis without war. He had eliminated from the American military the possibility of fighting a limited war to defend Berlin; the alternative that remained was too terrible to propose, so there was no war. Campbell Craig summarizes what happened:

> To avoid nuclear war Eisenhower wanted to make a deal on Berlin. But every one of his major national security advisors opposed compromise, preferring to force the Soviets to back down by pushing the crisis toward war. To make the task more difficult, Eisenhower could not simply state what he wanted, as if the debate were about the minimum wage or a highway program; the president was not going to say openly that he wanted to back down on Berlin, so he had to pretend that he also wanted to stare down the Russians. By using basic policy as a means of giving his advisors no reasonable military options, and then quietly attaching the Berlin diplomacy to that of the conciliatory British, Eisenhower was able to realize his objective.

Not every scholar examining Eisenhower's presidency agrees with Campbell Craig's interpretation. Did Ike really have this deliberate intent to arrange the all-or-nothing state of weaponry in order to forestall his own administration from dragging him into any smaller war (because he believed it would surely escalate into total war)? At least there were the objective facts: He did repeatedly and vociferously deplore the catastrophe of thermonuclear war; at the same time, he did resist the efforts, by Maxwell Taylor and others, to build the flexible response forces for smaller wars, insisting such a war with the Soviet Union would not remain small; he did say, often, that there would be no winner of a thermonuclear war between the great powers. And he did manage to preserve the peace throughout the crises of his presidency.

Dwight Eisenhower, for all his abhorrence of thermonuclear war, did not stop or slow the relentless production of the weapons by which it would be conducted. They continued to be piled up throughout his regime. The Kennedy administration scrambled to put in place more discriminate alternatives. But Ike's program had succeeded by this important criterion: There had been no such war.

In his last State of the Union address, Eisenhower struck a note that would resound, describing the vast permanent armaments industry and the immense expenditure on military security—more than the net income of all United States corporations. And he warned against the huge influence of a vast military establishment joined to a large arms industry, an influence felt in every city, every statehouse, and every office of the federal government.

> Our toil, resources and livelihood are all involved; so is the very structure of our society.
>
> In the councils of government, we must guard against the acquisition of unwarranted influence, whether sought or unsought, by the military-industrial complex.

Neither Harry Truman nor Dwight Eisenhower could reach the moral penetration to say (could a chief executive of the United States in those years have said this?) that we should not produce the monstrous thermonuclear weapons. The United States started turning them out in the last days of Truman's presidency and kept building these weapons steadily throughout Eisenhower's eight years. By the time Eisenhower turned the presidential office over to John Kennedy, the United States had enough of those weapons to destroy the Soviet Union, and much else, multiple times. But both of these presidents did find that when it came down to it, a thermonuclear war was not something one could risk. Like the scientists and policy makers who actually witnessed the eruptions at Eniwetok and Kazakhstan and Bikini, and who reported the strange feelings of awe and wonder when one actually saw acres of dead birds and saw an island disappear—the world being blown apart—these presidents, whose decisions might have brought incalculable destruction, looked at the destructive power of these instruments and said *no.*

Farewell

EISENHOWER IN THE White House never called on ex-president Truman for any advice, support, political service, or ceremonial representation, and did not in eight years ever seriously invite him to the White House. At least that is the Truman version of the story. Truman said he felt himself to be "the most snubbed former president in American history." In October 1953, the still fairly new president Eisenhower came to Kansas City to address the Future Farmers of America, and stayed at the Hotel Muehlbach, the downtown hotel across the street from the site, in the early twenties, of Truman's shirt shop. Ex-president Truman in Independence, now a virtual suburb of Kansas City, called the president's suite at the hotel, intending to drop by to pay his respects. An aide told Truman that the president was too busy and that a visit would be impossible. The Eisenhower White House later told the press they had no record of any such call, and that if there had been one, the aide who took it must have thought it was a prank. Harry Truman was not persuaded or mollified.

Much later, Eisenhower sources let it be known that the president had in fact invited the ex-president to his second inauguration in 1956, and, in 1959, to a small stag dinner for Winston Churchill, and perhaps to other events.

John Eisenhower wrote in his book *Strictly Personal* in 1974: "Several times during the Eisenhower administration Dad invited Truman to the White House. I drafted one of the letters. Truman always had cogent reasons not to attend." Truman, for his part, said that these "invitations" were to very formal occasions, and were offered in such a way that they had to be turned down.

As the Eisenhowers' only child, John Eisenhower has had a function with respect to these matters somewhat parallel to that of the Trumans' only child, Margaret. The defense by offspring tends to take this form: (1) there was no feud; (2) "Dad" (as they both call their fathers in their books) is too big to take part in the feud; and (3) the feud was the other man's fault.

Truman and his supporters could not help noticing the difference in the tax treatment of his memoirs and Eisenhower's book, *Crusade in Europe*. Ike's book was published while Truman was president and got a very favorable ruling. Truman's book was published while Eisenhower was president and got none.

Eisenhower, in his 1967 retirement book *At Ease,* described the deal he had received for *Crusade in Europe* with a detail that may make an uninitiated reader wonder, Why are the financial arrangements for book publication carefully set forth in this collection of amiable reminiscences? Eisenhower explains that he was advised by John Snyder, the secretary of the treasury (*Truman's* secretary of the treasury, of course, although Eisenhower does not put it that way), that if he followed certain rules, selling the book as a one-time unit sale to a buyer, then the returns could be treated as a capital gain, and taxed at only 25 percent because he was not a professional writer. Eisenhower kept more than $400,000, and was thereafter financially independent. Truman, on the other hand, in 1955–1956, having received the same sum ($630,000) from the same paired publishers (Doubleday and *Life* magazine), had to pay at the personal income tax rate, 67 percent; after subtracting expenses, he realized a net profit of only $37,000 for five years' work. Congress had in the meantime closed off the loophole that Eisenhower had used, but Truman could not help noticing that this time there was no advice from the secretary of the treasury, no favorable treatment from the IRS, no White House intervention.

The occasions on which the two men did thereafter encounter one another, after they bristled at each other at the 1952 inaugural ceremonies, were mostly funerals. Eisenhower and Truman both attended the funeral of Chief Justice Fred Vinson in 1953; of General George C. Marshall in 1959; of Speaker Sam Rayburn, in Bonham, Texas, in November 1961; of Eleanor Roosevelt, in Hyde Park, New York, in November 1962; and of John F. Kennedy in November 1963.

At Marshall's funeral at the Fort Myer Chapel, in October 1959, just before the family entered, ex-president Harry Truman and his aide Harry Vaughan came in, and then President of the United States Dwight Eisenhower and an aide followed, and the two presidents sat side by side in the same pew at the front, just across the aisle from the pews reserved for Mrs. Marshall and the family.

Between Marshall's funeral and Rayburn's, the two had encountered each other briefly at the inauguration of John Kennedy. Now it was Eisenhower's turn to be the outgoing president. President-elect Kennedy wore the traditional top hat, so President Eisenhower finally had to wear one, too. The Kennedys did accept the Eisenhowers' invitation to the White

House, and on inauguration day President-elect Kennedy and his wife sprang from their car with alacrity to go into the White House to greet the president. After the ceremony, Dwight Eisenhower went out a side door and into the curious American role of ex-president. No doubt a certain amount of air is let out of your balloon when you are no longer president.

On the first full day of John Kennedy's presidency, Harry Truman was pleased to be invited back to the White House for the first time (in his view) in eight years. Truman was later to say, jocularly, that he and Herbert Hoover had formed a "Former Presidents' Club," but that "the other fellow hasn't been taken in yet." (Truman, newly in the White House in 1945, had gone out of his way personally to invite Herbert Hoover, then the very lonely sole member of the ex-presidents' club, to come to the White House, to which Hoover—more snubbed than Truman ever would be—had never been invited through all the long years of Franklin Roosevelt's administration. Truman graciously brought Hoover back into the circle of public life.)

In November 1961, a committee of Kansas City citizens, chaired by Joyce C. Hall, founded to promote "international understanding" asked themselves, If we can have "international understanding," why not ex-presidential understanding? They noticed that they had near at hand, just ten minutes outside Kansas City, an ex-president of the United States, and they conceived the idea (one can imagine the moment some committee member or Mr. Hall himself came up with this inspiration, and the others excitedly endorsed it) of inviting the other ex-president, known to have icy relations with Truman, to attend the event also, so that a reconciliation might be effected. They put the question to Truman, who accepted, and then to Eisenhower, who agreed as well. They would speak in separate parts of the two-day ceremony rededicating the Kansas City Liberty Memorial, but the notable event came right at the start, when by the committee's arrangement Eisenhower was taken directly from the airport to the Truman Library, where Truman greeted him cordially at the door near his office, then gave him the beginnings of a tour of the library. Reporters were not told about this event until Eisenhower was headed for the library, so there was a certain amount of scrambling to get quotations from the two principals. Most of what the two presidents were heard to say—about how nice and pleasant and interesting the meeting and the tour and the library were—was bland enough to be printed on Hallmark cards, but there was one joke by Truman that might not be. He checked to be sure Eisenhower had signed the guest book and wisecracked, "Then if anything is missing we will know who to blame."

When Truman and Eisenhower had been seen on television, sitting in the same pew with President Kennedy at Sam Rayburn's funeral in November 1961, and again when the three had attended Eleanor Roosevelt's funeral in November 1962, the aging of the two ex-presidents, contrasted with the youth and vigor of the current president, was widely noticed. Yet the next in the sequence of November funerals was not that of either of the old men but of the vigorous young man. The two old men sat together in the same pew yet again at John F. Kennedy's funeral.

Softened a little, perhaps, by the sobering impact of Kennedy's assassination, as well as by the passage of some years and the repeated sharing of pews at funerals, the two came to a tentative reconciliation.

Eisenhower, staying at the Statler Hotel, tried to call the Trumans, staying at Blair House, but at first could not get through (among other things, it must be harder to get your telephone calls put through when you are only an ex-president). There was for a moment the danger of an inadvertent repetition-in-reverse of Truman's attempt to call Eisenhower at the Muehlbach years earlier, but Truman's onetime naval aide, Adm. Robert Denninson, who was with Truman and Margaret (Bess had not come) at Blair House, heard about the call and phoned Eisenhower back at the Statler. Eisenhower said that all he called for was to ask whether he and Mamie could pick up Truman and Margaret and take them to Washington National Cathedral. Dennison took the word to Truman, and Truman immediately accepted. The two older ex-presidents chatted on their way to the service for a slain younger president.

By William Ewald's account, Eisenhower opened with an echo of Mark Twain: "I believe the differences between us have been much exaggerated." By Margaret Truman's account, when she discovered that the Eisenhowers were not planning to stay in Washington, she invited them to stop at Blair House for something to eat before they headed back to Gettysburg. By the account of Admiral Dennison: "They just kept on having another drink and talking. I thought it would never end, but it was *really* heartwarming because they completely buried the hatchet and you'd think there had never been any differences between them."

The next presidential funerals would be their own—Eisenhower in 1969, Truman in 1972—after which the two middle Americans who had done their duty at the highest level, and had changed America's role in the world, would make their way, separately one may assume, to the special corner of heaven reserved for American presidents.

THE STORY OF THIS BOOK

Some years ago, in midcareer, I decided to write books about American historical episodes that had some strong moral content. I wrote about Thomas Jefferson's fight for religious liberty in Virginia and about James Madison in the 1780s, getting ready to go to the convention in Philadelphia, thinking through what a constitutional republic should be. I had planned to write about the letters between John and Abigail Adams, but that territory proved to be well occupied, and, in any case, I discovered a little-known tangent of great interest, the fight by their son John Quincy to make it possible to debate slavery in the House of Representatives. That was a story with a plot and a hero, and I told it in a book called *Arguing About Slavery.* I first wrote about Lincoln in an essay on the greatest of American speeches, Lincoln's Second Inaugural, and started work on what developed into two books on Lincoln. It was suggested that I write about some more recent figures and events, and I decided the similarities in the backgrounds of Presidents Truman and Eisenhower, together with their interaction in the twentieth century's great events, would make them a good subject for a book. I proposed working on these two in tandem to the Miller Center for Public Affairs at the University of Virginia, which has been my institutional sponsor throughout this series of books. My wife, Linda, and I drove to Abilene, Kansas, and Independence, Missouri, and spent valuable time in the Eisenhower library in Abilene and the Truman library in Independence; the staffs of the two libraries went out of their way to be helpful, and we returned with many folders of copied papers. I then produced a Miller Center paper on Ike and Harry, which was discussed in the center, to my benefit.

When I was well into the Ike and Harry project, I was startled to discover that there was a book, published in 2001, called *Harry and Ike,* written by the late Chicago newspaperman Steve Neal. A friend assured me that what I would write would be different enough from that book as to be no problem, and so it proved to be when I obtained Neal's book. For just one point, he shapes the treatment fundamentally around the implicit and explicit collaboration of the two men; the subtitle of his book is *The Partnership That Remade the Postwar World.* The two men in my book are not exactly partners.

Friends and colleagues who read some or all of this book include Truman scholar Robert Ferrell, the late Thomas C. Sorensen, William Freehling, Richard Bonnie, William May, and Marc Silverstone. Tom Core read the entire manuscript, to my benefit, as did Linda Miller, who assisted me in many other ways. No one who helped me should be blamed for any faults in this book, which are entirely my own. My editor, Jane Garrett, and her assistant, Leslie Levine, were unusually involved in the last stage of putting this book together, to my great profit.

SOME SOURCES FOR THIS BOOK

For reasons of geography, history, and the complications of life, it was not possible to assemble a full-fledged statement of the sources of particular references and quotations in this book; I hope the text itself includes clues that are of help. I list here some of the books and articles that were most helpful in producing this book. Needless to say, this list is by no means complete; the literature about these two presidents, the Cold War, and especially about World War II is immense, and I have drawn on more works than are listed here.

The quotations from, and references to, George Kennan in chapters 1, 6, 11, and 12 are all drawn from Kennan's *Memoirs,* of which there are two volumes: *Memoirs: 1925–1950* (Little, Brown, 1967) and *Memoirs: 1960–1963* (Pantheon, 1972).

For the life of Harry Truman, particularly in the first three chapters, I relied chiefly on three biographies: Alonzo Hamby, *Man of the People: A Life of Harry S Truman* (Oxford University Press, 1961); Robert Ferrell, *Harry S Truman: A Life* (University of Missouri Press, 1996); and David McCullough's widely read *Truman* (Simon & Schuster, 1992). I used McCullough somewhat sparingly exactly because it is widely read and also because, although it is an immensely readable narrative, it does not deal in interpretation, analysis, or concept. I referred to Richard Miller's *Truman: The Rise to Power* (McGraw-Hill, 1986) for areas of Truman's prepresidential life not covered by mainline biographies. Truman's own *Memoirs,* published in two volumes, like the efforts of most other presidents, do not have great value. Eisenhower's also uninspiring volumes, though, did provoke the article by Murray Kempton that I refer to in chapter 11 when treating the turnaround in Eisenhower studies.

It may be that before that turnaround Ike was more fully treated as a general than as a president. I thought the best book about him was Carlo D'Este, *Eisenhower: A Soldier's Life, 1890–1945* (Henry Holt, 2002), which stops with Ike's military career. Along with the many Eisenhower books by Stephen Ambrose, I used particularly *At Ease: Stories I Tell to Friends* (Doubleday, 1967), Eisenhower's amiable book of reminiscences, written during his retirement.

Books by the fine historian John S. D. Eisenhower, Ike's son, were doubly interesting because of that connection. His book *The Bitter Woods* (De Capo, 1995) is the definitive book about the Battle of the Bulge; *Allies* (De Capo, 1982) is a fine treatment of the tribulations of high command, coping with the Allies; and *Strictly Personal* (Doubleday, 1974) is just what its title indicates.

William Ewald's *Eisenhower the President* (Prentice Hall, 1981) gives inside views. Ewald was a presidential assistant and speechwriter, and he assisted in writing Eisenhower's memoir *Mandate for Change.*

The changing appraisal of Eisenhower is introduced in chapter 11 by references to, and quotations from, a striking magazine article by the brilliant journalist Murray Kempton published in *Esquire* in September 1967. The essay, entitled "The Underestimation of Dwight Eisenhower," was reprinted in a collection of Kempton's pieces, *Rebellions, Perversities, and Main Events* (Times Books, 1995).

The revised appraisal of Ike began with the work of political scientist Fred Greenstein. The title reveals the book's striking theme: *The Hidden-Hand Presidency: Eisenhower as Leader* (Basic Books, 1982; rev. ed., Johns Hopkins University Press, 1994).

For the history of World War II, two books were recommended to me, to my great benefit: Richard Overby's *Why the Allies Won* (Norton, 1996), which deals with the contingent and problematic—it was not certain from the start, or from superior resources, that the Allies would win; and Eric Larrabee's *Commander in Chief: FDR Lieutenant's War* (HarperCollins, 1986), which is a rich book organized by commanders—Patton, Marshall, Stilwell, MacArthur, "Hap" Arnold—and gives a full story of the war and much about Eisenhower.

For the overarching story of World War II, I used not only Ike's own good book *Crusade in Europe* but also John Keegan's classic *Second World War* (Penguin, 2005). The book by Alan Brooke, the British equivalent of George Marshall, put together by Arthur Bryant from his diary, is *The Turn of the Tide* (Grafton, 1986). His is a particularly valuable corrective to purely American sources.

For the outrageous story of the internment of Japanese-Americans, touched on in chapter 4, I relied particularly on Greg Robinson's *By Order of the President* (Harvard University Press, 2003), which underlines Roosevelt's role in the evil deed, and on a short section in Milton Eisenhower's book, *The President Is Calling* (Doubleday, 1984).

For the landing-craft story in both war chapters, and the role of Andrew Higgins within it, I drew upon Jerry E. Strahan's *Andrew Jackson Higgins and the Boat That Won World War II* (Louisiana State University Press, 1994).

For chapter 7, I draw first of all on Kennan but also on John Lewis Gaddis, *Strategies of Containment: A Critical Appraisal of American National Security Policy during the Cold War* (Oxford University Press, 1982; rev. ed., with Cold War developments, 2005).

Dean Acheson is at once a key figure in the Truman administration and a key witness and interpreter in his book *Present at the Creation* (Norton, 1987). The title means he was present at the creation of the postwar American foreign policy; there are quotations from that book throughout chapter 7.

For information about the men in the policy-making circles of those days, I drew upon Walter Isaacson and Evan Thomas, *The Wise Men* (Faber and Faber, 1987), which deals with six of them, and *The Hawk and the Dove,* by Nicholas Thompson (Holt, 2009), which deals with Paul Nitze and George Kennan.

For chapter 8, I used in particular the last book David Halberstam wrote, *The Coldest Winter: America and the Korean War* (Hyperion, 2007).

In chapter 10, the pungent and pointed quotation about Truman and Eisenhower on page 275 comes from the little biography by the English parliamentarian and political author Roy Jenkins. See *Truman* (Harper & Row, 1986), p. 203.

The most important source for chapter 12 was the classic treatment by Richard Rovere, *Senator Joe McCarthy* (University of California Press, 1970). Clark Clifford's book, important in several Truman settings, figures large in this: *Counsel to the President: A Memoir* (Random House, 1991). The story about Carl Bernstein's parents appears in McCullough's *Truman,* p. 553. I went back to those days and resurrected a most interesting article by a victim of the Eisenhower acquiescence to McCarthyism: Martin Merson, "My Education in Government," which appeared in *The Reporter,* October 7, 1954.

For chapter 13, David Nichols's *A Matter of Justice* (Simon & Schuster, 2007) has been of large importance, a corrective to much that had gone before in the scholarly and popular treatment of Eisenhower on race. As I noted in this chapter, one does not want to overdo the accepting response to Eisenhower or the parallel disparaging of Harry Truman's efforts. A solid defense of Truman's role is Michael R. Gardner's *Harry Truman and Civil Rights: Moral Courage and Political Risks* (Southern Illinois University Press, 2002). I extracted one episode from a journalist's biography of Truman: Alfred Steinberg's *The Man from Missouri: The Life and Times of Harry S. Truman* (Putnam, 1962).

For chapter 14, two of the key books I used are by the distinguished Cold War historian John Lewis Gaddis: his revision of thinking about the war, *We Now Know: Rethinking Cold War History* (Oxford University Press, 1997), and his brief distillation of the whole story, *The Cold War: A New History* (Penguin, 2006). Professor Campbell Craig set forth his interpretation of Eisenhower's policy on the bomb in *Destroying the Village* (Columbia University Press, 1998).

INDEX

A NOTE ABOUT THE AUTHOR

William Lee Miller, Scholar in Ethics and Institutions at the Miller Center of the University of Virginia, has taught at Yale, Smith College, and Indiana University. His previous books include *Arguing About Slavery, Lincoln's Virtues,* and *President Lincoln: The Duty of a Statesman.*

A NOTE ON THE TYPE

This book was set in Adobe Garamond. Designed for the Adobe Corporation by Robert Slimbach, the fonts are based on types first cut by Claude Garamond (c. 1480–1561).

Composed by Scribe, Philadelphia, Pennsylvania
Printed and bound by Berryville Graphics, Berryville, Virginia
Book design by Robert C. Olsson